Cambridge Studies in Early Modern British History

THOMAS STARKEY
AND THE COMMONWEAL

Cambridge Studies in Early Modern British History

Series editors

ANTHONY FLETCHER
Professor of Modern History, University of Durham

JOHN GUY
Reader in British History, University of Bristol

and JOHN MORRILL
*Lecturer in History, University of Cambridge, and
Fellow and Tutor of Selwyn College*

This is a series of monographs and studies covering many aspects of the history of the British Isles between the late fifteenth century and the early eighteenth century. It includes the work of established scholars and pioneering work by a new generation of scholars. It includes both reviews and revisions of major topics and books which open up new historical terrain or which reveal startling new perspectives on familiar subjects. All the volumes set detailed research into broader perspectives and the books are intended for the use of students as well as of their teachers.

THOMAS STARKEY
AND THE COMMONWEAL

Humanist politics and religion in the reign of Henry VIII

THOMAS F. MAYER

Assistant Professor of History,
Augustana College, Rock Island, Illinois

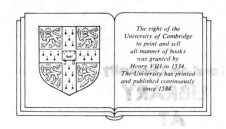

The right of the
University of Cambridge
to print and sell
all manner of books
was granted by
Henry VIII in 1534.
The University has printed
and published continuously
since 1584.

CAMBRIDGE UNIVERSITY PRESS

Cambridge
New York   New Rochelle
Melbourne   Sydney

Published by the Press Syndicate of the University of Cambridge
The Pitt Building, Trumpington Street, Cambridge CB2 1RP
32 East 57th Street, New York, NY 10022, USA
10 Stamford Road, Oakleigh, Melbourne 3166, Australia

© Cambridge University Press 1989

First published 1989

Printed in Great Britain by
Redwood Burn Limited, Trowbridge, Wiltshire

British Library cataloguing in publication data

Mayer, Thomas
Thomas Starkey and the commonweal: humanist
politics and religion in the reign of
Henry VIII – (Cambridge studies in early
modern British history).
1. England. Starkey, Thomas, 1499? 1538
I. Title
942.05'2'0924

Library of Congress cataloguing in publication data

Mayer, Thomas F. (Thomas Frederick), 1951–
Thomas Starkey and the commonweal: humanist politics and religion
in the reign of Henry VIII/Thomas F. Mayer.
p.   cm. – (Cambridge studies in early modern British history)
Bibliography: p.
Includes index.
ISBN 0–521–36104–4
1. Starkey, Thomas, d. 1538.   2. Reformation – England.
3. Sociology, Christian – History of doctrines – 16th century.
4. England – Church history – 16th century.   5. Great Britain –
Politics and government – 1509–1547.   6. Christianity and politics –
History of doctrines – 16th century.   7. Humanities – England –
History – 16th century.   I. Title.   II. Series.
BR350.S7M39   1989
942.05'2'0924 – dc19   88–26000   CIP

CONTENTS

ACKNOWLEDGEMENTS

I have incurred many debts in the researching and writing of this book over the last ten years. When I was just beginning, Marjorie Gesner tolerated and then encouraged a study well out of her usual territory, as did Gordon Stewart and Fred Graham. Stanford Lehmberg, my former adviser, has done and continues to do more than one can reasonably expect, both in the way of academic assistance and of friendship. Perhaps most crucial, he let me go my own way even when neither of us was quite sure where I was headed. At the outset of this project's second *aetas* George Huppert forcefully pulled me out of a disastrous way of thinking. As my work picked up speed, Joe Slavin insisted that I learn to write and has helped since with some of my most fundamental ideas. Geoffrey Elton has taken a keen interest almost from the first and I have always profited from his trenchant criticism, especially of the penultimate draft. Quentin Skinner has read much of my work for almost as long; I am grateful for his encouragement to write this book.

Others have provided fora or stimulus at crucial moments. John Guy invited me to speak to his seminar on British political thought at the Folger Shakespeare Library at an ideal time, and this book has since profited greatly from his criticism; my thanks to him, the steering committee of the Center for the History of British Political Thought, particularly John Pocock, and to Lena Cowen Orlin of the Folger Institute. David Starkey has had a great deal to do with shaping my argument, even if I have sometimes resisted the force of his suggestions. Charles Schmitt was constantly helpful. In Padua, Gregorio Piaia gave me the benefit of his enormous knowledge of Marsilio of Padua and his successors and has read several versions of my work on Marco Mantova Benavides since then. Antonio Padoa Schioppa was the perfect host at the Istituto per la storia di diritto italiano in the University of Milan. Robert Tittler gave me another welcome opportunity to try out some of my ideas both about Starkey and his Paduan environment at Concordia University, Montreal. The Reverend Alan Clarke generously put his knowledge of the parish of Wrenbury at my disposal, and the Reverend Brian Castle welcomed me to North Petherton and assisted with the photography for the illustration which appears on this book's dust jacket. Dennis Gilkey guided my initial forays into literature, and Elizabeth Gleason gave me the courage to float my argument that Starkey was as Italian in religion as in most other respects. Diana Robin, classicist extraordinaire, discussed some of my peculiar notions at great length and then generously read several chapters at a particularly bad time.

She was one of the many people I met while on the second of two fellowships at the Newberry Library, for both of which I am very grateful. This book could not have been whatever it is without my residences there. Likewise, the Graduate School of the University of Minnesota supported an extended trip to Europe as well as a summer at the Folger. The Center for Reformation Research gave me a fellowship during which I began my essential training in palaeography with Alan Bernstein, and the Vatican Film Library, St Louis University, twice awarded me Andrew W. Mellon Fellowships. The editors of *The historical journal* and *History of political thought* gave me permission to incorporate in chapters three, four and five heavily revised sections of pieces which they first published, as did the editor of the *Journal of the history of ideas*, who allowed me to reprint material scattered through chapters two, seven and eight. I owe a large but alas impersonal debt to the staffs of: Interlibrary Loan at the University of Minnesota, Southwest Missouri State University and Augustana College; the Folger Shakespeare Library; the British Library; the Public Record Office; the Institute of Historical Research; the Cambridge University Library; the Biblioteca nazionale 'Marciana', Venice; the Biblioteca universitaria, the Biblioteca communale, and the Biblioteca del seminario vescovile, Padua; the Istituto per la storia di diritto italiano, Milan, especially Alberto Pastore; the Nantwich City Library; and the Record Offices of Devon, Hampshire, Staffordshire, West Sussex and Wiltshire, especially the County Archivist of the latter, K. H. Rogers. Special thanks to Terry L. Taylor for some last moment assistance, and to the School Journey Association and especially its office staff who endured the typing of the final version of this book.

Finally, I must single out three people who made this study possible in yet more basic ways. First, my father introduced me to Collingwood and Toynbee at the age of what now seems to have been three and set a standard of effective historical communication which I have yet to reach. Second, Lynn Zastoupil's imposing intellect challenged me constantly during the later phases of our graduate careers. Last, I owe much more than any conventional phrases could convey to my wife, Jan Popehn. She has put up with the usual abuse from a writer of dissertations and books, with long stretches in London when she would much rather have been in the countryside, with vacations deferred or cancelled, and with the forced migrations of a late-twentieth-century American academic. All this is secondary to my real debt which I

could not put into words and certainly not in public. I dedicate this book to
her in part recompense.

A NOTE ON CITATIONS AND ABBREVIATIONS

I cite Starkey's Dialogue in a slightly modified form of Fredson Bowers's system of diplomatic transcription. An asterisk indicates that all text between it and the next set of square brackets is governed by the information in those brackets, unless a double asterisk intervenes, in which case the next brackets belong with it, and the next after them with the original asterisk. For example, the hypothetical instance '*and wyth myselfe longe have communyd [*ab. del*. "I have so consyderyd"]' means that Starkey interlineated the phrase between asterisk and brackets above the phrase within the brackets, which he crossed out. Square brackets without a preceding asterisk apply only to the previous word.

Abbreviations should be clear. The Dialogue and all other sources have been rendered in original spelling, except for u/v and i/j, and I have preserved original punctuation to avoid any modern impositions of meaning. I have referred to Starkey's major work only as the Dialogue in order to correct the impression left by earlier editors that Starkey completed it.

In order to hold the already large number of footnotes to a minimum, I have usually put the first reference to a work into a note, and then incorporated subsequent references in contiguity to the original in round brackets in the text. I have also omitted page, folio or *sigillum* abbreviations when it is clear which is meant from the first citation. All works are cited by short title in the notes; full particulars may be found in the bibliography. Unless otherwise indicated, all numbers in the notes refer to pages, except for the following, where they refer to documents: *CSPSp*; *CSPV*; *LP*; and *Op. Ep. Er.*

ARG	*Archiv für Reformationsgeschichte*
BL	British Library
Burton	Thomas Starkey, *A dialogue between Reginald Pole and Thomas Lupset*, ed. Kathleen M. Burton

CSPSp	*Calendar of letters, despatches and state papers relating to the negotiations between England and Spain*, ed. Pascual de Gazangos, et al.
CSPV	*Calendar of state papers and manuscripts, relating to English affairs in the archives and collections of Venice*, ed. Rawdon Brown, IV and V
DBI	*Dizionario biografico degli italiani*, ed. A. M. Ghisalberti
DNB	*Dictionary of national biography*, ed. Leslie Stephen and Sidney Lee
EETS	Early English text society
ERP	*Epistolarum Reginaldi Poli*, ed. A. M. Quirini
Exhortation	Thomas Starkey, *An exhortation to the people instructynge theym to Unitie and Obedience* (London: Thomas Berthelet, 1536)
HJ	*Historical journal*
LP	*Letters and papers, foreign and domestic of the reign of Henry VIII*, ed. J. S. Brewer, et al.
Op. Ep. Er.	*Opus epistolarum Desiderii Erasmi roterodami*, ed. P. S. Allen, H. M. Allen and H. W. Garrod
PRO	Public Record Office, London
RQ	*Renaissance quarterly*
SCJ	*Sixteenth century journal*
SP	State papers of the reign of Henry VIII, PRO
VCH	*Victoria county history*

INTRODUCTION

> Far be it from me to espouse the genius of a single man in its totality because of one or two well-formulated phrases ... He who wants to be safe in praising the entire man must see, examine, and estimate the entire man.
>
> Petrarch, *De ignorantia*

Although Petrarch meant his words to apply only to philosophers, they still well describe the ends of this first thorough intellectual and biographical study of Thomas Starkey. Petrarch's subjects were also well known, but this cannot be said of Starkey. He was born about the end of the fifteenth century into a reasonably well-off Cheshire family which paid for his education at Magdalen College, Oxford. In addition to an initiation into a rudimentary variety of humanism, Starkey there met the man who would have the most decisive impact on his life, Reginald Pole, grandson of the Duke of Clarence and protégé of Henry VIII. After gaining his MA in 1521, Starkey probably made his first trip to Italy, the determining event in his life. He would spend about a decade out of the next thirteen years acquiring an Italian education, mainly while moving in Pole's circle in Padua. His training there, first in natural science and then in civil law, prepared him to fulfil his ambition to enter royal service.

If it had not developed before, Starkey's aim to attract Henry's patronage matured in the last years of the 1520s, which he divided about equally between England and France. This is the time when he wrote his most famous work, the Dialogue between Pole and (Thomas) Lupset. Starkey did not choose these two as his interlocutors by coincidence. Both then stood high in royal favour, especially after their success helping to persuade the Parisian theologians to give a favourable opinion on Henry's divorce. But Pole refused to follow Starkey's plan to lure him into high office as leader of a reformed nobility. Starkey therefore separated from Pole in early 1532 and began the study of civil law in Avignon, his most overt step yet towards the king's service. After a short time in the south of France, he rejoined Pole in Padua where he took his degree in both laws before returning home in late 1534.

Very soon after his arrival in England, Starkey successfully caught the eye

1

of Henry's chief minister, Thomas Cromwell. Cromwell could not miss Starkey's value as a man recently returned from Italy, and the secretary recruited him in the first place to handle intelligence reports from friends in Venice and Padua. A little later Cromwell put Starkey to work corresponding with Pole in an effort to learn his true opinion of the divorce. Even though part of the reason for Starkey's departure from Pole in 1532 had probably been Pole's refusal to have anything further to do with Henry's attempts to rid himself of Catherine, neither Starkey nor Henry took Pole at his word. Starkey and Cromwell appear to have got along reasonably well; at least Starkey's correspondence with Cromwell contains many references to discussions between the two. One subject they talked about was doubtless religion, and at first this helped to draw the two together. Cromwell shortly gave Starkey the chance to fulfil his ultimate ambition of becoming a preacher, and in late 1535 Starkey finished a lengthy sermon entitled *An exhortation to the people instructynge theym to Unitie and Obedience*, his only work published during his lifetime.

In early 1536, then, the future looked promising. Pole was shortly to deliver his opinion, and Starkey's correspondents assured him it would be impressive. Starkey had just published a book, was enjoying a royal chaplaincy and his career seemed set fair for success. In mid-year, however, the bubble deflated. Disgrace did not burst it, because Starkey only temporarily fell out of favour. Compounded of concern over his preaching in the first place and his failure to induce Pole to give the proper opinion in the second, the cloud over Starkey lifted when he successfully defended his preaching and some of those in power – if not Cromwell – decided to give Pole yet another chance. In the midst of all this, Starkey made one last bid to attract Henry's attention in the cause of reform, and sent the king a letter detailing how to handle religious dissent, defending religious conservatives and moderates, and advising Henry what to do with the proceeds from the dissolution of the monasteries. The letter had no effect. At least it did not anger Henry, for in December 1536 Starkey added a rich benefice in London to his growing list of ecclesiastical preferments. Probably about the same time he began a tract against the Pilgrimage of Grace, but completed only a few lines. This may have been a sign of Starkey's ambivalence both about Henry's government and the rebels, now that neither the king nor Pole, whom the pope sent to aid the Pilgrims, would embrace reform.

Even though his fall proved temporary, Starkey had lost Cromwell's confidence and his career came to a standstill in 1537, save for his participation in a debate with the bishops over various theological questions. As a result, and as often happened when secular ambitions met frustration, Starkey's religious bent became increasingly pronounced. He turned to the Old Testament for inspiration and by October he had finished a set of notes on it which manifested his growing discontent with the course of policy in England. Only obliquely hidden under many remarks on prophets and the kings who refused to hear them was the figure of his old master Pole. Starkey kept in touch with Pole, and at least once provided him with crucial intelligence of moves against him. Starkey was drifting into opposition.

In the beginning of 1538, Starkey's hopes probably revived somewhat when he was first asked to preach before the king at York Place and then added to a commission charged to investigate an incident of witchcraft in London. About the middle of the year, Starkey undertook his most ambitious piece of writing, a detailed refutation of Albert Pighe's massive *Hierarchiae ecclesiasticae assertio*, part of which attacked Henry. Starkey did not live to bring the work past the stage of notes and a sketch of his counter-argument, but it still clearly embodies his typical moderation. That was a commodity in increasingly short supply. Starkey's death in August cheated the headsman. Shortly after he died in Somerset, where he seems almost to have fled, Starkey narrowly escaped indictment for treason as a member of the so-called Exeter conspiracy.

Starkey's is not a life of outstanding accomplishment, but it does define a series of contexts which can help to make sense of his ideas.[1] Starkey has always been regarded as important above all for them, particularly those which fall within the realm of the history of political thought. This book endorses that assessment, even as it strips Starkey of much of his traditional significance. My argument is often negative, and designed to clear away fifty or more years of unhelpful analysis. I shall argue that Starkey was not a follower of Marsilio of Padua, nor a Lutheran (or any kind of Protestant), nor a proto-Roundhead, nor even an enthusiastic partisan and intellectual companion of Cromwell. Instead, I shall present Starkey as the most Italianate Englishman of his generation and among the most eager importers of Italian concepts in the sixteenth century. The manner in which he combined various European traditions – Paduan, Venetian, Florentine, Parisian – with English ideas constitues his greatest significance. This claim could be phrased in such a way as to label Starkey a harbinger or anticipation of his Elizabethan successors, but that would be to read history backwards. He skilfully, if not always clearly, wielded Italian categories of political analysis, both secular and ecclesiastical, together with Italian religious beliefs to make sense of English 'reality'. He was especially good at stretching the parlous English vernacular to cover the much more sophisticated coinage of Italian political

---

[1] Dominick LaCapra warns historians against the dangers of placing ideas in context, and especially against the problems in a 'life and works' approach in his 'Rethinking intellectual history and reading texts', 55ff. and 60–1. Starkey's social ideas, which A. B. Ferguson studied in *The articulate citizen*, will receive less attention than his political and religious thought in this book.

discourse. Study of his language then can contribute to understanding how ideas move from one culture to another.

As ideas, so the manner in which they were presented, and Starkey further deserves attention as the first writer of a humanist political dialogue in English. This he has almost never had. On the score of both his play with language and his skill in weaving it into a larger literary representation, Starkey fits Richard Lanham's portrait of the 'playful' rhetorician. Therefore a study of him can contribute to the new 'literary' history Lanham seeks, a history 'essentially literary ... animated by dramatic motive, play instead of purpose' or, more tamely put, to the sort of 'fully serious history [which] will combine both conceptions of event: purposive and playful'.[2] This biography thus essays to bridge the gap Barbara Shapiro decries between narrowly focused intellectual history and literary studies.[3] Lanham calls the relationship between play and purpose, philosophy and rhetoric 'symbiotic', and this is certainly true of Starkey's career.[4] Beneath a spate of highly aureate diction lay a political purpose, and a perfectly serious motive under markedly rhetorical intentions. The resulting ambiguity in Starkey's thought will require careful study. This problem again is partly a function of Starkey's Italian experience. The study of the Dialogue offered here is the first attempt to put any such Henrician work into its Italian context.

But Starkey also played some role in English politics, if again not quite the one he has usually been given. He shaped his career and his thinking around a double loyalty, to Pole (and his fellow nobles) and to prince, but Starkey would support neither unless they answered his call to reform. The tension between these two allegiances helps to account for much of the peculiarity of Starkey's thought. Starkey's plans look odd, even 'radical', because he put his humanist education to the conservative end of restoring Pole and his fellow reformed aristocrats to dominance. Pole thus emerges as the central force in Starkey's life. His importance to Starkey has not gone unnoticed, but the implications of the link between them have not been properly appreciated. Pole, like Starkey, has borne the label 'liberal' and been seen as yet another of those pushing Starkey into modernity. In fact, Pole was perhaps the Englishman best placed to put Starkey in contact with the traditions of the high nobility, and he certainly behaved on several well-known occasions a good deal like his maternal grandfather. It must be emphasized that Pole was in an unusual position: a scion of the high nobility, thrown down from that eminence by Henry VII, only to be rescued and well educated by Henry VIII in precisely the humanist fashion Starkey was. This is not to suggest 'influence', but it seems most likely that if Starkey debated his ideas with anyone, that

---

[2] R. A. Lanham, *The motives of eloquence: literary rhetoric in the renaissance*, 20.
[3] Review of L. Martines, *Society and history in English renaissance verse*, 1191.
[4] Lanham, *Motives*, 34.

person was Pole, not Richard Morison.[5] Alas, next to nothing is known of Pole's ideas before he wrote *De unitate*, his savage attack on King Henry. The usual argument that Starkey faithfully reproduced Pole's thinking in the Dialogue could be stood on its head to make of Pole an ambitious man, eager to pursue the active life. That, of course, was no longer his view by 1536. A long, drawn-out process stretched between Dialogue and *De unitate*, but very little of it can be sufficiently documented to allow us to say much about Pole's impact on Starkey.

Nevertheless, it seems that Starkey saw himself as the spokesman for a party of the high nobility, centred around Pole. Its membership can be roughly reconstructed from the names of those who either certainly or probably favoured Pole during his legation of 1537, to judge from the very likely deliberately bungled efforts to settle the threat Pole posed.[6] The members of the Carewe–Exeter faction head the list, especially the Marquis of Exeter himself and Pole's brothers, Henry Lord Montagu and Sir Geoffrey Pole, not to mention his mother, the Countess of Salisbury. Sir John Wallop, then one of the English ambassadors in Paris, expressed open support for Pole, and Stephen Gardiner and Francis Bryan, on a special mission to Francis's court, behaved in such a way as to raise strong suspicions that they also favoured Pole. Further, at least four leading members of the king's council should probably be counted as real or potential sympathizers. One of Henry's most senior advisers, William Lord Sandys, was a notorious opponent of Cromwell and had contemplated open opposition a year or two earlier.[7] Sir William Paulet certainly helped one of Pole's clients who had fled England for religious reasons. His neighbour in Hampshire and fellow councillor Sir William Fitzwilliam did his best to cover up the first signs of Sir Geoffrey Pole's misdeeds in 1538. And Sir John Russell had earlier openly supported Pole and was certainly much less than enthusiastic about Anne. The council's principal secretary, Thomas Wriothesley, who also had an estate in Hampshire should be added to the list, too. Several bishops and members of the council ought not to be excluded, especially Richard Sampson and Cuthbert Tunstall, even though the latter was by 1536 being kept away from council meetings.[8] Three other great lords belong in the same region of the political landscape: Delawarr, Abergavenny, and perhaps Baron Hastings, son of the Earl of Huntingdon. One of Paulet's near neighbours in

---

[5] D. S. Berkowitz suggested in his introduction to *Humanist scholarship and public order*, 43, that Morison and Starkey must have talked over their work in Padua. In my view, Morison loses his traditionally important place in Starkey's life, because he was not close to Starkey in Padua, he and Starkey used a common language to different ends, and we have next to no evidence for the period when they may have acted together in 1536.

[6] For most of this, see my 'A diet for Henry VIII: the failure of Reginald Pole's 1537 legation', 323–27.

[7] For Sandys, see chapt. seven, n. 87, below.

[8] For Tunstall, see further chapt. 7, below.

Hampshire, Sir Antony Windsor, should also be included for the same reason as Paulet. Sir Antony served as receiver-general to Lord Lisle, who would be brought down in 1540 partly on charges of having met secretly with Pole.

Much of this party never achieved 'reality', but if we are to restore contingency to the study of Tudor history, we might profitably think in terms of options, of what might have been.[9] J.-P. Moreau has recently suggested that the Pilgrimage could have enjoyed much greater success if it had availed itself of Pole's leadership, especially because he could have provided it with a programme.[10] Doubtless this is right, and Pole's ideas came close to what many of the Pilgrims believed in an inarticulate way, but then Starkey's platform did, too. As J. A. Guy demonstrates, many of the Pilgrims' leaders supported conciliar government and were given to using the language of the commonwealth.[11] They may have been thinking more traditionally than Starkey in both cases, but Starkey's positive programme offered them much more than Pole's essentially negative and defensive one, no less than the chance to take the theoretical and moral high ground against Cromwell in the name of reform. Thus by thinking in counter-factuals, it appears that Starkey's programme, together with his patron and near-claimant to the throne Pole, and the force assembled by the Pilgrims in 1536 and 1537, could have added up to a successful rebellion against Henry VIII. It did indeed misfire because Starkey had not yet moved all the way to covert opposition (although the potential was there from the beginning of his thinking life), Pole was tardy, and the Pilgrims a little too trusting, but all the elements were present. It may even be that Starkey shows us the end of an evolution like Thomas More began but did not live to complete, from the reforming impulses and career-seeking of *Utopia* (no matter how ironically masked) to passive resistance to a king who had disappointed More's hopes.

Starkey also acquires new significance in the history of the Reformation, which important new materials dating from the last two formerly almost entirely dark years of his life support. Here we are on firmer ground. Starkey represented the thinking of a middle party, anti-papal but not Protestant, and not much concerned about doctrinal niceties. Once again, contingency must enter in if we are not to view the Reformation as a foregone conclusion. Starkey's views well illustrate recent efforts to stress the religious heterogeneity of pre-Reformation Christianity both in England and in the rest of Europe. Unlike many of his religious allies at home, Starkey's inspiration was

[9] This study thus joins the emphasis of many of the essays in D. Starkey and C. Coleman, eds., *Revolution reassessed*, especially those by J. A. Guy and J. D. Alsop. Cf. also D. Starkey's conclusion, 201.

[10] J.-P. Moreau, *Rome ou l'Angleterre?*, 248.

[11] J. A. Guy, 'The king's council and political participation', in J. A. Guy and A. Fox, *Reassessing the Henrician age*, 121–2.

once again Italian, stemming from the group known as Italian Evangelicals or *spirituali*, one of whose leaders was Pole. It may even be that some members of this party regarded Starkey as an emissary to England. Another of its leaders, Pole's close friend Gianmatteo Giberti, had earlier made vigorous efforts to recruit Tunstall, friend of More and Pole, to join him in Rome to reform the church, and it appears that someone (perhaps the third member of the central leadership of the *spirituali*, Gasparo Contarini) made vigorous attempts to keep lines of communication open to England even after the apparent fiasco of Pole's intemperate attack on Henry. However this may be, Starkey manifested the typically irenic attitude of the *spirituali*, and used their nondogmatic Pauline language skilfully.

It was this, along with his training in the civil law, which probably accounts for Starkey's appeal to Cromwell and for his brief moment of prominence. This has never been missed, but I shall suggest that from the outset Starkey and Cromwell were speaking superficially similar languages, while using them to quite different ends. Cromwell's intention to employ Starkey as a master intelligence-gatherer while Starkey wished only to preach illustrates this neatly. Neither Cromwell nor Starkey noticed their divergence at first, but gradually they drifted apart until finally Cromwell authorized Starkey's indictment for treason a few months after his death. Even though the indictment was not proceeded with, part of the cause for it was Starkey's continued support and covert assistance to Pole. It is probable that his religious and political principles continued to coalesce in his erstwhile patron. And it must be emphasized that prior to Cromwell's swoop on the Exeter conspiracy in 1538, this course of action was not dangerous. The middle party, even with the 'renegade' Pole as its standard-bearer and even after the Pilgrimage, retained life.

So much for Starkey's intellectual and political significance, the latter proving the harder to assess. The problem here lies more in the yardstick than in the object measured. The external standard of political or religious 'reality' is no longer adequate and it can certainly no longer be the exclusive means of judging importance, either for a political figure or for an intellectual one.[12] If Starkey never seems to have followed Pole in the typically Renaissance activity of self-fashioning or creating a new *persona* through literary means, he certainly engaged in the humanist practice of creating 'reality' through language.[13] This he did most clearly in his Dialogue, in both the 'objective'

---

[12] A. Lockyer, 'Traditions as context in the history of political thought', 203n; Robert Hariman argues that Machiavelli was making a rhetorical claim when he offered a more 'realistic' analysis of politics than his predecessors had, and that historians have been deceived by his device. 'Composing modernity in *The prince*'.

[13] S. J. Greenblatt, *Renaissance self-fashioning*, and T. F. Mayer, 'A mission worse than death: Reginald Pole and the Parisian theologians'.

sense of putting forward a manifesto of reform designed to influence events, and in the 'subjective' one of using words to bring a particular vision of things into existence, whatever its 'practical' impact.

Starkey's Dialogue has been accounted a classic of English political thought since the last century, even if it was left unpublished before that and probably had only a very limited circulation (if any) during Starkey's lifetime. This book hinges on it, in particular its constitutional ideas. Here, as in most of his works, Starkey adhered to an oligarchical model of secular government which drew ultimately on Aristotle. For most of his life, Starkey hoped to see sweeping institutional changes in England designed to restore the high nobility to leadership of the commonwealth. This is the basic argument of the Dialogue. Starkey blamed the ills in the body politic – his central metaphor – on the 'frencey' in its head, by which he meant first the prince and second the nobility. All his long catalogue of ills, from depopulation, through high prices, to the slow process of the law, could be cured if the nobles were trained in civic virtue. Once properly educated, the leading members of the nobility would regain their rightful place in two councils which Starkey proposed as a means to bridle the power of the prince. As is clear from the long debate between Pole and Lupset over the relative merits of the *vita activa* and the *vita contemplativa* at the beginning of the work, Starkey meant Pole to head this reordered government. But it would not be sufficient to restore the secular order alone; papal tyranny was as serious a problem as royal and Starkey once more proposed a conciliar solution. The pope should do nothing without the advice of the cardinals, who derived their authority from the general council.

Starkey argued further that this was both the natural system and accorded with natural law. Nature, however, played a much greater role in Starkey's theory than natural law. From the beginning of society, biology and native endowment counted for more than human action, even though social order was in part consensual. Humans had been brought to accept communal life by leaders of great prudence, which must have come to them naturally since Starkey offered no explanation of how they might otherwise have acquired their preeminence. The problem in Henrician England was that those natural leaders had become corrupted. But while Starkey argued that the choice of prince was in the hands of his subjects, he never swerved from his belief that they in turn were permanently of two sorts with no choice about their station. Some were nobles born to rule (at least once retrained) and the rest were destined to serve them. Some remained naturally superior to their fellows. And naturally they also needed more property to allow them to exercise rulership.

As Starkey finally assured his readers, these arrangements had been approved by Christ. For most of the Dialogue, Starkey displayed little more interest in religion. Near its end, however, he had 'Pole' and 'Lupset' turn to a discussion of salvation, allegedly drawing on Paul. In fact, Starkey embraced an idea of salvation through grace and one's own effort, but the latter was much deemphasized. This seems to have been the entering wedge for Starkey's gradual evolution into a believer in salvation through faith alone. From the conclusion of the Dialogue foreward, in any case, religious concerns bulked increasingly large in Starkey's mind.

Starkey made his case in most of his work through two means which often overlapped. Sometimes he used dialectical or 'demonstrative' arguments, and sometimes rhetorical or persuasive. The whole of the Dialogue is a heavily rhetorical work, replete with all the trappings of humanist literature. It is this and especially the humanist bent for eclecticism which largely accounts for the difficulty in interpreting the Dialogue. Starkey's humanist predilection for word play and historical precedents further complicates matters. The former means that most of his central terms can be translated into one another and the latter that he both drew on more or less 'accurate' versions of English history and also seems to have invented what he could not find. As Starkey learned from humanist rhetoricians like Rudfolf Agricola, what mattered was persuasion, not strict accuracy, verisimilitude not point-to-point realism. Lastly, the structure of the Dialogue can help to clarify Starkey's procedure. Starkey divided his work into three sections. It began with a description of the ideal commonwealth, proceeded to the general causes of its decay, and Starkey finally worked his way down to specifics, with the end in view of proposing remedies once the causes of problems had been isolated. This systematic procedure is usually well sign-posted, but the twistings and turnings of the dialogue between Pole and Lupset do not always stick to the straight line from one section to the next.

A word about the method of this book, especially lest this synopsis of Starkey's major ideas give a false impression that I shall be concerned to track 'influences' on Starkey's mind. G. R. Elton once warned that paucity of evidence renders biography among the worst approaches to the Henrician period in most cases, but enough material about Starkey survives to mean that Elton's stricture does not apply well to him.[14] Current emphasis on placing ideas in their proper context demands more attention to the lives of those who think them and reinforces the recommendation of a *Sitz-im-Leben* approach for the study of lesser humanists.[15] My *modus operandi* derives both directly and through various mediators from R. G. Collingwood's idealist model of history.[16] In particular, if Quentin Skinner's proposal to locate an idea in a context of speech acts and conventions is loosened up a

[14] G. R. Elton, *England 1200–1640*, 243–4.
[15] J. D. Tracy, 'Humanism and the reformation', in S. E. Ozment, ed., *Reformation Europe: a guide to research*, 42. Richard Tuck proposed a similar modification in the direction of biography to Quentin Skinner's influential emphasis on context, but on a broader scale. *Natural rights theories*, 4.
[16] R. G. Collingwood, *The idea of history*, part V, especially section 4.

little and translated into Conal Condren's notion of 'usage', and J. G. A. Pocock's concept of tradition (lately somewhat modified in the direction of 'language') is converted into a matter of a continuing discourse, as Andrew Lockyer suggests, then both will serve to locate Starkey in his linguistic context.[17] Unlike the hoary category of influence, usage is not an evaluative term and serves merely as shorthand 'that one writer has found another germane to his own enterprises'.[18] The vital point is that emphasis throughout must fall on redressing the balance between individual and tradition, as Condren insists, on how Starkey used the materials available to him, not the materials.[19] This is once more a matter of restoring contingency to Starkey's life. Hence the great stress I place on Starkey's contacts with friends, in which as much potential significance inheres as in his reading of books. The object is never establishing influence, for as both Skinner and Condren have shown this concept is nearly devoid of explanatory power.[20] Occasionally, it is clear that Starkey closely imitated a particular model, for example, Donato Giannotti's dialogue on Venice, and this is worth knowing. That sort of demonstration is not my usual concern. Instead, in order to define the limits on what Starkey could have thought, the resources on which he drew or could have drawn must be established. Thus this book endorses the focus on intention and language together with context and tradition which Donald Kelley recommends for the study of intellectual history.[21] Unlike Kelley and Skinner, I would argue that Starkey's motives should also be taken into account.[22] Motive is undoubtedly more difficult to deal with, in part because any number of motives may coalesce in a single intention. The former is also, of

---

[17] Both Skinner and Pocock, together with their critics, have created an imposing literature on method. Perhaps Skinner's most important thoughts are contained in 'Meaning and understanding in the history of ideas'; 'On performing and explaining linguistic actions'; '"Social meaning" and the explanation of social action'; and his reply to a critical symposium in 'Some problems in the analysis of political thought and action'. Pocock's chief contributions are 'The history of political thought: a methodological enquiry'; 'Time, institutions and action: an essay on traditions and their understanding'; most of the pieces in *Politics, language and time: essays on political thought and history*; his self-review, '*The Machiavellian moment* revisited: a study in history and ideology'; and 'Introduction: the state of the art', in *Virtue, commerce and history*. The second last piece cited provides a reasonably comprehensive bibliography of Pocock's critics, of whom C. Vasoli, '*The Machiavellian moment*: a grand ideological synthesis' and J. H. Geerken, 'Pocock and Machiavelli: structuralist explanation and history' should be singled out. Amongst Skinner's most important critics are C. D. Tarlton, 'History, meaning and revisionism in the study of political thought'; B. Parekh and R. N. Berki, 'The history of political ideas: a critique of Q. Skinner's methodology'; and LaCapra, 'Rethinking intellectual history', 55ff. C. Condren, *The status and appraisal of classic texts*, 139. Lockyer, 'Traditions', *passim*.

[18] Condren, *The status and appraisal of classic texts*, 139.   [19] *Ibid.*, 136.

[20] Skinner presents a radical attack in 'The limits of historical explanation', while Condren argues more moderately in *Classic texts*, chapter 5.

[21] D. R. Kelley, 'Horizons of intellectual history', 162.

[22] Skinner, '"Social meaning"', 144–7.

course, more deeply seated. Nevertheless, I have concentrated both on establishing what Starkey's texts said in his own words – his intentions in Skinner's terms – and also what reason (in Collingwood's sense) led him to put those intentions into prose. Whenever a conflict arises between interpretations based on intention and text or motive and life, I give somewhat greater weight to the latter in common with more traditional historians.

The first three chapters of this book concern Starkey's exposure to various traditions (or perhaps 'coherent sub-traditions' in George Logan's phrase) and languages during the early years of his education.[23] These included several fairly primitive forms of 'civic humanism' in England, together with the fully developed Venetian oligarchical variety, the Florentine–Venetian hybrid, and echoes of the once more robustly republican Paduan sort. Then, too, Starkey almost certainly knew several schools of conciliarist thought, including the Gallican type and its close analogue descending from Francesco Zabarella. During this time he also began his training in rhetoric, encompassing the again fairly unrefined English imitators of Cicero and the more polished littérateurs of Padua, and in dialectic. Here he probably learned both the new humanist mode of argument, typified by Agricola's transformation of dialectic into rhetoric, as well as the scientific method of the 'school of Padua' which blended a more rhetorical style with the logic of its scholastic predecessors. Finally, although religion would become more important later in Starkey's life, the Pauline Christianity of John Colet and the equally Pauline circle around Contarini helped to prepare an option for Starkey. Training in Padua and Paris gave Starkey an arsenal of concepts and a complete language which allowed him to describe English conditions in a much more sophisticated fashion than usual in the early sixteenth century, and to prescribe civic humanist remedies for the problems his analysis revealed.

Chapters 4 and 5 focus on the Dialogue itself. In the first of these I turn to Starkey's political vocabulary in order to pin down the language he used to construct his argument for a revived aristocracy. Chapter 5 documents that case within an ideological context both of traditional aristocratic political thought and of some of its forms contemporary with Starkey.[24] Beginning with chapter 6, the basic tension in Starkey as in all humanists between the active and contemplative lives manifests itself as I trace his attempts to prepare himself for government service at the same time as he developed an Italian Evangelical religious faith and decided on a career as a preacher. The last two chapters cover Starkey's brief moment near centre stage and the denouement of his career when he immersed himself in religion.

[23] G. M. Logan, 'Substance and form in renaissance humanism', 2, 30–1.
[24] This is the approach Skinner followed in 'History and ideology in the English revolution' and 'The ideological context of Hobbes's political thought'.

Much of my portrait of Starkey differs from the interpretations currently available. Most previous scholarship treated Starkey's language too imprecisely, even arbitrarily, and thereby imposed anachronistic categories on him, usually by means of linking him to previous or subsequent tradition without good cause. I will not constantly polemicize against the pandemic of Froude's disease afflicting scholars working on Starkey's biography. It stemmed from a willingness to treat Starkey himself as unimportant. His role as founder of Anglicanism, or the first modern liberal, or whatever was always most important. Indeed, despite changes in the political valence assigned to Starkey, most interpreters maintain remarkably consistently that somehow Starkey did not fit his immediate context. J. W. Allen judged that Starkey's belief that God had not bound humans to any particular political order left him 'in some respects isolated', F. L. Baumer that Starkey was a misplaced seventeenth-century republican, and A. B. Ferguson that Starkey 'followed the logic of his argument beyond the limits acceptable in Henrician England'. K. W. Beckmann endorsed Baumer's argument after a reasonably careful evaluation which seemed to demand a quite different conclusion, and even Skinner insisted on Starkey's radicalism.[25]

There have been only two dissenters. First, A. J. Carlyle thought Starkey would not be worth attention if his ideas did not 'coincide, in large measure, with those of other important writers of the time', but Carlyle seems to have had in mind chiefly continental writers, an angle on Starkey which both obliquely endorsed the majority position and would not be seriously followed before Beckmann.[26] Second, Elton gave Starkey and his ideas a secure home in the Cromwellian camp, which amounted to endorsing the usual position, too, since Starkey now came to qualify as an inhabitant of 1530s England only because one sector of that period had become even more revolutionary than he.[27]

One previous study of Starkey deserves special credit. Beckmann's Hamburg thesis, although often sketchy and marred by an anachronistic interpretive framework, touched on most of the points I have come to regard as crucial, and his conclusion anticipated one of my own. 'Starkey held on to typically English attitudes [to government], but he wanted to give them definite forms and entirely certain functions, which they had never had

---

[25] J. W. Allen, *A history of political thought in the sixteenth century*, 137; F. L. Baumer, 'Thomas Starkey and Marsilius of Padua'; Ferguson, *Articulate citizen*, 171 and cf. 328–9 where Ferguson thoroughly endorsed Baumer's case for a Starkey 'suspended ... between Marsilio of Padua and the seventeenth-century revolutionaries'; K. W. Beckmann, 'Staatstheorie und Kirchenpolitik im Werke des englischen Humanisten Thomas Starkey', 131–2; Q. Skinner, *Foundations of modern political thought*, I, *The renaissance*, 215.

[26] R. W. Carlyle and A. J. Carlyle, *A history of medieval political theory in the west*, 263.

[27] G. R. Elton, 'Reform by statute: Thomas Starkey's *Dialogue* and Thomas Cromwell's policy', and *Reform and renewal: Thomas Cromwell and the common weal*, 46ff.

before. The inspiration to that end stemmed from Venice.'[28] Beckmann thus focused on Contarini and his party, and on the 'Lancastrian constitution' as key elements in Starkey's political thought. Despite this promising orientation, Beckmann tried to make Starkey fit the theory of humanism espoused by his mentor, Ludwig Borinski. Thus Starkey became a 'bourgeois' thinker, a spokesman for the coalition which would later become the Whigs and a sort of proto-John Locke, as Beckmann nearly wrote.[29] Or in short, yet again a seventeenth-century Englishman out of his time.[30]

[28] Beckmann, 'Staatstheorie', 94. I am very grateful to N. L. Joners for bringing this work to my attention and helping me track down a copy. This facet of my study contributes a little to Christopher Hill's suggestion that 'there is a good book to be written on the overall influence of Venice and Padua on pre-revolutionary England'. *Intellectual origins of the English revolution*, 278.

[29] Beckmann, 'Staatstheorie', 77, 85–7, 100–6. Cf. L. Borinski and C. Uhlig, *Literatur der Renaissance*, 25–7. Borinski also apparently inculcated Beckmann's notion that the Dialogue belongs in the mirror of princes' tradition.

[30] Beckmann, 'Staatstheorie', 131, and cf. 3, where he explains Starkey's precocity by observing that he was 'einer der intelligentesten Männer seiner Zeit'.

※ 1 ※

Early life and education

In the first twenty or twenty-five years of his life, Thomas Starkey parlayed
social standing and moderate wealth in his native Cheshire into one of the
best humanist educations available in England. Perhaps the underpinnings of
his civic humanism had been laid even before he reached Magdalen College,
Oxford. While there he made contact with the most exalted circles of English
society and European learning. He probably counted both the speakers in his
Dialogue, Reginald Pole and Thomas Lupset, as his friends. Through Lupset
if not directly Starkey encountered the writings of John Colet, Erasmus and,
perhaps, Thomas More. The first and the last made a much greater impact on
Starkey, who embraced Colet's notion of church reform and probably also
pieces of his theology, even if Starkey picked and chose the parts which
interested him and even they did not root for a while. Neither Erasmus's
aloofness nor More's pessimism spoke to Starkey, but he did adopt much of
More's analysis of English social problems. In addition to this *copia* of ideas,
Starkey also gained a grounding in how to arrange it in the proper *dispositio*
necessary to make an impact on his hearers. For the moment, Starkey's chief
interests may have lain in the largely contemplative science of nature, but he
left Oxford with many of the elements which would convert him to the *vita
activa* and prepare him to pursue it successfully.

Thomas Starkey came from Cheshire, but to which branch of the Starkeys
he belonged and when he was born are much less clear. The only evidence
about Starkey's family comes from his will, which contained bequests to his
father Thomas and brother John. George Ormerod's genealogical tables,
together with the records of heraldic visitations in 1580 and 1613, make it
tolerably certain that Starkey belonged to the Wrenbury wing of the clan.[1]
According to the 1580 visitation, Ormerod made a mistake about the date of
death of the only Thomas Starkey succeeded by his son and heir John, putting
his demise into 20 Henry VIII instead of 34 Henry VIII. The latter date must

---

[1] G. Ormerod, *County palatine and city of Chester*, III, 205; J. P. Rylands, eds., *The visitation of
Cheshire, 1580*, 219, and G. J. Armytage and J. P. Rylands, eds., *The visitation of Cheshire,
1613*, 221. Starkey's will is in PRO, PCC Pynyng, register VI, fol. 45r.

be right if this was Starkey's father, since a bequest to him would have made no sense had he been dead for almost a decade when Starkey died in 1538. (We must hope that 1544 did not arise from a confusion with the probate of Thomas junior's will!) John, our Thomas's elder brother was thirty in 1528, so that we may infer that Starkey was born sometime after 1498. Working backwards from his BA in 1516 it appears that the two brothers must have been born close together. If the inventory of one John Starkey dated 1543, discovered by H. A. Clarke in the Cheshire Record Office, is of Starkey's brother, it would appear that he and his father must have died very close together.

Starkey's family ranked among the lesser gentry of Cheshire, but it was by no means poorly off. It had been sufficiently prominent to play a part in various military actions in the fourteenth and fifteenth centuries, and it remained well connected and reasonably prosperous in Starkey's day.[2] Starkey's mother was a daughter of John Mainwaring of Over Peover, who would be knighted after the 1513 expedition to France and was among the richest and most important men in the county. The Starkeys' tie to the Mainwarings went back at least to the early years of Henry VI, when the founder of Starkey's branch of the family had worn Mainwaring livery.[3] Starkey's brother John married a daughter of Sir John Warburton, and thus acquired a Stanley mother-in-law.[4] Through a senior branch of his family, Thomas was related to one of the other chief powers in Cheshire, Sir Randall Brereton, who would become a knight of the body to Henry VIII and whose son William acted as virtual viceroy for the county. John Starkey held Wrenbury of Sir John Savage, whose estate William Brereton controlled.[5] According to Ormerod, Starkey's family was distantly related to the Starkeys of Barnton, to whom Lawrence Starkey, a man of 'considerable importance' belonged.[6] Less can be said about Thomas Starkey senior's economic position, except that he did well enough out of his mixed farming to afford his son's Oxford education. This the early Tudor gentry rarely could, although perhaps things were better in Cheshire.[7] The inventory of John Starkey already noted gives concrete evidence of the family's wealth. The total value of his estate surpassed £100, and it included a large number of livestock and extensive

[2] M. J. Bennett, *Community, class and careerism*, 22n, 36, 41.

[3] J. T. Driver, *Cheshire in the later middle ages*, 21 and Bennett, *Community, class and careerism*, 41.

[4] See the Warburton pedigree in *The visitation of Cheshire, 1580*, 239.

[5] E. W. Ives, ed., *Letters and accounts of William Brereton of Malpas*, 137. See also Ives, 'Court and county palatine in the reign of Henry VIII'.

[6] S. J. Herrtage, *Starkey's life and letters*, v.

[7] N. Orme, *English schools in the middle ages*, 36, but cf. Bennett, *Community, class and careerism*, 141, for freeholders who sent their sons to university. J. Beck, *Tudor Cheshire*, 44, describes agriculture in Starkey's native region.

household furnishings.[8] Vague ties to the court apparently helped the Starkeys of Wrenbury. It seems likely that Starkey's father was that king's officer in Wales who received an annuity (together with John Dudley) of £26 13s. 11d. in 1526. If S. J. Herrtage is correct, the same Thomas drew an annuity of ten marks out of the earldom of March by grant of Henry VII, renewed by his son. Herrtage was right to describe Starkey's family as 'of high standing and considerable local influence in Cheshire', even if he mistook the branch from which Starkey came.[9]

On the face of it, a vast distance separates the Cheshire of *Sir Gawain and the green knight* and the intellectual world of the Oxford- and European-trained Starkey. There was certainly a gulf between the sometimes almost crude 'black-and-white' architecture with which Starkey would have been familiar, whether in his father's hall or perhaps in his parish church, and the elegance of the palaces he shared with Pole in Padua, and between the rather damp environs of Wrenbury and the bright Italian sunshine.[10] Nonetheless Starkey preserved some bits and pieces of his upbringing in an area which a few years earlier had supported a literary culture to rival Chaucer's London.[11] Perhaps most fundamental, Cheshire was largely devoid of nobles, which led the gentry and such nobility as there was to be thought of as one group. Consequently, rather than looking to service in a noble retinue to protect themselves, the Cheshire gentry relied on a system of 'mutual credit and collective security'. Cheshire's status as a palatinate reinforced this sense of solidarity: the county court, suitably reinforced, could function as a parliament, and Starkey's grandfather took part in at least one such assembly.[12] Starkey thus came from one of the areas of England (aside from London or one of the other incorporated cities) most like a classical or Italian republic.

Cheshire's unusually close ties to the royal family in the late middle ages made it peculiar, too, so that right from the beginning Starkey may have been after the royal patronage he later single-mindedly pursued. Other Cheshire

[8] H. A. Clarke, *History of the ancient parish of Wrenbury*, unpaginated, section 28. The original is Cheshire Record Office, EDA 2/1, fols. 221v-223r, dated 16 January 1542 (i.e. 1543).

[9] *LP*, IV:1, 1941, p. 873; Herrtage, *Starkey's life*, vi and iv for his genealogy of the Starkey family.

[10] The present parish church in Wrenbury is built of stone, but it, begun in the late fifteenth century, is not the building Starkey would have known. Its predecessor, according to Rev. Clarke, was probably a timber-framed building like the churches of St James's, Marton (its most likely analogue at least in scale) or of St Oswald's, Lower Peover. Clarke bases his deduction on the absence of any traces of even the foundations of an earlier church on the site. Then again, the Starkeys may not have frequented their parish church; at least there are very few traces of them in its later records. My thanks to Rev. Clarke for much help on these points. See also N. Pevsner and E. Hubbard, *The buildings of England: Cheshire*, 392.

[11] Bennett, *Community, class and careerism*, 232.

[12] *Ibid.*, 76, 31, 33 and 36. The major noble family in Lancashire and Cheshire, the Stanleys, maintained harmonious relations with the local gentry, which may have reinforced the impression of a homogeneous 'republican' community. B. Coward, *The Stanleys*, 116.

gentlemen besides his father realized the value of investing in an education for their sons. Several of the latter made highly successful clerical careers, especially Andrew Holes, who earned a doctorate in canon law at Padua and was briefly keeper of the privy seal under Henry VI. Even better from Starkey's point of view, Holes was a 'harbinger of the English Renaissance'.[13] Starkey might well have aspired to follow such examples through their training for the church and into a noble household, whence he could reasonably hope to enter royal service.[14]

That journey had to begin with a first step into school. Where Starkey went to grammar school is a matter for conjecture, and not perhaps of much importance, given how little is known about most such schools in the early sixteenth century. He seems to have made no use of the link between Wrenbury and Combermere Abbey, which held the impropriation of St Margaret's in Wrenbury, but was in any case in a decayed condition.[15] He probably had to leave home to begin his education, since Cheshire had only a few grammar schools. Sir Randall Brereton did not found the school at Malpas not far from Wrenbury until 1528, and the school at the abbey of St Werburgh in Chester apparently catered only for the monks.[16] Starkey's friendship with Robert Whittinton, together with his choice of college at Oxford, suggest that he may have gone to the dominant grammar school in England, Magdalen College School, which was attached to one of the foremost homes of the new learning.[17] Starkey would have left for school between the ages of nine and twelve and stayed for five or six years.[18] Once more counting from his BA in 1516, it must be that Starkey came to Magdalen nearer the former age than the latter. Then again, he could have studied at the school while an undergraduate.[19] The master during Starkey's probable residence was Thomas Bynknell, who did not distinguish himself as an educator in the way his predecessors John Anwykyll (who introduced Valla to his students and authored a twice-reprinted grammar) and John Stanbridge did, nor as much as Whittinton, who was officially never more than a pupil of the latter, but who claimed in 1513 to have 'informed' boys for twelve years.[20] Starkey's friendship with Edward Wotton may date from their days in the school, and Thomas Wolsey had studied there just before Starkey.[21]

---

[13] *Ibid.*, 143. If K. B. McFarlane correctly claimed that primogeniture was more effective after 1500 than before, and that knights tried to prevent their younger sons from being 'de-classed', this situation, and the example the knights set, might have affected the lower gentry and help to explain Starkey's father's actions. *The nobility of later medieval England*, 62, 71–2.

[14] *Ibid.*, 153 and 192.   [15] Clarke, *Wrenbury*, section 20.

[16] Orme, *Schools*, 310, and Driver, *Cheshire*, 148.   [17] Orme, *Schools*, 107 and 109.

[18] *Ibid.*, 117 and 133.

[19] N. Orme, 'An early Tudor Oxford schoolbook', 13.

[20] R. G. Stanier, *Magdalen school*, 62; Orme, *Schools*, 107; and D. Gilkey, 'The *Colloquies* of Erasmus', chapter 2, n. 87, who flatly calls Whittinton one of three *informatores* of the school, together with Anwykyll and Stanbridge.   [21] Stanier, *Magdalen school*, 65.

The survival of several sets of exercises designed to teach senior boys more complex translations of English into Latin, especially some by Whittinton, not only allows us to develop some idea of the teaching in Magdalen School, but also gives us a good picture of its intellectual climate.[22] K. J. Wilson singles these *vulgaria* out for their impact on the formation of humanist dialogue, calling them an intermediate step between scholasticism and humanist rhetoric.[23] Their form varied, but much of Whittinton's sample is a dialogue between master and student, as is the bulk of its fifteenth-century ancestor printed by William Nelson. Students did not have to wait until they went up to university to begin their training in disputation.[24] In some ways, this elementary teaching may have made more of an impact than later learning: as the students acquired language, they also absorbed the vehicle through which it was taught.[25] They further learned that eloquent language was only a means to a moral end. Almost from the beginning, exercises aimed to show the students that 'eliquens is a gay thing be the wich a man ma expresse all the consetes of his mynd ... yet me semyth eloqua[ns] withowt wisdom doth a man but lityll good'. Students should follow Cicero's advice and turn to philosophy, 'for of it cummyth all the abundant or ornat spech withowt the wich can be seid and expressid noo thyng wisely, no thyng excellently, no thyng abundantly'.[26] Cicero was frequently praised as a great light of both literature and philosophy, and on his authority the person who taught them was apostrophized as the greatest benefactor of the 'commonwelth'.[27]

Some of the same vaguely civic humanist attitude comes through in Nelson's anonymous *vulgaria*, one of which praised the 'olde Romans' who would rather kill themselves 'than they wolde departe from that that was the comyn welth'.[28] This commonwealth language is a pronounced feature of Whittinton's other works, but very little of it appears in his *vulgaria*.[29] Instead, Whittinton devoted them to moral exhortation and complaints about the evils of the world. He praised temperance over *crapula*, claimed that 'all the world wondreth & cryeth out of this penury & scantnes of all thynges', 'since beestes and cattell that we have seen to be plenteous here in englande were never so scaunte as nowe', but concluded with a tag from Augustine that 'continual healthe and abundaunce of ryches ... be most evydent tokens of damnacyon' (45–8). Whittinton summed up a long dialogue between master and student with a similar lament.

[22] Orme, *Schools*, 110.
[23] K. J. Wilson, *Incomplete fictions: the formation of English renaissance dialogue*, 60–1.
[24] *Ibid.*, 50–2 and Orme, 'Schoolbook', 18.
[25] See *ibid.*, 13–22 for a brief portrait of the teaching in Magdalen college school.
[26] *Ibid.*, 25.
[27] *Ibid.*, 28.
[28] W. Nelson, ed., *A fifteenth century school book*, 63.
[29] B. White, ed., *The vulgaria of Robert Whittinton*, 78.

Alakke this hevy world? wo is my herte to remembre ye felicyte yt hath be? poore men cryeth out of this scarsyte of al thynge? O ye felycyte of olde tyme? O this newe mysery? o good lord? refourme our maneris yt the olde wealth may renewe. (127–8)

These sentiments are identical to the underlying tone of complaint in Starkey's Dialogue, in which all these particular problems reappear. Like that work, Whittinton's exercises shared an interest in medicine and apparently in the cures it could work, as Whittinton's praise of Thomas Linacre's translation of Galen indicates (105–6).

To judge from these *vulgaria*, Whittinton had not yet developed the ambition he would later have in common with Starkey. At least he devoted a long passage to disparaging the life of the courtier who was forced to agree with everybody, 'cory favell craftely', be in attendance at all hours, and efface himself constantly, even if he excelled his superiors in any virtue. 'To be breve. the courte is ... as a monstre of many heedes: havynge moo eyes than Argus: lyfteth up as many eeres & openeth as many tongues as fleynge fame' (83 and 85). In light of the sequel, however, Whittinton's dim view was probably a function of the almost obligatory ambivalence among English humanists about royal service.

Little of this made an impression on Starkey, but much of the rest of Whittinton's language may have, and Whittinton's great interest in Stoicism may likewise have helped to induce Starkey's leanings in that direction. Starkey and Whittinton knew each other well enough to have dinner together, but the letter upbraiding Starkey for the drunken disturbance he had caused during the meal is undated and its sender cannot be identified.[30] Even if Starkey's friendship with Whittinton did not date from his student days, Whittinton's ideas still give a good idea of the intellectual climate in which Starkey moved, both at grammar school and at university.

Whittinton definitely changed his mind about government service by the time Starkey began work on his MA. In 1519 Wynkyn de Worde printed a volume of Whittinton's *opuscula* which contained a fulsome poem to Henry praising him as a peacemaker, and de Worde also issued '*De difficultate iusticiae servandae in republica administranda*', which Whittinton dedicated to Wolsey. (The fancy presentation manuscript is in the Bodleian, MS Bodl. 523.) Whittinton formed his perfectly conventional advice to Wolsey around medical and corporate images, likening Wolsey to Plato's good physician who would cure the wound of discord, and observing that an ailing treasury weakened all the other members of the body.[31] He called England a *respublica* which formed its *cives* according to the example set by their leaders, which

---

[30] SP 1/100, fol. 129 (*LP*, IX, 1159), printed in Herrtage, *Starkey's life*, lxx. The mere fact of its survival amongst Starkey's correspondence is a reasonably good argument in favour of it postdating his return to England in 1534.
[31] In *Opusculum Roberti Whittintoni*, sig. Aiiir–Bir and Biiir.

alone could bring the whole to its *commune bonum* (Biiir). To complete the sweep of standard metaphors, Whittinton advised Wolsey to steer his boat on a middle course between the Scylla of cruelty and the Charybdis of leniency in order to avoid a *naufragium* (Aiiiiv and Biiiv). Whittinton also addressed his '*Panegyricon, A laude quatuor virtutum Cardinalium*' in the same volume to Wolsey, and it contains a very similar vocabulary and argument. England was almost always called *Angliae respublica*, the 'public utility' of which kings were supposed to make flourish. The exercise of justice led to peace, plenty and felicity (Biiiiv and Bvv). The prudence of the rulers, the *principes et reipublicae gubernatores*, required reinforcement from counsel, even though Henry's prudence was sufficient to guide the ship through great storms and winds (Bvr). Elsewhere Whittinton praised Henry VII as 'a prynce bothe of famous vyctory also wonderous pollycy'.[32] These words and metaphors may all have been common currency, but Whittinton spent them as freely as Starkey.

This is fairly dilute civic humanism but Whittinton preserved his commitment to it, and some years later offered two translations of pseudo-Seneca as the quintessence of 'morall wysedome, whiche is the nexte meane to amplyfye and encrease the commen welthes'.[33] In the same preface to *The Myrrour or Glass of Manners*, Whittinton bemoaned that 'we judge nothynge to be good, but yt the opynyon of vulgare people dothe alowe whiche standeth ... in ye madde folly of blynde fortune'. As much like Starkey as this is, the rest of Whittinton's lament comes even closer. 'Comen profyt hathe decayed for carnal affectyon is encreased, avaryce augmented, sensualitie yt is an enemy to reason ruleth, and jugleth ... ye eyes of the soule, for yt it can not discerne that thynge whiche is good in dede'. Ignorance caused vice, as Starkey put it. Although it cannot be proved that Whittinton taught Seneca to his students, the sorrowful complaints in his *vulgaria* about the state of the world certainly lean in the direction of the Roman Stoic's attitude, and Beatrice White thought Whittinton's translations had been done some time before they were printed.[34]

It may well be that Whittinton and Starkey through him derived their Stoicism indirectly through another Roman, the great eclectic Cicero. Wherever Starkey encountered Cicero, his ideas provided one of the major foundations of Starkey's later work. There is more reason for an extended look at Whittinton's version than mere supposition, though. For one thing, although his translation of *De officiis* appeared in 1534, he must have taught the work earlier. Of even greater interest, Whittinton's habit of printing Latin and

---

[32] *Vulgaria*, xxvii and 60.

[33] *A Frutefull worke of Lucius Anneus Senecae. Called the myrrour or Glasse of maners and wysedome*, preface (unpaginated). This piece is now assigned to St Martin, Archbishop of Braga.

[34] *Vulgaria*, xxxiv.

English on facing pages facilitates a study of how he shaped his vernacular to its classical original. Since his vocabulary and Starkey's are so similar, this allows some insight into how Starkey may have modelled his English, and helps to explain why Starkey treated so many terms as nearly interchangeable.

Whittinton ran up against the limits of English almost immediately, and often dealt with the problem by indulging a marked propensity for humanist word play. Where Cicero had written *et authoritate meae gravissimum*, Whittinton read 'also to my dignitie most agreyng'. *Utilia* equalled 'profit'. *Neque publicis* became 'in causes commune', *malorum et bonorum finibus* 'endes of mysery and felycities'.[35] Whittinton's tendency to outdo Cicero and expand his allegedly perfect eloquence also cropped up very early. Cicero's *de officio*, for example, was twice transmuted into 'of offyce and honesty', while honesty also rendered *honestatem* and, more strangely, *nobilitatem* (A3v–A4r; A7v).

Cicero's moral vocabulary underwent further mutations in Whittinton's hands. He almost never translated *officium* by a single word and almost never made duty one of them. He did, however, equate *officia* and 'benefytes', and occasionally render *officium* as 'offyce', but with 'of humanyte' attached (C7r). 'Offyce and humanyte' also stood for *officia, naturaque*, Whittinton thereby mixing up three key terms in a noticeably Stoic fashion (13r). Other words could mean 'offyce', among them *munus*, and phrases like 'the due offyce of an offycer' did not embarrass Whittinton (G8v). His handling of the central term *virtus* recalls Machiavelli's definition of its Italian cognate. *Virtus* meant either 'vertue & manhode' or more bluntly 'manhode in warre' (C4r). Whittinton frequently took the opportunity of underlining the masculinity of his idea of virtue, whether by substituting 'polytyke manlynes of herte' for *sapiens animi magnitudo*, or offering 'valyant and manly stomake' for *fortis animi, magnique* (D5r and D6r).

In common with other sixteenth-century Englishmen, Whittinton had trouble when it came to translating words for political and social order. Like Starkey, Whittinton used the English 'society' sparingly, preferring to translate its Latin original into 'unyte' or 'company' or even 'felowshyp & unyte of this lyfe' (*e.g.*, Br and B6r). When faced with the notoriously difficult *res publica*, Whittinton first made do by inventing 'commentye'. That became his most frequent usage, but he also employed the more usual 'commune welthe', and sometimes interchanged the two translations (B4r, D2r, I7r, I8r). The last could also translate *communem utilitatem* where one might have

---

[35] *The thre bookes of Tullius offyce*, sig. A2v–A3r. Only the reference to the English will be given, since the Latin original is always on the facing page. 'Felicity' was Whittinton's standard offering for *finem bonorum*.

expected common benefit, and *communem societatem* where common company might have been looked for (Dr and Q3r). Perhaps Thomas Elyot's objection to the translation of *res publica* as commonwealth had registered with Whittinton. Then again, Whittinton was probably merely experimenting, since he also translated *rebus agendis* by 'mynystracion of the commen welthe', and *salute communi* into 'commen welthe', too (B2r and D4r). In any case, he does not seem to have suffered from quite as virulent an antipathy against the lower orders as Elyot, since Whittinton could translate *negotiis publiciis* into 'busynesse in the commenty' and in one place even went so far as to render *multitudo* as 'commenty' (D7r and L6v). There were, however, grades of 'commentyes': *omnibus opulentis populis* meant 'all welthy commentyes' (O6r). But Whittinton was not finished with stretching 'commen'. It also had to do duty for *vulgus* (as in 'commen people') and – joined to 'vulgare' – for *popularis* (Mr).

The closely connected set of words around the stem 'poli–' also figured prominently in Whittinton's version of *De officiis*, beyond the attachment of 'polityke' to manliness. *Togatorum consilio* suggested 'the polityke counsayle of governours', so that their *ingeniis* naturally became 'polityke wyttes', and *animi efficitur* came out 'brought to passe by policy of wytte' (E2r and E3v). Whittinton inserted 'polytike' to modify Cicero's plain *cunctando* (E7r). By the same token, *Cedant arma togae* was turned into 'Let warre gyve place to policy', and Whittinton pursued Cicero's comparison of politics with warfare, substituting policy where necessary for terms like *opera* or *decernendi ratio* (E2v, E4r, E3v). Whittinton differed from Starkey in his use of this whole complex by refusing to employ policy in the sense of constitutional order, probably because he did not know Greek and therefore missed the possibilities in πολιτεια.

As the first specimen of Whittinton's translating practice indicated, he mingled together two other important but only dimly understood terms, dignity and authority. Sometimes he gave what amounted to an explicit definition, as when he turned *administrandae potestatem* into 'auctoritie', but he then added a glimpse of the inner reaches of sixteenth-century political psychology by further defining *administrandis* as 'ordringe' (Er and L6v). Sometimes Whittinton simply substituted the English cognate for the Latin, as 'honour & dignyte' for *honoris & dignitatis* (C3r and cf. G8v). On other occasions he offered a description, as when he converted *quanto superiores sumus* into 'the hygher we be in auctorite' (Fr). Once he turned *dignitatis* into 'of authoritie' and plain *authoritas* into 'authorite & counsayle', almost in the same stroke of the pen (N8r and V7r). Whittinton could also give a neatly exact translation of *imperio* as 'authoritie', but elsewhere offer the equally literal rendering of *ad opes tuendas, ac tenendas* into 'to defende and kepe rychesse and authoritie' (L2v). Wealth connoted authority to Whittinton.

Finally, Whittinton shared Starkey's ambivalence over the term 'liberty', an attitude they probably absorbed directly from Cicero, but one reinforced by sixteenth-century social and political circumstances. 'Liberty' carried equally strong positive and negative connotations. It was simultaneously the goal of the civic life and the greatest threat to its fulfilment, depending upon the social class to which it referred. Early on, Whittinton employed the positive overtones of the word when he offered it as equivalent for *ius* (A3v). Or, in a clearly Stoic translation, *solitudinis munus* became 'lybertye of mynde' (P5r). But a few pages later the negative side of the word appeared in Whittinton's rendering of *magnam licentiam* as 'great lyberty' (Q3v). Another revealing substitution helps to clarify the social dimension of Whittinton's notion of liberty. He converted Cicero's simple *hac vi* into 'this power and lybertye' (T3r). The two went hand in hand; only those with 'authoritie' deserved both. When Whittinton offered that 'free lybertye' meant 'to lyve as thou wylt', he both defined the word and described the original state of things which had since degenerated into tyranny (D7r).

Like Starkey, Whittinton absorbed some of Cicero's urban bias and tried hard to make Cicero's discussion of Roman republican politics fit English monarchical circumstances. He equated 'commenty' with 'towne' in one place, but also stretched *civitas* into 'cyte or the commen welthe' (S7r). On the other hand, Whittinton knew no other word for the members of a commonwealth save 'citizen', rendering *& civibus, & reipub. salutaris* as 'both to the cytezyns it was holsome and also the commenwelthe' (O3v). *Cives* were always either 'cytezynys' or 'men of the cyte' (L4v). Nevertheless, the process of assimilation between Whittinton's England and Cicero's Rome went both ways. Cicero's *senatus* could only be Whittinton's 'parliament' (C4r and E3r). Finally, Cicero's words and Whittinton's translation of them may have helped to shape Starkey's idea of representation by a similar amalgamation of classical and contemporary concepts. As Cicero put it, a magistrate had to remember that *se gerere personam civitatis* which Whittinton phrased as 'that he beareth the personage of the cytie and that he is bounde to sustayne and kepe his dignyte ... and to declare the nature of the lawe' (G8v). Whittinton's excruciatingly literal translation lays bare the difficulty of the idea of representation in the sixteenth century, which his employment of the term to translate *similitudo* and other words meaning 'likeness' underscores. Whittinton's 'beareth the personage of the cytie' has very little in common with modern notions of representation, but it does have close affinities to Roman flaw ideas about the literal substitution of one person for another which ran parallel to medieval notions about 'symbolic' representation (see chapt. 5).

All in all, White's description of Whittinton's effort as 'diligent ... put pedestrian' is too limited. His translation illustrates the long-drawn-out process of creating a vocabulary of politics in English, as well as how faithfully Whittinton reproduced Cicero's meaning. Whittinton's Stoic reading of Cicero could well have steered Starkey's understanding of one of the sixteenth-century's favourite texts.[36] Starkey probably read other of Cicero's works, but the most obviously relevant *De republica* was known only in part. The first printed edition, containing about forty per cent of the present text, did not appear until 1538.[37] It is thus safe to conclude that Starkey drew mainly on *De officiis* for his knowledge of Cicero's political ideas, and no exaggeration to say that it contains virtually the whole of Starkey's argument in his Dialogue.

Cicero played down contemplative knowledge because it could not 'dispute of offyce and honesty', and wisdom not applied to the good of one's fellows was only a beginning.[38] Those who pursued 'scyence unyversall' acted against honesty if their interest took them away from administering the commonwealth, 'for all the laude of vertue standeth in effectuall exercyse' (B2r). Put even more bluntly, Cicero insisted that:

These that have by nature ayde and helpe to governe / all slacknesse caste away they must obtayne offyces / and rule commen welthes. For none otherwise eyther a cytie may be governed or the valyaunce of stomake may be shewed. (Er)

The highest 'sapyence' concerned the 'companye and felowshyppe of god and men amonge them selfe togythers'. Consequently, 'that offyce and honesty that is deduced of company and felowshyp is chefe & princypall' (I6r). 'Phylosophers or studyentes' made unsatisfactory governors because they were too much immersed in their 'study of lernyng'. Worse, their concentration on getting knowledge led them to 'forsake them whom they ought to defende' (B6r).

Instead, wise men should give their attention to moral questions, especially 'the defynicion of felycities' and the determination of precepts which led 'to the ende of felycite' through 'the commune ordre of mannes lyfe' (A5r). Once they had learned to make the choice of the 'perfect office' through a judgment of honesty and profit, they would know 'honesty of nature, whose sedes be gyven of nature to men' (A6r). That honesty consisted chiefly of the four cardinal virtues and especially 'kepynge of unyte bytwene man and man' (Br). The prudence of rulers had to rest on justice and liberality, by means of which 'we be bounde to folowe nature as a gyde / & to mynistre profites indifferently one to another' (B3r).

Cicero described a society both natural and consensual. Those with superior gifts were compelled to share them with others because society was

[36] *Vulgaria*, xxxv.

[37] E. Heck, *Die Bezeugung von Ciceros Schrift De re publica*, 3–4, 225. Quentin Skinner emphasizes the centrality of *De officiis* in 'Sir Thomas More's *Utopia* and the language of renaissance humanism', 129.

[38] Cicero/Whittinton, A4r and I6r.

held together by 'reason and communycacyon / whiche in teachyng / com-munyng / disputynge / and judgement doth allure & companyeth men to-gyther by a naturall socyete and famyliaritie' (C8v). Society arose originally through natural reproduction within the bonds of marriage, but the ties of kinship came to be replaced by connections based on 'benefytes gyven and taken' (D2r–D3r). This reciprocity meant that although valour was still a prime requisite, it consisted in achieving one's ends through 'policy of wytte / & not by strength of body' (E3v). Legitimate contention for the honours of office did not countenance stooping to terror tactics to maintain one's pos-ition. That was tyranny, which worked not at all to preserve 'rychesse and authoritie'. It was much better to be loved than 'dradde' (L2v). Cicero drew two rules from Plato for 'suche as beare rule in the commenty'.

One is that they shal defende so the welthe of the cytyzyns / that what so ever they do they shall have ever regarde therunto / forgettynge their owne private profyte. The other is that they shall respect the hole body of the commenty / leste whyyle they defende the one parte they leave the rest destitute / for lyke as the defence / so the procurynge of the commen welthe is to be referred to the profyte of them whiche be under their tuytion / and not to them to whome tuycion and governaunce is commyt-ted. For they that provyde for one parte of the citezyns & respeck not the other / they induce a mischevous thyng in to a cyte / as sedycion & debate. (E7r)

Ideally, individual and social profit would coalesce. 'It is necessary after the same nature that profyte of all men be commen and indyfferent / whiche if it be so we be contayned all under one lawe / & the same lawe of nature' (Q6r). Thus Cicero brought his whole apparatus of governing back to its grounding in nature, to what 'is called perfyte felycyte of Socrates folowers / to lyve accordynge to the law of nature' (P8r).

Cicero and Starkey shared many other ideas, from the necessity of control-ling how houses were built and the importance of seizing opportunities, to more fundamental notions of kingship (H8r). Cicero realized that kings had once ruled Rome, but theorized that they had been elected as a remedy for oligarchy. By defending the weaker party in a struggle, the king kept both the contenders within the same law and established equity. 'And this was the selfe same cause to make lawes / that was the cause of electyon of kynges / for ryght was ever sought egally' (M4r). This suggestion that kings and laws were interchangeable responses to the same problem may have underlain Starkey's complicated alternative solutions to English tyranny.

As Whittinton's translation of Cicero reveals, from his early teaching aids through to his late translations of pseudo-Seneca, he adhered to a heavily Stoic but still roughly civic humanist position. This might not have mattered much to the schoolboy Starkey, but the mere presence of a figure like Whittinton in Oxford indicates that even if the Renaissance arrived there late, one of its dominant strains quickly made an impact. When Starkey moved up to Magdalen College, he would have had a chance to pursue similar interests in the most humanist college in Oxford.[39]

Magdalen had been founded in 1448 as a hall and reformed in 1457 by William Waynflete, bishop of Winchester and lord chancellor in 1456. By its statutes of 1483 the college had a president, forty indigent scholars of theology and philosophy, thirty demies or undergraduates, four chaplains, eight clerks and sixteen choristers. The fellows were to be drawn especially from the counties of Lincoln and Oxford, and the dioceses of Winchester (to which the college was attached) and Norwich. The degree of either BA or MA was required for election. Fellows received £20 *per annum* and commons, a goodly stipend. They also played an important role in collegiate governance, since they elected the president, who was expected to consult them in important matters. He could be removed if necessary. The president and the thirteen senior fellows elected the vice-president.[40] As these statutes make clear, colleges were perhaps the institutions in England most like either an ancient *civitas* or an Italian commune, and Starkey's experience in Magdalen would therefore have reinforced Whittinton's tuition.

The second and third presidents of Magdalen tied it closely into national politics and international culture, as did perhaps its most famous alumnus, Wolsey. Richard Mayhew, the second president, was Henry VII's almoner and negotiated Catherine of Aragon's marriage treaty. He became a bishop in 1504. His successor John Claymond was a friend of Erasmus and More, a 'distinguished humanist' and a man of rigorous piety.[41] He served as president of Richard Fox's new foundation of Corpus Christi beginning in 1516. Richard Morwent and some other Magdalen fellows accompanied him. Wolsey, as bursar of Magdalen sometime before 1500, had exercised his office in a building campaign which included the tower of the chapel. In his days of power, Wolsey drew liberally on Magdalen men.[42] Someone made a wise choice when they sent Starkey to that college. And a deliberate choice this must have been. Whoever made it ignored the connection between Cheshire and Brasenose College. Sir Richard Sutton, member of an old Cheshire gentry family and politically prominent under Henry VII founded

[39] M. Dowling, *Humanism in the reign of Henry VIII*, 27, slights Magdalen's importance to English humanism. Oxford generally resisted humanist inroads fairly successfully, but Magdalen still stood out as one of the new learning's most important centres. J. K. McConica, 'The rise of the undergraduate college', 4, and J. M. Fletcher, 'The faculty of arts', 159, in J. K. McConica, ed., *History of the university of Oxford*, III.

[40] C. E. Mallett, *A history of the university of Oxford*, I, 385–97 and II, 29–32, and McConica, 'Undergraduate college', 3–7.

[41] W. Schenk, *Reginald Pole*, 6.

[42] Mallett, *Oxford*, I, 392 and Claire Cross, 'Oxford and the Tudor state from the accession of Henry VIII to the death of Mary', in McConica, *Oxford*, 121. For example, his chancellor, Lawrence Stubbes, came from Magdalen, despite earlier service with Wolsey's arch-enemy, the Duke of Buckingham. C. Rawcliffe, *The Staffords*, 230, and B. J. Harris, *Edward Stafford*, 219.

the college just about the time Starkey should have gone up. Perhaps it seemed too untried a proposition.[43]

Starkey's years as an undergraduate have left no trace in the university records apart from his degree, but it seems likely that he arrived in 1513 and studied the prescribed four years before receiving his BA in 1516. Starkey's father paid his son's way as a demy, and Starkey probably meant the £40 he left to his father as repayment. That sum equals the estimated cost of the period required for inception.[44] Dispensation for shorter terms of study was not uncommon, however, and three years or even less might have sufficed for a BA.[45] If Starkey did indeed arrive in 1513, then he entered Magdalen at the same time as his future patron Pole. They may have been in the same place, but they probably did not immediately move in the same circles. As a scion of the high nobility Pole lived in president Claymond's lodging, and there is no warrant for Fritz Caspari's claim that he and Starkey shared lessons from William Latimer.[46]

In order to earn a BA, Starkey had to acquire a grounding in the two parts of the medieval arts course, the *trivium* and the *quadrivium*. The former included grammar, rhetoric and dialectic, and the latter embraced arithmetic, astronomy, geometry and music, as well as the three philosophies: natural, moral and metaphysical. Priscian and Donatus were still the basic grammar texts in Starkey's day, while rhetoric rested on Boethius and Cicero, including the pseudo-Ciceronian *Ad Herrenium*. Dialectic was taught first from Aristotle, then from Boethius, and finally from two scholastic treatises, especially Petrus Hispanus's *Parva logicalia*. The philosophical part of Starkey's education was supposed to come again chiefly from Aristotle, including both his *Ethica nicomachea* and *Politica*.[47]

Starkey may have left the university for a time after gaining his BA. His MA did not come until 1521, and if he had worked continuously towards it after 1516, he would have put in two more years than the three required. On the other hand, if he left his studies until his election as a fellow of Magdalen in 1518, that would fit the statutory period between determination and inception exactly.[48] Towards the end of his residence in Magdalen, Starkey

---

[43] McConica, 'Undergraduate college', 7–17, esp. 9 and 13.

[44] PRO PCC Pynyng, VI, fol. 45r for the bequest, and Mallett, *Oxford*, I, 186 for costs.

[45] W. T. Mitchell, ed., *Epistolae academicae 1508–1596*, xxiv, and Fletcher, 'Faculty of arts', 165–71 for dispensation and the statutory prescriptions. See also S. Gibson, ed., *Statuta antiqua universitatis oxoniensis*, lxxxviii–cii.

[46] Schenk, *Pole*, 6 and F. Caspari, *Humanism and the social order*, 25.

[47] This curriculum reconstructed by analogy to that at Cambridge. See L. Jardine, 'The place of dialectic teaching in sixteenth-century Cambridge', 32–4, and *idem, Bacon*, 19–23 for a lucid discussion of instruction in dialectic. Oxford began to experience changes in both curriculum and pedagogy already at the beginning of the century, but more significant modifications came only in the reign of Elizabeth. See McConica, 'Undergraduate college', 60ff.

[48] Fletcher, 'Faculty of arts', 181–98.

apparently gave the lectures required of a regent master.[49] His teaching covered his first love, natural philosophy. About the same time in 1522 Starkey caught Cardinal Wolsey's eye, and was appointed a proctor to settle an election dispute.[50] Lawrence Barber, who had been William Grocyn's executor, joined Starkey in office.[51] In making these appointments, Wolsey overrode Congregation's recommendation of two other men, so that he must have known something of Starkey. On paper, Wolsey limited these two proctors to the powers of Masters of the Schools, but they seem to have exercised full proctorial powers beyond simply control over academic affairs. Starkey and Barber held office for about six months between May and October.[52]

Fourteenth-century proctors had been powerful men, but it is unclear how much authority their sixteenth-century successors still had. In the earlier period proctors could remove the chancellor and one of them acting alone could veto legislation by refusing to assemble the faculty of arts.[53] Some experience in the notoriously 'republican' university government may have contributed to Starkey's later political ideas, as has been argued for other conciliarists. Whatever its powers, Starkey's contemporaries continued to fight over the office of proctor, perhaps with financial gain chiefly in mind.[54] The system by which proctors were elected seems to have invited abuses by putting effective control into the hands of only eight men. W. T. Mitchell thinks the position attracted 'young men of a thrusting disposition', but there is no way to tell whether this description fits Starkey.[55]

W. Dunn Macray's painstaking labours uncovered a great deal of information about the fellows of Magdalen during Starkey's tenure. In the 1520 visitation of the college we even catch a glimpse of Starkey as more than a disembodied brain. He, Anthony Sutton, Thomas Marshall and Roger Baynthorpe were scolded for frequently leaving hall during meals.[56] Marshall and

---

[49] *Epistolae academicae*, xxiv and W. D. Macray, *Register of St Mary Magdalen college*, I, 158. See Fletcher, 'Faculty of arts', 185 for changes in the regency system. It was apparently falling into desuetude in Cambridge. D. R. Leader, 'Professorships and academic reform at Cambridge', 215.

[50] *Epistolae academicae*, 123–8.

[51] A. B. Emden, *Biographical register of the university of Oxford A.D. 1501 to 1540*, 23.

[52] *Epistolae academicae*, 381n. Mitchell corrected the date for the termination of Starkey's proctorship given by C. W. Boase in *Register of the university of Oxford*, I, 100. Boase must have taken literally Wolsey's promise to make other arrangements (immediately) after Michaelmas. See also Cross, 'Oxford and the Tudor state', 122 for the situation in 1522. D. G. Newcombe takes Starkey's proctorship as both a reward for Starkey's scholarship and a sign that he was one of those recruited later for Cardinal's College, but this is unlikely. Starkey was in Italy at the time. '"Due order & reasonabul mean"', 11.

[53] Mallett, *Oxford*, I, 170–5, and *Statuta antiqua*, lxxv–lxxvi. The proctors are mentioned only in passing in Cross, 'Oxford and the Tudor state', 118–19.

[54] *Epistolae academicae*, xxviii.　　　[55] *Ibid.*, xxvii–viii.　　　[56] Macray, *Fellows*, 74.

Baynthorpe regularly ran amok. Together or singly they were charged with frequenting taverns and female beer-sellers, writing a threatening letter to the president and sending it, being too familiar with masters and not paying due reverence to the president and other officers, as well as scaling walls and getting into rooms by windows. More seriously, Baynthorpe was dis-commoned and denied his share of the distribution for failure to progress academically. He overcame this temporary setback quickly, taking his MA in the next year and remaining at Magdalen until sometime before 1525.[57] Marshall received his MA at the same time as Starkey did after also having to wait for election as a fellow.

A pity more cannot be learned about this group of friends. They may have typified Magdalen men in one way, since comparatively few went on for higher degrees, but those who did overwhelmingly studied theology.[58] Per-haps these escapades testify to the decline of late medieval Oxford. Even though Starkey remained an unindicted co-conspirator in his friends' more heinous offences, a love letter to a woman almost certainly written after Starkey had been ordained as a priest, a life-long battle against celibacy and some measure of fondness for drink may yet have been legacies from his student days. Herrtage gave Starkey some benefit of the doubt and dated the letter before 1522, but Starkey's statement that he was in a strange land whose language he could speak only imperfectly – the letter is written in an odd French – fits any of several later periods better.[59] He and his fellow dangerous malefactors ultimately reformed and Marshall and Sutton pur-sued strictly academic careers.[60] Starkey outstripped them all.

Besides eventually coming to know Pole, Starkey made four other enduring friends at Magdalen, two of them important to his intellectual development. The two less significant friends were John Hales and John Walker, who probably knew one another at Oxford. Starkey may have met them through Pole.[61] Pole later patronized Hales, Starkey acting as intermediary, and the John Walker who was appointed university messenger in 1509 is probably the same man as Pole's faithful servant.[62] Unfortunately, in the cases of both Starkey's more important friends little more concrete is known of their years in Oxford than about a fellow of Magdalen like Nicholas Cartwright, who was twice lecturer in moral philosophy and later consulted about the divorce. Nevertheless, Starkey was later very close to Wotton and Lupset. Both

---

[57] *Ibid.*, 72, 75, 163–4.   [58] T. H. Aston, 'Oxford's medieval alumni', 12–13.

[59] Herrtage, *Starkey's life*, lxviii-xix printed the letter and discussed Starkey's postprandial drunkenness on lxx.

[60] Dowling, *Humanism*, 85, identifies Marshall as the son of Cromwell's sometime contro-versialist William.

[61] For both Hales and Walker, see Hales's letter to Starkey in SP 1/68, fol. 55r (*LP*, V, 530).

[62] For Pole's patronage, see chapter three below. *Epistolae academicae*, 8 for Walker's Oxford career.

played vital roles at two points in Starkey's life. He made the first the executor of his will and the second potentially a ticket to advancement as one of the two speakers in his Dialogue. Through Wotton Starkey stayed up to date on medical matters, and through Lupset (and to a lesser degree Pole) he made contact with the legacy of Colet.

Wotton lectured in moral philosophy at Magdalen for three years, and later in Greek at Corpus. Conversations with him may thus have helped to form Starkey's political ideas, as well as his Greek. Wotton's career began in earnest when Bishop Fox made him *socius compar* of Corpus in order to allow him to study medicine in Italy.[63] Starkey witnessed Wotton's successful defence of his medical degree at Padua in 1525. Wotton parlayed his new credentials into incorporation at Oxford in 1526 and soon thereafter he was proposed as physician to Princess Mary.[64] Although he or his father refused that prestigious appointment on grounds of inexperience, Wotton became a fellow of the Royal College of Physicians in 1528, and was employed by both Norfolk and the Countess of Salisbury.[65] He remained close to her son Reginald and acted as his London agent in 1532.[66] Starkey's later comrade-in-arms John Leland studied under Wotton, perhaps in Greek.[67]

It cannot be proved that Lupset and Starkey met in Oxford, but Starkey would not have passed up Lupset's lectures in Corpus, which began probably in the fall of 1519.[68] J. A. Gee thought it 'quite possible' that Lupset was in the university in 1517–18 and he certainly visited Magdalen for supper in December 1516.[69] He apparently stayed beyond the last reference to him in June 1522, perhaps until he left England in the spring of the next year.[70] Lupset may well have known Wotton as a family friend even before they were in Oxford: at least he later acted as executor to Lupset's mother.[71] Lupset had been a friend and protégé of Erasmus, who had entrusted the draft of his highly sensitive *Julius exclusus* to the young Englishman.[72]

Before Lupset entered Erasmus's circle, he had lived in Colet's household for about five years between 1508 and 1513, and Colet had doubtless had a great impact on his charge.[73] Lupset may have been only a part of a broad

---

[63] The material on Wotton to this point drawn from the *DNB*.
[64] See the next chapter for Starkey in Padua, and *LP*, IV:2, 2395, for Wotton's proposed appointment.
[65] Emden, *Register*, 639.   [66] M. Hallé, *Reginald Pole*, 89.
[67] W. G. Zeeveld, *Foundations of Tudor policy*, 56. Wotton cannot serve as a link between Starkey and either Juan Luis Vives or the Duke of Buckingham. He was no relation to Vives's favourite pupil Nicholas Wotton, and there is no evidence to connect him to Thomas Wotton, a member of Buckingham's household until at least 1520. *DNB* for Nicholas, and Rawcliffe, *Staffords*, 231 for Thomas.
[68] J. A. Gee, *Thomas Lupset*, 90 and 95.   [69] *Ibid.*, 58 and 67.   [70] *Ibid.*, 101.
[71] *Ibid.*, 22.   [72] *Ibid.*, 53 and 55.   [73] *Ibid.*, 36–8, 40, 176–8, 28.

Coletian movement in Magdalen, but he put Starkey in most direct contact with the ideas of his master.[74] Colet offered Starkey an almost prototypical example of the dialectic in humanism between 'Stoicism' and 'Augustinianism', identified by W. J. Bouwsma. Colet's disdainfully Pauline attitude to worldly pleasures came very close to a Stoic outlook, while his Augustinian language had many points of contact with Starkey's civic humanist preparation and helped to provide a more explicitly religious justification for Starkey's reform programme, some points of which he borrowed from Colet. For a while Colet's notion of justification appealed to Starkey, but in the long run Colet's reliance on Paul probably helped to point the way to a much different soteriology. Colet's heavily neo-platonic cosmology and psychology made little impression on Starkey, even if he shared Colet's passion for hierarchy.

Most of these aspects of Colet's thinking appear in the second of his three lectures on Paul's Epistle to the Romans, and his fragment on the church and famous sermon to convocation underscore them. In the lectures which he delivered in Oxford between 1497 and 1500, Colet turned first to the subject of justification. Natural law was not a means to salvation, he argued, but served rather to give sinners a knowledge of their sin.[75] The fall of Adam and Eve accounted for the power of the animal part of human nature, the degeneracy of which made a human commonwealth impossible. Instead of mutual action, each citizen pursued his own private advantage, while laws designed to restrain anti-social behaviour had no effect.[76] The weakness of nature led to disorder and almost overwhelmed the soul, the higher part of both human body and commonwealth.[77] The remedy was to make the body obedient to reason. This would allow the soul to unite 'the conflicting natures whereof it consists', and by analogy society to submit to the spirit of God.[78] Thus the body would become 'wholly spiritual' and the commonwealth united and, more important, justified.[79] The whole city (*civitas*) would take on a 'fair order'. This all sounds like civic humanist language, but when Colet continued that 'He [God] calls whom he will to his city, and justifies those whom he has called; that of men so justified he may form ... a righteous city, to be called the city of God', his Augustinian inspiration manifested itself.[80]

---

[74] D. Fenlon, *Heresy and obedience*, 2–3, and Schenk, *Pole*, 6.
[75] John Colet, *Enarratio . . . Romanos*, 4, 9–10, 19. Cf. S. Jayne, *John Colet and Marsilio Ficino*, 23 and 33.
[76] John Colet, *Opuscula theologica*, 32.
[77] *Ibid.*, 33, and *Enarratio*, 17.
[78] *Opuscula*, 34–5.
[79] *Enarratio*, 25; cf. *Opuscula*, 35.
[80] *Opuscula*, 35. Lupton's translation, but substituting 'city' for his rendering of *civitas* as 'commonwealth'.

Then Colet's neo-platonism took over to explain that the spirit of God
communicated 'both spiritual being and working' to all the members of the
commonwealth, forming them into a homogeneous whole, shaped like
Christ.[81]

Colet fleshed out this conception more fully when explaining the twelfth
chapter of Romans. As the body obeys the soul, it became 'in a measure
rational; and the body and soul of man, by being subject and surrendered to
God, may itself become divine'. 'So long as he retains this enlightenment, man
... appears to be not so much man as God and he does retain it ... so long as
his own soul keeps his body in check'.[82] Or as Colet phrased the same idea
even more strongly in his lectures on Corinthians, men had to 'be made
godlike and refashioned to a divine condition, and become gods, by being
made like unto God, that they may represent God'.[83] Nearly the same thing
happened to the body politic 'through the harmonizing effect of the natural
life, that flowed from the body's head to all the joints and members' and
created 'a united whole composed of several parts'. 'The silent teaching of
instinct, a singular desire for fellowship and unity and the welfare of the
whole body' held them together. Colet offered this nearly Aristotelian vision
of natural sociability as a model for the Christian community, but he assured
his hearers that Christ stood behind nature in the first place. 'It was the
purpose of Christ, himself the author of nature, to express nature herself
among men, and to bring back to the order and beauty of nature what had
diverged from order.'[84] Finally, Colet appealed to a neo-platonist interpretation of the relation between individual beings in the universe to define what
he meant by nature. Everything was connected in a hierarchy, those lower
depending on those higher. 'Wherefore there is nothing more agreeable to
nature or pleasing to God, than that beings, singly deficient, should seek
sufficiency in the bonds of society.' Men managed 'through some weakness or
other and perverseness' to be the only creatures to resist the natural instinct to
species-feeling.[85]

Hence the need for justification and a greater power to bring humans
together. The problem to Colet, as to Starkey, lay in ignorance. Because
humans could never know enough to save themselves, they had no choice but
to hope that God would rescue them through His love.[86] Colet, like Lupset
and Pole, was much more pessimistic than Starkey about the powers of
human intellect.[87] Since it could never attain to divine truth, faith in God had
to replace inquiry into His nature and intentions.[88] Faith was the most

---

[81] *Ibid.*, 38; cf. *Enarratio*, 74.   [82] *Enarratio*, 59.
[83] E. W. Hunt, *Dean Colet and his theology*, 118.   [84] *Enarratio*, 71.
[85] *Ibid.*, 74.   [86] *Ibid.*, 12 and 30.   [87] *Ibid.*, 44.   [88] *Ibid.*, 46.

important element of the 'working' which the Spirit infused into believers. As Colet put it in his fragment on the church, 'if men believe the gospel, they are saved ... Men will be saved, not by righteousness from the law, but by righteousness from faith.' *Vita eterna erit ex justicia fidei sola.*[89] Peter Kaufman concludes that Colet meant that prevenient grace was indispensable, but human effort had to complete it by giving up 'self-reliance' and performing good works which could earn divine favour.[90] Starkey leaned more on what human reason could accomplish by following natural law, but by the end of his Dialogue he too had adopted justification *sola fide* and would adhere to it consistently thereafter. Neither for Colet nor for Starkey did this ever remotely signal a Lutheran allegiance. For both it came straight from Paul, as for many other late medieval believers (see chapt. 7).

Colet's soteriology issued in an emphasis on the *vita activa*. This combined with his belief in hierarchy led to his deep conviction that reform of the church must come from the top. Colet sprinkled sharp remarks about the clerical estate throughout his writing, but he saved some of the most cutting for his commentaries on Ps.-Dionysius's *Celestial hierarchies* and, of course, for his sermon to Convocation.[91] Starkey is especially likely to have known both through Lupset. He translated the sermon in its entirety, apparently near the end of his life in 1530 when Starkey was deep in writing the Dialogue, and the most important part of the *Hierarchies* – an attack on secular interference in episcopal elections – must have inspired Lupset's lost work condemning the same abuse in very similar language.[92]

In his sermon, Colet began with an attack on the worldly living of clergy who failed to heed Paul's admonition 'be not carnal, but spiritual'. He traced the root cause of the church's problems to the clergy's refusal to follow Paul's model. They therefore set a poor example to their charges.[93] Colet spoke more diplomatically here than he had in his comments on the *Hierarchies*. Then he flayed canon lawyers as an 'atrocious race of men! deadliest plague to the Church of Christ' for failing to teach their flock 'by precept and example', and inveighed as well against 'the detestable boldness of wicked men in this our generation! O the abominable impiety of these miserable priests ... who fear not to rush from the bosom of some foul harlot into the temple of the church' (69 and 71). Only beginning with its heads could restore the church.

---

[89] *Opuscula*, 62 and 209.
[90] P. I. Kaufman, *Augustinian piety*, chapter 3, esp. 58, 69–72.
[91] Jayne, *Colet*, 33 for the date.
[92] B. O'Kelly and C. A. L. Jarrott, eds., *Colet's commentary on first Corinthians*, 59 and Gee, *Lupset*, 169–70 for the sermon and 172–3 for the lost work, which I suggest owed something to Colet.
[93] J. H. Lupton, *John Colet*, appendix, 294 and 295.

'You spirituall phisitions, fyrste taste you this medicine of purgation of maners, and than after offre us the same to taste' (299). Colet concluded with an exordium promising the assembled clergy that if they reformed themselves, they would gain obedience, honour, money and ecclesiastical liberties from the people (302–3).

The present mess arose because what Colet called the four worldly evils had taken deep root in the church: pride ('gredynes & appetite of honour & dignitie'); concupiscence; covetousness (which led to pluralism and myriad other evils in abuse of the legal system of the church, 'and to conclude at one worde: all corruptness, all the decaye of the churche, all the offences of the worlde, come of the covetousness of prestes'); and involvement in secular business (295–6). Despite this long catalogue of problems, Colet proposed a simple solution. The church should enforce existing legislation, beginning with that governing ordination which would ensure a clergy of pure life. Only those worthy should receive benefices and promotions. Simony should be eradicated. All clergy should reside in their cures, and adhere religiously to laws regulating their conduct, especially of monks and canons (300–1).

As much as Colet's reform seemed to depend on individual effort, at bottom it rested on administrative change. Kaufman labels Colet a reactionary reformer who looked forward to the withering way of the church. Undoubtedly Colet would have restricted its powers over laymen, since 'only God binds and looses' and clergy should minister, not govern.[94] Nevertheless, he blamed the church's problems on its institutional arrangements. They all followed from the fundamental problem of non-canonical election of bishops. Colet again addressed convocation more circumspectly than he wrote in his commentary on Ps.-Dionysius. In 1511 he merely noted the abuse and insisted that it be remedied, along with other faults in the episcopate, including non-residence and the failure to preach, hear poor men's cases, do good deeds and spend revenues properly.[95] Ten years earlier, probably in his study and certainly in no more public a venue than an Oxford lecture hall, Colet lashed out at the interference of temporal rulers in clerical elections.

Wherefore, one may here express an abhorrence of the detestable custom which ... is at the present time deep rooted almost to the destruction of the Christian commonwealth, whereby temporal princes, void of reason, &, under the name of Christians, open enemies and foes of God [etc.] not with humble and pious, but with proud and rash minds, not in consecrated and holy places, but in chambers and at banquets, appoint bishops to rule the Church of Christ; and those too (heinous crime!) men ignorant of all that is sacred, skilled in all that is profane; even to whom they have already shamelessly sold these very bishoprics ... All order is being overthrown; the flesh waxes wanton; the spirit is quenched; all things are distorted and foul ... For how

---

[94] Kaufman, *Colet*, 102–3.   [95] Lupton, *Colet*, 301.

shall that endure, which is being administered with destructive counsels and murderous hands? (72)

By comparison, Colet's demand to convocation that the church be left free to govern itself through frequent councils, both general and provincial, seems a model of moderation (302).

Colet may have supported his position with different theological and philosophical arguments than Starkey did, but both men offered similarly active, ultimately institutional reforms beginning at the top. If Starkey did find major inspiration in Colet, he was only one of many to do so. During his years at Magdalen Starkey probably encountered the works of Erasmus and More, who have often been tabbed both as followers of Colet and also as providing key elements in Starkey's thinking. Recent scholarship has begun to introduce more careful distinctions between similar-looking positions, though. Richard Marius has tried to separate More and Erasmus, Kaufman Erasmus and Colet, and Alistair Fox Erasmus and Starkey.[96] The grounds for thinking Starkey may have made something of More's *Utopia* are much better, but that in itself suggests that those who question the depth of the coalescence between More and Erasmus are right.

Fox has wrecked whatever substance the party label Erasmian humanism ever had as applied to England.[97] He shows that Erasmus always pursued transcendental withdrawal, rather than the cut and thrust of the court. At most, Erasmus counselled those who would involve themselves in politics to put their eloquence to the task of persuading the prince to act morally. Fox concedes that Erasmus's ideas had a great impact in the spheres of religion and education in England, but concludes that 'many of the English were suspicious of the political implications of Erasmian humanism from the outset'. More may have borrowed some of the specific elements of *Utopia* from Erasmus, but as long as a public career beckoned, he concluded that most of what Erasmus wanted was politically unfeasible. As a politician born, More used the dialogue form to test Erasmus's plans and to mask the conflict between them and reality.[98] By contrast, Elyot embodied the 'idealistic, didactic element in Erasmian humanism', but never quite got around to

[96] Kaufman, *Colet*, 49–54 for the distortions of Erasmus's biography of his friend, and R. Marius, *Thomas More*, esp. chapter 6.

[97] As George Logan notes, Elton typified the older view in *Reform and reformation*, 15. Elton also claimed that Starkey 'fully embraced the "Erasmian" Christian humanism' of Pole's household in Italy (165), but the inverted commas around Erasmian may have indicated the beginning of doubts. Logan expressed a few reservations like Alistair Fox's (see next note) about the 'essentially monolithic and static' nature of Erasmian humanism, but still concluded that an Erasmian subtradition in England should include More. G. M. Logan, *More's 'Utopia'*, 255 and n.

[98] A. Fox, 'English humanism and the body politic', in A. Fox and J. A. Guy, *Reassessing the Henrician age*, 34–51, quotation at 37.

translating his moral precepts, into proposals for reform.[99] Needless to say, Starkey did not suffer from Elyot's problem, even if in the long run his political career also failed to accomplish much. The activist Starkey had little in common with the retiring Erasmus. It is significant that the two works of Erasmus which Starkey recommended in his Dialogue both dealt with religion, not politics.

Lupset did not succeed in inducing in Starkey his own Erasmian ambivalence about political action, and the underlying pessimism of More's *Utopia* failed to affect Starkey, too. The ironic discourse in which both Erasmus and More specialized apparently had no attractions for a serious reformer like Starkey. Of course, it may well be that Starkey largely ignored More and Erasmus during his Oxford days. His studies in natural science may not have left much time or interest to consider political and moral questions, whether ironically or in any other way. Nevertheless, any budding English humanist would have found it hard to resist reading *Utopia*, especially if like Starkey he were friendly with Lupset, who had seen the Paris edition through the press.[100] Whenever Starkey read *Utopia*, he took it all in earnest and transformed much of More's ironic commentary into planks of a seriously intended programme of reform.

Many commentators have noted the similarity between Starkey's discussion of the merits of political involvement and the 'dialogue of counsel' in *Utopia*, but Starkey's Dialogue reflected the substance of More's proposals much more clearly.[101] Starkey changed the outcome of More's fictitious debate, perhaps in light of the knowledge that More had rejected Hythloday's attempts to dissuade 'Morus' from entering royal service. In any case, Starkey reversed the protagonists' roles in his dialogue as 'Lupset' tried to argue 'Pole' *into* royal service and few of 'Pole's' objections match Hythloday's. On the other hand, many of 'Morus's' criticisms of English society in his speech to Cardinal Morton reappear in Starkey's Dialogue, from the excessive cruelty of punishment for theft, through concern for the impotent poor, to man-eating sheep and the scarcity and high price of commodities.[102] Here Starkey borrowed more than the complaints. He took over More's analysis of the causes of and remedies for these social ills, too. He did the same in the case of 'Morus's' diatribe against the nobles and their retainers, which became one of the cornerstones of Starkey's effort to reform the high nobility. Starkey of course agreed that bad education was the basic difficulty, and that the

---

[99] *Ibid.*, 44 and for a case study of 'why Erasmian humanism ... had very little influence on political affairs in England', see 'Sir Thomas Elyot and the humanist dilemma' in the same volume, 52–73.

[100] T. More, *Utopia*, ed. J. H. Hexter and E. Surtz, clxxxv.

[101] For example, S. E. Lehmberg, 'English humanists', 88.   [102] *Utopia*, 61–9.

example of Rome should have priority in matters of government.[103]

Fewer of the peculiar features of the commonwealth of Utopia made it into Starkey's work, doubtless because he knew their impracticality as well as More did. Starkey did not altogether ignore the concerns they reflected, especially the Utopians' attention to their institutions and the quality of their magistrates, both of which had to function as well in Starkey's common-wealth as in theirs. Starkey was much more 'tolerant' than More, especially in religious matters, but neither of them could overlook the worst vice, pride. Ultimately there still remains the basic difference that Starkey refused to follow More into ironical detachment. The final sentence of *Utopia* encapsulated this difference between the two, which may have been rooted in More's greater experience of practical affairs. Starkey could never have included a disclaimer 'but I readily admit that there are very many features in the Utopian commonwealth which it is easier for me to wish for in our countries than to have any hope of seeing realized'.[104]

G. M. Logan's interpretation of *Utopia* sounds very much like the portrait of Starkey offered here. Logan argues that in his most famous work More tried to 'fuse' the scholastic (Aristotelian) and humanist (Platonic) traditions identified by Quentin Skinner in the same way as contemporary Italian humanists did.[105] In other words, More set out to blend the characteristic emphasis of the former on institutions with that of the latter on individual moral development.[106] Logan claims that only More made this significant 'advance', which may be true as of 1515, but is so no longer fifteen years later. From More's 'systemic approach' derived from Greek political thought, to his attempt to save the premises of Stoic thought by an analysis based on 'city-state theory', most of Logan's case applies equally well if not better to Starkey, who, unlike More, followed out the full implications not only of Greek method, but of Greek politics.[107] Starkey used 'city-state theory' as more than an analytical device. Logan defines *Utopia* as a humanist work because it fits between his two hallmarks of that tradition, rhetoric and history. The latter held greater importance for More than the former. He employed 'humanist criticial procedures' which taught him to see a text whole and in context, which in turn made possible his 'theoretical advances', and also engendered the 'complex tone' of the work. More's keen historical sense led him to see that anything he could do had to be relative, and that he

---

[103] *Ibid.*, 71.   [104] *Ibid.*, 247.

[105] Logan, *Utopia*, x. Logan somewhat overstates Skinner's case. Skinner wrote only that the 'two main strands' of republican analysis underwent 'incomparably rich development' in the late fifteenth and sixteenth centuries, not that they coalesced. *Foundations of modern political thought*, I, 144.

[106] Logan, *Utopia*, 82–3.   [107] *Ibid.*, 94, 100–1.

should therefore view his success with scepticism. From the 'pragmatic rhetorical tradition' More drew his predilection for 'concretion over abstraction' or concern with 'substantive questions'. In short, More 'fused' 'city-state theory with universal-state theory by reconciling Aristotle's empirical approach with the idealism of universal-state theory, and by bringing the analytic methods of city-state theory to bear on the problem of realizing Stoic and Christian ideals'.[108] This conclusion introduces some large abstractions, but it still basically describes Starkey at least as well as More.

Aside from standard educational texts, Colet, More and perhaps Erasmus, we know little about Starkey's reading at Oxford. Next to nothing is known of Magdalen's library in the early sixteenth century, Starkey's own bequest of books has disappeared, and John Bale's *Index* is an unreliable guide.[109] The first fairly complete catalogues of Magdalen's collection date from the early seventeenth century.[110] Nevertheless, Bale recorded some works which may have interested Starkey, among them parts of his fellow Cheshireman Ranulf Higden's *Polychronicon*.[111] Starkey certainly read some such pro-baronial chronicle, but Higden's became very thin by the time it reached the period when both offices which most interested Starkey – the constable and the steward – took on greatest constitutional significance.[112] Starkey may have found other expressions of resistance to monarchical pretensions in his college's library, including a petition from the Kentish rebels of 1450 which asserted that the king was not above the law, nor able to make it at his pleasure.[113] Some would say that the manuscript in Magdalen's collection which Starkey would use best was a copy of Marsilio of Padua's *Defensor pacis*, attributed to William of Ockham.[114] Starkey may have read it, but he made little out of it (see chapt. 5).

A grounding in how to argue persuasively, especially through dialogue, gave Starkey the final component of his Oxford education. Starkey learned scholastic logic, but it seems likely that he also picked up newer humanist notions of dialectic, which came close to obliterating the distinction between logic and rhetoric and melded both into an argument offered as a piece of oratorical persuasion. Dialectic became a sort of ordinary language philosophy in the early sixteenth century, as Lisa Jardine put it.[115] More important,

---

[108] *Ibid.*, 265–8.

[109] John Bale, *Index Britanniae scriptorum*, ed. R. L. Poole and M. Bateson does not list owners of MSS. Sir Thomas Smith's bequest of 300 books also disappeared altogether. M. Dewar, *Sir Thomas Smith*, 203.

[110] Neither lists donors. Thomas James's monumental catalogue of the Bodleian appeared only in 1620. S. Jayne, *Library catalogues*, 75 and 36.

[111] *Index*, 489 and 492. John Taylor lists five other MSS presently in Magdalen's library, but whether they were already there in Starkey's day is unknown. *Ranulf Higden*, 157.

[112] Higden skipped over *Magna charta* altogether, but he generally sympathized with the barons, especially *ipse justus* Simon de Montfort. *Polychronicon Ranulphi Higden*, 250.

[113] S. B. Chrimes, *English constitutional ideas*, 20, provenance unknown.

[114] Bale, *Index*, 141.   [115] Jardine, *Bacon*, 26.

both scholastic and humanist dialectic may well have reinforced one another. K. J. Wilson argues that practice in scholastic disputation formed an important matrix for the creation of humanist dialogue.[116] W. J. Ong made the same point in more detail in the course of his analysis of the 'oral residue' in Tudor prose style. Ong traced the Tudor 'tendency to a loosely strung-out, episodic style' to the ineluctable connection between partisanship and expression. An agonistic training forced Tudor littérateurs to take sides, and left them with the permanent impression that any debate had to be oral, even if written down.[117] Joan Lechner seconds Ong's stress on the humanist addiction to oratory by suggesting that training in epideictic rhetoric (how to apportion praise and blame) may have been all the education in writing offered.[118]

Roger Deakins goes furthest of all to blur the distinction between arguing and persuading by maintaining that Rudolf Agricola's treatise on dialectic served as a manual of how to write a dialogue, including Starkey's.[119] Agricola's concern with probable arguments led him to develop what Lisa Jardine calls a 'largely descriptive study of language usage'.[120] Once again, Ong made a similar point. He argued that the absence of any human sciences forced sixteenth-century thinkers to turn to dialogue, in which they dealt oratorically with all manner of general problems 'in the guise of personal concerns'.[121] This characterizes Agricola's intention perfectly. He meant his method to apply indifferently to investigations in the hard sciences and in the more doubtful areas of law, medicine and theology where nothing more than probable arguments were possible.[122]

Deakin's case for Agricola's impact on dialogue does not engender entire conviction, but his most penetrating critic agrees with him about Agricola's importance to English dialogue.[123] Unfortunately, Agricola's work did not certainly appear in Oxford until Thomas Cromwell's ordinances of 1535. Cambridge students apparently read it well before that, that is if John Fisher's praise of Agricola arose from his experience as an undergraduate.[124] The stream of sixteenth-century printed editions of *De inventione dialectica* began in 1515, and four more editions appeared during Starkey's time at Oxford.[125] His contact with Lupset may have led Starkey to Agricola, whom Erasmus had praised extravagantly.[126]

---

[116] Wilson, *Incomplete fictions*, 55.
[117] W. J. Ong, 'Oral residue in Tudor prose style', 28 and 38, and 'Tudor writings on rhetoric, poetic and literary theory', 65, in *Rhetoric, romance and technology*.
[118] J. M. Lechner, *Renaissance concepts of the commonplaces*, 7.
[119] R. Deakins, 'The Tudor prose dialogue', 6–7.
[120] Jardine, *Bacon*, 32.   [121] 'Oral residue', 44.
[122] C. Vasoli, *La dialettica e la retorica dell'Umanesimo*, 167 and 169.
[123] See below, chapt. 2. Gilkey, '*Colloquies* of Erasmus', chapter 4, 4.
[124] Deakins, 'Tudor prose dialogue', 7.   [125] Vasoli, *Dialettica*, 252.
[126] W. J. Ong, *Ramus, method and the decay of dialogue*, 94.

Another possible channel between humanist dialectic and Starkey must be closed. Although Juan Luis Vives nailed his colours to the Agricolan mast in 1519 with his *In pseudodialecticos* and he continued to develop a view of the relations between rhetoric and dialectic like Agricola's, neither Pole nor Starkey could have heard him lecture in Oxford.[127] Pole's alleged discipleship hinges on the belief that he resided as a fellow of Corpus at the time of Vives's first extended visit to England in 1523–4, but Pole was then certainly in Padua. Perhaps Bishop Fox merely proposed Pole for the fellowship but the college did not admit him, or Fox may have worked out an arrangement similar to Wotton's *socius compar*. In any case, none of the sources for Vives's students in Oxford name Pole.[128] Starkey may have met Vives on the latter's flying visit to Oxford in late 1522, but if Starkey left for Italy with Lupset as seems likely, he could not have attended any of Vives's later courses of lectures.

Despite the uncertainty over precisely how Starkey came into contact with Agricola, the way Starkey presented and argued his political project a few years afterwards closely resembled Agricola's recommendations, and Starkey later called his other large-scale political work, the *Exhortation*, a piece of 'probabyl persuasyon'.[129] Although Agricola counselled an orator to strive for pithy definitions which avoided ambiguous or obscure words, the method he proposed for arriving at definitions led him to subvert his earlier advice. This practice and its outcome are true of Starkey with a vengeance, and some of Agricola's illustrations could almost have served as a blueprint for several of Starkey's major definitions.[130] *Copia*, or the full *enumeratio* of the parts of any phenomenon would best distinguish it from any similar thing, and Agricola demonstrated on *civitas* in such a way as to remind one very strongly

[127] Vasoli, *Dialettica*, part III, chapter 3.

[128] J. K. McConica confirmed J. Foster Watson's claim that Pole was one of Fox's original Fellows, from which Henry de Vocht and Carlos G. Noreña had deduced that Pole studied under Vives. McConica, 'Elizabethan Oxford: the collegiate society', in McConica, ed., *Oxford*, 668 and 677; Foster Watson, *Las relaccions de Juan Lluis Vives amb es anglesos i amb L'Angleterra*, 267–9; de Vocht, 'Vives and his visits to England', in *Monumenta humanistica lovaniensa*, 4, 13, 20; Noreña, *Juan Luis Vives*, 85. Hallé suggested that Pole may merely have been proposed, but McConica seems to have disposed of that solution, drawing on the *libri admissionum*; Hallé, *Pole*, 28. For Wotton's special arrangement, see McConica, 'Undergraduate college', 25, who also noted that Wotton was admitted as reader in Greek, a post he executed until 1527/8. *Socius compar* may have been the theory, but the interpretation in the *DNB* that the arrangement was a fiction in order to support Wotton's study in Italy must be nearer the truth – Wotton took his degree in medicine in Padua in 1525, two years before McConica seems to think he went there. Neither John Helyar's letter, cited by de Vocht, nor Vives's own letter about his student Nicholas Udall, nor John Twyne's later recollections, named Pole as Vives's student. De Vocht, 'Vives', 8, 587 (text of letter, 14–16); Juan Luis Vives, *Opera omnia*, II, 309; and J. Twyne, *De rebus Albionicis*, ed. T. Twyne, 6–7.

[129] SP 1/89, fol. 178r. Cf. Vasoli, *Dialettica*, 156 and 176 for Agricola's stress on probable arguments.

[130] Rudolf Agricola, *De inventione dialectica*, 28.

of Starkey's involved discussion of the related English term civility (see chapt. 4).

Agricola tried to base his dialectic on Aristotelian science, but he wound up going far beyond its safe confines by placing great emphasis on teaching, rather than grasping 'the thing in itself'. A 'similitude' would best convey an object to a student (142–4). Such was Starkey's body politic. This point illustrates Agricola's tendency to identify dialectic with rhetoric. Book II of *De inventione* began with the assertion that the *instrumentum* of dialectic was the oration. Dialectic no longer served to discover the truth. Instead, Agricola posited that 'this therefore is the end of dialectic … to find those things which are fitted to creating faith, and disposing the things found in order that they be arranged in a way most fitting to teaching' (197; cf. 154 and 258). Pleasing terms would induce belief in a listener, even if the whole oration still had to rest on causes, not only in general 'but in the individual parts of the exposition' (298–9). Imagery offered the best tool to persuade an audience to take action. An oration first needed 'the movements of animals, conversations of persons, counsels and undecided happenings of events'. Pleasure came not from the subject of the oration, but from its *imitatio* of its subject. As in painting, the audience of an oration admired the verisimilitude of the characters and their conversations, and the effect this *figura* had on them. Poetry made the best impression, followed by history, but the same principle applied in political oratory. Agricola recommended Plato's dialogues for their use of experts in philosophy as speakers (397). Any kind of *oratio*, whether a speech or a dialogue, had to be life-like if it would persuade. The speaker should arrange his arguments in the manner which he thought would work best (435). In addition to explaining how Starkey could combine dialectical and rhetorical purposes in his Dialogue, Agricola's disinterest in form cleared the way for Starkey's immersion in the rough-and-tumble climate he would meet in Padua. Truth-to-life offered licence to reproduce all the hurly-burly and downright confusion of human existence.

Thomas Starkey senior may not have meant to give his son the chance to learn such a comparatively unbuttoned approach when dispatching Thomas to Oxford, but Starkey's early education laid the groundwork for his later outspokenly critical approach to English politics and society. S. E. Lehmberg's new statistics on the highest ranking English cathedral clergy in the sixteenth century reinforce Starkey's unusualness, as well as perhaps suggesting the sort of career his father had in mind for him. Lehmberg's numbers are often too small to support confident generalizations, but they nonetheless suggest patterns. Fully 40 per cent of Lehmberg's sample of 208 cathedral clergy or about 7 per cent of the total came from the gentry and the nobility, the vast bulk of them from the former. Lehmberg also found 'a regional rather than national market for the talents of young clerics'. Starkey may well have

hoped to escape this constraint, even though the first stage of his career –
study at Oxford, the nearer of the two universities – fits the usual pattern. The
next phase, however, put Starkey into select company. Of the 166 men whose
grammar school can be identified, only eight went on to study abroad and,
even more striking, a total of only thirty-three or thirty-four of 1493 known
graduates went overseas for schooling. The cathedral clergy may have formed
an intellectual élite, but Starkey would come to stand on a rung even above
them. Nevertheless, Lehmberg found a strong correlation between higher
degrees and advancement, which in retrospect seems to have been Starkey's
aim.[131] All of his education in England pointed in the direction both of more
schooling and towards the best place to get it, Italy.

[131] S. E. Lehmberg, *The reformation of cathedrals*, forthcoming, Princeton University Press.

2

Humanism from the source

Thin evidence leaves us more dependent than usual on supposition to reconstruct Starkey's movements for much of the decade of the 1520s. Most previous claims about his activities cannot be supported – from the reasonably likely one that he lived in Pole's household in Padua through the more remote possibility that he served as Pole's chaplain to the ludicrous suggestion that he was set to spy on Pole. We have even fewer chronological landmarks than for Starkey's earlier life, as George Parks well summed up when he admitted that Starkey was in Padua, 'though we do not know when he came or how long he stayed'.[1] Nevertheless, a few new data about Starkey have turned up since Parks and W. Gordon Zeeveld wrote, together with much new evidence about the intellectual environment of Padua.

Placing Starkey into the proper context often remains difficult, but enough signposts exist to allow reasonable conjectures. Thus it seems likely enough that Starkey soon realized, like the boy in one of the *vulgaria* he may have translated as a youth, that he would have to go to Italy to complete his education and only a little less likely that he went there in company with Thomas Lupset in 1523.[2] Again, it matters comparatively little where Starkey lived in Padua, but even if Starkey were not in Pole's employ, as old friends they would at least have known many of the same people. Pole's social standing doubtless accounted for the tributes he received from the Signory of Venice and the accolades to his good learning offered by Venetian humanists like Andrea Navagero. They nonetheless provided an entrée to the circle of the dominant Paduan humanist, Pietro Bembo.[3] Starkey probably learned from his example, that of his friends, and from Niccolò Leonico. Although neither Pole nor Starkey met Gasparo Contarini until later, Starkey must have shared much of Contarini's educational and political milieu, to judge from their strikingly similar ideas. Yet another of Bembo's satellites in the mid-1520s, the Florentine exile Donato Giannotti, had at least an equal effect

---

[1] G. B. Parks, *The English traveller to Italy*, 478–9.
[2] N. Orme, 'An early-Tudor Oxford schoolbook', 35.
[3] Pole to Henry VIII, BL Cotton MS Nero B VI, fol. 118r (*LP*, III:1, 198).

43

on Starkey, contributing both the form and much of the content of his Dialogue.

Starkey gained more than intellectual and literary tools in Padua. While there he lived through the deep crisis which shook Italy in the early sixteenth century and gave questions of politics, literature and religion new urgency. As might be expected, the upheaval hit men of letters particularly hard.[4] It dislocated Venice and Padua acutely, but the Florentine republic also suffered through the death agony before its final collapse in 1530. By accident, Starkey was in Padua precisely when Florentine refugees and Venetian patricians on the defensive blended their two distinct civic humanisms into a new oligarchical form which could suit English circumstances much better than older republican varieties. The 'myth of Venice' became one of Starkey's most important political devices. By the same token, he was in Padua just as the full consequences of its submission to Venice were reinforced. This produced another dimension in civic humanism which would make it more adaptable to the new courts, whether in Italy or in England.

The Venetian defeat at Agnadello in 1509 triggered most of these developments. Both in Padua and in Venice it exacerbated the profound tension between the *vita activa* and the *vita contemplativa*, very much like that which Pole and Lupset would undergo beginning in 1530. Reacting immediately to the strain, in the early teens members of some of Venice's most distinguished families turned their backs on civic obligation and entered a life of religion.[5] Contarini was intimately involved, as two of his closest friends withdrew to the strict monastery of Camaldoli and tried to induce him and his teacher Giovanni Battista Egnazio to follow them.[6] The native Paduan élite perhaps suffered even more. Ever since the Venetian conquest in 1405 opportunity had become increasingly limited for Paduan nobles and members of the litterati. They learned how to praise Venice in the course of the fifteenth century, but the formulaic nature of their encomia together with the increasing separation of Paduan political and literary pursuits testifies to the ideological pressure which Venice applied to Padua.[7]

Padua still resented Venetian dominance in the early sixteenth century. The lack of solidarity amongst Italian city-states in the face of trying times was a constant refrain in humanist political literature, but Padua not only failed to help Venice, it also seized the opportunity offered in 1509 to rebel. That rankled in Venice, and twenty years later the Venetians commemorated (and rubbed in) their victory by erecting two new city gates in Padua, which still exist. They symbolized the closing of ranks against Padua, which meant

[4] A. Pastore, 'Giacomo Tiburzi', 70.
[5] F. Gilbert, 'Venice in the crisis of the league of Cambrai' and 'Religion and politics in the thought of Gasparo Contarini'.
[6] J. B. Ross, 'Gasparo Contarini and his friends', 192–232.
[7] G. Ronconi, 'Il giurista Lauro Palazzolo', 63–5.

opportunities for its nobles would henceforth be even more restricted. The Paduans responded with 'a steady stream of poems of protest'.[8] The carnivalesque plays of Angelo Beolco, called Ruzante, illustrate this very clearly. His vicious social satire repeatedly scored Venetian aristocrats.[9]

Ultimately, the strain produced a complex reaction known variously as Italian Evangelism or the party of the *spirituali*.[10] It was born in the circles in which Pole moved during Starkey's two residences. In the course of his first visit, this group wove concern for personal salvation (symbolized by belief in *sola fide*), humanism in the narrower sense of linguistic method, and various varieties of republicanism into something new, which then came to define a broad party of reform by the time of Starkey's second stay in the early 1530s. Evangelicals like Contarini who chose to remain in the world continued to espouse loyalty to republican or civic humanist ideals, but often in muted form. In Padua, where public life was no longer the arena for the exercise of *virtù* it had once been, republicanism was first transmuted into new theories of courtly behaviour and then went underground once more and emerged in the form of conciliarism, as it had done already in the fifteenth century. Republicanism or conciliarism also frequently reinforced the call for reform of the institutional church generated by a quest for a more personal religion. Finally, these activists expressed their republicanism and religious striving through literary endeavours. This description also fits Starkey almost perfectly. The struggle to hold these three elements in suspension helped to produce the profound ambiguities and ambivalences in early *cinquecento* Venetian and Paduan thought, many of which Starkey reproduced.[11]

The final step on the way to Evangelism – belief in justification by faith – caused the most trouble. Like Starkey himself, many of his Italian friends embraced a more personal religion reluctantly. They hesitated partly because of the ingrained Venetian patrician attitude that religion was a function of the state and reform largely a matter of institutions.[12] The conversion of Venice from a mixed state to a closed oligarchy hinged on the decade between 1516 and 1526, and the confrontation between religion and politics was part of that movement.[13] Religion necessarily depended on the correct political organization, in the same way as the moral and social hierarchy were interchangeable.[14] As the ruling class entrenched itself, it emphasized inevitably conservative disciplinary and liturgical reforms, designed to produce unity.[15]

[8] L. L. Carroll, 'Carnival rites as vehicles of protest', 496.   [9] *Ibid.*, 491–2 and 494.

[10] E. G. Gleason, 'Sixteenth-century Italian evangelism', 21.

[11] W. J. Bouwsma, *Venice and the defense of republican liberty*, 123 and T. F. Mayer, 'Marco Mantova and the Paduan religious crisis'.

[12] I. Cervelli, *Machiavelli e la crisi dello stato veneziano*, 11, 14, 70.

[13] *Ibid.*, 294, 308; Gilbert, 'Religion and politics in the thought of Gasparo Contarini', 109–10.

[14] Cervelli, *Crisi*, 317.   [15] L. Donvito, 'La "religione cittadina"', 442–3.

The Evangelicals shared many of the same social attitudes as the patriciate. For example, as early as 1514 Contarini wrote to Vincenzo Querini that the problems of the church could be laid to 'the example of these who have governed' it in the past.[16] Querini shared Contarini's judgment, observing that the Christian people had no hope, since their heads were weaker than they.[17] When Contarini offered his model of the ideal bishop, he focused exclusively on the man, and said next to nothing about institutions.[18] Nevertheless, that attitude reinforced the first part of the notion of reform Starkey had absorbed from Colet, while the more general Venetian commitment to disciplining the faithful underscored Colet's stress on institutions.

If Starkey's religion did not change much yet, his literary and political ideas – the almost invariably united second and third elements of the Evangelical triad – grew to maturity during his first visit to Padua. Despite a marked decline from its glory days at the turn of the fourteenth century, Paduan humanism still deserves the label civic in the early sixteenth. Whatever might be true of the 'degeneracy' of Paduan humanism in the narrow sense, even Eugenio Garin conceded that some members of Pole's circle were accomplished humanists, especially Bembo and Leonico.[19] In cases like Leonico's we can demonstrate that Starkey knew particular figures, in others we can infer that he did because Pole was acquainted with them, and in yet others similarities of ideas together with evidence that Starkey and an individual were at least in proximity to one another must do.

Starkey certainly arrived in the city Erasmus called the Athens of Europe and Pier Paolo Vergerio *il teatro del mondo* by 1525 when he witnessed Edward Wotton's MD examination.[20] He could not have gone to Italy on either of Pole's first two trips in 1519 and 1521, but Lupset's report to Erasmus on 21 April 1523 that an unidentified Thomas was with him in Constance could well refer to Starkey en route to Italy with Lupset.[21] Both P. S. Allen and Lupset's biographer J. A. Gee thought it 'very likely' or at least

---

[16] G. Fragnito, 'Cultura umanistica e riforma religiosa', 115.   [17] *Ibid.*, 117.

[18] *Ibid.*, 184.   [19] E. Garin, *L'Umanesimo italiano*, 157–8.

[20] *Op. Ep. Er.*, VIII, 389; L. A. Ferrai, 'Pier Paolo Vergerio il giovane a Padova', 73; for Wotton's examination on 10 April 1525 see E. Martellozzo Forin, ed., *Acta graduum academicorum*, I, 414.

[21] No one doubts that Pole was in Italy in 1521, but whether he had made another trip before that has caused difficulties. Ludovico Beccadelli, Pole's first biographer wrote that he originally made his way to Italy at the age of nineteen (i.e., in 1519), although Beccadelli obscured the issue by adding *intorno al 1520*, but Pole's friendship with Christophorus Longolius provides the best evidence for his earliest visit. Longolius must have known Pole before 18 August 1520 when he bemoaned the absence of everyone, including Pole, from Padua. At least the balance of probability from Longolius's cryptic Latin is that he and Pole had already met. L. Beccadelli, 'Vita del cardinale Reginaldo Polo', 281, and *ERP*, I, 381–2 (*LP*, III:1, 1267) for Longolius's letter. Lupset's letter to Erasmus in *Op. Ep. Er.*, V, 1360, p. 279.

'probable' that this was Thomas Winter, Cardinal Wolsey's illegitimate son.[22] Neither Allen nor Gee developed conclusive demonstrations. Allen contented himself with observing that Winter was in Italy in December 1523 and later at Paris with Lupset.[23] Gee presented a much more elaborate argument. He admitted that 'the identification rests largely on circumstantial evidence', which consisted of two main points. First, Lupset's failure to give his travelling partner's last name meant that he was either very young or Lupset wished to keep his identity a secret. Second, Lupset's journey through Constance dovetailed with Winter's presence in Trent in May. Therefore, they made the trip together.[24] Gee's second point founders on geography. The shortest route from Constance to Italy ran via the St Gotthard pass which led to Milan, not Trent. The most direct line from England to Trent went over either the Reschen or the Brenner, both to the east of the St Gotthard. Far from English travellers having any reason to avoid Milan in 1523, the alliance then in force between Henry and Charles V might have encouraged them to visit the city.[25] The omission of 'Thomas's' family name indicates little about his age, too. As just one example, Jacopo Sadoleto referred to Starkey as *Thomae tuo* in a letter to Pole when Starkey must have been at least thirty-five.[26] Gee offered no reason why Lupset should have concealed his companion's identity.

So much for Gee's two main points. He presented some subsidiary support. A letter from Leonico to Pole of 26 June 1524 was exhibit 'C'. Leonico asked Pole to 'let me know that you and Lupset, and the other Thomas, are well'.[27] Gee thought Leonico meant to put all three on the same social level.[28] However that may be, neither Lupset nor Starkey nor (in Pole's eyes, anyway) Winter were on a par with a near relative of the crown, and Lupset and Starkey's standing was no worse than even since Lupset was the son of a London goldsmith. Gee himself offered an objection to the identification of Leonico's Thomas with Winter, noting that if Winter were still in Italy in June of 1524, he would have overstayed the limit of March laid down by his physicians.[29] Gee borrowed his final point from Allen, but it was ill chosen. The evidence of Lupset's tutelage of Winter which Gee cited seems to make against any close connection between them as early as 1523. In August 1525 Lupset reported on his pupil to Erasmus in singularly reserved terms. He merely noted that Winter was well-born, had collected a number of benefices,

---

[22] *Ibid.*, and J. A. Gee, *Thomas Lupset*, 106.   [23] *Ibid.*, 128ff.   [24] *Ibid.*, 105.
[25] G. R. Elton, ed., *The new Cambridge modern history*, II, *The reformation*, 341.
[26] *ERP*, I, 407 (15 July 1533).
[27] Biblioteca apostolica vaticana, Rome, Codex Rossiana 997, fol. 38v.
[28] Gee, *Lupset*, 106–7.   [29] *Ibid.*, 110.

and been proposed as husband for the Earl of Essex's daughter.[30] Winter never impressed anyone with his brilliance, but the lack of even conventional praise for Winter's virtue or learning suggests that the relation between Lupset and Winter had only just begun.

The identification of Lupset's Thomas with Starkey is no more doubtful than Gee's case, and fits the known chronology of Starkey's career. His friendship with Lupset and the dedicatory letter for his Dialogue provide some positive evidence for the suggestion that they journeyed together in 1523. First, the trip would have come shortly after the expiration of Starkey's Magdalen Fellowship. It seems unlikely that a man who had impressed Wolsey could have remained in Oxford without leaving any further trace. If Starkey went with Lupset, he would have left at almost precisely the moment he disappeared from Oxford records. Second, Starkey wrote to Cromwell in 1535 saying that he had left Oxford for Italy, and in the letter dedicating his Dialogue he added that he had wished to go 'strayght in to the cuntre of Italy' after his youthful study of philosophy.[31] According to the literal meaning of Starkey's phrase, he must have been in Italy for some time before his presence is recorded in 1525.

Finally, the evidence of Starkey's relations with Leonico supports that conclusion. In March 1529, Leonico asked Pole to 'salute all friends, especially Tunstall, Latimer and Starkey'. This is very select company for Starkey in the midst of two other men who could only be described as Leonico's old friends.[32] This seems to indicate a long-standing acquaintance with Starkey as well, dating at least from Leonico's 1524 enquiries after 'the other Thomas'. If this argument is accepted, then Starkey shared Pole's tutor Leonico almost from the beginning.[33] By early 1529 Leonico knew Starkey well enough to write him a long letter assuring Starkey that experience had convinced Leonico of Starkey's good will toward him, which two recent letters had confirmed.[34]

Pole quickly came to know many people in Contarini's circle, even if it appears that these two future allies did not meet face to face until sometime in 1533 or 1534. In September 1534, Pole introduced Contarini to Sadoleto by letter, but in terms which leave open the possibility that Sadoleto already knew him. Whether or not that was the case, apparently Pole and Sadoleto had not talked about Contarini during Pole's brief visit to Sadoleto in

[30] *Ibid.*, 318.

[31] BL Harleian MS 283, fol. 129v and PRO, SP 1/90, fol. 1r.

[32] A. Gasquet, *Cardinal Pole and his early friends*, 107. Tunstall and Leonico had been together at Padua in the 1490s (*ibid.*, 46) and Latimer was probably there at the same time (F. Caspari, *Humanism and the social order in Tudor England*, 24).

[33] *ERP*, I, 387 (Pietro Bembo-Pole, 24 December 1523). See Daniella de Bellis, 'La vita e l'ambiente di Niccolò Leonico Tomeo' for a brief capsule of Leonico's life.

[34] Rossiana 997, fol. 29r.

mid-1532, which seems to mean that neither he nor Sadoleto could have known Contarini that early.[35] Contarini's letter to Charles V of June 1535 confirmed that he had only known Pole for a short time, but as is often the case in the sixteenth century, it is difficult to say how long Contarini meant.[36] Starkey could mean anything up to eighteen months by 'now a late'. Bembo was among the first people Pole met, and he encountered other members of Bembo's circle fairly quickly, including his closest friend, Trifone Gabriele.[37] Therefore, Starkey probably at least learned of Bembo's importance very soon, too, but neither Pole's later distaste for royal service nor Bembo's reputation as a thoroughgoing platonist gives the proper impression of what they could have offered Starkey. Gabriele, known as the Venetian Socrates (despite his almost permanent residence in Padua), was primarily a grammarian and critic, and took the part of the *vita contemplativa* in a philosophical correspondence with Contarini about the value of the active life, among other things.[38] Gabriele no more than Bembo or Leonico led a noticeably public life. It might therefore appear that the allegedly shy, retiring Pole and they would have got along perfectly, far from the bustle of an engaged life.

Pole's friendship with Christophorus Longolius suggests instead that he may have been much less hostile than he later became to the ideals of civic humanism, to which all three of these friends at least paid lip service. Longolius was among Pole's earliest friends in Padua and he lived in Pole's household for a while before his early death. Before he met Pole's friend Richard Pace, but after he apparently knew Pole, Longolius wrote to Pole that the attribute above all others which attracted him to Pace was 'that quality you would like to see in the majority of all responsible men these days – a talent perfectly suited to the running of affairs of state', *ingenium ad gerendam Rempublicam aptissimum.*[39] Pole may or may not have shared his friend's civic humanist enthusiasm, but it is worth noting that Longolius thought he did. Longolius's own interest in political discussion dated from at least his days in Rome.[40]

W. J. Bouwsma doubts the strength of both Bembo's and Gabriele's republicanism, and Leonico's pronounced neo-platonist bent might well have operated as such beliefs did in late *quattrocento* Florence to push him into

[35] *ERP*, I, 408.   [36] *CSPSp*, V:1, 172.

[37] For Pole's contacts, see two letters from Bembo to Pole in *ERP*, I, 383 (for meeting with Bembo himself, 15 July 1521) and 381 (for Gabriele, 31 December 1524). Pietro Verrua called Pole 'specially intimate' with Gabriele by 1532. *Umanisti ed altri 'studiosi viri'*, 81.

[38] F. Dittrich, *Gasparo Contarini*, 204, 209, 260–2. Sperone Speroni and Pietro Aretino praised Gabriele's literary efforts. V. Cian, *Un decennio della vita di M. Pietro Bembo (1521–1531)*, 120–1. C. Cairns quotes Aretino's laudatory verse in *Pietro Aretino and the republic of Venice*, 236.

[39] *ERP*, I, 381 (Longolius–Pole, 18 August 1520). Cf. note 21 above.

[40] Pastore, 'Giacomo Tiburzi', 80, citing Tiburzi's letter to Girolamo Castiglione.

withdrawal. Nevertheless, these three men's decisions to live quietly did not necessarily spring from political principles. Bouwsma plays down Bembo's appearance as the defender of liberty in his friend Baldessare Castiglione's *Il cortegiano*, but Castiglione's choice deserves to be credited, especially since most critics agree that he was after a realistic dialogue.[41] Bembo's turgid official history of Venice may be only in part a product of his failings as a historian.[42] As a Paduan noble at least by choice, his heart may not have been in the assignment. Similarly, Bouwsma admits that Gabriele accepted the Florentine interpretation of Roman history which made Julius Caesar a tyrant for having destroyed liberty, but he minimizes the significance of the ardently republican Giannotti's choice of Gabriele as main speaker in *Della repubblica de' Veneziani*.[43] Giannotti's dialogue reflects his similarly positive attitude toward Bembo's circle. It was set in Bembo's garden and Bembo later urged Giannotti to have it printed.[44]

Giannotti also had a sufficiently high opinion of Leonico to recommend his political wisdom near the end of the work. Leonico was to have centre-stage in a planned sequel on the republic in the abstract which Giannotti never wrote.[45] Giannotti's patron Alessandro de' Pazzi dedicated his translation of Aristotle's *Politics* to Leonico, who corrected it along with Contarini during Pazzi's stay in Venice in 1527.[46] Giannotti and Pazzi may have had solid grounds for relying on Leonico. At the beginning of a dialogue Leonico wrote to console himself on the death of his brother, one of the characters extolled the power of the condolences offered by the learned and experienced leaders of the *republica veneta*. This may have been a conventionally pious sentiment, but it was not obligatory, especially not in a dialogue on such a subject.[47] It would thus be as true to say that Gabriele and Leonico played important roles in Paduan civic humanism as to doubt their commitment to it. Gabriele helped to introduce the mainstream of Florentine republicanism to Padua and Leonico did not stand in its way, while both contributed to the nascent myth of Venice, at least through the *personae* that Giannotti created for them. Margaret King goes further and points to Leonico as a specimen of how Venetian and Paduan humanists created a 'profound fusion of Aristotelian philosophy and Venetian political principles'.[48] It might be safe to

---

[41] B. Castiglione, *Il cortegiano*, ed. V. Cian, I, chapter 20, 429–30. Bouwsma, *Venice*, 136 and 155. Bouwsma conceded that some 'personal exchange' with Bembo might have lain behind Castiglione's choice. If so, this casts further doubt on Bouwsma's reservations about Bembo. G. Spini, *Antonio Brucioli*, 148 in common with other critics emphasized Castiglione's realism.

[42] P. Bembo, *Prose e rime*, ed. C. Dionisotti, 52.

[43] *Venice*, 158. Cf. H. Baron, *The crisis of the early Italian renaissance*, 53n.

[44] D. Giannotti, *Lettere a Piero Vettori*, ed. R. Ridolfi and C. Roth, 68.

[45] D. Giannotti, *Della repubblica de' Veneziani*, ed. G. Rosini, 242.

[46] De Bellis, 'Leonico', 69.   [47] N. Leonico, *Dialogi*, sig. LVIIIv.

[48] M. L. King, *Venetian humanism in an age of patrician dominance*, 182. For Leonico's science, see below, 73–74.

conclude that Bembo and his friends were *Vernunftrepublikaner*, the species which abounded in the Weimar Republic: content to profess themselves sound, but perhaps not much to be relied upon in a crisis.

Even while overstating the case, Wilhelm Schenk came close to the mark when he took Castiglione's fiction as almost a literal transcription of Bembo's views, which he thought 'informed' the ideas about tyranny which 'Pole' expressed in Starkey's Dialogue.[49] It may be that Bembo offered Starkey even more, quite apart from his theory of language, which will be considered later. Literary historians have usually treated Bembo in an apolitical way. Carlo Dionisotti, the great expert on Bembo, singled out Bembo's concern with style and deemphasized much of the content of his works. An overriding concern with appearances accounts for the mediocrity of his history of Venice, according to Dionisotti.[50] But this stylistic approach does not give enough credit to Bembo's experience in the courts of Ferrara and Urbino and its consequences for his politics. Piero Floriani maintains that Bembo's great concern with language sprang from the necessity of finding an instrument to express the new reality of the courts.[51] Hence in *Gli asolani* Bembo actually experimented both with inventing a new courtly society and in giving it a form to express itself, instead of composing a platonic exercise in contemplation.[52] More important, it was Bembo's first essay in an ongoing exploration of the relation between intellectuals and power-wielders of the sort Castiglione also pursued.[53] A personal trial playing the courtier dissatisfied Bembo and he retired to Padua, where his experience was available to Starkey.

Not all of Pole's and Starkey's friends were overtly or covertly political. Pole became a student of Lazzaro Bonamico, for example, sometime before 1528, while Starkey became close to him at least before leaving Padua in 1534.[54] Starkey's friendship with Bonamico may well provide another bit of evidence in the effort to pin down when Pole came to know him, and hence when Starkey may have met him originally. Giuseppe Marangoni confused an obviously inaccurate narrative by another student of Bonamico with the story of Pole's trip to Rome in 1525 and concluded that Pole took Bonamico with him on that journey.[55] Despite misreading the evidence, Marangoni could still be correct that Pole and Bonamico met in 1525, the year Bonamico

---

[49] W. Schenk, *Reginald Pole*, 40.   [50] Bembo, *Prose e rime*, 52.
[51] P. Floriani, *Bembo e Castiglione*, 13–14.   [52] *Ibid.*, 17–19.   [53] *Ibid.*, 27.
[54] See below, chapt. 6.
[55] G. Marangoni, 'Lazzaro Bonamico e lo studio padovano', II, 314. He adopted Giambattista Verci's notion that Bonamico had gone to Rome on Pole's advice, a year before Pole was born. M. Hallé reached the same conclusion. *Reginald Pole*, 21. J. V. Pollet's claim that Pole and Bonamico met in Rome in 1527 cannot be supported, either. J. V. Pollet, ed., *Julius Pflug Correspondence*, I (*1510–39*), 312.

returned from a stint in Bologna. Then again, they may have met during Pole's first visit when Bonamico was in Padua for a year.[56] More recently, Rino Avesani claims that Pole did not know Bonamico before 1532.[57] Leonico's letter to Pole of 7 February 1531 seems to support Avesani. Leonico praised 'Lazarus, named Bonamico from the city of Bassiano' who had begun to contribute mightily to the good state of the humanities in Padua.[58] Two letters from Pole to Sadoleto, however, clinch the case for an earlier meeting between Pole and Bonamico. In September 1534, about the time Starkey left Padua, Pole wrote to Sadoleto saying that he was trying to recapture his youth by bringing Bonamico, whom he had known as master and 'quasi-tutor', into his household.[59] In November 1532 he wrote that he had not read as much Latin in four years as he was then writing to the bishop.[60] Thus his tutelage under Bonamico must have come no later than about 1528.

Like his master Leonico, Bonamico was a punctilious Ciceronian.[61] He learned Greek from Contarini's teacher Marco Musuro and Leonico refined it; his mastery has recently been judged more than passable.[62] In the course of his arts studies at Padua beginning in 1499, Bonamico became a close follower of Pietro Pomponazzi and put his language skills to good use by providing his master with fresh readings of Aristotle.[63] He later followed Pomponazzi to Bologna and served as one of his executors. Sperone Speroni, another 'zealous custodian of the memory of Pomponazzi' joined Bonamico in the Paduan literary academy of *gl'Infiammati*.[64] Speroni certainly followed Pomponazzi's precept that man was cut out for moral action, as did other of Bonamico's fellow students and friends.[65] Contarini, Pomponazzi's star pupil in the first decade of the century, must have known Bonamico well. In 1532 he opposed a project to lure Bonamico to Bologna and succeeded in having his friend's salary augmented.[66] Perhaps some of Contarini's activism rubbed off on Bonamico.

Neither Bonamico's politics nor his contemporary fame as a teacher have left much trace.[67] A hint of the former may appear in his acid lament to Aldo Manuzio in 1509 that the siege and the behaviour of Venetian troops made it impossible for him to write Greek 'in this Paduan barbarism'.[68] A set of

[56] Marangoni, 'Bonamico', II, 312–14.   [57] R. Avesani, 'Bonamico, Lazaro', *DBI*.
[58] Rossiana 997, fol. 55v (Gasquet, *Pole*, 114–15).   [59] *ERP*, I, 410 (13 September 1534).
[60] *Ibid.*, 401. The vagaries of an old man's memory may then have influenced Leonico's letter.
[61] De Bellis, 'Leonico', 67 for the two.
[62] G. Marangoni, 'Lazzaro Bonamico e lo studio padovano', III, 168 and A. Meschini, 'Inediti greci di Lazaro Bonamico', 54–5 and 68.
[63] A. Stella, 'Tradizione razionalistica patavina', 279.
[64] B. Nardi, *Saggi sull'aristotelismo padovano*, 341.
[65] A. B. Collins, *The secular is sacred*, 4.   [66] Avesani, 'Bonamico'.
[67] Meschini, 'Bonamico', 51–2 for his reputation as an educator.   [68] *Ibid.*, 56–7.

lecture notes gives some idea of what Bonamico taught. His comment on Cicero's *Pro lege manilia*, delivered between November 1530 and December 1531, mainly summarized the oration and occasionally commented on form and style. Bonamico emphasized Cicero's dedication to the *res publica* and its *libertas* and *utilitas*, but the only hint of his own attitude does not square well with the careerism reflected in Cicero's maiden political speech.[69] Bonamico's auditor noted an *ADMONITIO LAZARI* that 'there is never glory in external goods'.[70] These notes do not offer much support for Bonamico's students' claim that deep philosophical questions interested him. One of them linked him with Leonico as an antidote to Marcantonio Zimara, but none of his friends' urgings could induce him to commit himself to any full-dress consideration of such problems.[71] Whatever the content of his teaching, Bonamico took students without any regard to their religious or political views. He sheltered the violently anti-papal Jakob Ziegler in 1528–9, well after Ziegler had gone over to the Reformation, and taught Benedetto Varchi, a Florentine republican exile. Bonamico and Varchi probably shared their neo-platonism.[72]

Many of Pole's fellow students also became his friends, among them Pier Paolo Vergerio the younger, Pietro Martire Vermigli (Peter Martyr), Marcantonio Flaminio, and four others who were later among his closest allies and supporters: Vittore Soranzo, Tommaso Sanfelice, Giovanni Morone and Pole's life-long companion, Alvise Priuli.[73] Very little is known about the last four at this early period, but Vergerio and Martire could have been especially important to Starkey. Vergerio had studied in Padua and taught there for a while in both the notarial and legal faculties. Vergerio remained in Padua until 1527 at least and in Venice until 1532. During this time he joined the ranks of Paduan dialogue writers with his *De republica veneta*, but never got around to its promised sequel on Venetian government.[74] Martire had come to the monastery of S. Giovanni da Vedara in Padua in 1518, attracted by its humanist prior Alberto da Verona. Martire's literary tastes no doubt account for his close friendship with Bembo, which Phillip McNair called 'the only reasonable explanation' for the assertion of Martire's sixteenth-century biographer that Pole was 'sometime a speciall friend of Martyr'.[75] Martire's stout

---

[69] Biblioteca Ambrosiana, Milan, MS H 28 inf. 54, fol. 1r–v.   [70] *Ibid.*, fol. 6r.

[71] Marangoni, II, 307; Stella, 'Tradizione', 279.   [72] Marangoni, III, 146.

[73] D. Fenlon, *Heresy and obedience in Tridentine Italy*, 25.

[74] A. J. Schutte, *Pier Paolo Vergerio*, chapt. 1, especially 36–8. If Edmund Harvel was in a position to know, Starkey did not know Vergerio. In a postscript to a letter of October 1535 Harvel told Starkey that 'one petrus pau[lus] vergerius [has been] sent to ferdinando and al other princes of almayn' about the convocation of a council. BL Cotton Nero B VI, fol. 139v.

[75] P. McNair, *Peter Martyr in Italy*, 97–8 and 100.

Aristotelianism arose from his Paduan education, and his political thinking in particular rested on Aristotle.[76] Martire's friend, Gerolamo Cardano, rector of the university in 1525 bitterly opposed all tyranny.[77] No one has ever detected any obvious political views in Flaminio, but he had spent a year in Castiglione's household in 1514 and 1515. Flaminio would go even further in the direction of personal religion and inner retreat than Pole and would appear as the defender of monarchy in Marco Girolamo Vida's *De dignitate reipublicae* (*c.* 1545), which was dedicated to Pole.[78] On the other hand, Flaminio was close to Giannotti.[79] Leaving Flaminio and Bonamico aside, most of Pole's friends seem to have had reasonably strong political convictions at least leaning in the direction of republicanism.

So did the Venetian humanists with whom Pole and Starkey probably came in contact, most of whom resembled Contarini both politically and religiously. This is especially true of Egnazio, who was one of Contarini's closest friends.[80] Egnazio later taught Starkey's friend George Lily and he was well enough known to Englishmen for Richard Croke to solicit Egnazio's help in 1530.[81] Egnazio had another tie to Pole through Romolo Amaseo, whom Pole later tried to recruit for Wolsey's new college at Oxford.[82] The Aldine academy counted him a founding member and he edited both Cicero's *De officiis* (1517) and *Epistolae familiares* (1509) for Aldus.[83] He had gone farther than Contarini in the direction of withdrawal, actually cloistering himself at Camaldoli for a time.[84] Egnazio decided such a life was not for him, and pursued a career as a public orator and teacher of eloquence.[85] The political views expressed in Egnazio's *De caesaribus libri III* resembled Gabriele's and Cardano's, or what Hans Baron has called the 'new Guelphism' of the later fifteenth century which rested on opposition to tyrants in both church and secular world, beginning with Caesar.[86] John Libby calls

[76] *Ibid.*, 106–7 and R. M. Kingdon, *The political thought of Peter Martyr Vermigli*, VII–VIII.
[77] *Ibid.*, 99 and R. de Mattei, 'Il problema della tirannide', 396–7.
[78] C. Maddison, *Marcantonio Flaminio*, 14; E. G. Gleason, ed. and trans., *Reform thought in sixteenth-century Italy*, 47, and M. Firpo, review of Marcantonio Flaminio, *Lettere*, ed. A. Pastore, 660; and *CSPV*, V, p. x.
[79] Giannotti, *Lettere a Vettori*, 19.
[80] G. degli Agostini, 'Battista Egnazio sacerdoto viniziano', 58. For the most recent summary of his life, see J. B. Ross, 'Venetian schools and teachers fourteenth to early sixteenth century', 536–56.
[81] *LP*, IV:3, 6236 and for Lily, his letter to Starkey, BL Nero B VI, fol. 166r (22 April 1535).
[82] E. Billanovich, 'Intorno a Romolo Amaseo', 532–3.
[83] M. E. Cosenza, *Biographical and bibliographical dictionary of the Italian humanists*, II, 1280.
[84] Ross, 'Contarini and his friends', 195.   [85] *Enciclopedia cattolica*, X, 386.
[86] *De caesaribus libri III a dictatore Caesare ad Constantinum Palaeologum, hinc a Carolo Magno ad Maximilianum caesarem*, sig. A6r; Baron, 'Die politische Entwicklung der italienischen Renaissance', 48ff.

Egnazio's outlook 'traditional' rather than republican, and faults him for failing to understand 'the significance of the Venetian struggle with despotic Milan', but this may give Egnazio too little credit for his forthright stand against tyranny in *De caesaribus* and condemn him by a standard which would have found most other humanists wanting, too.[87] Egnazio's later religion continued to fit the Evangelical mould. In 1536 his library held the best book on ancient councils which an ally of Contarini's could find, and near the end of his life he sheltered the fugitive Vergerio, even though Egnazio claimed to have thrown Vergerio out when he realized the bishop was no longer a *buono cattolico*.[88] Vergerio may have been Egnazio's student' and he certainly trained the Evangelically inclined Paolo Manuzio and the Genesio-Lutheran Matthias Flaccius Illyricus.[89]

Exiles from Florence and Venetians and Paduans willing to help them form one last group around Pole and Starkey. Some of them are of special significance for their hand in amalgamating Florentine and Venetian civic humanism into a new theory of government by the *ottimati*, or the oligarchy cooperating with the ruler.[90] Others remained unreconstructed republicans, following more closely in Machiavelli's footsteps. One of the most important of the first group was Alessandro de' Pazzi de' Medici. In 1521 Pazzi had begun the creation of an oligarchical theory of the Florentine constitution in response to a request from Giulio de' Medici. He had asked Pazzi to come up with an argument to refute the *Consiglio Grande*'s claim to sovereignty, and Pazzi put forward the contention that the principate should run Florence together with *il governo degli ottimati e di polizia*. The example of Venice provided the underpinning for this new system.[91] The use of *polizia* as an apparent synonym for oligarchy is worth remembering.

It may be that the purest form of Florentine aristocratic thought also found its way to Venice through Pole's friend Gianmatteo Giberti, who developed a 'relationship of great trust' with Francesco Guicciardini in 1526.[92] Bembo put Pole in touch with the papal datary Giberti just before that.[93] Pole could

---

[87] 'Venetian history and political thought after 1509', 9, 33, 37.

[88] F. Dittrich, *Regesten und Briefen des Cardinals Gasparo Contarini*, 91 for his book. For Egnazio and Vergerio, see F. Sarri, 'Giovanni Fabrini da Figlione (1516–1580?)', 627–31; Ross, 'Egnazio', 549; and Schutte, *Vergerio*, 230, who cites Girolamo Muzio's possibly unreliable report that Vergerio had not only stayed with Egnazio, but actually given readings from his works in Egnazio's house.

[89] *Enc. catt., s.n.*; Cosenza, *Dictionary, s.n.*; and G. Piaia, *Marsilio da Padova nella riforma e nella controriforma*, 92.

[90] See especially R. Pecchioli, *Dal 'mito' di Venezia all' 'ideologia americana'*, 43–73.

[91] R. von Albertini, *Das florentinisches Staatsbewusstsein in Übergang von der Republik zum Principat*, 85–7.

[92] A. Prosperi, *G. M. Giberti*, 65–6 and Albertini, *Staatsbewusstsein*, 94ff.

[93] Bembo wrote to Pole on 24 December 1524, saying that he had sent Pole's letters to Giberti and on 23 January passed on Giberti's opinion of them. *ERP*, I, 385 and 387.

aready have heard of Giberti by reputation, since Giberti had visited England in 1522 and met Cuthbert Tunstall, John Fisher, Thomas More and Antonio Bonvisi, all of whom knew Pole. Giberti tried hard to persuade Tunstall and Fisher to return to Rome with him to undertake the reform of the church from the top down.[94] Henry and Wolsey counted him a friend in the Curia and Giberti's retirement to his see after the sack of Rome disappointed them.[95] Giberti may well have been sympathetic to Guicciardini's ideas, because Guicciardini drew on the example of Venice and Giberti was at one time its partisan.[96] He converted his erstwhile political sympathies into religious reform after he retired to his diocese of Verona in 1527.[97]

Giannotti best represents the tendency to justify oligarchical government, which Quentin Skinner terms 'aristocratic republicanism'.[98] He was in Venice from June 1525 until November 1526, and then again for six months in 1527.[99] Giannotti acted as secretary both for Pazzi during part of the latter's stay, and perhaps also for a Venetian notable.[100] In the former case he declared a new party allegiance, and in the latter he may have gained some first-hand experience of Venetian politics. Giannotti had been a student of the Florentine Platonist Francesco Diaceto, but his reading of Aristotle inspired him much more. By the time he left Florence, he was almost certainly an adherent of the aristocratic opposition, Niccolò 'Capponi's man', as Randolph Starn put it. Giannotti formulated his new oligarchical republicanism in the course of *Della repubblica*.[101] Thus he may well have passed on the ardour of the new convert to Starkey, the more so because Giannotti made religious reform a function of his republicanism.[102] Among his friends were Antonio Brucioli, Pier Vettori, Pierfrancesco Portinari, and Filippo and Lorenzo Strozzi.[103] He was also close to Flaminio and Amaseo.[104]

One of the earliest of the second class of Florentine exiles – the committed republicans – was Brucioli, who had been a member of Machiavelli's circle in the Orti Oricellari. He came to Venice in 1522 and returned there before the end of 1526 after trips to France and Germany.[105] For some of this time Brucioli lived with Contarini's friend Carlo Cappello, who regarded Florentine

---

[94] Prosperi, *Giberti*, 110.   [95] *Ibid.*, 85.   [96] Pecchioli, 'Mito', 68–9.
[97] Prosperi, *Giberti*, 47.
[98] Q. Skinner, *Foundations of modern political thought*, I, *The renaissance*, 160–1.
[99] R. Starn, *Donato Giannotti and his epistolae*, 20.
[100] Albertini, *Staatsbewusstsein*, 150 and Giannotti, *Lettere a Vettori*, 6.
[101] Starn, *Giannotti*, 15, 19–21. Capponi became the last *gonfalionere* before the Medici conquest.
[102] J. G. A. Pocock, *The Machiavellian moment: Florentine political thought and the atlantic republican tradition*, 293.
[103] G. Bisaccia, *La 'Repubblica fiorentina' di Donato Giannotti*, 14.
[104] Giannotti, *Lettere a Vettori*, 19 and 23.   [105] Spini, *Brucioli*, 39, 40–55.

republicans very sympathetically. He was ambassador to the Florentine republic in its last days, when he did all he could to aid it.[106] The republican Machiavelli of the then unpublished *Discorsi* arrived in Venice through Brucioli.[107] Lorenzo Strozzi, the dedicatee of Machiavelli's *Arte della guerra* doubtless helped. It is difficult to determine whether Pole or Starkey had direct contacts with any of these Florentines, but Richard Morison's familiarity with Machiavelli proves that some Englishmen in Venice and Padua availed themselves of the exiles' knowledge, and Bouwsma and Myron Gilmore both think that Contarini could have known the *Discorsi* before composing his own *De magistratibus et republica venetorum*.[108] Other exiles who may have arrived in Venice before the final collapse of the Florentine republic in 1530 included Giacopo Nardi, Pier Filippo Pandolfini and Silvestro Aldobrandini, not to mention Giannotti and his friend Giovanni Borgherini, Capponi's son-in-law.[109]

Machiavelli's ideas may or may not have had much importance in Venice and Padua, but there can be no question of how much Starkey depended on the 'myth of Venice'. Margaret King's brilliant new synthesis of how fifteenth-century Venetian humanists elaborated that myth casts a flood of light on what Starkey meant to do, even if he drew on a later and more hybrid version of it.[110] To King's humanists, Venice had been founded on the principles of liberty and justice, which made it 'intrinsically righteous'. As the darling of providence, it would last forever. Getting to the political nub, they argued that the Venetian nobility enshrined hereditary virtue and ruled selflessly. The *doge*, the best of the best, governed 'without ambition and subject to the law'. The people had sufficient material goods and were convinced of the justice of the system, and therefore never even thought about rebellion. Starkey deviated from this paradigm only in thinking the nobility's virtue needed to be recharged.

More than the surface elements of the myth, Starkey shared its underpinnings as well, what King calls 'an armature, a context, a metaphysics for the

---

[106] L. Firpo, ed., *Ambasciatori veneti in Inghilterra*, xix. Cappello shared Musuro's tutelage in Greek as well as similar literary tastes with Contarini. As a young man, Cappello wrote literary and philosophical works, including Platonic dialogues.

[107] Spini, *Brucioli*, 27. See also Q. Skinner, *Machiavelli*, 50.

[108] W. G. Zeeveld, *Foundations of Tudor policy*, 184–9 argues strongly that Morison had read Machiavelli, a point contested by D. S. Berkowitz in his introduction to *Humanist scholarship and public order*, 70–8. Both their cases are open to doubt, but Morison must somehow have encountered Machiavelli. See my review of Berkowitz's edition in *SCJ*, XVI:4 (1985), 540–1. Bouwsma, *Venice*, 149, 16–17 and M. P. Gilmore, 'Myth and reality in Venetian political theory', 433.

[109] Albertini, *Staatsbewusstsein*, 143 and *passim*.

[110] The following discussion drawn from King, *Venetian humanism in an age of patrician dominance*, 174–91.

mythic vision'. The world was an ordered place, not the potential chaos Florentine humanists saw. This vision produced the Venetians' distinctive attitude which 'subordinated[d] the individual to the group, and place[d] both in a timeless hierarchical universe' inherited from their ancestors and resting on the authority of Aristotle and Christ. Starkey, too, proposed severe curbs on the individual lest his passions disturb the commonwealth, but he changed the content of his moral code from the more 'medieval' one the Venetians espoused. Nevertheless, he and they had the same end. The ruling nobility, by exercising self-control or what Starkey would call the discipline of the commonwealth, and providing a model of the virtues formed the whole of Venice into a 'single personality', united by love and symbolized by the *doge*. Hierarchy meant concord, tranquillity and, ultimately, atemporality. But in order to preserve this system, change had to be avoided at all costs, even if that meant ambivalence about, or even suspicion of, liberty. Hence Starkey's deep concern over this fundamental value was of a piece with his Venetian predecessors'. Finally, both turned to Aristotle's 'comprehensive vision' for legitimation either of 'Venice's highly stratified, rigid, and authoritarian society', or of exactly the same system transported to England.

King spells out the social and political function of Venetian humanism, which was fundamentally 'uncritical' and designed to 'affirm, not challenge, Venetian culture'. Unlike Florentine civic humanism, Venetian 'civicism' was not a new thing, but rather a matter of expressing 'old concepts in new forms'. English humanism of a civic stripe almost had to be more critical, but that did not mean that it had necessarily to ride roughshod over old standards and values. King's explanation of the nature and role of the basic Venetian humanist value of *unanimitas* clarifies exactly what Starkey hoped to do.

Rid of the potentially corrosive notions of individual freedom, attitudinal openness, cosmic dynamism, it became the vehicle of accepted values and familiar ideas shaped to new precision ... To natives, it compelled acquiescence, for how is it possible to protest against an order that is righteous and synchronous with a heavenly order of ineffable perfection? ... Thus patrician intellectuals [and their clients] guided the formation of a humanist culture that would help protect patrician hegemony by anticipating any challenge to it ... Benevolent policies and constitutional structures alike served as prophylaxis against social unrest.

Starkey was not a patrician, but his patron Reginald Pole most assuredly was.

Starkey probably had most direct contact with this powerful myth through Contarini's circle. Contarini's *De magistratibus* crystallized 'public opinion' into a nearly archetypal work, as its rapid ascent to the status of a classic text in the creation of the 'myth of Venice' indicates.[111] Contarini began it in the

---

[111] The most recent survey of the vast literature on the *mito di Venezia* is in the first chapter of Edward Muir's intriguing *Civic ritual in renaissance Venice*. Muir notes that the myth

early 1520s when he was mainly employed as Venetian envoy to Charles V, although he did not complete it until a decade later and probably kept it out of public view until it was finished.[112] Neither Giannotti nor Starkey made explicit reference to *De magistratibus*, no doubt because they had not read it, but there is no particular reason why Contarini would not have talked about his work.[113] The similarities between all three of these works, including Starkey's Dialogue, make them all a part of Venetian political discussions. Gigliola Fragnito suggested this when she hypothesized that *De magistratibus* reflected the talk in Pole's household as recorded in Starkey's Dialogue, but those relations should probably be reversed.[114] Rather than emphasize at every turn the similarities between Contarini and Starkey, suffice it to say once that Contarini's work deserves extended treatment, because on virtually every point singled out it resembled Starkey's ideas closely.

Most humanists tolerated contradiction as a way of life, and so did Contarini and Starkey. They held many of the same incompatible ideas and may therefore have lived in what Bouwsma calls a 'state of tension' which issued in both Evangelical religious beliefs and republicanism.[115] Bouwsma's list of basic oppositions in Contarini's thought could have been drawn from Starkey's Dialogue. They all fit Bouwsma's dialectic between Augustinianism and Stoicism as well as the fundamental dialectic John Pocock has identified in Renaissance republicanism between 'particularity and time', or nature and supernature, whether Christian grace or humanist *virtù*.[116] The problem lay in how to assure the stability of an actual political unit in historical time, without abstracting it from that time or propping it up by supernatural means. Both Contarini and Starkey got themselves into particular trouble here. As Bouwsma summed up, the good Aristotelian Contarini believed the state was natural and therefore subject to decay, but the peculiar constitution of Venice made it an exception to the rule. The reason, alas, was the qualities nature had given it. Contarini thus defined nature ambiguously. He usually meant the 'eternal order of things', but it could also be 'the world of time' with its cycles of growth and decline.[117] Likewise, Contarini asserted that

especially attracted Englishmen by its emphasis on liberty, but he discusses no English contributions before the reign of Elizabeth, 52.
[112] F. Gilbert, 'The date of the composition of Contarini's and Giannotti's books on Venice', 176 and 182.
[113] Schutte, *Vergerio*, 37. K. W. Beckmann also suggested the importance of Contarini's work to Starkey, but through a more rigorous (and therefore problematic, given the dating of the two works) comparison of *De magistratibus* and Dialogue. 'Staatstheorie und Kirchenpolitik im Werke des englischen Humanisten Thomas Starkey', 88–92.
[114] Fragnito, 'Cultura umanistica', 114.   [115] Bouwsma, *Venice*, 123 and 41.
[116] Pocock, *Machiavellian moment*, part 1. For more on this point, see the conclusion below.
[117] Bouwsma, *Venice*, 152–3.

Venice was eternal, but carefully described its historical development.[118] Contarini combined nature, history and virtue to argue that 'our ancestors therefore by the imitation of nature ... have therein used the iust temperature and excellent moderation, that none ... may any way blame or finde fault with a government so vertuously established, and so temperately main-tayned'.[119] In common with Starkey and many of their contemporaries, Contarini framed his analysis on the twin principles of unity and hierarchy, which can operate in tandem only in a hierocratic or at least extremely autocratic system, but not easily in a republic.[120] These two came into open but unresolved conflict in Contarini's explanation of the *doge*'s position both by the great chain of being and by the superior prudence of old men. (Both are basic Aristotelian positions, although Bouwsma does not note this.)

Contarini designed *De magistratibus* to explain the institutions and laws of Venice, which were equivalent to true reason and produced the form of the commonwealth (5–6/263). He began by explaining why the laws must govern on the basis of an Aristotelian account of man's civil nature which led him to associate with his fellows in order to achieve happiness through the exercise of virtue (8/264). Therefore the ruler must provide a commonwealth 'accommodated to vertue', and himself be modelled on the rationality of the human mind 'being by nature granted in us as a beam of the heavenly brightnes'. That meant a single man could not rule because 'inferior and brutish powers' too often diverted him from the rational course. Instead, the laws should govern (9–10/265). Once enacted, they provide a certain guarantee against 'the greatest and most dangerous contagion' of sedition, since no one could complain that any individual man had caught him out (11/266). Contarini quoted Aristotle's simile of 'God in the university of things as an ancient lawe in a civill company' to conclude his discussion of law (12/266F).

Cold, unemotional law having been enshrined, Contarini turned to the question of who should administer it, act as its lieutenant, and decide cases to which the law did not extend. As ancient history confirmed, a multitude would do better than a king, but the many could not govern because it lacked unity. As Contarini put it succinctly, 'civill society ... consisteth in a certaine unity'. Thus the best form of government was 'a temperature betweene the state of nobility and popular sort', or a mixed state (12–14/266H–267A). Contarini supported the point with the same historical examples Starkey would use, the Lacedemonians, Athenians and Romans (267B–C). But Contarini quickly got around to putting the nobility in control. At the outset he

---

[118] *Ibid.*, 145–6.
[119] Gasparo Contarini, *De magistratibus et republica venetorum*, 326F. I cite the English translation of Lewes Lewkenor, *The Commonwealth and Government of Venice*, 149. Future references will be to the English translation, followed by the Latin text.
[120] Bouwsma, *Venice*, 147.

had tabbed it as responsible for the success of Venice. From the moment when all the nobles consented to create the state they had never paid any attention to 'their owne private glorie or commodity' (6/263). Now he did not actually intend to say that the mean fell between aristocracy and people, but rather that aristocracy came between prince and people. Venice, of course, showed the best example of such a mixed government. The *doge* represented royal power, the *consiglio maggiore* the populace, and the *dieci* and the *pregadi* holding the mean between them stood in for the nobility (18–19/269B and 65/290H). Contarini may have picked up the idea of the mixed state from Machiavelli whose Florentine pessimism would have reinforced Contarini's dim view of human nature, but trying to pin down a source for the wide-spread notion of mixed government is probably even more pointless a task in the Renaissance than it is in the classical world.[121] It was probably already the standard interpretation of the Venetian constitution in Venice itself.[122]

Contarini leaned almost as heavily on the corporate metaphor as did Starkey. Contarini appealed to both macrocosm and microcosm to prove that someone wielding authority in the commonwealth was necessary in order to bind all the rest into 'one entire body'. Just as everything in the universe was subject to the will of 'one heavenly and eternall mover', 'and as in a living creature there are many and diverse members, whose functions are sundrie and different: yet nevertheless are all comprised under one onely life and member, which is the hart', so in a multitude (38/278G–H). As Bouswma noted, unity very quickly gave way to hierarchy even while Contarini continued to operate within the corporate metaphor. Following Aristotle once again Contarini concluded that 'olde men should be placed at the helme' according to the 'wisedome & policie of nature' (64/290F). Some of them would be members of the *dieci* who preserved Venice from sedition, or the equivalent of 'the corruption and putrefaction of one humour' which led to 'many & most daungerous diseases' in a human body. Contarini emphasized how the Venetians' ancestors had established laws together with the *dieci* to avoid 'an intestine enemy, or civill strife & sedition among the citizens' (77/195D). (They had, of course, drawn on ancient precedent [78/296E].) Finally, it was up to the 'eyes of the citie', the gentlemen, to act as reason and cooperate with the less noble officers to make 'a happie and wel compacted bodie' (149/326E). Here the *doge* played his most important role by seeing to it that every officer did his duty (41/279D).

We do not know what Contarini thought about the English constitution, but others of his compatriots left enough comments to make clear that Starkey shared their analysis of its fundamental weaknesses. A series of three

---

[121] Bouwsma, *Venice*, 149, 16–17. For the caution, see F. W. Walbank, *Polybius*, 137.
[122] F. Gilbert, 'The Venetian constitution in Florentine political thought', 466–70.

relazioni delivered to the Venetian Senate by returning ambassadors between 1535 and 1558 together with one anonymous set of observations dating from 1498 afford a remarkably consistent picture.

Someone in the suite of ambassador Andrea Trevisan began by noting that the English did not abide by imperial law, and he went on at length about the faults of English criminal procedure.[123] Of more constitutional significance, the anonymous author complained that the king was not elected and often came to the throne by force of arms, despite the principle of hereditary succession (40). It is worth noting that the constable – the head of Starkey's chief council – came first in the discussion of great officers of state and household (46–7). When Cappello returned from England he delivered some barbed criticisms. As had the earlier writer, he pointed out the connection between the English refusal to adopt imperial law and their 'many bad laws and constitutions', but he went further than his predecessor and traced them, including feudal tenure, back to *'Guilelmo bastardo* who ruled there and had dominion' (54). Apparently the 'Norman yoke' had some Italian origins or perhaps Cappello had talked to the same people as Starkey did. Three later ambassadors offered much the same interpretation. Daniele Barbaro, ambassador under Edward VI, viewed the English political system less hostilely than some of his peers and consequently imposed Venetian standards on it even more rigorously. He interpreted the coronation ritual as an election procedure and concluded that although the crown was hereditary, 'it needs the consent of the lords and of the people'.[124] Giovanni Michele, who left England at the end of Mary's reign, adopted most of Cappello's report on the idiosyncratic English legal system, including its establishment by William.[125] All the laws worked to the advantage of the king, 'because they were established by a nation, than which there is none in the whole world more learned in the lies and delays of suits than that of Normandy' (316). Michele made no mention of the succession, but he did compare the monarch to the Grand Turk, who called parliament only out of *modestia*. Originally the king had been a 'political and civil head', rather than a 'lord and monarch' as he had become (316 and 318). Then parliament had much more freedom. It would be most interesting to know where these ambassadors got their information. Perhaps they continued to confer with the likes of the Duke of Buckingham, as they had earlier.[126]

Such ideas shaped Starkey's political attitudes, as they did Giannotti's.

---

[123] Firpo, ed., *Ambasciatori veneti*, 28–9. This report is available in English in *A relation, or rather a true account of the islands of England*, trans. with notes by C. A. Sneyd.

[124] E. Albèri, ed., *Relazioni degli ambasciatori veneti al senato*, 229. For Barbaro, see G. Alberigo's article in *DBI*, where Alberigo characterized his account as 'rather a literary exercise than an effective contribution to the Signory's political action', 91.

[125] *Relazioni*, 315.

[126] B. J. Harris, *Edward Stafford*, 171. These conferences were held at Venetian behest.

Both drew much from the Venetian ethos which Contarini represented. Yet Contarini on the one hand and Giannotti and Starkey on the other differed over how to express their ideas. Starkey and Giannotti saw eye to eye in considering a dialogue, not a treatise, the most effective means to communicate political ideas. Thus far neither historians nor literary scholars have paid much attention to the form of either of their works. Nevertheless, the genre of Starkey's work must be established in order to determine how it limited what he could have said.[127] Experience in Padua probably had a decisive impact on the literary tastes of both Starkey and Giannotti, but the latter's *De' Veneziani* could almost have served as the former's blueprint. Current practice in Padua would have encouraged these two to believe that just about anything could pass for a dialogue which could be put to nearly any end.[128] Neither classical literature nor his own vernacular offered Starkey any better models than those abounding in the literary circles of Padua. Dialogue best suited their tastes, and wide-open experimentation continued to be the rule.[129] Starkey's dependence on only two characters, as well as his blending of scientific method and literary form, fit the species of literally 'free-form' early *cinquecento* dialogue denizenated in Padua. Not even Paduan practice, however, can account for the most peculiar feature of Starkey's work: its pronounced hortatory 'aim' at one of its two characters. Starkey praised Pole's talents as a statesman, not his own, in the process of urging his patron to admit his responsibilities. Nonetheless, the Paduans willingly, indeed exuberantly, experimented with Starkey's chosen mode of communicating with Pole, and their example could surely have had an impact even on this nearly unique feature of Starkey's work.

The study of sixteenth-century dialogue – whether English or continental – is in its infancy, despite the long-standing recognition of the humanist predilection for political dialogue in particular.[130] Summarizing content has been the dominant approach to dialogue, and form has attracted virtually no attention.[131] That situation began to change when Francesco Tateo suggested that concentrating on content obscured 'the truest sense of discourse'. He argued that the form of a dialogue could reveal much more about the 'mental

---

127 E. D. Hirsch, *Validity in interpretation*, 74 and 76.
128 Gilbert, 'Venetian constitution', 492 suggests that Vergerio's and Brucioli's dialogues may have stimulated Giannotti, but he did not realize how intense the preoccupation with the form was.
129 Sixteenth-century dialogue writers followed their fifteenth-century predecessors in their relative unconcern for formal rules. F. Tateo, *Tradizione e realtà nell'Umanesimo italiano*, 224, and G. Mazzacurati, *Conflitti di culture nel cinquecento*, 229.
130 D. Cantimori, 'Rhetoric and politics in Italian humanism', 93, and H. H. Gray, 'Renaissance humanism: the pursuit of eloquence', 214–15.
131 The classic study by R. Hirzel, *Der Dialog. Ein literarhistorischer Versuch* set the pattern. Hirzel's work consists almost entirely of plot summaries.

processes' encapsulated in it.[132] The debate over Renaissance English dialogue presently turns on the question of whether or not the form constituted a genre, as Tateo insisted it had not in the fifteenth century.[133] Those who believe it does have recently begun the arduous search for common features amongst the mountains of English specimens. So far, results are disappointing, especially the judgment that Starkey wrote one of only five 'genre' dialogues in sixteenth-century England.[134] According to this argument, the dialectical or genre dialogue began with Sir John Fortescue in the fifteenth century, but its form has been explicated from the model offered by Carlo Sigonio in 1561, and from Rudolf Agricola's treatise on dialectic.[135] Other critics doubt that Agricola was used for more than the construction of speeches. The larger formal elements came from 'the tradition of dialogue literature', which still did not constitute a genre. Few writers paid any attention to genre rules.[136]

The latest contribution to the debate emphatically concludes that humanist dialogue did not form a genre.[137] Instead, K. J. Wilson argues that it offered 'a mode for probing the conflicting ideas and indistinct feelings of self-consciousness'.[138] Writers of dialogues set out not to create a true fiction, but rather to imitate 'discursive experience'. Their medium offered them a peculiarly apt form for focusing 'binocular vision' simultaneously on past and present, while constructing works doomed to shift uneasily between philosophy and rhetoric.[139] This judgment is, of course, of a piece with Pocock's interpretation of humanism, but none of the contributors to the debate over English dialogue, while recognizing the importance of Italian models, has thus far tried to place any particular specimen into an Italian context and demonstrate how an author's exposure to it shaped his efforts. This can at least be sketched in the case of Starkey's pioneering effort in the English vernacular dialogue.

In keeping with Renaissance literary theory, Starkey should have followed one of several models in the creation of his work. Starkey would have known of the famous controversy between Bembo and G. F. Pico over imitation, if he had not learned this lesson elsewhere.[140] Starkey doubtless gained a great deal from Cicero and Plato. But his Dialogue is still peculiar in its abbreviated cast of characters. Starkey's purpose dictated that he focus very narrowly on Pole and Lupset as his ticket into royal service. While in practice many classical dialogues quickly turned into a conversation between only two speakers, they

---

132 *Tradizione e realtà*, 225–6.   133 *Ibid.*, 223.
134 R. Deakins, 'The Tudor prose dialogue', 16.   135 *Ibid.*, 7, 8–11.
136 D. M. Gilkey, 'The *Colloquies* of Erasmus and the literature of the renaissance', chapter 4.
137 K. J. Wilson, *Incomplete fictions: the formation of English renaissance dialogue*, 20.
138 *Ibid.*, 177.   139 *Ibid.*, chapter 1 *passim*.
140 G. W. Pigman III, 'Versions of imitation in the renaissance', 7–12, 20 (for Bembo).

almost always began with a larger number. Even the nearest Greek or Roman candidate would have required Starkey to invert both its message and the roles of its characters. On the one hand, 'Socrates' in the Platonic *Alcibiades* bore the brunt of the conversation as he tried to persuade the title character of his unsuitability for public office, while on the other hand 'Lupset' tried to argue the Dialogue's main speaker, 'Pole', into royal service, for which he was obviously eminently qualified.

Native English dialogue literature would not have helped Starkey much. It might have reinforced his decision to restrict the number of characters in his dialogue, but it would not have sanctioned discussion of matters of high policy in the vernacular nor an elaborate form. Starkey's contemporaries relied greatly on dialogue, but usually as a heavy-handed educational device. So even More's first effort in English, which dates from roughly the same time as Starkey wrote. Aside from his own character, More never cast real people in his English dialogues, and aimed all but one of them at a popular audience, as prose written in English should have been.[141] The wooden creations of Christopher St German are even more typical. He used dialogue as an excuse to break treatises into smaller pieces. By-play between the characters in *Doctor and Student*, for example, or any attempt at realistic setting or lively conversation did not interest him. St German's work fits the mould of the Answerer–Objector format with a vengeance. Likewise, even though Thomas Elyot chose English for his *The Governour* (1531) when he tried his hand at dialogue two years later in *Pasquil the Playne*, he produced a purely didactic effort with its stock comic characters, including the statue of the title which does most of the talking. The simple fact that Starkey aimed his work at two people, neither of whom would qualify as a *rudis*, indicates that he meant to do something more sophisticated than most of his compatriots. The English dialogue was still a rather 'backwoods' affair in Starkey's day.

Not so the Italian version. Real characters, statecraft as subject matter and all manner of structures and purposes abounded in the Paduan dialogue. During and shortly after Starkey's first residence, Bembo, Leonico, Speroni and Marco Mantova Benavides, not to mention Giannotti, all produced respectable numbers of dialogues. Of these, Leonico and, to a much lesser degree, Bembo imitated recognizably classical form. Not by accident, of the four only Leonico wrote exclusively in Latin, and Bembo vigorously espoused 'Ciceronianism', although championing the *volgare*. Leonico repeatedly claimed to have written Platonic dialogues, but Bembo's look as much like Bocaccio's *novelle* as they do their alleged Platonic original.[142] Neither probably had much effect on the form Starkey chose to adopt, but Bembo's

---

[141] R. F. Jones, *The triumph of the English language*, 39, 96 and chapter 2 *passim*.

[142] *Pietro Bembo's Gli asolani*, trans. R. B. Gottfried, xvii.

praise of the vernacular and Leonico's demonstration of how to blend scientific and literary goals probably interested him. Bembo made a concerted effort to win converts to Italian after the success of his theoretical dialogue *Prose della volgar lingua* (1525), and his example could have pushed Starkey toward English.[143] Leonico's ideas of method will be considered further below.

One of Bembo's followers may have made more of an impact on Starkey specifically as a writer of dialogues. Marco Mantova, who suffered through an almost paradigmatic religious crisis during Starkey's first visit to Padua and may later have taught him a little law, invested a good deal in literary productions from *L'heremita* (1521) and some nearly contemporary *novelle*, through his *Dialogus de concilio* (1541) to *Discorsi sopra i dialogi di M. Speron Speroni* (1561).[144] *L'heremita* probably drew on Bembo's *Gli asolani*. Its setting in the Colli euganei outside Padua is nearly identical to the hills around Asolo, and Mantova's work turned on an interchange between 'Mantova' (a character in all three of these dialogues) and a hermit, like that between Lavinello and another recluse which concluded Bembo's dialogue.[145] Mantova interspersed 'crowd scenes' in the story of his character's spiritual struggle, which first-person narration and dialogue carried forward. The work dwelt on scene and Mantova painted his character full-length. Perhaps the amount of experience Mantova put into this youthful dialogue accounts for some of its liveliness. At any rate, this effort was better realized than Mantova's later dialogues, even though he continued to aim for a high degree of verisimilitude. *De concilio* and the *Discorsi* signify the depth of Mantova's commitment to a two-character format, as do his didactic question and answer dialogues designed for beginning law students, while *L'heremita* and its Bembonian model indicate the strength of the impulse to experiment in sixteenth-century Padua.

But Speroni made the dialogue form peculiarly (in all senses of the word) his own. Most of Speroni's dialogues came early in his career in the 1520s and early 1530s, so Starkey could have known of them.[146] Perhaps most of these were merely sketches for Speroni's full-dress efforts like his more famous *Delle lingue*, but they appeared in print and Speroni did not disavow them. If we confine ourselves strictly to his two-character (or fewer!) dialogues, we

---

[143] C. Dionisotti, 'Bembo, Pietro', *DBI*, 142.　　　[144] Mayer, 'Religious crisis', *passim*.

[145] My thanks to R. H. Terpening for pointing out this parallel. For what follows, see Mayer, 'Religious crisis', 46–9. R. H. Terpening, 'Pietro Bembo and the cardinalate', 75–86 discusses some of the links between Bembo and Mantova. See also M. Pastore Stocchi, 'Marco Manotva Benavides e i trecentisti maggiori', especially 256–7 where he agrees that Mantova was probably a disciple of Bembo, though a singularly maladroit one and not much of a humanist, either.

[146] Sperone Speroni, *Dialogo delle lingue*, ed. and trans. H. Harth, 8.

find that formal constraints sat very lightly on his shoulders. *Della dignità delle donne*, like many of Speroni's efforts, presented a conversation between two historical Venetian aristocrats, but it lacked setting and characterization. Its argument proceeded in much the desultory fashion of *Gli asolani*. Nor did Speroni even stick to his original interlocutors. Near the end, the only *donna* discussed, Beatrice Pia degli Obizi, and *Il conte* turned up, and while the lady simply smiled, the fourth character 'unexpectedly' spoke to close the work.[147] The *Dialogo del tempo del partorire*, appended to *Delle donne*, has a yet stranger form. As its eighteenth-century editor noted, 'it appears to be more a letter than a dialogue', but Speroni insisted that he meant it as the latter in his *Apologia* for his work in that genre.[148] Marco Forcellini judged too cautiously: *Del partorire* is a letter. It begins 'You ask me if I think that a baby girl born in one hundred sixty days and a few hours … can live naturally the whole space of our life. A good subject for disputation [or conversation: *da ragionare*]', replied Speroni, but he ignored his own prescription and launched into a monologic treatment of the case.[149] The succeeding *Della cura della famiglia* is an oration on the occasion of a wedding in 1533. Speroni not only put this speech into Pomponazzi's mouth, but alleged that Pomponazzi had originally authored it himself for his own daughter's nuptials. Speroni had simply copied it.[150] Short snatches of third-person narration broke up the speech, and aside from the occasion(s), *Della cura* has no setting and, naturally, no characterization. These are typical of Speroni's early dialogues. Of them, only *Del partorire* contained the semblance of an argument. Speroni's insistence in his *Apologia* that making a point did not interest him rings true, however much self-serving motives may have entered in by 1574. Speroni really did regard his work as rhetorical exercises (as he almost wrote) or *giuochi* to be tossed off in his spare time (as he did write).[151]

Not so the sober exile Giannotti, nor his compatriot Brucioli who contributed four books of dialogues which ran through numerous sixteenth-century editions.[152] Giannotti's *De' Veneziani* is more interesting. Since we lack certain evidence to link Giannotti and Starkey, for the moment it must remain a marked coincidence that Starkey began to write his only dialogue drawing heavily on the example of Venice to undergird improvements in the English polity just after Giannotti attempted to sell Venetian reforms to republican Florence. By another strange coincidence, most of Giannotti's dialogue involves only two characters, both historical. One may discount the impact of the Paduan mania for dialogue, but when Giannotti came to treat the Florentine constitution in depth he chose to write a treatise. The content, purpose

[147] Sperone Speroni, *Opera di M. Sperone Speroni*, ed. M. Forcellini and N. dalle Laste, I, 46–63.
[148] *Opera*, I, 64.   [149] *Ibid.*   [150] *Ibid.*, 75.   [151] *Ibid.*, 268–70, 273.
[152] G. Spini, 'Bibliografia delle opere di Antonio Brucioli', 129ff.

and audience of Giannotti's dialogue also strikingly resemble Starkey's. Giannotti tried to explain to his circle of Florentine aristocrats how they could satisfy the lower orders after a successful coup by offering impartial administration of justice. This comes very close to Starkey's plan to make the English nobility responsible for its actions, primarily by overhauling the legal system. And like Starkey (but in common with their generation) Giannotti impatiently dismissed earlier humanists' ideal commonwealths.[153] Gilmore's complaint about the lack of political theory in *De' Veneziani* thus missed the point, although he was surely correct that the work is about superiors and servitors.[154]

Giannotti cast Bembo's close friend Gabriele and his own intimate Borgherini as the speakers in his work. Neither got much of a character, and Giannotti had some trouble deciding exactly what kind of work he wished to write. A first-person *proemio* sketched an ambitious plan (9). The first conversation, but the only one written, would deal with Venetian administration; the second its magistracy; and the third *la forma e composizione* of the republic. The last would have been Leonico's star turn. Giannotti moved from the introduction to set the stage by writing that he had been Bembo's guest in Padua and his host had wanted Giannotti to see everything (10). Consequently they had gone to visit Trifone when he came to Bembo's house. Once they were seated, Giannotti disappeared from the action and Giovanni and Trifone exchanged compliments (11). Borgherini proposed a parallel between Trifone and Cicero's friend Atticus as a means to compare the late Roman republic with early sixteenth-century Italy, but this gambit did not initiate a historical discussion (12). Instead, it allowed Trifone to explain why he chose not to lead the *vita attiva* while nonetheless establishing his credentials as an expert on Venice. Trifone assured Giovanni that he had not withdrawn because the republic was corrupt, but rather because he was not needed (17–18). Giovanni picked up the comparison between Venice and Rome which he finally induced Trifone to accept. From the outset, Gabriele sounded like Contarini. Giovanni had to learn about Venetian administration because the republic was a natural body, formed by art. Just as nature intended to give a man *una università*, so it provided a republic with members, all of whom the government had to keep in a 'certain proportion' (21). After further attention to setting, Trifone laid out the manner of proceeding and encouraged Giovanni to ask questions (23–25).

Trifone's first speech and Giovanni's response exemplify the workings of most of the dialogue. Trifone held forth for nine pages on Venice's geographical setting and resources in order to prove that it lacked for nothing (25–33).

---

[153] Cf. Gilbert, 'Venetian constitution', 494 and 497 on Giannotti's motives. Bouwsma, *Venice*, 156 offers a brief comparison of Giannotti and Contarini.
[154] Gilmore, 'Myth and reality', 436.

Did I miss anything? he asked Giovanni, while at the same time acknowledging that Borgherini probably already knew all this. Giovanni agreed, but said he did not mind hearing it again, although he did want to know why Trifone began with geography. Gabriele gave two reasons: first, one must know the *forze* as well as the *custumi* of any republic; and second, philosophers worked from the general to the particular. He would follow the same method (34–5).

Next among Venice's resources after her setting was her people, the components of her government. Trifone distinguished between the class of nobles and gentlemen or the citizens, and the people, but when he came to fit them into the four 'members' of the republic, he wound up dealing only with the first group. They alone could belong to the *consiglio grande*, the *pregadi*, and the *collegio* and from them alone came the *principe*. The republic was thus composed only of the governors, whom Giannotti likened to its nerves (35–47 and 51). Giannotti then had Trifone take the usual step from organic metaphor to historical support by recounting the origin of the *consiglio*. The *doge*'s immoderate exercise of his unrestrained authority had led 'our ancestors' to replace him with a *maestro de' cavalieri*. That office had lasted only a short time before the citizens reinstituted the *doge*, but this time they quickly realized the necessity of bridling his power (55 and 62). Trifone learned this key bit of history not from the defective official chronicles, but from a manuscript fragment he had read in Leonico's house (57 and 64).

Thus far Giannotti's text has been generally similar to Starkey's, but this passage is almost identical to one of the greatest peculiarities in Starkey's history of the English constitution, the role of the constable. As Starkey put it, 'our old aunceturys the instytutorys of our lawys & ordur of our reame ... ordeynyd a comustable of englond to conturpaise the authoryte of the prynce and tempur the same'.[155] This officer lasted longer than Giannotti's *maestro de' cavalieri,* but his competence and his title are virtually the same. The Master of the Knights = The Master of the Horse. Giannotti may also have drawn on classical precedent. He modelled his description of the Venetian constitution on the Roman republic, as he made explicit when he compared the *dieci* to the Roman dictator. The only difference between them was that the former was permanent (168). Since the *dieci* was superior to the *doge*, Giannotti came close to reproducing the relation between a Roman dictator and his master of the horse. This is also very similar to Starkey's constitution. It looks as if Giannotti's story of the evolution of the *doge* helped to produce Starkey's interpretation of English constitutional history.

After describing this short-lived expedient, Trifone continued his explanation of how the *consiglio maggiore* had come to have ultimate authority.

---

[155] SP 1/90, fol. 110ɼ (Burton, 165–6).

Electing the *doge* not only failed to restrain his *licenza* and excessive authority, but it had led to great popular tumults. The solution was to turn over both the *doge*'s authority and his selection to the *consiglio*, thereby cutting out both the one and the many (70–1). The transfer of the *doge*'s whole authority made the republic freer, quieter and more civil, and modelling the new council on the *doge*'s own council allowed it to operate in similar unity (72–4). Giannotti's bias in favour of an oligarchical constitution then cropped up in the discussion of the final element in the creation of the council, the confining of its membership to the nobility. Trifone knew why the council was closed – in order to preserve *tutto il fiore de' Cittadini della Città* from dilution by foreign blood – but not the origin of the citizen class (78). That he proposed to leave in shadow, because he lacked 'certain knowledge'. The entirety of this historical section had necessarily to rest on conjecture and probability (76–82).

Throughout this key passage, Giovanni exercised his assignment *da dubitare*, and his objections and questions gathered momentum as the dialogue progressed (e.g., 102 and 114). Sometimes Trifone confessed he could not produce probable and true reasons for Venetian customs because of their antiquity, but rather than pressing him Giovanni praised him for speaking 'prudently' (116). Giannotti's largely descriptive purpose allowed him to duck some issues which Starkey's more activist agenda required him to handle. A detailed description of the operation of the other public offices of Venice occupied the remainder of the work, which concluded with Giovanni expressing his complete satisfaction in Trifone's exposition (242).

Giannotti deliberately chose not to go into the theory of the republic in this dialogue, but the discussion he offered in his later work on Florence drew heavily on Aristotle to produce a picture of the best Florentine republic. It looked much like Starkey's England and Contarini's Venice.[156] The proper form of the republic, its soul, most interested Giannotti. He could afford to skip over perfectly obvious questions which the ancients had already settled like the definition of a city and a citizen, as well as the detail of the distinctions in wealth and dignity between Florentine citizens. Existing stratification was simply accepted (9). How to preserve the political body from corruption posed the real problem. That meant first describing the possible forms of the republic, then laying out the defects of Florence, next devising their cures, and finally providing the city with means for self-defence (10). That would reestablish the life which God and nature intended for the city: the *ben vivere comune degli abitanti* (11). In order to do that, the disorder of the multitude had to be regulated by the republic, 'a certain institution, or ordering of the

---

156 Donato Giannotti, *Della repubblica fiorentina, Opere*, II, 12. According to Bisaccia, *Repubblica fiorentina*, 15–16, Giannotti wrote his second constitutional work between 1531 and 1536.

inhabitants of the city'. If this order were directed to the common good, all would be well (12). Giannotti allowed that a community could be administered in different ways, but only rule by the 'many' was 'properly a republic' (13). Those who would settle for a prince lacked ambition; those who brimmed with *virtù* (especially in a military sense) had to have a republic (13–14). In all this Giannotti departed from Aristotle and Starkey only by introducing Polybius's constitutional cycle to explain how republics decayed (17).

Thus Giannotti's ideas fitted perfectly into the heavily Aristotelian climate of Padua, and for a time his literary inclinations did, too. Giannotti's stay there may or may not have induced his foray into dialogue, and the similarities between his single essay in that form and Starkey's only such effort may be no more than coincidence. Nevertheless, the marked parallels between the two works suggest that both picked up a powerful alembic in Padua to the use of dialogue for the discussion of the most serious political problems. It likely sprang from Bembo and his followers. As the original impulse spread outwards, the range of possible shapes for the genre became almost boundless. Even if most of Bembo's circle usually turned their hands to topics other than politics, they were keenly interested in those who were willing to study them. Starkey's exposure to Paduan models, then, would have told him he might write a dialogue to serve any purpose, direct it to any audience, and execute it in any form, a judgment which his Oxford education and any knowledge of contemporary northern theorists of dialectic would have reinforced. As it happened, Starkey may well have found a precise guide for his plan to reform the English commonwealth in Giannotti's similar design for Florence.

In addition to content and form, Starkey's experience in Padua furthered his grounding in the method and language needed to make a case and persuade an audience to accept it. All came together in dialogue, the representation of 'actual verbal argument'.[157] In theory, not all kinds of argument could fit into a dialogue. Dialogue inevitably proceeded by what Juan Luis Vives, following Cicero, called 'a certain mutual comparing of opinions and reasonings', because it dealt with subjects which deductive method could not handle.[158] As the case of Vives also demonstrates, the strict theoretical separation between rhetorical persuasion and scientific demonstration often became blurred and 'probable reasons' gave place to the truth.[159] Writers of dialogues may have deliberately aimed at greater openness than the authors of demonstrative treatises could, but they still made use of dialectic and they still had to allow their individual characters to argue coherently.

---

[157] R. Pineas, *Thomas More and Tudor polemics*, 81.
[158] C. J. R. Armstrong, 'The dialectial road to truth: the dialogue', 42.   [159] *Ibid.*, 40–4.

Leonico's adherence to Latin may have limited his impact on Starkey's thinking about form and language, but along with Leonico's commentaries on Aristotle, his dialogues place him in the ranks of the 'school of Padua' or those predecessors of Galileo who invented the resoluto-compositive method, which Starkey followed in his Dialogue. Starkey's friendship with Wotton, membership in the 'collective' which produced the first printed edition of Galen, and his life-long interest in medicine reinforced the lessons he learned from Leonico. If Starkey already knew Marcantonio de Genova, the dominant figure amongst Paduan Aristotelians a few years later, he would have been exposed to de Genova's similar ideas about method (see below, chapt. 6). As Starkey told Thomas Cromwell some years later, during his years in Italy natural science attracted him so strongly that he had intended to make it his career. Starkey changed his mind, but he did not therefore forget what he had learned about method from Paduan scientists.

Leonico's dialogues vary a good deal in literary polish. He usually set the stage, but often with a minimum of dressing. Only *Trophonius* unfolded within a fully developed scene including a change of venue and prayer before 'Leonicus' entered the question (sig. IIv–Xv). Leonico wasted little time on his characters, unless one grants that his own character's extended monologues sound as he must have in a Paduan lecture hall. Many of the dialogues were written in the first person, but Leonico often made another character the main speaker, even if that meant transforming Bembo into a systematic philosopher or Sadoleto into a neo-platonist. What Leonico lost in realism by stinting his actors of both character and distinctive speech, he made up in clarity of presentation. Leonico frequently laid out exactly what he intended to do, as in *Trophonius* when he proposed to apply the method of *divisio* in order to determine to which genus of art divination belonged (XIr). His character broke the problem into two parts: the nature of divination, and what caused it. The point of the whole dialogue was to isolate the causes of oracles in order to answer the question whether they could come in dreams (VIIv and IIIr). Leonico did the same in *Sadoletus* where he had the title character first describe prayer and then lay out how he proposed to explain it. He called his approach *academicorum mos*, which proceeded by the setting of propositions followed by questions.[160] In the terms used by his Academic models, Leonico began with 'description and explanation of the form' of prayer, since if the disputants remained ignorant of its nature, they would wind up accomplishing nothing in the rest of their discussion (153). As in *Trophonius*, Leonico had 'Sadoletus' lay out the types of prayer, which led to the conclusion that all sorts proceeded from God and returned to him. (Leonico supported this point by citing Ps.-Dionysius, on whom he leaned heavily throughout this dialogue.) Once the general nature of prayer was

---

[160] *Dialogi* (2nd edn), 151.

established, 'Sadoletus' spent a lot of time detailing its natural workings, before arriving at the *divisio* of the parts of prayer (159). This in turn produced a definition of prayer, which allowed 'Sadoletus' to conclude that it had five of the six causes, lacking only the instrumental (160).

Thus Academic or 'Socratic' procedure ultimately always led Leonico to the causes of the phenomenon under investigation, which alone could provide *certissimam sententiam* or, in a virtually interchangeable phrase for Leonico, *certam cognitionem* (LXVv and LVIr). In short, Leonico used his dialogues to present a dissertation in slightly disguised fashion.

Despite the fact that his dialogues often dealt with matters not usually regarded as part of merely probable knowledge, Leonico adhered to the Aristotelian distinction between noble and ignoble disciplines, between those which could penetrate to the essence of things as they proceed from immediate causes and those which had to make do with a more confused *cognitio* based on remoter and more material causes.[161] His commentary on Aristotle's *De partibus animalium* gives a capsule summary both of Leonico's philosophy of science and, more important, his notion of method. Natural *scientia* was not properly called *scientia* at all, but rather *peritia* or *eruditio* (118). Nevertheless, the modern fashion of beginning with formal causes could lead these *physicae demonstrationes* closer to essences. If one began with common elements rather than *differentia*, this would bring results closer to higher reality. In other words, one began with species and then compared all the accidents encountered in order to see if they fit universal nature (122). Leonico adopted the Aristotelian scheme of four causes, except that he concluded that the formal and final cause were nearly identical (130–1). The great gulf fixed between the formal and the efficient cause meant that the natural scientist had to abandon the model of astronomy and turn instead to that of medicine (128 and 134). A physician knew the object of his intervention in advance, health, but he could also perceive the effect of his efforts through his senses. Thus he came close to knowing the formal cause of something – a disease – which was not a part of contemplative knowledge (135). Yet he finally could not, and Leonico turned most of his attention to identifying the material causes which any physical scientist could determine from the effects which he perceived (139 and 145).

Once he had established his philosophy of science, Leonico turned to the difficult question of method. Leonico began with a summary of Plato's dialectic, which he called *divisiva et definitiva methodus* [*sic*] thereby coming very near to other terms for the resoluto-compositive method (196). As Leonico explained, Plato's method had the power 'to divide one properly into many, and we can knowledgeably divide and determine, and by resolving many into one deduce [its nature]'. In the cases at hand, Plato's dialectic

---

[161] Niccolò Leonico, *De partibus animalium*, 114.

operated fundamentally by bifurcating an animal into *membra* and *contraria* (197). As Aristotle pointed out, that method failed when it encountered two *accidentia* which appeared to separate creatures into two species, while it actually missed their common essence (199 and 201). Thus the only safe method was to divide all *genera* into as many *differentia* as one could, in order to incorporate the maximum amount of sense data into the search for their essence (227). In short, *divisio* into *bifaria* had to be replaced by *divisio* into the number of observable *differentia*, since the ultimate goal was understanding the action of all parts of the body (235 and 264).

Starkey almost certainly heard this exhortation to observation rather than the pursuit of eternal truth, if not quite in this precise form then in the course of Leonico's explanation of the 'philosophical parts' of Galen, which he probably passed on to his pupil Pole.[162] Leonico's approach closely approximated Galen's in *De metodo medendi*, no doubt because they began with the same Platonic and Aristotelian texts.[163] Like Leonico, Galen had argued that medicine contained elements of both *ratio* and *experientia*, even if they had to be kept rigorously distinct (XXIIIr and XXIVr). The physician's first goal had to be the discovery (*inventio*) of the sort of disease(s) afflicting a patient, but he would never find them unless he had some notion of what he was looking for before he began (VIr and VIIIr). That in turn rested on knowledge of how a human body worked. Thus medicine became the art of restoring natural function, and that meant above all *claritatis causa particulas aliquas* (VIIIv). Clear understanding of the problem would allow determination of its causes, but connecting an effect to its cause required a thorough knowledge both of the body's actions and its constitution (IXr; cf. XIIIr–v). Of course, clarity of information had to be translated into precise terminology (XIIIv). In short, Galen came very close to the method the fifteenth- and sixteenth-century Paduans would refine according to which observation broke a phenomenon down into its parts, and reason would then reassemble them. The understanding produced by this operation could lead as easily to medical interventions as to knowledge of the cosmos, or to their intersection in man and the commonwealth.[164] Leonico was hardly the only humanist to interest himself in medicine or in Galen. The career of the Padua-trained, perfectly ordinary physician Giacomo Tiburzi emphasizes how much other Paduans owed to Galen. Tiburzi treated him as an authority not only on medicine, but also on grammar, rhetoric and history. Tiburzi moved in some of the same circles as Starkey would later, and was apparently especially close to Federigo

162 Rossiana 997, fol. 30v.
163 Galen, *Methodus medendi*, ed. Thomas Linacre, fol. Vv.
164 J. H. Randall offered the classic formulation of Paduan scientific method in his 'The development of scientific method in the school of Padua', 215–51, and see also G. Moria, 'Struttura logica e consapevolezza epistemologica in alcuni trattatisti padovani di medicina del sec. XV', especially 390–1 on Giacopo della Torre.

Fregoso. It may be that he, too, was an Evangelical, whatever that may have to do with his opinion of Galen.[165]

Leonico offered Starkey one more lesson connected to Galen's emphasis on careful use of terms, which acquaintance with Bembo would have heightened. In his dialogue *Peripateticus, sive de nominum inventione* Leonico argued in favour of natural language as against the artificial dialectic of philosophers. Names expressed the nature of things, and therefore required careful handling.[166] Bembo, too, pursued a natural language, even if he thought it could only be the vernacular. Leonico would have disagreed with Bembo on specifics, but not with Bembo's passionate concern for the proper means of expression. Bembo's attachment to language was of a piece with a long humanist tradition arising ultimately from Cicero, who had maintained stoutly that successful oratory rested on 'the language of everyday life'.[167] Bembo may have been less certain that the orator's polished speaking led men to civility and protected the *res publica*, but he could not have disagreed with the necessity of *eloquentia*, nor that both style and wisdom went into it.[168]

Knowledge of whatever sort required the means to express it, and Bembo believed unequivocally that any good humanist had to write in the *volgare*. The success of his *Prose della volgar lingua*, which he wrote during Starkey's first visit to Padua, helped to make his house a rallying point for young authors, including, perhaps, Starkey.[169] Bembo insisted on the dynamism of language, but at the same time he argued that experiments in the *volgare* had to be anchored in good models lest they become barbaric or artificial like the court language of Rome.[170] This argument has helped to earn him a reputation for slavish dependence on Cicero, but Bembo's point had been to encourage not imitation, but emulation, the surpassing of one's model.[171] Bembo may have been unusually interested in style, but not for its own sake.[172] Rather, the goal remained persuasion, and it was that which drove him to assert that an author had to test *ogni minuta parte* of his work to see if it would reach his reader.[173] In order to ensure his effectiveness, an author should employ not only the language of his audience, but stories and illustrative examples suited to it (82–3). Perhaps an awareness of the limits to an intellectual's impact helped to inspire Bembo's leanings to stylistic experimentation instead of to more overtly political activity. But

165 Pastore, 'Tiburzi', 79–83.
166 G. Saitta, *Il pensiero italiano nell'Umanesimo e nel rinascimento*, I, 457.
167 Cicero, *De oratore*, ed. E. W. Sutton and H. Rackham, 10–11.
168 *Ibid.*, 26 and Gray, 'Renaissance humanism', 202.   169 Bembo, *Prose*, 52.
170 G. Santangelo, *Il Bembo critico e il principio d'imitazione*, 76 and 80, and Bembo, *Prose*, 45.
171 G. Santangelo, ed., *Le epistole 'de imitatione' di Giovanfrancesco Pico della Mirandola e di Pietro Bembo*, 56 and 58, and Santangelo, *Bembo critico*, 29.
172 *Ibid.*, 38 and 40; Bembo, *Prose*, 44–5; and Mazzacurati, *Classicismo*, 152.
173 Bembo, *Prose*, 174.

Bembo's championing of the *volgare* together with his heavy emphasis on the overarching importance of a style which could effectively persuade, no matter the labour it might take to acquire, seem to have appealed to Starkey. Starkey could well have blended Leonico's admonition about how to do good science with Bembo's about how to write good literature to produce the carefully involved English of his Dialogue. The example both Leonico and Bembo set of an intellectual, erstwhile republican responding to a rapidly changing (and shrinking) court culture could have stayed with Starkey and inspired him to try to avoid drawing Bembo's conclusion. Then all that he lacked was an occasion to exercise his principles and his skills. The vicissitudes of Starkey's relation to Pole soon provided that.

3

'Occasyon and tyme wyl never be restoryd agayne': Pole, Paris, and the Dialogue

Probably sometime in 1528 Pole and Starkey returned to England. Starkey reacted enthusiastically, seeing 'thys occasyon' as his chance to begin a career in service to the commonwealth. Now that he and Pole had finished their education in Padua, the two of them would put their skills to practical use. Starkey's ambitions took on solid form in the elaborate reform programme offered in his Dialogue, which he composed in the main between 1529 and 1532. Pole's prospects encouraged Starkey to hope that he could gain office himself on Pole's coat-tails. They would have pulled strongly because of Pole's successful mission to the Parisian theologians in 1529–30, combined with the general lack of obvious direction from the centre in England. Starkey already had most of the pieces of his design for secular government in place when he began to write the Dialogue, but it seems likely that he gained some new ideas about ecclesiastical power while with Pole in Paris. The vibrant conciliarist tradition descending from Jean Gerson probably helped to foster Starkey's emphasis on cardinals and council. Debates in the theological faculty may have inspired some other aspects of the Dialogue as well. Pole's diplomatic assignment also brought Starkey into close contact with Englishmen interested in conciliarism and aware of the direction of policy at home.

Conflicting testimony and lack of much direct evidence continue to obscure Starkey's movements in the late 1520s, but now they affect our knowledge of Pole's actions, too. G. R. Elton most recently asserted that the two parted company as Starkey stayed in France between 1528 and 1530 reading law and 'the great political works of Aristotle and Marsilio', while Pole returned to England.[1] This theory would seem to fit the facts of 1532–3 much better when Starkey stayed behind in Avignon studying law and Pole went on to Padua. Starkey surely did not wait so long to read Aristotle, and it remains to be proved that he ever gave Marsilio much time. However Starkey occupied himself during Elton's period, the only evidence from it continues to link Pole and Starkey. Pole's first biographer, Ludovico Beccadelli, made it appear that

---

[1] G. R. Elton, *Reform and reformation*, 165.

his subject returned to England shortly after a flying visit to Rome for the Jubilee of 1525.[2] After a stopover in Paris, Pole retired to the house John Colet had built for himself at Sheen.[3] The only independently documented retreat there came in 1530–1. Beccadelli was not close to Pole in this early period and probably had to go by Pole's notoriously inaccurate memory. Later biographers have relied almost entirely on Beccadelli, claiming that no other evidence of Pole's doings exists. However, three letters from Pole to Romolo Amaseo, dated Padua, June and September 1528, indicate that Pole must either have returned to Italy by then, or never have left. He was certainly back in London by 27 January 1529.[4] Starkey's expense ledger for Pole covering a stay in Paris and return to England may support part of Beccadelli's account, although it may equally well refer to Pole's later mission. Zeeveld assumed that it did, probably because it is currently bound after a memo from Pole to Starkey which clearly came from the latter trip. Their departure from Dieppe, not Calais, as Zeeveld had it, might indicate that Pole was headed to the homes of relatives near Portsmouth and thus in no hurry, as he should have been in 1530; but another payment reveals that his destination was London after all. This document's glimpse of Pole's travelling household, which included Starkey's friends Bernardino Sandro and Richard Pate, does not help either. There is no independent evidence for Sandro's movements and Pate must have been in Paris at least through 1529 and perhaps later.[5]

It did not take long after Pole's return to London for someone to realize how valuable he could be in the effort to solicit favourable opinions on the divorce.[6] In October 1529 he was sent back to Paris along with Starkey and, for part of the time, Lupset. All of them may have regarded their task with some ambivalence, and they probably looked upon the prospect of royal service with the degree of doubt usual among Tudor humanists. Nevertheless, Pole and Lupset executed their assignment successfully and were rewarded accordingly. Lupset accepted a gift of money and several benefices, but Pole turned down Henry's offer of his choice of either York or Winchester, and from that point in late 1530 began to drift into open opposition. There is no sign that he had begun that evolution any earlier. He cooperated fully with Edward Foxe, one of the architects of the policy of circularizing the uni-

---

[2] Ludovico Beccadelli, 'Vita del cardinale Reginaldo Polo', 282.   [3] *Ibid.*, 283.
[4] BL Egerton 1998, fols. 2r–5r (*LP*, IV:3, 4405, 4756 and 5224). The first is the one from London. Cf. W. G. Zeeveld, *Foundations of Tudor policy*, 66n.
[5] SP 1/55, fol. 194r–v and Zeeveld, *Foundations*, 66–7.
[6] This is unsurprising in light of Virginia Murphy's finding that Henry directed a coherent policy on the divorce from at least 1527. 'The debate over Henry VIII's first divorce: an analysis of the contemporary treatises', 31–2, 67, 80, 87–90, 181–2, 217, 262.

versities. Starkey apparently worked closely with Foxe, too, as his memo of instructions from Pole to Lupset indicates.[7] It is probably not a coincidence that Starkey was presented to the living of Great Mongeham, Kent, on 31 July 1530, almost precisely the time that he, Pole and Lupset must have returned from Paris. If, as seems likely, this was a reward for services rendered, a benefice worth £20 per year suggests that Starkey did more than handle Pole's household affairs in Paris.[8]

The English legation showed a good deal of interest in individual conciliarists and conciliarist ideas. Foxe had not yet begun to write his *Collectanea satis copiosa*, which contained many conciliarist arguments against papal power, but he probably spent some of his time in Paris assembling material for it.[9] Pole's instruction to Lupset 'to demand off monsieur [Guillaume] de langy ii bokes for mr fox', one of them a *librum conciliorum*, and Starkey's item of expense 'for byndyng of the conseylys' probably refer to such activity.[10] Graham Nicholson identified the *librum* as the 1530 Cologne edition of Jacques Merlin's *Conciliorum quattuor generalium tomus primus*.[11] Pole, too, may have shown an interest now, even if he was anything but a conciliarist later. When he died, Pole's library contained the first volume of the Parisian edition of Gerson's *Opera omnia*, which included all his major conciliarist writings.[12] John Stokesley, another important member of the English legation, must have been in contact at this time with John Mair, one of the two most prominent Parisian conciliarists.[13] Not that such men were hard to find. They cropped up on both sides of the divorce case, and even

---

[7] SP 1/55, fol. 193r (*LP*, IV:3, 6004). Pole's activities are detailed in T. F. Mayer, 'A mission worse than death: Reginald Pole and the Parisian theologians'.

[8] S. J. Herrtage, *Starkey's life and letters*, viii.

[9] G. Nicholson, 'The nature and function of historical argument in the Henrician reformation', 76. Nicholson thought Foxe might have begun work on the *Collectanea* as early as the autumn of 1530.

[10] SP 1/55, fol. 193r.

[11] Nicholson, 'Historical argument', 116. For more on this work, see J. V. Mehl, 'The first printed editions of the history of church councils'. Despite Merlin's preparation of two editions of this work, Mehl finds no evidence that the views of his fellow students at the Collège de Navarre, including John Mair, affected Merlin.

[12] A. Pastore, 'Due biblioteche umanistiche del Cinquecento', 278. The Jean Petit and François Regnault 1521 edition included, among others, *De potestate ecclesiastica*, *De auferibilitate pape ab ecclesia*, and *Tractatus de unitate ecclesiastica*. It may be that Foxe, and perhaps Pole as well, backed a plan to gain Henry's divorce through an appeal to a general council. Many of the extracts in the *Collectanea* concern the council and an appeal to one was certainly an option then under consideration. The possibility that Foxe and Pole favoured such a course of action needs further attention. It might help to explain Pole's abrupt change of heart from enthusiastic royal servant in Paris to *refusenik* just a few months later.

[13] *LP*, V, 84 is Stokesley's report of a conversation with Mair. See further J. E. Bigane, III, *Faith, Christ or Peter*, 78 and 87.

counted one of Catherine's most fervent partisans, the Spaniard Pedro de Garay, among their number.[14]

Starkey almost certainly did not miss the opportunity to reinforce his aristocratic leanings with Parisian conciliarism. Unfortunately, it is unlikely that he studied formally at the University of Paris, as did Pole and Pate.[15] The matriculation lists of the theology faculty, which are thought to be complete, have no trace of Starkey, nor do any other university records yet studied.[16] Then again, George Lily's claim that Lupset returned 'ad pristina sacrarum literarum studia' in Paris is similarly unsubstantiated.[17] In the fifteenth century, theologians had to put in six years before proceeding to their licentiate, and that time requirement was usually carefully observed. Students from outside the university had to study even longer. At the time Starkey might have studied, all licentiates went on to their doctoral degree.[18]

Yet somehow Starkey acquired an STP before his presentation to St Mary's (or Fishbourne) chantry in Holy Trinity, Bosham, on 8 May 1531.[19] A check of other STPs in Bishop Sherborne's register as well as Stephen Gardiner's indicates that they all held doctoral degrees in theology, that is if Venn and Emden can be trusted.[20] The chronology of studies offered in Starkey's various autobiographies points to Paris (or at least this time period) as the only chance he could have had to study theology at all seriously. One of his letters to Cromwell of early 1535 claimed 'I applyd myselfe to the redyng of holy scrypture' after studies in Oxford and Italy (the latter in natural science) and before reading civil law 'thes last yerys past', that is in 1533 and 1534 in

---

[14] Between 1529 and 1531 Pedro de Garay bombarded Charles V with reports on the progress of English attempts to secure a favourable opinion on Henry's divorce from the theologians of the university of Paris. He closed a letter of 2 February 1530 by hoping that God would watch over the emperor 'de manera que se formado el estado de la iglesia con un concilio general De que tanta necessidad ay y extirpadas las heregias y males en la cristianidad', as had been the case in *la primitiva iglesia* (and as Starkey would argue in 1533). Haus-, Hof-, und Staatsarchiv, Vienna, Frankreich Varia 1, fol. 37r (?). James K. Farge collects the few details known about Garay in his *Biographical register of Paris doctors of theology*, 187.

[15] Farge, *Register*, 437 for Pole. Pate is listed in the *Conclusiones* of the English–German nation as *licentiatus & inceptor* in 1529 (Archives de l'université de Paris [Sorbonne] 91, fol. 261r) and in the *Liber receptoris nationis Alamanie*, 1494–1530 (AU 15, fols. 182r–v and 183r) as both BA and MA in the same year. Neither was noticed in 1530. My thanks to Prof. Farge for loan of a microfilm of these two documents and much advice.

[16] Farge, *Register*, 457. Professor Astrik Gabriel concurs in private correspondence.

[17] E. L. Hirsh, 'George Lily', 15.

[18] L. W. B. Brockliss, 'Patterns of attendance at the university of Paris, 1400–1800', 506 and 513.

[19] West Sussex Record Office, Ep 1/1/4 (Bishop Sherborne, Register II, Institutions and collocations), fol. 72r–v. Edmund Harvel addressed Starkey as doctor in a letter of 18 June 1531 (BL Nero B VI, fol. 169r), but he did not congratulate Starkey, which suggests that his degree must have been relatively old.

[20] In at least one other case, Emden cannot. He claimed Richard Borde, STP as a Paris DTh, but he is no better documented there than Starkey.

Avignon and Padua.[21] Starkey's complete lack of interest in theology, and nearly complete absence of acquaintances among teachers of theology in Padua reinforces this report. None of his correspondents ever sent word about any Paduan theologians, with one exception, while keeping him steadily informed about rhetoricians and the medical faculty. In October 1535 John Friar reported that Simone Ardeo, professor of Scotist theology from 1517 until his death twenty years later, had resigned, but had immediately come out of retirement when another Franciscan was appointed in his place.[22] Ardeo and Niccolò Leonico were well acquainted and Ardeo had played a major role in securing a favourable opinion on the divorce from the Paduan theological faculty, so that Starkey could well have known him in a non-professional capacity.[23]

A theological degree for Starkey from another French university might seem likely, but there is no evidence he attended any other school save Avignon, where he studied civil law. Starkey is not known to have spent any time in the German-speaking part of the Empire, either; the Cologne matriculation lists bear no sign of him.[24] That leaves only one other reasonably live possibility, Louvain. It attracted large numbers of other English students, many more than Paris, and the recent founding of the humanist Collegium trilingue would have enhanced its appeal to men like Starkey. Once again, no evidence that he was ever there has turned up. Starkey does not appear in the printed edition of Louvain's matriculation registers, at least not under any recognizable corruption of his name.[25] J. F. van de Velde's eighteenth-century abstract from the *Acta* of the theological faculty (now lost) usually noted merely the number of students at various levels and only occasionally any of their names.[26] Henry de Vocht's excerpts from the *Liber tertius intitulatorum* do not pretend to completeness, but he called the MS record highly unreliable.[27] Nevertheless, some study in Louvain is not incompatible with other evidence about Starkey's career. He claimed to have spent time in Flanders, enough to learn about the model poor ordinance of Ypres.[28] The ordinance itself was not printed, although a commentary on it appeared at Antwerp in 1531.[29] This is thin evidence, especially since the law became well enough known to form a subject of debate in the Paris theological faculty in 1531.[30] Starkey's friendship with Jan van Kampen may be more help. From the tone of two letters from Kampen to Starkey in 1535, it appears that they were

[21] BL Harl. 283, fol. 129v.
[22] Nero B VI, fol. 147r.   [23] E. Surtz, *Henry VIII's great matter in Italy*, 199.
[24] My thanks to Prof. C. G. Nauert for checking his copy of Hermann Keussen, ed., *Der Matrikel der Universität Köln*.   [25] A. Schillings, ed., *Matricule de l'université de Louvain*, III–IV.
[26] H. de Jongh, *L'ancienne faculté de theologie de Louvain*, 38*–62*.
[27] H. de Vocht, 'Excerpts from the register of Louvain university from 1405 to 1527', 89.
[28] SP 1/90, fols. 60r, 73v and 107v.
[29] O. Winckelmann, 'Die Armenordung von Ypern (1525)', 257.   [30] Farge, *Register*, 306.

reasonably close, even allowing for humanist effusion. If they met in Pole's household at Padua, they could have known each other for only about six weeks. Kampen, however, had been on the faculty of the Collegium trilingue until 1531, so that Starkey could have met him there (see below, chapt. 7).

Starkey's lack of interest in formal theology makes establishing where he received his degree comparatively unimportant. The Bible and especially the letters of Paul would become very important to Starkey later, but he could well almost have taught himself in them or perhaps learned something from Kampen in Padua or elsewhere, or even from Jacopo Sadoleto. Much greater significance attaches to Starkey's knowledge of Parisian conciliarism than to his knowledge of the rest of its theology, as he himself testified. Starkey noted very near the end of his life that he had always followed Gerson 'and the Parisian school' on the constitution of the church.[31] That school originated at the beginning of the fourteenth century in John of Paris, a contemporary of Marsilio. Much of John's thinking went beyond the mainstream, but toward the end of the century Pierre d'Ailly took in John's central point that the church was a mixed government, domesticated it, and made it a distinguishing mark of Parisian conciliarism.[32] From this contention flowed almost all the Parisians' corollaries limiting papal power and enhancing that of the council. Even more important to Starkey, d'Ailly regularly appealed to secular analogies and thought the concept of mixed government applied to any 'rightly ordained polity'.[33] Thus d'Ailly made a major contribution to 'faltering moves toward the institutionalization' of checks on ecclesiastical government.[34] D'Ailly's mixed constitution in the church remained current in Starkey's England, as the Scottish theologian Alexander Alesius's (Ales) *A treatise concernynge generalle councilles* (Berthelet, 1538) demonstrated.[35]

D'Ailly's ideas about the origin of papal power and the relation between pope and council also proved long-lived. Even though the pope's power came *principaliter* from God, it nevertheless 'depended *ministerialiter* from human power'. In other words, the cardinals elected a particular man to the divinely established office of pope. Their power went back to the natural right of all Christians to choose successors to Peter.[36] D'Ailly drew on the nominalist distinction between God's absolute and ordained power to argue that according to the latter, human signs, including election, designated who actually exercised divine power.[37] Here d'Ailly followed the common late medieval

[31] SP 1/141, fol. 190r, col. 1.
[32] F. Oakley, *The political thought of Pierre d'Ailly*, 118, 204. Oakley argued that d'Ailly's conciliarism owed more to John than to William of Ockham, 205.
[33] *Ibid.*, 128–9.   [34] *Ibid.*, 117.   [35] Nicholson, 'Historical argument', 239.
[36] Oakley, *D'Ailly*, 63.   [37] *Ibid.*, 89.

argument that the divine reason (or source of authority) required human mediation (or the setting up of a particular government).[38] Election was not the only valid route to power, but the equally acceptable means of inheritance did not reduce the importance of the popular origin of royal authority.[39] Because power originally came from the community, the pope's exercise of the plenitude of power could be restrained by the authority 'latent' in the body of the church. D'Ailly proposed to regularize the community's oversight of papal power by requiring councils every thirty to fifty years.[40] The problem of how to assemble a council if the pope refused was solved by an appeal to *epiekeia*, a concept drawn from Aristotle and similar to equity. Since a positive law could not remove a natural right, if the pope refused to accede to the people's call for a council, then they could call one themselves.[41]

D'Ailly's pupil Jean Gerson preserved much of his master's teaching. Although the mystical underpinnings of Gerson's conciliarism and reforming inclinations might not have appealed to Starkey, and some basic differences do separate them, most of Gerson's constitutional ideas and the impulse behind them closely resemble Starkey's. Gerson held an intensely hierarchical view of the church, which led him to argue that its *prelati*, the clergy, were responsible for all the rest of its members.[42] Their obligation to see to the church's reform led to his conciliarism. The power of the *prelati* assembled in council, 'the most perfect representation of the church', offered the best means of creating unity and the only hope of remedying the schism.[43] As the primary agent for the exercise of *epiekeia* and the supreme legislator, the council could assemble itself, and then became the legitimate embodiment of the church because all consented to its assembly. Nevertheless, the council so acted only in an emergency. Under ordinary circumstances it could never presume to set itself above the divinely established papacy.[44]

Aside from the immutable headship of the pope, Gerson's view of the ecclesiastical constitution was identical to Starkey's. Some years later Starkey would defend Gerson's chief work on that subject, *De potestate ecclesiastica*, against Albert Pighe's attacks. Gerson was more chary than d'Ailly of drawing parallels between secular and ecclesiastical power, because the church was not a natural community like the secular state.[45] All the same, both were mixed polities, as Gerson demonstrated from the example of Moses's rule of

---

[38] *Ibid.*, 134.   [39] *Ibid.*, 140.   [40] *Ibid.*, 122–3.   [41] *Ibid.*, 160–1.

[42] L. B. Pascoe, 'Jean Gerson: mysticism, conciliarism and reform', 150.

[43] *Ibid.*, 142 and L. B. Pascoe, *Jean Gerson: principles of church reform*, 74.

[44] Pascoe, *Gerson*, 71–4, 22, 26–8.

[45] Quentin Skinner may overstress Gerson's attention to the parallels and underestimate d'Ailly's thinking in claiming this as one of Gerson's two 'radical' contributions. *Foundations of modern political thought*, II, 116.

the Old Testament church. Moses represented royal power, the seventy elders aristocratic, and the 'rectors' of the tribes 'timocratic'.[46] In his conclusion Gerson stressed that the church as a *societas perfecta* (Starkey's 'hole congregation & perfyte') had to be a mixture of all three polities, even though it had a supernatural end.[47]

A similar structure shaped the contemporary western church. The pope might be divinely established, but the college of cardinals was, too. God had given them to the pope 'as coassistants and as if an aristocratic community' to moderate his power and prevent him from abusing the order set up by the perfect legislator, Christ. Either the whole church or a council would in turn correct their excesses.[48] The church regularly acted through the cardinals, but through its 'representative' the council in an emergency. The whole community also retained the power to legislate, if only potentially.[49] This regress of power again rested on the requirement that the church established by Christ be perfect and its *potestas* remain unified. In representing the church – in presenting the most complete image of it – the council embraced all its power 'virtually', including that of the pope.[50] The church also retained the power to elect individual popes, as well as all other ecclesiastical ministers, granting them authority 'mediately', just as it had originally delegated the power of dispensation to the popes.[51] The utility of a single head with his council of cardinals to moderate disputes had initially led kings to give them the power of making and interpreting laws, instead of constantly recurring to a council.[52] Almost all of these ideas crop up in Starkey, who may also have been attracted by Gerson's legal theory. His notion of adiaphora – things which should be left indifferent – is closely related to Gerson's *epiekeia*; both were means of moderating the rigour of the law.[53]

Francis Oakley emphasizes the degree of continuity between Gerson and the early sixteenth-century Parisian Gallicans Jacques Almain and John Mair, but as Oakley has also pointed out, they introduced two major discontinuities into the tradition: they either ignored the cardinals (Mair) or deprecated their position (Almain); and displayed little interest in reform.[54] Consequently, although both continued to draw comparisons between secular and ecclesiastical government, they either explicitly (Mair) or tacitly (Almain) denied that

[46] Jean Gerson, *De potestate ecclesiastica*, 225.   [47] *Ibid.*, 248.   [48] *Ibid.*, 233.
[49] *Ibid.*, 217.   [50] *Ibid.*, 222.   [51] *Ibid.*, 226, 225 and 228.   [52] *Ibid.*, 229 and 228.
[53] T. F. Mayer, 'The sources of the political ideas of Thomas Starkey', 50–3.
[54] F. Oakley, 'Almain and Major: conciliar theory on the eve of the reformation', 686. Perhaps the similarities between Almain and Mair arose from their training in the Collège de Navarre under Pedro de Valla, a conciliarist and Gallican despite his Spanish origin. He also taught Jacques Merlin. R. G. Villoslada, *La universidad de Paris durante los estudios de Francesco de Vitoria*, 129–30, 166.

either was a mixed polity.[55] Nevertheless, both allowed the legitimacy of a non-monarchical constitution.[56] Almain treated this point less doctrinairely than Mair, admitting that a secular monarchy could be converted into an aristocracy or a democracy because it was not rooted in divine law.[57] Almain and Mair may have plumped for monarchy, but Almain at least clung to the principle of popular sovereignty.[58] Otherwise, Almain (died 1515) adhered very closely to Gerson.[59] He also at least knew the ideas of Marsilio of Padua.[60] Thus Starkey would have drawn less from his conciliarist contemporaries in Paris than from their master Gerson. Almain's and Mair's specific innovations left few traces in Starkey.

Mair was a much more considerable figure than Almain and his thought more complex. R. G. Villoslada may have exaggerated in calling him 'the most authoritative theologian in the university', but Villoslada's claim that Mair's teaching dominated all the Parisian colleges after 1515 seems closer to the mark.[61] From his base in the Collège de Montaigu and through his nucleus of pupils, Mair's eclectic nominalism became 'the most typical incarnation of the scholasticism of that time', to quote Villoslada again.[62] Wolsey tried to lure Mair to Oxford in 1525, and Mair dedicated his commentary on Aristotle's *Ethics* to the cardinal.[63] Interest in such works characterized Mair. He gave a heavily moral imprint to his teaching, and insisted that all moral questions (including, for example, Henry's divorce) were the preserve of theologians.[64]

Mair moved as easily as d'Ailly between civil and ecclesiastical forms of government, but took a fundamentally different view of both.[65] He agreed with Gerson that the divine ordination of the church imposed basic differences on its constitution, but refused to follow either d'Ailly or Gerson in the belief that the ecclesiastical polity must be mixed.[66] Mair also failed to emphasize the institutional dimension of conciliarism when discussing either king or pope. He preferred the rule of a good man to the best laws, because the ruler was a living law, and both source and interpreter of the other laws. The ruler's prudence provided the very framework of society.[67] Of

---

[55] F. Oakley, 'Conciliarism in the sixteenth century: Jacques Almain again', 116, and J. H. Burns, '*Politia regalis & optima*: the political ideas of John Mair', 32, for their use of parallels. Oakley, 'Almain and Major', 683 and Burns, 'Mair', 53–4, discuss Mair's rejection of Gerson's theory, while F. Merzbacher considers Almain in 'Die Kirchen- und Staatsgewalt bei J. Almain', 306 and 308.

[56] Burns, 'Mair', 35.   [57] Merzbacher, 'Almain', 308.   [58] *Ibid.*, 309 and 306.

[59] Oakley, 'Almain', *passim*, and see also Merzbacher, 'Almain', 304.

[60] Merzbacher, 'Almain', 303, and G. Piaia, *Marsilio da Padova nella riforma e nella controriforma, s.n.*

[61] Villoslada, *Universidad*, 37 and 114.   [62] *Ibid.*, 128, 106–7 for his students.

[63] *Ibid.*, 135.   [64] *Ibid.*, 121 and 140.   [65] Burns, 'Mair', 32.   [66] *Ibid.*, 51.

[67] *Ibid.*, 34 and 35.

course, he should take advice, but ultimate authority remained his. That power, however, rested on consent as expressed through those 'qui vicem gerunt totius communitatis', whether peers of the realm, the three estates or imperial electors.[68] The rest of the community was therefore in some sense superior to its head, but this would rarely be obvious. Mair preferred hereditary succession to election, which meant that consent usually operated simply by the people failing to do anything at all about the ruler. True, the community retained the right to depose a ruler who failed to govern 'pro communi populi utilitate et non pro sua', but only its representatives could exercise this right.[69] Mair apparently believed that the origin of society rested on consent, but he was unclear about the implications of his theory.[70]

When discussing the ecclesiastical constitution, Mair maintained again that '*politia regalis et optima*' meant a combination of absolute authority for the ruler and safeguards for the community against its misuse.[71] Thus he almost automatically adhered to Parisian conciliarism in some sense, but Mair's view of the ordinary power of the pope accorded him every bit as much authority as a secular monarch. The council, defined as 'an assembly of all grades of the hierarchy who have a right to be present, convoked by those to whom it pertains to deal with the *utilitate publica christiana* in a common spirit', was superior to the pope only in an emergency. In no sense did it and he share power otherwise.[72] John E. Bigane, citing Mair's commentaries on Matthew 16:18 (*Tu es Petrus*), went so far as to claim that Mair diluted his already weak conciliarism by 1529 to the point where he had almost become a papalist.[73]

In short, J. H. Burns judges that Mair fitted perfectly into his French intellectual context. He defended monarchy while resisting absolutism in exactly the same way Claude de Seyssel did.[74] Neither stood alone. Contemporary French legists of the stamp of Jean Montaigne commenting on the powers of the *parlements* belong to the same tradition.[75] All fit into the variety of European constitutional thought analysed by J. H. Hexter.[76] De Seyssel and Montaigne could have drawn on 'populist' readings of French constitutional history and theory for many of the same points, which had some-

---

[68] *Ibid.*, 37.
[69] *Ibid.*, 38, 41 and 43. See also F. Oakley, 'On the road from Constance to 1688: the political thought of John Major and George Buchanan', 15 and 17.
[70] Burns, 'Mair', 57.
[71] *Ibid.*, 49.   [72] *Ibid.*, 52–3.
[73] Bigane, *Faith*, 69–76, but see my review in *SCJ*, XIII:3 (1982), 128. For Mair, see also Skinner, *Foundations*, II, *passim*.
[74] Burns, 'Mair', 60–1.
[75] J. H. Franklin, 'Jean Bodin and the end of medieval constitutionalism', 157–61, especially 162.
[76] J. H. Hexter, *The vision of politics on the eve of the reformation*, chapter 5.

times been made in forms even closer to Starkey's thinking. For example, until the late fifteenth century, the Estates General had the right to appoint the king's council, and the 'popular' party made much of this right. It derived, so they argued, from the people's original election of the king, and was merely a part of their sovereign authority over the commonwealth. In a minority like that in 1484, power devolved again on the people.[77] And while theory about the constable may not have helped Starkey much, Anne de Montmorency's domination of the government from that office at least underlined Starkey's attachment to the position.[78] Starkey may well have picked up such ideas in Paris and could have read the French lawyers a few years later while studying law in Avignon, but its seems almost as certain that he must have been exposed to de Seyssel somewhere as that he read Gerson. Some of their similarities may have arisen from a common emphasis on practicalities, but de Seyssel's *Monarchie de France* is the same sort of eclectic work as Starkey's Dialogue, drawing on medieval jurisprudence, Gallicanism, Aristotelianism, Italian diplomacy, institutional history, social analysis, and the literature of mirrors of princes and the art of war to bridge the gap between theory and practice.[79]

De Seyssel began his analysis with the fundamental concept of *police* which meant 'not only a theoretical constitutional structure but more specifically the legislative tradition of the French monarchy expressed in the royal ordinances', or, even more strongly put, the 'whole social-political structure of the community'.[80] Descending ultimately from Aristotle's notion of *politia, police* was one of the three 'bridles' on royal authority, which would render it neither 'totally absolute nor yet too much restrained'.[81] De Seyssel used *police* as a multi-purpose word for an entire political system, in the same way 'pollycy' functioned for Starkey.

A theoretical discussion of the best form of government did not interest de Seyssel, although he did deign to mention the three-fold classification of constitutions in order to argue that 'monarchy is the best if the prince is good and has the sense, the experience, and the good will to govern justly'. De Seyssel was not prepared to leave the monarch's behaviour to chance. He pointed out the rarity of a paragon, and suggested instead that it was better to install an aristocracy which 'seems the more reasonable and praiseworthy since it is more lasting, better founded, and easier to bear, being composed of

[77] J. H. Shennan, *The parlement of Paris*, 190, and J. R. Major, *Representative institutions in renaissance France, 1421–1559*, 81 and 88.
[78] R. Doucet, *Les institutions de la France au XVIe siècle*, I, 112–13 and R. J. Knecht, *Francis I*, 253.
[79] Claude de Seyssel, *The monarchy of France*, 2.
[80] *Ibid.*, 19 and N. O. Keohane, *Philosophy and the state in France*, 40.   [81] *Monarchy*, 51.

the persons selected by the assembly or a part of them'. This system would not do, either. De Seyssel returned to the title of this section to argue 'that it [the monarchical state] is better than any other' after detailing the danger that an aristocracy would degenerate into an oligarchy (38–9). In an earlier work de Seyssel had maintained that 'taken as a whole the French realm participates in all three ways of political governance', and it might be expected that the failings of a bad prince and greedy aristocrats would lead him to fall back on the mixed constitution.[82] This de Seyssel did not quite do. The excesses of the lower orders probably scared him away from allowing any admixture of democracy in his constitution, and in the *Monarchie* he concluded that kingship was the best form of government, provided that it partook of some aristocratic elements, especially the 'fundamental necessity' of good counsel. This platitude did not content de Seyssel, who went on to spell out a system of advising the king through three councils, based on an analogy to the seventy-two elders, the twelve disciples and the trinity (? the king's most secret council of three) (71–3). Unlike Starkey, de Seyssel did not particularly care where the members of these councils came from: the king could even appoint his own advisers (75–6). Like Starkey, de Seyssel opted for a hereditary monarchy because of the dangers of election, but he did not explicitly make his system of councils a remedy for the failings of the royal blood.

De Seyssel rested his discussion on the ever-popular medical metaphor of the four humours and the increasingly common example of Venice. The governance of leading citizens and good laws accounted for Venice's success. It had 'some trace of monarchy in the *doge*', but not a glimmer of the popular. The people were 'entirely subject to the signory', which both kept them in place through strict laws and preserved their rights so that they would have no pretext for rebellion. 'In truth it is the most perfect and best policed empire and republican state which we have seen or read about' (42–3). Not even Venice was eternal, though. Anything sublunary could not avoid decay. Mystical bodies behaved like physical ones 'created and composed of four contrary elements and humours' and they were subject to an ineluctable cycle of 'increase, stability and decline'. Trying to support the weakest humour to keep them all in balance inevitably injured the others (43–4). Unlike Polybius or Starkey, de Seyssel did not believe the mixed constitution could remedy the bleak prospect of inevitable decline.

Some of de Seyssel's ideas about practical reforms, like his image of Venice, were similar to Starkey's. Episcopal non-residence, for example, posed the basic problem of the church. If bishops lived in their dioceses and offered the good example they should, all would be well (87–8). But de Seyssel's attitude to the nobility and his designs to keep it in power might have endeared him even more to Starkey. Even if the king must maintain the nobility, it had to

---

[82] Keohane, *Philosophy*, 34.

deserve office. Although blood should not count above all else, the king had no choice but to prefer competent nobles to any other candidates (95–6). He was also obligated to control the expenses of law suits which allowed the middle sort to profit exorbitantly and thus tread on the toes of the nobility, and he must further keep a tight rein on foreign trade, lest the merchandise brought in tempt the nobles into ostentatious display, 'the most pernicious of all' the problems of the commonwealth. Their finery was a big enough waste in itself, but it led the nobility's inferiors to imitate them, and that was unreasonable. The king should set an example of moderate display, and the lower orders had to be prevented from aping their betters (99–102).

In this congenial political environment, Starkey probably began to write his 'justly famous' Dialogue.[83] Experience in Paris and its university, including Pole's successful mission, stimulated both Starkey's mind and ambition. The rise of his friend and probable teacher Robert Whittinton to the post of schoolmaster of the henchmen at a salary of £20 per annum in 1529 no doubt helped.[84] Starkey would produce a sweeping reform programme, centred on Pole, but leaving plenty of room for himself.[85] This small audience dictated two perhaps conflicting purposes for Starkey and largely accounts for the difficulty of interpreting the work. Yet these two intentions and the motives underlying them can be reconstructed by restoring the Dialogue to its proper context in Starkey's life.[86] When Starkey originally conceived the work, he meant it as a manifesto to persuade his patron to assume the place in English public life expected of him. This intention, of course, was hardly chimerical at a time when Henry dogged Pole's footsteps with offers of high ecclesiastical preferments. Starkey had other ideas. He envisioned Pole as the leader of a group of aristocratic reformers, perhaps centred on the nascent Aragonese party and particularly its old nobility wing. Or perhaps Starkey saw Pole as heir to the Duke of Buckingham, who would not make the same mistake of failing to launch a broad-based movement. Pole's refusal to succumb to Henry's blandishments and capitalize on his own success frustrated Starkey's original design. Between late 1530 and early 1532 when Pole and Starkey again left England for Italy, Starkey decided to leave Pole's

---

[83] The description is A. J. Slavin's. 'Profitable studies: humanists and government in early Tudor England', 321. In what follows I extensively revise an argument which first appeared in *HJ*, XXVIII:1 (1985). The notes to this earlier version contain fuller quotations from Starkey's works than I cite here.

[84] *The vulgaria of John Stanbridge and the vulgaria of Robert Whittinton*, ed. Beatrice White, xxx.

[85] W. Schenk, *Reginald Pole*, 43 put both points too mildly. 'Starkey seems to have had some political ambitions and may well have considered it his duty to draw his friend's attention to these problems, in the hope of persuading him to devote himself to politics'. Schenk also thought the Dialogue was written in Padua.

[86] Skinner sketches the useful distinction between motive and intention in '"Social meaning" and the explanation of social action', 144–7. See also the introduction above.

household and enter the king's. Then his second motive for the Dialogue came into play. It became the centrepiece of Starkey's own credentials, no longer an advertisement for Pole. Starkey completed his dossier with some advice on the divorce and a covering letter for the Dialogue spelling out his qualifications for government service. All were largely completed by late 1532, although Starkey may have dusted off the Dialogue when another opportunity seemed to offer in 1536. Most of the case for the earlier date rests on palaeographical and diplomatic evidence, neither of which does much to support a later revision.

Unfortunately, the depredations of nineteenth-century archivists piled on top of those of earlier miscreants make it impossible to determine the Dialogue's place in Starkey's archive and hence to explain how and why he preserved it. They have also led to the alarmingly rapid deterioration of the only MS and made it impossible to continue to debate some palaeographical questions.[87] The manuscript no doubt outlasted Starkey because of Cromwell's seizure of his papers when Starkey came within a few months of indictment for treason in 1538. Two years later Cromwell's papers in turn fell into the crown's hands, and Starkey's work probably found its way among the records kept in the Treasury of the Receipt.

Scholarship on Starkey's work has passed considerably beyond F. L. Baumer's pessimistic judgments that both its date and purpose were doomed to remain 'unanswerable enigmas', and attempted solutions could generate nothing but 'hopeless controversy'.[88] There has, it is true, been a great deal of the latter, largely because no commentator before G. R. Elton possessed either the skill or the will to take the decisive first step out of this morass by examining the MS to see what information it might yield about the Dialogue's composition. Thirty years after Baumer, Elton found two points at which he thought Starkey had broken off writing which fall in Kathleen Burton's edition at pages 134 and 183. Elton assumed that Starkey composed each of these three sections continuously, and he therefore dated the middle piece to 1533 by its reference to Sadoleto's *De liberis recte instituendis*. Starkey must thus have written the first part of the work sometime in 1532. That left only the short conclusion. Fritz Caspari had suggested that Starkey was thinking of Erasmus's *Ecclesiastes sive de ratione concionandi* when recommending his 'boke of the prechar'. Elton accepted this identification, which meant that Starkey must then have added the Dialogue's tailpiece in 1535 after Erasmus's work appeared. Elton also noted revisions in the text and took these to mean that Starkey thought to present the work to Henry as late as 1536, perhaps at Cromwell's urging.[89]

---

[87] My forthcoming diplomatic edition for the Camden Series will preserve all the remaining information in the MS.

[88] F. L. Baumer, 'Thomas Starkey and Marsilius of Padua', 189.

[89] G. R. Elton, 'Reform by statute: Thomas Starkey's *Dialogue* and Thomas Cromwell's policy', 167–8.

Despite Elton's care, problems remain in his description of the MS and in his reasoning about it. Most important, the MS was written in only two sections, not three. Elton supposed that Starkey paused at the bottom of fol. 121r, where the sentence he took as Starkey's original conclusion falls.[90] But this is not the final sentence on that page, nor is there any blank space between foot and dorse. The only such gap in the last five or six folios occurs at the bottom of fol. 124r, after Starkey wrote out the long discussion of aediles and censors and marked it for insertion at the foot of fol. 121r. The white space on fol. 124r could well represent a mental pause while Starkey resumed his train of thought, or he may simply have miscalculated how much paper he would need for the insertion. In any case, there is no discontinuity between the passage at the top of fol. 124v and that to which it was attached on 121r, even though Starkey began on 124v with words which sound as if he had laid the pen down for a while and then changed directions.

That had already happened on 121v where Starkey concluded his consideration of the proper education of priests and appended a summary of the work thus far, which he had begun on 121r. That done, Starkey had 'Lupset' introduce a fundamental objection to everything that had gone before, but without interrupting his writing. Even though 'Pole's' ordinances for the perfection of the civil life were all very nice, said 'Lupset', they could not bring man to virtue. 'Lupset' here executed an abrupt about-face and abandoned his earlier assurances to 'Pole' that the natural law could well lead to salvation by itself and that Englishmen in particular had no cause for concern since Christ had established all their civil laws.[91] The overtly religious note at the beginning of what Elton took to be the second section signalled this change of emphasis. After leaving more than three-quarters of fol. 92v blank, Starkey presented his characters having a mass celebrated in order to gain divine inspiration as they searched for remedies to all the problems they had uncovered. A set of solutions, however, kept to the plan of the work, which Starkey had announced at the end of the introduction on fol. 17r–v. Thus the mass followed the last hiatus in the MS and introduced the whole of the work's remainder. Starkey prepared the 'new' approach on fol. 121v long before he reached it. He did not interrupt his writing there, nor anywhere else in the last eight or nine folios, with the exception of the inserted section on fols. 123v–124r. In short, Elton's final interruption is spurious.

Possibly the recommendation of the 'boke of the prechar' contributed to Elton's belief in a second division of the MS. By Elton's own demonstration, Starkey could not have written the whole of the work as late as 1535. Therefore, the section containing a reference to a book printed in that year must have been tacked on. In fact, Starkey added the reference, not the segment. Nevertheless, this one small *marginalium* provides the strongest

[90] Elton, '*Dialogue*', 168.
[91] SP 1/90, fols. 13r–14r (Burton, 34–5).

palaeographical evidence that Starkey did work over his MS after 1532, but it is hardly irrefutable proof.[92] Erasmus worked on *Ecclesiastes* for twelve years, and periodically announced its completion.[93] He promised John à Lasco that he would finish by the winter of 1528, and John Fisher had earlier prodded him several times to hurry the work along.[94] Either Lupset or Pole could have channelled misinformation like this to Starkey. Pole had been in communication with Erasmus since 1523 and Lupset had been his star pupil in the previous decade.[95]

Starkey referred to another of Erasmus's works in this final section, but it is harder to tell what Starkey meant when he praised the 'Instructyon of a Chrystun man' and called for its translation into English. The most likely candidate reinforces an early date for the completion of the Dialogue. Reading the translated title literally, Caspari pointed to the *Christiani hominis institutio* (1514), and suggested as an alternative that Starkey may have confused it with the *Institutio principis christiani*, since the former was not a book.[96] Here Caspari probably erred: just about anything, printed or not, of any length, could be called a book in the sixteenth century.[97] Nevertheless, Burton's suggestion of the *Enchiridion militis christiani* (1503) is much more plausible on the basis of content. If she is correct, then the final section must have been written before 1533 when de Worde produced an English translation.[98]

Elton pointed to two other additions to support a 1536 revision, but neither does. The main text contains parallels both to an encomium of Henry designed to sugar-coat the proposal for an elective monarchy, and to the suggested conversion of Westminster and St Albans into schools.[99] The first of these made direct reference to part of the opening section.[100] Starkey wrote the second in the margin of a text proposing that 'we schold now folow' the example of the original founders of monasteries 'in byldyng placys for the instytutyon of the nobylyte, or els in chaungyng some of thes *to that use [ab.]

---

[92] For more on this point, see chapt. 7 below.   [93] *Op. Ep. Er.*, XI, 189.

[94] *Ibid.*, V, 1489, 4 September 1524. For other such promises see Charles Béné, *Érasme et Saint Augustin*, 373–5 and J. M. Weiss, '*Ecclesiastes* and Erasmus: the mirror and the image', 85 and *passim* for more on the work's composition.

[95] J. A. Gee, *Thomas Lupset*, 53–5 and *Op. Ep. Er.*, VI, 1627. This first letter of Erasmus to Pole introduced the latter to à Lasco when both were in Padua.

[96] F. Caspari, *Humanism and the social order in Tudor England*, 258.

[97] For some good examples, see N. L. Jones, *Faith by statute: parliament and the settlement of religion 1559*, 125–6, 128.

[98] Burton, 188. E. J. Devereux, *A checklist of English translations of Erasmus to 1700*, 15 records the edition. William Tyndale did the translation in about 1522, but the printed version was anonymous. J. F. Mozley, *Coverdale and his Bibles*, 28.

[99] Elton, '*Dialogue*', 169–70.

[100] SP 1/90, fol. 104r (Burton, 154) made reference to fol. 16v (Burton, 28).

bycause ther be over many *of thys sort now in our days [*ab. del.* 'to thys use']'.[101] He probably added the two specific examples as further rhetorical reinforcement of the point, as the last phrase was. Neither passage changes the sense of the original. Nor were these new ideas for Starkey. He certainly did not need to wait until 1536 to flatter Henry fulsomely – his 'divorce opinion' did the same thing.[102] Besides, other passages in the Dialogue's original text eased the acceptance of Starkey's elective monarchy, and he let stand some harsh attacks on hereditary succession, the virtue of the present prince notwithstanding.[103] The specific form of Starkey's attack on the monasteries clinches the case against his adding it in 1536. By then he had given up on the nobility and proposed instead that some of the monasteries be converted into communal dormitories for younger sons to whom they should be leased for farming, and that others become educational institutions, apparently for all comers (see below, chapt. 7). Even then, he would not have needed the stimulus of the dissolution of the small, corrupt houses to attack large ones, which could hardly have appeared doomed.[104] Numerous precedents for the conversion of monasteries to more socially useful ends existed, from Wolsey's to those current around Starkey in Italy.[105] John Fisher apparently feared that Henry intended to dissolve the lesser monasteries already in 1529.[106]

So much for a 1535 conclusion and most of the evidence for a 1536 overhaul. In all likelihood, Starkey finished the work before Elton's proposed *terminus ad quem* of 1533. Elton rested his case partly on the redundancy of many of Starkey's reforms after that, but mainly on Sadoleto's *De liberis*. The manner in which Starkey heralded the appearance of Sadoleto's book 'of late days' seems to support Elton, or perhaps even W. Gordon Zeeveld's claim for 1534.[107] Starkey used this phrase only once when we can get even a crude idea of how much time it measured. Then it meant between fifteen and eighteen months.[108] The printed edition of Sadoleto's work did indeed appear in 1533, but Starkey learned of *De liberis* in August 1532 when Sadoleto gave Pole a

---

[101] SP 1/90, fols. 112v–113r.   [102] SP 1/75, e.g., fols. 230r, 234r.

[103] E.g., SP 1/90, fol. 17r. For attacks, see fols. 65v (Burton, 99), 68r–v (102), 70r, 70v (both 104), 109v (164) and 111v (168).

[104] J. J. Scarisbrick, *The reformation and the English people*, 68–9.

[105] For example, the Florentine exile Antonio Brucioli proposed that the monasteries in his native city should be replaced by 'dieci o dodici scuole per i giovani e cinque o sei per le giovane, dove ogni giorno una lettione delle sacre lettere nella materna lingua si legesse et appresso che nella metà di quelle de'giovani le lettere hebraice, grece et latine'. Quoted from one of Brucioli's *Dialogi* (published 1526) by G. Spini, *Antonio Brucioli*, 162.

[106] J.-P. Moreau, *Rome ou l'Angleterre?*, 32.

[107] SP 1/90, fol. 121r. Zeeveld, *Foundations*, 144–5.

[108] *Exhortation*, fol. 45v. Writing in early or mid-1536, Starkey used 'now of late, at such time as I returned out of Italye' to refer to late 1534.

copy of the MS to take to their mutual friends in Venice.[109] On the basis of this evidence, Starkey could not have finished the Dialogue any later than the end of 1533, and possibly as early as the summer of 1532. Starkey's failure to mention Thomas Elyot's *Boke of the Governour* (1531) probably also supports an early date, as does his unfamiliarity with (or lack of interest in) scripture. At one key point in his discussion of papal authority, Starkey refused to go into any biblical grounds for it.[110]

While Elton could therefore still be correct that Starkey wrote the rest of the Dialogue earlier in 1532, the changing identity of 'Pole's' interlocutor makes that unlikely. Throughout nearly all of his work Starkey originally named 'Pole's' companion 'mr. le'. This was almost certainly Geoffrey Lee, a member of Pole's college and client of his family, brother of Edward Lee, and family friend of Thomas More.[111] Lee had been at Magdalen until 1517, where Starkey would have known him for perhaps three or four years. Better yet, Lee delivered Pole's exhibition for Paris in 1529, so that it may even be that Lee's reappearance in Pole's circle pins down when Starkey began to write the Dialogue. Starkey continued to work on it in Paris, but there he came into very close contact with Lupset who rejoined Pole's household. He died in December 1530. Starkey's decision to alter his speakers therefore strongly suggests that he wrote most of his work before Lupset's death, perhaps drawing on conversations between him and Pole. It would have been odd enough deliberately to choose a dead man for a character, but to substitute him for a live person would have been strange indeed.

Starkey's alteration of the second speaker's identity seems to have rested on a very nice calculation of advantage, but Lupset may have done more for the Dialogue than merely stimulate Starkey's ambition. Starkey may well have chosen Lee in the first place because his mission as paymaster to Pole marked him as a royal favourite. Once arrived in Paris, Starkey renewed his friendship

---

[109] Sadoleto apparently completed the work in the summer of 1530 and sent a copy of it to cardinal Ercole Gonzaga in January 1531. Jacopo Sadoleto, *Epistolae quotquot extant proprio nomine scriptae*, ed. V. A. Costanzi, I, 383–7, to Gonzaga, 25 January 1531. Sadoleto for some reason waited until 3 September 1532 to send a copy to his old friend Pietro Bembo, with whom he had worked closely on literary matters when both were papal secretaries. J. F. D'Amico, *Renaissance humanism in papal Rome*, 108. From the covering letter, which asks Bembo to read the work and show it to other learned men for their reactions, it appears that this version was only recently completed. Sadoleto wrote to his almost equally close friend Lazzaro Bonamico in similar terms on the same date. Since Sadoleto gave the work to Pole to carry to Bembo, it seems more likely that Starkey heard of it then rather than when Sadoleto first let it out of his hands. Jacopo Sadoleto, *Opera quae exstant omnia*, I, 34–5 (*Epistolae*, II, no. 6) and II, 146 (*Ibid.*, XXVII, no. 5).

[110] SP 1/90, fol. 81r.

[111] S. E. Lehmberg, *The reformation parliament*, 28, 30 and S. T. Bindoff, ed., *The house of commons 1509–1558*, II, 506–7.

with Lupset, who discharged his role in the negotiations with the Parisian theologians brilliantly. Starkey therefore switched horses, expecting almost as great things from hitching his wagon to Lupset as to Pole. Unfortunately, Lupset died before Starkey could capitalize fully on his friend's success. Lupset still left Starkey a worthwhile legacy. During the last months of his life in Paris he wrote his *Treatyse teachinge the waye of dieyng well* and probably also translated Colet's sermon to convocation.[112] Stoicism heavily imbued Lupset's treatise, like the rest of his writings, from contempt for the body to the idea that perfect virtue could be achieved on earth.[113] Lupset's conversation might thus both have helped to keep Starkey's Stoic leanings firm, as well as remind him of Colet's reforming tradition. And More had just opened parliament by announcing that the clergy needed reform. He differed from Colet and Lupset by looking to the king as agent of clerical renewal, but they (and Starkey) all agreed about the problem.[114]

A few other clues hint that Starkey may have drafted his Dialogue even earlier, and that the surviving MS is not the original. In many places Starkey repeated words or phrases as he might have done if his eye had slipped while reading from another MS.[115] A number of tags in the bottom margin of folios point more definitely to recopying. If these tags fell between quires, that would provide proof positive, but they do not fit such a pattern. Alternatively, some of them may have signalled the order of the pieces of an already written MS, but not all fit that pattern, either.[116]

When combined with watermark evidence which by itself is also inconclusive, these tags support the case for a recopied MS. Starkey used four different papers. For the first thirty-two folios he wrote on paper with a pot watermark reminiscent of Briquet's 11344 (Harcourt, 1531). Its earliest near relative in a long series came from Lisieux and was dated 1526. This family of papers enjoyed great popularity in England, as a glance through many volumes of State Papers will confirm. Folios 33 to 43 were written on a lighter paper, bearing a hand-and-flower watermark nearly identical to Briquet's 12660. This specimen, dated 1534, turned up in Brussels. After another long run of the first paper, Starkey switched to a waxy, cheap paper bearing no maker's design, only to replace it after twelve folios with the final, similarly waxy, type. Its watermark resembles Briquet's series 11912–14, all found in Padua

---

[112] B. O'Kelly and C. A. L. Jarrott, *John Colet's commentary on First Corinthians*, 59.

[113] All in Gee, *Lupset: Dieyng*, 263–90, *passim*; cf. *A treatise of charitie*, 208 and 212, and *An Exhortation to yonge men*, 239, 245, 261–2.

[114] J. A. Guy, *The public career of Sir Thomas More*, 113–15.

[115] E.g., fols. 17r–v, 37v, 50v, 70r, etc.

[116] The tags fall between fols. 24 and 25, 25 and 26, 32 and 33, 44 and 45, 58 and 59. From fol. 32 on they fit the greyer folios, which must once have been exposed to the air more than the rest.

between 1515 and 1552.[117] This might seem to support Elton's case, but the lack of any interruption in the composition tied to a change of paper means that Starkey must simply have carried a stock of writing materials around with him.

The evidence of the change from 'Lee' to 'Lupset' and of recopying shows that Starkey undoubtedly laboured over his writing, and probably revised the existing MS a total of three times. First, he corrected some errors in the process of copying. Then a second set of corrections and additions was made while Starkey still designated the second character 'mr. le', and he finally emended his text one last time after 'le' became 'lup'. It appears that Starkey used different inks and pens in these three revisions, but the present condition of the MS makes it very difficult if not impossible to distinguish between them.

Unlike the messy text of the Dialogue, the dedicatory letter is written out fair in a clerk's hand, although it contains scribal errors. This may well indicate exactly how brief Starkey judged the opportunity for presentation: he had time only for a letter, not for a fair copy of the whole Dialogue. When did he make that decision? Although he does not say so, Elton appeared to believe that the dedicatory letter succeeded the Dialogue's putative final revision. In light of Starkey's career and of English politics, however, the letter more likely followed hard on the heels of the completion of the Dialogue's first draft no later than the end of 1532. Starkey had finished the whole of the work or at least planned it substantially when he wrote the letter. In it he described all three sections of the present work, including the last covering how 'thes abusys both in custum and law may be reformyd and the treu commyn wele a mong us restoryd'.[118]

Starkey introduced himself to Henry in the letter and assured the king that 'except in some perte occatyon serve me to satysfye the same [his desire to serve the king] the rest of my lyfe schall appere ... tedyouse and displeas-ant'.[119] Both introduction and place-hunting would have been unnecessary after Starkey's entry to royal service and interview with Henry in early 1535. His conversation with the king should also have affected how Starkey recited his credentials. While both his 1535 letters to Cromwell made much of his studies of law and scripture, he mentioned neither in the dedicatory letter.[120] Starkey would certainly have mentioned at least the latter to Henry after the king had faulted his insufficiently scriptural reasoning with Richard

---

[117] Not surprisingly, the middle third of the MS, which includes the poorest quality paper, is in the worst shape. Starkey's ink may have been inferior, but the surface to which he applied it is the more likely culprit. For the watermarks of his papers, see C. M. Briquet, *Les filigranes. Dictionnaire historique des marques du papier*.

[118] SP 1/90, fol. 2r.   [119] *Ibid.*, fol. 1r, repeated on fol. 1v.

[120] SP 1/89, fol. 175r and Harl. 283, fol. 129v.

Reynolds.[121] Instead, Starkey wrote merely that 'aftur that I had spent perte of my youth in the study of philosophi … I went streyght in to the cuntre of Italy, as to the place most famys both with grete lerning and gud and iust pollyci'. That experience made him 'somewhat better instructe at my returne in to myn owne cuntrey indyfferently to considur & wey the custummys & mannerys … with the pollyty usyd here'.[122]

Zeeveld took Starkey's search for employment in this letter together with his description of composing 'now a late in leyser & quietnes' to put both letter and Dialogue into the period after Starkey returned from Italy in late 1534.[123] Zeeveld cannot be right about the date, but he was correct to stress the importance of a period in retirement. Starkey would have needed a long period free of pressing business in order to write the Dialogue. The only documented interval of that sort came during Pole's retreat to Sheen in 1530 and 1531, which Starkey shared. Immediately before that, Starkey and Pole were deeply engaged in Paris. Immediately after, Starkey began his study of civil law.

Starkey engaged in high-minded pursuits during his retirement in addition to continuing to act as Pole's secretary, and his patron's behaviour probably continued to encourage him. As Edmund Harvel lamented in June 1531, 'you have inclosid yourselff in the charter howse wher it semith that you have dedicate al you [sic] worke to perpetual philosophye but whether tendith soche pertinacye?' Harvel's tone indicates that he had drawn an inference about Starkey's activity at Sheen from the mere fact that Starkey had gone into a monastic retreat. Starkey almost certainly never needed the prodding of Harvel's next question 'wil you not comme forthe & teche other qualiter sit humanum vivendum, and helpe to take out al barbarous custom [?] and bring the realme to an antike form of good living?'[124] In late 1531, Starkey received two letters from his old friend John Hales, asking him to secure Pole's help. The matter apparently concerned Hales's benefice in Wimborne Minster, which he held by Pole's appointment.[125] Starkey may or may not have succeeded on Hales's behalf, but the evidence suggests that Starkey thought Pole would still aid Starkey's grand plans. According to Pole's biographer Beccadelli, he retreated to Sheen in order to avoid giving Henry any cause for suspicion and to satisfy his family.[126] This account doubtless descends from Pole's own later interpretation, according to which he had begged Henry for a

---

[121] SP 1/92, fol. 59v. [122] SP 1/90, fol. 1v. [123] Zeeveld, *Foundations*, 145n.
[124] Nero B VI, fol. 169r.
[125] SP 1/68, fols. 54 and 55r (*LP*, V, 529 and 530); *LP*, V, 1443 confirms Pole's patronage of Hales when reporting the latter's death in October 1532. See further, N. Orme, *Education in the west of England 1066–1548*, 184–5.
[126] Beccadelli, 'Vita', 285.

leave of absence in order to avoid 'another storm ... much graver and more dangerous [than Paris]'.[127] If Pole had done no more than try to avoid controversy as he always had, he would not have upset Starkey's ambitions. If he also tried to please his family, that would have played even further into Starkey's hands. Their object – Pole's honourable preferment – was the same as Starkey's.

As we have seen, Starkey's 'now a late' to fix the time of his retreat meant that it could have fallen anywhere within the previous eighteen months. Starkey's earnestness in this letter makes it impossible that he could have thought to present his work in its existing form any later than the outside limit calculated from completion mainly by 1531, that is, 1533. To borrow a leaf from Elton's method of dating the Dialogue, by 1534 many of the reform proposals to which Starkey's letter pointed had already been embodied in legislation.[128] This is a strong argument as far as it goes, but it stops short of the full implications of the 1534 legislation for Starkey's platform. The Dialogue lost more than some of its ideas: its spiritual and secular heart had been cut out by March of that year. Just as rule by the prince's unbridled will and fantasy had been the greatest cause of the destruction of commonwealths, so the chief fault in the spirituality lay in the authority 'gyven to the hede or els by many yerys usurpyd apon us tyrannycally' of dispensation from all laws of God and man.[129] Sharing the monarch's power would remedy both problems, whether with parliament and various councils, or with cardinals and general council.[130] The Act for the Exoneration of Exactions, however, not only outlawed papal dispensation, but also recognized that only 'your royal majesty and your lords spiritual and temporal and commons' could dispense 'all human laws of this your realm', exactly as Starkey had recommended.[131]

In dedicating his Dialogue, Starkey wrote about his interlocutors in a way that suggests an early date for his letter. His hope that Pole was 'yet I trust in lyfe' reveals that Starkey was no longer living in Pole's household, and Starkey closely connected this sentiment to Lupset's death. Had he not died, Henry 'shold have had true & fayfull servyce' from him. Pole still had a chance and Starkey was confident that

yf he coud have seen that thing, by his lernyng wych your most notabull clarkys in your reame and many other hath approvyd your heynes schold have had before this certayne and sure experyence, of the wych thing also yet I dow not utterly dyspeare, for I trust hyt schal not be long before he shall declare unto your grace of his wysedome & jugement playne and manyfest argment [sic].[132]

127 Reginald Pole, 'Epistola ad Eduardum VI Angliae regem', in *ERP*, IV, 313.
128 Elton, '*Dialogue*', 168.   129 SP 1/90, fols. 65v and 80v (Burton, 99 and 118).
130 *Ibid.*, fols. 66v and 118r–v (Burton, 100 and 178).
131 G. R. Elton, *The Tudor constitution*, 351, 352.   132 SP 1/90, fols. 1v, 2r (quotation).

The close proximity of this passage to Starkey's encomium of Lupset, to-gether with one reading of its second clause and Starkey's confidence that Pole would agree with the divorce all support an earlier rather than a later date for the letter.

The second phrase quoted could refer to the determination of the uni-versities in favour of Henry's divorce. If so, it should be read: if Pole, by his learning, could have seen that thing, which your most notable clerks, etc. This reading is as plausible as taking the sentence as written. Starkey often sep-arated his relatives from their referents, as did many sixteenth-century Englishmen.[133] Then again, plenty of clerks (clerics or writers?) offered tributes to Pole's learning, as Starkey's sentence could also appear to read, but most who had thus far gone on record were foreigners.[134] Contemporary meanings of 'approve' would support either sense. The balance of probability is that Starkey intended the first meaning suggested and drew on his recent experience in Paris in citing the opinion of the 'clarkys', or the theologians of Paris. If Starkey did indeed refer to their and other determinations, he must have cited them before Cranmer's annulment of the marriage to Catherine in May 1533. The university opinions served a purpose in 1530 and 1531, but by 1533 they would have made a much weaker reed for domestic consump-tion, anyway, than the judgment of the Archbishop of Canterbury.[135] Star-key's certainty about Pole's cooperation would also have been much more plausible before Pole's first 'position paper' on the divorce in 1530 or 1531 than during the negotiations of 1535 and 1536. Starkey later remembered having read Pole's earliest opinion, which showed the king 'the daungerys wych hangyd apon wordly pollycy' in such a convincing fashion 'that hyt put me in a feare *of daungerys to cum [ab.]'.[136] Even an optimist like Starkey would have had to have been much more uncertain about Pole's malleability after that, especially if Pole's piece made such a strong impression. The brazen assurance of the passage in the dedicatory letter contrasts strongly with the cautious line Starkey followed in 1535 and 1536 when he did his best to persuade both Henry and Cromwell first, that he had no idea what Pole then thought, and second that he had never imagined Pole could have thought *that* (see below, chap. 7).

On the face of it, Starkey's praise for Henry's superior 'lyght of jugement' 'by the reson wherof yow have utterly plukkyd up the rote of all abuses, this utward powar and intollerabul tyranny of rome', square better with a date after the same 1533–4 legislation implementing the Supremacy.[137] But once

---

[133] For a random sample of Starkey's practice, see *Exhortation*, sig. a[iv], 41v, 42v, 45v.

[134] Beccadelli, 'Vita', 284.

[135] As Dr Murphy also concludes in her painstaking study 'discussion over the marriage had become an academic question by 1533'. 'The debate', 259.

[136] BL Cleop. E VI, fol. 376r.   [137] SP 1/90, fol. 2r.

again, it would have looked peculiar after the spring of 1533 to hope that uprooting the papacy's external power would lead to a whole series of reforms, including presumably those adumbrated in the Dialogue, when many of them had become redundant, and as we shall see other conservatives regarded the manoeuvres of 1531–2 as tantamount to the destruction of papal authority in England. Thus the apparent contradiction between the letter and the course of events earlier than the traditional date assigned to it can be explained by assigning the letter to the same period as the original composition of the Dialogue.

In both letter and Dialogue Starkey considered only the external power of the papacy and left its spiritual authority untouched (see below, chapt. 6). The Dialogue defined papal tyranny as the usurpation of power in temporal affairs. The pope retained the power of absolution, and Starkey still conceded him control over cases of schism. This could be exactly what Starkey meant in the dedicatory letter and no more. [138] Such an attitude comes very close to the tenor of the campaign against the pope in the early part of 1531, including Norfolk's famous taunt that Henry would be absolute master in his realm and Henry's threat to limit the clergy's power to absolution only.[139] If the similarity between Starkey's ideas and Norfolk's manoeuvres is more than superficial, it may be that Starkey attributed more importance than some modern historians to convocation's acceptance of the Supreme Headship in February 1531, or he may have been thinking of the submission of the clergy in May 1532.

Although Starkey never had a fair copy of his work made, he kept it in mind, watching for opportunities when he might yet use it. He set the stage for the Dialogue's revival in a passage of the *Exhortation to the people*, completed before September 1535. More important for present purposes, in the same text he attacked the papacy in a way which seems to suggest that the dedicatory letter was written at this time, after all. When Starkey tried to discover why the commonwealth 'was slypped from that hevenly perfection' of pure Christianity, he found the principal cause to be 'this usurped long and many yeres superioritie of the pope'. He concluded this broadside by observing that upon his return to England he had found the 'pluckynge awaye [of] this superioritie' 'partly put in effecte'.[140] This apparently means that the dedicatory letter's praise for its complete removal would have to follow the *Exhortation*, but in the same place Starkey insisted how long and how ardently he had wished for an end to papal primacy; meaning to flatter at an

---

[138] SP 1/90, fol. 118v (Burton, 178).
[139] *CSPSp*, IV:2, 598, fol. 27 and Moreau, *Rome ou l'Angleterre?*, 33.
[140] *Exhortation*, sig. 44r–45v.

earlier date, he could have made too much of a previous 'uprooting'. The account of Starkey's education in this passage supports this argument. As in the letters to Cromwell of the first half of 1535, Starkey emphasized his training in scripture, which the dedicatory letter conspicuously lacks. There he merely reported that after study of nature and 'thinges perteynyng to the maners of man in the civile and polytike lyfe' (which must include his legal training), he had gone directly to the Bible. It would seem safer to make as much of Starkey's personal chronology as possible, than of his references to external events. His remembrances of his education probably provide a much more reliable standard than anything he said about the vicissitudes of English attitudes to the papacy, and his own thinking about the pope is much too complex and full of twistings and turnings to serve as a yardstick of chronology.

Nevertheless, Starkey's words about the pope in the dedicatory letter may provide a clue about his factional leanings, which his original choice of characters and some of his constitutional proposals reinforce. If it is correct that the promulgation of the Headship triggered Starkey's claim that the papacy had been uprooted, then he espoused the same interpretation advanced by the Aragonese party, even if it turned out that both had over-reacted. Eustace Chapuys twice reported Henry's establishment as pope in England and noted the queen's extreme alarm. In the second instance, Chapuys also observed how upset More and Fisher were.[141] Another of this party's allies, Cuthbert Tunstall, protested against the Headship in terms which could indicate a similar reaction.[142] Even some months later the papal nuncio warned Clement VII that he ought to grant Norfolk a dispensation for one of his nephews 'in these times, when we are threatened by the [papal] jurisdiction being removed'.[143] Pole was probably close to this party, so that Starkey could easily have taken its violently negative reaction and turned it upside down into equally intemperate approval.[144]

Unfortunately, Pole's attitude to the Headship is obscure, but a slight balance of the exceptionally difficult evidence suggests that Pole opposed that solution to the divorce from the beginning. Gilbert Burnet claimed that Pole was present when convocation accepted the Headship and that he too acquiesced in it. Burnet adduced as evidence a passage from *De unitate* written some five years after the event, together with the fact that Pole lost none of his

---

[141] *CSPSp*, IV:2, 635 and 641, February 1531. Eric Ives takes Chapuys's alarm more seriously than most of his predecessors. *Anne Boleyn*, 169.
[142] D. Wilkins, ed., *Concilia magnae Britanniae et Hiberniae*, III, cc. 745–6.
[143] *Römische Dokumente zur Geschichte der Ehescheidung Heinrichs VIII von England 1527–1534*, ed. Stephan Ehses, 178 (1 July 1531).
[144] Lehmberg, *Reformation parliament*, 30.

benefices when he left England, in particular not the deanery of Exeter.[145] Burnet did not make his reference clear, but it appears to be the following:

What shall I say about the honor [the Headship] that has been conferred upon you in the midst of great dissension among the bishops themselves? ... I shall certainly say that you should not seek this honor, that you should not strive to obtain it by using threats, that you should not compel such recognition from unwilling persons even as I have seen you do. Contrary to the desire of some, you refused to subscribe certain documents containing promise of large amounts of money granted to you. You refused ... unless it were also stated in the document that this financial obligation was to be discharged to you in the capacity of supreme head of the Church in England.[146]

The circumstantial detail and Pole's claim to have been an eye witness certainly seem to mean that he had been in convocation, and the reference to monetary concessions must refer to the events of 1531. Pole was out of England at the time of both the submission of the clergy and the final implementation of the Supremacy which began in mid-1533. The difficulty is that he called the latter the Headship, too. Elsewhere in *De unitate* he chided Richard Sampson 'that you have endured more serious troubles in the space of the three years since the king has been placed over you in the distinguished and especially desirable position of head' than in all the centuries of papal supremacy before that.[147] This must have been written after January 1536 when Pole received Sampson's *Oratio de obedientia*, and must therefore refer to the creation of the Supremacy.[148] Pole had left England in January 1532 precisely because he had threatened to oppose the Supremacy, according to Chapuys.[149] Pole's memory was notoriously unreliable, so that he could have miscounted the number of years between 1536 and passage of the Headship, or perhaps he meant Headship in the first instance and the legislative package of 1533–4 in the second.[150]

　　Pole later claimed that he had opposed the divorce and thus probably the Headship from the very first, but his contemporary opinion on the former apparently made no mention of the latter. Cranmer said nothing about it in his 13 June 1531 summary of Pole's lost 'book'. It may be, however, that Pole ignored the Supremacy because he wrote before convocation accepted it on 11 February. In an account of this crucial period tendered to Protector

---

[145] G. Burnet, *The history of the reformation of the church of England*, ed. N. Pocock, I, 353 and 191.

[146] *Reginaldi Poli ad Henricum octavum Britanniae regem, pro ecclesiasticae unitatis defensione*, fol. XIXr–v. English quoted from *Pole's defense of the unity of the church*, trans. and intro. J. G. Dwyer, 47.

[147] Pole, *De unitate*, fols. 35v–36r, and *Pole's defense*, 88.

[148] *ERP*, I, 429.　　　[149] *LP*, V, 737.

[150] Paul van Dyke, 'Reginald Pole and Thomas Cromwell: an examination of the *Apologia ad Carolum quintum*', documents the clearest case thus far of the tricks Pole's memory played on him. Cf. also G. R. Elton, 'The political creed of Thomas Cromwell', 215–20, and *The Tudor revolution in government*, 73–4.

Somerset nearly twenty years later, Pole made it appear that he had handed in his opinion on the divorce shortly after his interview with Henry in December 1530. He also wrote that Henry had kept Pole's opinion close between himself, Norfolk and Pole's brother Montagu, at least for a while.[151] Therefore, Cranmer, not yet a very important figure, may simply have had to wait to see a document which no longer accurately reflected Pole's views. By 1539 Pole certainly regarded the Supreme Headship as the root of all evil, and his chronology of Cromwell's rise to power indicates that Pole must again have been thinking of 1531, not 1533.[152] The accepted view of the genesis of Pole's opposition to Henry, which largely rests on this and similar statements from Pole's own pen, supports this case.[153]

Starkey's original interlocutor may well have shared Pole's attitude to the Headship and divorce and Starkey's choice of Geoffrey Lee therefore reveals something of his own factional leanings. Unfortunately, there is no direct evidence that Lee played a part in the Aragonese circles of the Reformation Parliament, even though he probably owed his seat at Portsmouth to the Countess of Salisbury's patronage. All the same, the circumstantial evidence cited above makes him a solid candidate for a supporter of More's resistance.

This faction seems to have had very little by way of a clear programme in the early 1530s, and its position was undermined by its inability to overcome the anti-clericalism of its most natural supporters among the high nobility, who were otherwise rock-ribbed religious conservatives.[154] If Pole had made a choice between them, he might well have gone with his friend More, rather than with his fellow aristocrats.[155] In many ways, Starkey attempted to blend both parties' attitudes in his Dialogue, but his more specifically constitutional arrangements suggest that he saw his work as either reflecting or justifying the designs of a narrower aristocratic faction, unless he were careless or callous. Although Starkey's proposals for an elective monarchy, appointed king's council and revived constable to head it and 'conturpaise' the king have been

---

[151] *CSPV*, V, 575, pp. 243–4.

[152] Reginald Pole, 'Apologia ad Carolum quintum caesarem', in *ERP*, I, 132–3. Pole dated his interview with Cromwell immediately, or nearly so, before his flight from England in early 1532.

[153] By the time of his letter to Charles, Pole had decided that he had already been forced to flee England in 1529 (*ibid.*, 136). By 1547 in his *apologia* to Edward VI this had become the official version, with added drama. Pole treated the divorce as the *fons et origo* of all the 'tempests' raging over the realm. He himself had behaved as 'beasts are wont to do, wandering in an open field when they are faced with an approaching storm. They take themselves into a wood or some cave'. Pole alleged that he had thought like this even before his legation to the university of Paris in 1529. His request to Henry for permission to go there to study theology had been partly a ruse 'by which he should more easily dismiss me'. 'And so immediately I left, hoping to find a place where no part of the impending storm should touch me' (*ERP*, IV, 312).

[154] Guy, *The public career of Sir Thomas More*, 106–7 and appendix 2.

[155] Lehmberg, *Reformation parliament*, 30, and R. W. Chambers, *Thomas More*, 182.

dismissed as mere pipedreams, Starkey must have known the fate of the last constable, the Duke of Buckingham. Buckingham may have been politically isolated before his fall, but his fate offered a clear *exemplum*.

Many others of the high and mighty greatly respected Pole, including a somewhat more adroit politician from the same old nobility wing as Buckingham, the Marquess of Exeter. His faction would serve as a focal point of discontent in the later 1530s, often in conjunction with Pole. Exeter had high hopes for Pole and his departure from England in 1532 severely disappointed the marquess.[156] Norfolk held a similarly high opinion of Pole, to judge from the letter of congratulations he ordered sent to Pole after the doings in Paris.[157] Sir John Russell, by Pole's testimony, thought so well of Pole that 'knowing me [Pole] as he did – he would present the writing [Pole's divorce opinion] without any hesitation, let happen whatever pleased God'.[158] Even Cranmer praised the intelligence displayed in that opinion. Henry, of course, both offered Pole two choice bishoprics and supposedly told Montagu after his second disappointing interview with Pole that should Pole change his mind 'no one should be dearer to me'.[159]

Despite Pole's refusal to support the divorce, his standing was then perhaps at its zenith and it seems likely that Starkey meant to take full advantage by proposing that Pole take the office of constable, the central cog in Starkey's system of conciliar restraints on the monarch.[160] Wilhelm Schenk and A. B. Ferguson are surely correct that Starkey aimed his Dialogue first at Pole, and Schenk read Starkey's purpose more clearly than other historians. Starkey meant to draw Pole into politics.[161] The Dialogue was unquestionably addressed to Pole and on a definite occasion. This is clear from its opening lines where 'Lupset' exclaimed 'I have much & many tymys marvelyd ... why *you mr. pole [ab.] ... have [ab. del. 'that you'] not *before thys [ab.] settyllyd [alt. from 'set quyat', 'q' left as 'y', final 'at' del.] your selfe, [&] applyd your mynd to the handelyng of the materys of the commyn wele'.[162] 'Lupset' spent the rest of the first part of the work in an attempt to persuade Pole to accept high office in England. In both 1529 and 1532, the two probable *termini* for the Dialogue's composition, the Lord Chancellorship – one of the offices which could make its holder head of government, like Starkey's constable –

---

156 *CSPV*, V, 806.   157 *LP*, IV, 6252.

158 *CSPV*, V, 575 (quoting the calendar's summary).

159 At least by Pole's own account in his letter to Edward (*ERP*, IV, 332).

160 Even those who would canonize Pole admit the auguries for his career in Henry's service looked particularly good in 1530. Schenk, *Pole*, 21 and 24 and M. Hallé, *Reginald Pole*, 75–6.

161 Schenk, *Pole*, 36 and 43; A. B. Ferguson, *The articulate citizen and the English renaissance*, 182.

162 SP 1/90, fol. 2v (?). The foliation at the beginning of this volume does not come out quite right.

was open. Lupset urged Pole throughout not to 'let thys occasyon slype', and to have proper 'respecte both of tyme & of place', especially since the king had assembled parliament for the reformation of abuses. '[L]et not occasyon slyppe, suffur not your tyme vaynly to pas, wych wythout recovery fleth a way, *for as they say [*ab.*] occasyon & tyme wyl never be restoryd agayne [*ab.*], therfor as I have sayd to you before … *loke to that whych above al ys **your offyce & duty [*mar.*] [*ab.*]'.[163] The Dialogue concluded in an exordium to Pole to act, and act quickly. Starkey attempted to motivate Pole by adding an apostrophe to the 'gret nobility' of Pole's ancestors.[164] Starkey's obvious intent combined with Pole's proximity to the throne and Henry's vendetta against Buckingham, motivated in part by the duke's claim to the succession, would have made Pole's position in Starkey's plan highly exposed. Nor would Pole as constable have seemed such an odd idea to either Starkey or Henry, even if Henry had indeed decided to leave the office open after the failure of Buckingham's suit for its restoration.[165] After all, another self-styled scholarly, retiring type was then chancellor, and More had none of Pole's advantages of birth. He may have had more experience, but Henry had not jibbed at offering the callow Pole an archbishopric.

It is critical to realize that Starkey could not have misrepresented his patron's views if he hoped to gain from Pole, and Pole may not have been as innocent of ambition as he later claimed. Beccadelli made a great deal of Pole's Plantagenet descent, after a detailed discussion of the faction struggles which preceded the accession of the Tudors. Pole himself expatiated on his ancestry in a section of *De unitate* which Contarini persuaded him to cut. If these passages in any way reflect Pole's own outlook, he might have been guilty of the same sort of indiscrete presumption as Buckingham, who boasted of his descent from Edward III (see below, chapt. 5).

Thus Starkey's plans and Pole's aristocratic pride meant that Starkey and the party he saw himself representing would have run some risk if his plans were put forward publicly, but a risk definitely worthwhile in the fluid circumstances of 1529–32. Starkey may not have originally seen the danger, since he intended to dedicate his dialogue in turn to Pole and Henry. Like contradictions pervade Starkey's thought, but he knew well enough how the system worked – the promotion of his patron could hardly have failed to benefit Starkey. When he began writing he could easily have expected Pole to fulfil the role sketched for him, on Pole's own initiative. After Pole refused, Starkey simply redirected the work to Henry, hoping that he would draw the obvious conclusion and force Pole's hand. Starkey may never have realized that he was trying to serve two masters.

[163] SP 1/90, fols. 128r, 16r–17r (Burton, 190, 38–9).
[164] SP 1/90, fol. 1r.
[165] H. Miller, *Henry VIII and the english nobility*, 166.

4

A responsible aristocracy

The content and presentation of Starkey's Dialogue reveal that he had profited from Bembo's and Sadoleto's examples and acquired skills vital to any courtier, especially the ability to write and speak ambiguously. Since Starkey's major work lacks a title, we must assume with its nineteenth-century editor that Starkey meant it to be a dialogue. This, of course, means little given the vast sprawl of that form in the early sixteenth century, so that it is not surprising that commentators disagree over how well Starkey followed the example of his fifteenth-century predecessors. Joel Altman praises Starkey's 'remarkable work' because it 'suggests how constructively the spirit of debate, exercising its ethical neutrality, may be applied to public business'.[1] Altman would probably accept for Starkey Dennis Gilkey's characterization of the dialogues of More or Erasmus, which showed the reader 'in an open-minded, open-ended way [how] to enter into and continue a dialogue of ideas, cultures, and customs'.[2] Alistair Fox says much the same thing.[3] It would then appear that the same sort of 'polyphonic' structure which Artur Blaim detects in *Utopia* also characterized the Dialogue. In both, independent points of view clashed constantly, and thereby shaped the form of the work.[4] John King does not agree, contending that Starkey's work clearly led 'Pole' along, even if it was not as one-sided as More's polemical dialogues.[5] One can agree with King that Starkey aimed his work at Pole and with a resolutely serious purpose, but not necessarily that his own point of view or the nature of the argument is clear.

If the 'plot', the line of discourse, of the Dialogue can be hard to follow, Starkey's marked fondness for playing with words does not help. Richard Lanham is surely right that humanist writing ought to be read rhetorically,

[1] J. B. Altman, *The Tudor play of mind*, 36–8.
[2] D. M. Gilkey, 'The *Colloquies* of Erasmus and the literature of the renaissance', iv.
[3] A. Fox, 'English humanism and the body politic', in A. Fox and J. A. Guy, *Reassessing the Henrician age*, 47. Cf. also in general, G. M. Logan, 'Substance and form in renaissance humanism', 34, labelling dialogue one of the 'forms for tentative, ambivalent thought'.
[4] A. Blaim, 'More's *Utopia*: persuasion or polyphony?', 13–14.
[5] J. N. King, *English reformation literature*, 286.

and without prejudice against 'overblown' style. As Lanham points out, style is a function of the reality one sees or hopes to construct. A humanist almost automatically did the latter, and therefore threw himself wholeheartedly into rhetorical and stylistic exuberance. This is certainly true of Starkey's dialogue.[6] Starkey's prose style contains a thick 'oral residue' in its enormously long periods and almost randomly placed relative clauses.[7] Further, the union of wisdom and rhetoric in the humanist ideal of *eloquentia* could become almost an instrument of obfuscation and it surely gave a powerful impetus to the temptation to achieve a grand synthesis of the most diverse elements.[8] Similarly, Starkey's training in rhetorical dialectic means that it is nearly impossible to extract satisfactorily neat and static definitions of key terms, which overlapped one another by design: pollycy, commyn wele, cyvylyte, vertue, nature, authoryte, state, lyberty, tyranny. The Dialogue simply cannot wear the anachronistic strait-jacket of consistency and coherence. Nevertheless, a study of its structure, method, vocabulary and argument point to the conclusion that Starkey intended his reform programme to be taken seriously as a plan to rehabilitate the high nobility and restore it to its proper place at the head of the English commonwealth.[9]

We have seen that Starkey worked over his MS again and again. His modifications naturally helped to determine what he said. Starkey usually revised by expansion, by toning down extreme statements, or by struggling for precision. The first sort of very common correction likely resulted from Starkey's working too long on his text, although he may have been following Bembo's advice to test 'every little part' of his work to be certain it would persuade. If so, Starkey's efforts did not always meet with success. 'You have made me therwyth somewhat sory, *ye & to lament wyth myselfe [*ab*.]' is only long-winded (SP 1/90, fol. 39r). Many times Starkey reversed word order without gaining noticeably in effect (e.g., 51r, 103r). Starkey clearly had no use for the anti-rhetorical school. Sometimes revision for rhetorical reasons improved the give and take of the conversation and broke up treatise-like passages (e.g., 109r). More often Starkey simply inserted 'mr. le/lup' or 'mr. pole' to that end, but he at least recognized the problem. In this, as in his use of language, Starkey stood out.

A striking instance of how Starkey softened hyperbole occurred when he presented a central proposal for a set of councils to ride herd on a hereditary

[6] R. A. Lanham, *The motives of eloquence: literary rhetoric in the renaissance*, chapter 1, esp. 28 and 33, where he writes about the 'stylistic explosion' in the Renaissance and humanist 'adolescent infatuation' with language.

[7] H. H. Gray, 'Renaissance humanism: the pursuit of eloquence', 200 and 209.

[8] W. J. Ong, 'Oral residue in Tudor prose style', in Ong, *Rhetoric, romance, and technology*, 25–6.

[9] This at least principally concerned Starkey throughout most of the Dialogue. Near its end, it (and Starkey's career plans) veered into religion, but these new designs fit more conveniently into the treatment of Starkey's later evolution in chapter 6 below.

monarch. Despite their vital role, Starkey not only hedged on their necessity by altering 'the seconde mean ys' to 'the seconde mean * as me semyth may wel [ab.] be', but also rewrote his prescription that the king must not act without his council's advice as encouragement that he should not (104v). Starkey often insisted that the problem or solution under consideration was the most important of all, for example, when he asserted that one proposed remedy would produce 'al the wele of man', but then reduced that to 'a grete parte of' it (22r; cf. 105v). Revision usually meant toning down, but not invariably. Starkey could change a suggestion ('they may be applyd') to a requirement ('the wych therfor must be'; 72r). The same impulse which led Starkey to modify extreme statements probably lay behind his attempts to use terms more precisely. Perhaps the best example appears in his struggle over the technical vocabulary for English agricultural productivity. He tried three different terms for arable land, beginning with 'cuntry', then 'ground' before he finally settled on 'erthe' (48r; cf. 63r). Starkey treated some of his constitutional terms in a similar way, perhaps in an effort to square his Italian experience with English conditions. Near the beginning, for instance, he originally wrote only of the king's 'wyse conseyl' undertaking the reform of the commonwealth, but then recognized parliament's role by inserting it before the council. Then again, this could be another sign that Starkey began work even before the Reformation Parliament assembled in November 1529.

Starkey based his plans for England in part on foreign models, but some of his revisions reveal that he understood English insularity and also chose his examples according to how they fitted his politics. When 'Pole' first tried to persuade 'Lupset' that England was underpopulated, Starkey had Pole adumbrate the examples of 'france, flaundres almayn & italy', but he knew there were limits to how much an English audience, even Pole, would know of the continent. That awareness probably led Starkey to delete 'ipar' (Ypres) and call it simply 'a cyte in flaundres' (107v). Evidence of the virtues of Ypres's citizens could stand, even if it had to become anonymous, but not even that cloak would cover an appeal to Florence's agricultural success – 'as at florence above al cytes in our tyme, ys manyfest argument' (48r). This example had to go, and it seems likely that the reason was not a sudden collapse of Florentine agriculture, but rather the city's loss of civic liberty to the Medici in 1530.

Thus some of the changes Starkey introduced into his work can be relatively easily explained. Starkey's work also suffered from both over- and under-writing, in the sense that it is clearly not finished. Yet the evidence of the dedicatory letter reveals that Starkey considered some form of his work suitable for presentation. There is really nothing to say that the present and probably second version of the MS is the final copy Starkey meant to present. He may not have had a chance to impose even as much order on his work as humanist standards demanded. Nevertheless, the grand structure of the work seems clear, and Starkey several times explicitly described the method he proposed to follow.

Starkey's approach was both rhetorical and scientific. He called his dialogue a 'communycatyon', thereby underlining its rhetorical nature (e.g., 47r). He also had 'Pole' identify it as a 'commentary to conserve & kepe in memory', at the same time that the character optimistically forecast that it would take fifteen days to find detailed solutions to all the problems he and 'Lupset' had isolated (101v). A more dramatic illustration of early Tudor 'orality' would be hard to imagine – fifteen days of talking would suffice to cure all England's ills! An oral memory system underlay Starkey's work, even if it only occasionally showed, as when Starkey inserted '& also a deer' after noting that a sheep liked dry fodder, despite the complete irrelevance of the deer to the line of his argument (63v).

That sort of flourish is very common, and would alone indicate how heavily Starkey relied on rhetoric, but he explicitly claimed allegiance to rhetorical method when he had 'Lupset' lay down that their object should be 'the inventyon of the truth' through 'dowtyng & laying somewhat agayne' the truth, which made it 'to appere more manyfest & playn' (76r–v; cf. 18r where Lupset first suggested this approach). This procedure is not merely a function of the dialogue form, as Fox suggests.[10] Starkey probably followed Rudolf Agricola's new method of invention, and certainly maintained like Agricola that he was after 'probabul arguments' (117v). Often Starkey substituted persuasion for even rhetorical argument, ending discussion by having one of the characters insist that 'you may clerly perceyve', or that his case was 'so evydent & playn ... that hyt nedyth no profe, hyt nedyth no long declaratyon' (36v, 41r).

Starkey's preference for arguments based on example grew out of the same inclination to rhetoric. Starkey rested the 'ground' of his case on three means of presenting evidence, neatly collected in his claim that 'we see dayly in commyn experyence, we nede not to seke for reson or exampul to prove & confyrme hyt' (24r). Fox conflates the first two of these in his claim that Starkey preferred 'to work rationally and empirically, using the findings of experience and common sense', while nevertheless thinking they should be kept separate.[11] Any one of these three – experience, example and reason – could appear in any position in a particular argument, but experience usually came last. In many of his key arguments, Starkey leaned on example. In fact, he called the whole of his description of the true 'commyn wele' an 'exampul ... wych schalbe to us ever as a rule to examyn the rest of our communcatyon

---

[10] Fox, 'English humanism', 47.
[11] A. Fox, 'Facts and fallacies: interpreting English humanism', in Fox and Guy, *Henrician age*, 25.

by' (45r). In order to prove that men living in the countryside were more
virtuous than their city cousins, Starkey began with Aristotle and then turned
to common experience (4v), and he later offered both reason and example
before turning to experience (24r). Aristotle in the first instance provided an
example, not a specimen of reason (5r).

Example more often than not came from history, although it could also
derive from nature (94r). Near the beginning of the work, 'Lupset' decided to
forego giving 'Pole' any examples because of the latter's greater knowledge of
history (3r). When 'Lupset' asked for a definition of 'pollycy', 'Pole' responded with a history of the golden age (34r).[12] Again, Starkey alluded to many
unspecified 'exampullys' which alone made his case about sedition (44r). The
same thing happened when he asserted that the record of princely tyranny –
even though Starkey did not recount it – made proof unnecessary (110r).
Starkey similarly alleged that he could document papal tyranny through
history, but once again forebore (118v). Some of the claims Starkey rested on
history were a little strange, at least by English standards. For example, he
maintained that private property had been at the disposal of good policy, an
argument which underpinned his attack on wardship (72v). The yardstick for
both secular and ecclesiastical reform was the original status of church and
polity, 'the ordynance of the church at the fyrst instytutyon', or 'the tyme of
nature, *to the wych we wold forme our commyn wele [ab.]' (83v and 76r).

Starkey treated his historical examples as nearly equivalent to a claim of
reasonableness, but he was not always clear about how reason operated in his
arguments. Sometimes Starkey appealed to reason against custom (65r), and
sometimes he used the former to defend the latter, only to remove it by better
reasons (69v). 'Lupset' drew a sharp distinction between the two when he
admitted that 'Pole's' 'resonys' were 'probabyl & lyke the truth', but an
argument from experience resting on custom still swayed him (69r). When
'Pole' replied, he appealed first to nature, then to reason, and finally to
historical examples, and substituted present experience for history in a
second round (70r).

Ultimately, Starkey probably concerned himself very little about formal
rules of argument. Whatever seemed persuasive went in. An example will
demonstrate: when Starkey set out to establish that England suffered from a
dearth of people, he began with experience, but continued immediately that
'argumentys' would lead to the same conclusion. This promise replaced a
rhetorical sally which merely asserted that urban areas lacked people. Starkey
offered four arguments, interspersed with rhetorical encouragement to belief,
before concluding with a similar flourish. Cities and towns were formerly

---

[12] This is only one obvious point at which Starkey turned to classical sources and models to
support his politics. Fox's notion that Starkey never did that is strange. 'Interpreting English
humanism', 24.

more populous, because there are now many decayed houses, 'wherby playnly ys perceyvyd ... the grete lake of pepul'. Furthermore, he wrote, look at the decayed villages throughout England, which contain only cattle and sheep. 'Wherfor hyt ys not to be dowtyd, but that [*ab.*] thys dekey both [*ab.*] of cytes & townys ... declaryth [*ab. del.* 'rysyth'] playnly a [*ab. del.* 'of'] lake of pepul'. Thirdly, Starkey relied on a favourite rhetorical device, an enthymeme (a syllogism with one premise missing). The decay of crafts, which could be seen 'manyfestely in every place ... schowyth ... lake of pepul', but Starkey failed to argue that crafts required people. Finally, Starkey offered a complete syllogism, based on the amount of untilled ground in England. The major premise claimed that if there were as many people there as overseas, that ground would be tilled. The minor premise contained two subsidiary points to support England's fertility, which rested on experience. The conclusion: the waste was due not to the nature of the soil, but to lack of people. Starkey wrapped up the whole argument with more declamation: 'playnly perceyvyd', 'we may surely affyrme' (47r–v). 'Lupset's' rejoinder that negligence not depopulation caused scarcity was argued through in a similarly highly rhetorical fashion, if at much greater length (48r–57r).

This is what Starkey meant by the 'processe' or 'processe & ordur' of his dialogue, the 'methodus futurorum', as a marginal note put it (46r–v). The Latin term reveals that all was not rhetoric. Starkey might have employed the rhetorical device of a 'symylytude' to organize his work around the central image of the body politic, but this Ciceronian *collatio* also reflected his underlying scientific method, largely borrowed from the school of Padua (29v–30r and *passim*; it could have a more restricted meaning, e.g., 41v, 42r).[13] 'Pole' proposed that they should follow 'thys general rule of experte physcyonys in curyng of bodyly dyseasys ... fyrst to inserch out the cause of the dyseasys wythout the wych the applying of remedys lytyl avaylyth', and Starkey observed the necessity of 'resolving' or isolating causes throughout (94v, e.g., 89r, 95r). He also followed the second step of the Paduans, by providing for reassembling ('composing') the body he had broken into pieces, once it was healed. A sickness in any part probably indicated a 'mysordur in the hole body', and both had to be cured together (101v). Starkey very likely went back to Galen, whose attack on bad physicians who disputed while the patient died Starkey reproduced (96r). Technical medical terms were also assigned to the 'diseases' of the body politic (e.g., 57r). Starkey explicitly paralleled the practice of statecraft to medicine, adopting a common analogy. As physicians had to know the 'complexyon ... & most perfayt state' of the body, as well as its sicknesses, so rulers had to know both how to engage in 'unyversal & phylosophycal [*ab. undel.* 'scolastycal'] consyderatyon of a

---

[13] For *collatio*, see M. O. Boyle, 'Erasmus and the "modern question": was he semi-Pelagian?', 61.

veray & true commyn wele' and also its 'commyn fautys & general mysor-durys' (45v).

The relatively parlous state of English vocabulary in the early sixteenth century forced many of Starkey's vast collection of words to cover a broad range of meanings. As just one example, he at one point inserted 'gud pollycy' to translate 'the ordur ys gud, & dyrectyd to gud cyvylyte' (35r), but he earlier had used the adjectives from 'pollycy' and 'cyvylyte' to define the 'cyvyle lyfe' as 'lyvyng togyddur in gud & polytyke ordur' (7r). He probably also learned a good deal about giving words multiple meanings from his master Aristotle.[14] This causes perhaps the most basic problem in untangling their significations. Starkey often ran up against the limits of English and tried to stretch them by importing more terms from Latin, Greek and other vernaculars than many of his contemporaries were willing to allow.[15] Starkey's late notes on the Old Testament bear evidence that he apparently thought in Italian at times, even when writing Latin. At one point he switched to Italian to describe *la bellezza de li tabernaculi* of Jacob for no apparent reason, and even more revealingly, he later wrote the Italian conjunction *o* in place of *vel* or some other Latin word.[16] Starkey seems to have worked in as many as five different languages, sometimes almost simultaneously. It should come as no surprise that his idiom is a little peculiar, even by contemporary standards.

Alas, borrowing foreign terms forced Starkey to bring along many of their resonances as well as stretch their English equivalents. Elasticity of meaning necessarily resulted. In the passages just quoted where 'pollycy' and 'cyvylyte' became synonymous, Starkey combined their respective Greek and Latin roots to identify the *polis* with the *civitas*. Setting one term at null and trying to calibrate all the rest of Starkey's usages by it is a chimerical task. Instead, his words must be treated in relation to one another, but even then the full range of contacts between terms will elude us. Therefore, I will explicitly spell out only some interconnections, but these terms and their cognates relate closely to almost any other in Starkey's usage. Starkey circled constantly around this core of words, leaving any single occurrence in tension with many others. How much of this was deliberate is difficult, if not impossible, to say. Perhaps if one does not set out in quest of definitions like those Thomas Elyot habitually offered, and expects Starkey to play with words, something of his meaning can be discovered, even if it must always be provisional.[17] Instances of terms in pairings and series will be studied first, then any explicit definitions Starkey offered, and finally associations with other words, particularly those in the central complex.

[14] G. Bien, *Die Grundlegung der politischen Philosophie bei Aristoteles*, 318.
[15] R. F. Jones, *The triumph of the English language*, chapter four.
[16] BL Royal 7 C XVI, fols. 214r col. 2 and 216r/2.
[17] Jones, *English language*, 78–82, discusses Elyot's prowess at defining words, especially borrowings.

Pollycy and its cognates sooner or later touch virtually every other term in the Dialogue. It is coupled with 'wysdome' and then directly paralleled to it as that which brings men to civil order and political life (3r, 16r, 34v, 39v). Similarly, it provides the means by which man subdues the rest of the earth (34r and 8r). Starkey connected pollycy with 'justyce' (5v), with 'wyt' and 'lernyng' (7r) and 'gret wytt ... wyth perfayt eloquence & hye phylsophy' (34r and 8r), with 'labur' (as the means to successful agriculture), and with 'commyn counsel'. This last apparently indicated an intellectual virtue, a positive quality without which humans could scarcely survive (46v). The linkage of pollycy and the cardinal political virtue of 'prudence' reinforces this meaning, especially when Starkey had 'Pole' leave minute study of his plans to 'them wych in every cause have ordur [ab. del. 'presydence'] & rule, whose prudence *& pollycy [ab.] schal ever see ... the partycular remedye' (98r). Starkey's alteration of pollycy into wysedome in another coupling with prudence demonstrates that these three terms functioned as very near equivalents (3v; other joint usages of prudence and pollycy at, e.g., 4v, 5v [twice], 36r). Starkey also pointed to 'lawys wych mannys wyt hath devysyd *by pollycy [ab.]', thereby making pollycy a function of wyt and 'lawys' the product of their interaction (4v).

In a second sense, pollycy and lawys were functions of one another, and here pollycy appears to come near 'polity' in the meaning of type of constitution. According to Starkey, 'gud ordur & pollycy' was 'by gud lawys stablyschyd & set, & by hedys & rularys put in effect' (33r). (Is this an unintentional rhyme, or perhaps an echo of one of the *vulgaria* Starkey studied as a youth?) This is its sense when parallelled by 'cyvyle ordur and rule' (60v and 66r), by 'the ordur of the law' (77v), in the couplet 'exacte law *& pollycy [ab.]' (34v), and when Starkey wrote about the 'state of chrystys church', he called it a kind of pollycy, which seems to mean constitution, too (39r). One of Starkey's definitions of pollycy clearly means constitution: 'a commynalty to lyve other under a prynce or a commyn counsel in cytes & townys' (6v). Sometimes when joined with law and ordur pollycy had an ambiguous meaning, as in the phrase 'from the pryncys & rularys of the state commyth al lawys ordur & pollycy' (31v), which could mean pollycy as either political wisdom or constitution. Likewise, the impossibility of '*gud pollycy [ab.] wher the jugement of the pepul ys corrupt by false opynyon' (43v) leans in the direction of the intellectual virtue, but could still mean political system. To further complicate matters, Starkey also argued that 'gud pollycy' was the equivalent of gud ordur and led to 'gud cyvylyte' (35r). Pollycy provides a textbook example of how Starkey borrowed a Greek and a French and an Italian term, together with all their overtones.

In Starkey's simile for the soul of the body politic, he linked his two most important terms by connecting pollycy to 'the maner of admynystratyon of our commyn wele' (108v). Earlier he had apparently set them equal in the phrase 'no commyn welthe nor pollycy' (21v). Near the beginning of his text, Starkey added pollycy to the commyn wele (3v), but in another place besides that noted above (108v), he made pollycy a condition or, perhaps, a function of the commyn wele (41r). This meaning of pollycy falls in between those of wisdom/prudence and constitution, combining the two most important dimensions of the commyn wele. What Starkey meant when he added pollycy to 'commyn state' (104v) is completely obscure, as will emerge from the discussion of 'state' below. Nevertheless, at the risk of employing redundant terms, an essentially two-fold meaning of pollycy emerges: a sort of political wisdom; and a framework for politics. Their overlap and the resultant ambiguous usages sprang from the same mix of moral and practical political concerns in Starkey's thought which led him to define pollycy as commyn welthe. Starkey's prescription that the 'prudent & polytyke man' ought to communicate his virtues to others clinches the case for this hybrid meaning (5r).

'Polytyke' appears frequently as an adjective, with much the same meanings as its root. For example, 'polytyke personys' were to keep an eye on the commyn wele (21v), and Starkey often coupled polytyke with 'wyse' (e.g., 7v and 14v) and sometimes with 'prudent' (103r). Polytyke served to modify Starkey's key metaphor of the 'polytyke body', which frequently seems to mean the physical aspect of a group of people, for example, when Starkey discussed 'procuryng fode & thyngys necessary for the hole polytyke body' (36r), or later when he wrote that he would '*receyvyng of nature the mater therof [ab.] forme & adorne thys polytyke body' (94v). Polytyke, of course, often paralleled 'cyvyle' (virtually *passim*, but see for example 3r, 6r, 29v, etc.).[18]

In this last, more constitutional meaning, pollycy/polytyke has many close ties to the 'ordur/ordynance' complex, which in turn bleeds over into 'fastyon' (fashion), a highly interesting transference. Law and ordur and pollycy have already been observed in conjunction, and Starkey also placed pollycy in a triad with ordur and rule (40r). The second two-thirds of that linkage appears independently (4v and 56r), but Starkey wrote little about what rule indicated. Ordynance formed part of the pollycy/polytyke complex ('cyvyle ordynance & polytyke mean', for instance [13r]), and came close to the standard meaning of order (e.g., 13v). In addition, it occurred frequently in the phrase 'lawys statutys and ordynancys', although it is doubtful if Starkey

---

[18] Starkey's usage resembles that of his continental predecessors, especially de Seyssel and even Machiavelli. It also comes close to that of Fortescue. For all these, the adjective *politicus* or its vernacular equivalent had a primarily constitutional meaning, usually referring to institutions designed to restrain monarchical power. Nicolai Rubinstein, 'The history of the word *politicus* in early modern Europe'. Rubinstein does not emphasize the moral meaning of the term, although he does note that it acquired negative moral connotations later in the sixteenth century, 54.

meant this to have a technical legal meaning (8v). He also wrote about the 'ordynance of the law', and to keep things moving the 'cyvyle ordynance' which established 'lawys and ordynancys', and thereby pulled Starkey's two primary meanings close together (13v). Ordur sometimes had hierarchical overtones, most explicitly when joined to 'degre', especially when the latter was inserted (23v, 84r). On other occasions ordur seems to mean framework, most clearly when linked with the inserted 'frame', but also in the phrase 'hole ordur & processe of the law' (77r). In this last sense, Starkey connected 'cyvyle ordur, *& polytyke fastyon [ab.]' (95r). Fastyon, however, was also joined to the 'forme' of the commonwealth (60r), and treated as the substantive product of the act of forming, as in the clause 'forme hym [the prince] aftur hys [man's] owne fastyon' (102v). Thus just as many Renaissance figures hoped to 'fashion' their own *personae*, so Starkey intended to 'fashion' a moral order on a precise analogy to human personality.[19] He planned to induce men to 'exercyse themselfe in some fascyon of lyve convenyent to the dygnyte & nature of man' (51r).

Pollycy in either sense served to establish the 'commyn wele', but both could appear in tandem (3v, 21v). The commyn wele could be either an aspect of or synonymous with the political system which pollycy represented (e.g., 39r). Starkey offered an explicit definition of a commyn wele, which he tagged in the margin. It was 'the prosperouse & most perfayt state of a multytud assemblyd togyddur in any cuntrey cyty or towne governyd vertusely in cyvyle lyfe accordyng to the nature & dygnyte of man' (36v). The 'multytude' was 'as hyt were the ground & fundatyon of thys our commyn wele' (94v). Again, on the next folio after the definition just quoted, Starkey introduced the commyn wele into his central corporate metaphor, while also connecting it to 'polytyke ordur & gud cyvylyte'. 'Thys true commyn wele [ab.] in thys polytyke body, stondyth not in the wele & prosperouse state of any partycular parte separat from other, but in every parte couplyd togyddur unyte & knyte as membrys of one body by love as by the commyn bande of al polytyke ordur & gud cyvylyte' (37v; cf. 35v for the link to cyvylyte).

The political connotations of commyn wele appear in part in its linkage to 'state', but this term itself resists definition. The commyn wele 'determyth to hyt no partycular state', but the 'state of a prynce' is best 'for the mayntenance & long contynuance of thys commyn wele, & polytyke rule' (38r). Whatever its form, 'a true commyn wele' was a function of 'a perfayt state' (75v). Those

[19] See especially S. Greenblatt, *Renaissance self-fashioning*. David Norbrook also helps to explain the connection between fashioning and the commonwealth by noting that the latter, although not necessarily a radical term, nevertheless connoted that 'the state [was] an artifice that had been created by a collective agency, rather than a natural hierarchy embodied in the person of the monarch'. D. Norbrook, *Poetry and politics in the English renaissance*, 49. As we shall see, 'state' is the wrong word for Starkey, who was also not particularly concerned about collective effort.

who looked after 'the hole state' were also called, unsurprisingly, 'conserva-
torys of the commyn wele' (123v). The ambiguity in Starkey's use of state will
come out more clearly when we return to that term below. The commyn wele
could be administered (5r), and those with 'hye authoryte & rule, al ambycyouse affectyon set apert [who] only procure the true commyn wele' would
do that best (16r). The prince had the 'cure of hys commyn wele' printed in his
breast, which meant the 'admynystratyon of justyce & settyng forth of equyte
& ryght' (16v). The legal overtones in that last phrase appear more clearly in
Starkey's assertion that denying appeal by writ 'ys agayne the ordur of any
commyn wele, where as appellatyon ys ever admyttyd to the hede' (82r).

In addition to this mainly political and legal content, commyn wele had
physical extension together with much moral content, as might be expected.
It had 'ornamentys' 'as gudly cytes castellys & townys' (107v), and commyn
weles could die (16r). But despite this organic analogy and the use of commyn
wele in the corporate metaphor, the term was not often explicitly coupled
with 'nature'. In the clearest instance, Starkey added 'to the wych we wold
forme our commyn wele' to 'the tyme of nature' (76r). Commyn weles were
sometimes the same thing as 'cuntreys', but here the word once again quickly
acquired political and moral content (17r and 82r). Wise men who turned
their backs on the commyn wele hurt their 'hole cuntrey' (14v). Instead, they
should join the 'polytyke personys havyng regard of the commyn wele' (21v).
A major plank of Starkey's programme called for nobles to be sent to
converted monasteries in order to 'lerne ther the dyscyplyne of the commyn
wele' (113r). Although these men figured most prominently in Starkey's
solution, their flight from the commyn wele was only part of the general
difficulty which arose because 'every man sekyth hys owne profyt' (18v), or
'when men pryvatly abuse theyr owne godys to [*ab.*] the hurte of the commyn
wele' (119v). Starkey often proposed remedies 'orderyd to the commyn wele
wythout regard of pryvate gayn *& profyt [*ab.*].' (106r).

Starkey set up an opposition between commyn and 'pryvate' welth, but
neither the meaning of commyn nor of welth is self-evident. 'Commynalty'
appears almost as a synonym of commyn wele, both when Starkey coupled it
with 'reame' (realm) as the basis of the 'polytyke body' (46v) and when he
called 'the hole body of the reame' 'the hole commynalty' (110r), or when he
joined commynalty to 'cyty & cuntrey' or added 'cuntrey' alone to it (29v and
30v; cf. 45v). The two terms came very close when Starkey wrote both that
the end of 'cyvyle lyfe' was the 'true admynystratyon of the commyn wele'
(5r) and also that 'the end of al mannys studys & carys [is] the welth of the
commynalty' (16v). Just as commyn wele was a function of the state, so was
the commynalty, here set equivalent to 'polytyke state' (31v). Or again, a
prince governed the 'state of the commynalty' (35r). Most of the time
commynalty is a collective noun which seems to include all Englishmen, as

when Starkey described the 'end of all conseyllys & parlyamentys in any commynalty assemblyd togyddur, here in thys our owne cuntrey' (45r), or doubted 'so many wyse men in a commynalty to fynd I thynke hyt playn impossybul' (102r). Then again, Starkey once deleted commynalty and replaced it with 'the pepul commynly' (73v) and the 'pepul & hole commynalty' meant the 'multytud' (35r). In another place Starkey spoke of the 'private state of the sympul commynalty' (66r–v). The latter must be restrictive, and in light of Starkey's use of 'pepul', the former uses probably are, too. In one place Starkey substituted pepul for 'commyns' when speaking of the ill effects of 'commyn tavernys' (61v), and he also sometimes used the substantive 'commyns' in the technical sense of one of the three estates, which he did not usually employ. He observed the trouble caused by setting 'the commyns agayne the nobullys' (53v) and also claimed that the king received 'hys regal powar' 'by the consent of the hole commynys' (67v), which may or may not be the technical meaning. Blending the technical and the inclusive senses, Starkey boasted that 'our pepul of englond ... [are the] most rych & welthy of any commyns aboute us' (58v). Both the general and the particular senses appear together when Starkey argued that 'hedys & rularys' were 'to se the admynystratyon of justyce to the hole commynalty ... for the wych purpos they are thys maynteynyd ... by the labur & travayle of the pore commynalty' (36r). The noun only occasionally had plainly negative connotations for Starkey, however widely it might stretch.

That is also the case for the verb, but not entirely true of the adjective or adverb. As a verb, 'to commyn' was a synonym of 'talke' (2v), and Starkey usually thought it was laudable, indeed necessary, for a wise and virtuous man 'to commyn such gyftys' (3r) or 'commyn the same perfectyon to other', just as 'vertue & lernyng not communyd to other' went to waste (5r). The adjective and adverb carry more overtones. Their basic meaning was 'general' or 'shared', as in those things which nature had made 'commyn to al mankynd' (9r). They could also mean 'frequently observed' or 'usual' as in 'commyn fautys & mysordurys', or the lament that 'men commynly gyve themselfe to such inordynat dyat' (21v). Commyn might also denote 'togyddur' or jointly (116v). This distributive meaning is reflected in Starkey's proposal for a council to 'represent the hole *body of the pepul wythout [ab.] parlyament', which he also wrote should 'represent the hole state commynly' (110r). In the sense of ordinary commyn occurs frequently, sometimes in a clearly disdainful context, as in the phrase 'controversy ... betwyx the commyn sort & lernyd' (18v). On the other hand, Starkey noted that 'arystotyl [by] more conformyng hymselfe to the commune jugement of man' had arrived at a more plausible opinion on the causes of evil behaviour than Plato (19v), and linked commyn to one of his most positive terms, 'cyvyle' (102r).

The other component of commyn wele, 'welth', is a surprisingly slippery word and leads the commyn wele into a non-political realm. Frequently, welth (or wele) meant 'profyt' (e.g., 18v, 24r, 64r), or appeared in series with both 'plesure & profyt' (35r and 43r). Starkey once substituted profyt for 'value' (67r), and once joined it to 'lucre' (77v), but at another time he linked it to 'syngular comfort' (75r), and at yet another to 'utylyte' (5r). The connection of wele to 'felycyte' says much more about its meaning and enhances the moral connotations of the word. Of course, Starkey's toying with his signifiers sometimes produced near double-talk here, too, as when he blithely asserted that the 'wele & felycyte of every partycular man' depended on his being 'in prosperouse state [*ab.*] & felycyte' (25r), but wele and 'prosperouse state *& felycyte [*ab.*]' were synonyms (25v; cf. 24v), and Starkey often added one or the other of these to whichever he had already written (e.g., 7r). Virtue led to 'wele & felycytye' (25v and 40v), even though all men 'can not attayne to hyest degre therof' (28v, 29r). Nevertheless, 'no man ys *by nature [*ab.*] excludyd from felycyte' (28v). All it took was the diligence 'god requyryth ... of man in al such thyng as perteynyth to hys felycyte' (102v). This could be of two different, but related sorts, depending on whether the reference was earthly or heavenly, in so far as these can be distinguished. The 'commyn wele of any cuntrey cyty or towne' was the same thing as the 'felycyte of any partycular man' (40v). Felycyte arose in the 'cyvyle lyfe' (102v) and Starkey equated cyvylyte and 'quyetnes & hye [*ab.*] felycyte' (35v), but there was more. 'Aftur thys wordly & cyvyle lyfe' men would 'attayne such end & felycyte' as was 'determyd to the excellent dygnyte & nature of man' (36v), which meant 'ever lastyng lyfe, *& felycyte [*ab.*]' (39v).

Linking secular and spiritual well-being was a bold enough departure from medieval precedents for a northern European, even if Italian humanists commonly did that. When Starkey rounded out his description of political society with the collection of words around the root 'cyvyle', he went further than any of his contemporaries by coining a term from Latin (perhaps through the medium of French) as the antonym to 'rudenes'. 'Cyvylyte' functioned exactly as 'civilization' now does. Drawing on the seminal work of George Huppert, A. B. Ferguson maintained that no such English term existed, even though Tudor intellectuals displayed awareness of 'the elements that came to be expressed by it'.[20] Huppert followed Émile Benveniste and distinguished two senses of civilization, a process and a result. Benveniste tied the appearance of the term to the development of a historical, optimistic and non-theological view of society, indissolubly linked to the idea of progress. Like Ferguson, Huppert admitted that the idea may have existed before the word, but its only symbol in French, *civilisé*, usually meant 'civil, urbane,

---

[20] A. B. Ferguson, *Clio unbound: perception of the social and cultural past in renaissance England*, 346.

courteous'; it could not have been widely used in the sense of civilized. Although the word probably arose as a translation of Cicero's complex of *humanitas* and *civilitas*, Huppert found few clear instances of the 'modern' meaning before the 1560s.[21] The *Oxford English Dictionary* agrees with Ferguson and Huppert, citing two passages from the Dialogue in the very closely allied senses of 'polity' and 'good polity', while its first instance of the newer meaning comes only from 1549.[22] But Huppert's character sketch of the person likely to adopt the new usage fits Starkey almost perfectly. He had a classical education, studied Roman law (although not with any explicitly humanist jurisprudents, as Huppert stipulates), was a member of the English analogue of the French magisterial class, certainly interested in history, and a writer in the vernacular. He was a man, as Huppert summed up, 'whose mind wanders freely in the past but who prefers the present'.[23]

Man was born 'to a cyvylyte & to lyve in polytyke ordur' according to Starkey, which meant that each should '*be redy [*ab.*] to helpe a nother' (6v). As quick as Starkey was to introduce the term, he was almost as quick to contrast it with life in the 'cuntrey', the 'rude lyfe'. Following Cicero, Starkey argued historically that men had come to cyvylyte from 'rudenes & bestyal lyfe' through the 'persuasyon of wyse men' (7r–v). Starkey criticized ancient philosophers who 'abhorryd *thys from the polytyke lyfe & [*ab.*] from thys commynyng of theyr vertues to the profyt of other *in cyvylyte [*ab.*]' (6r). True, once men arrived at cyvylyte, Starkey regarded that state in almost exclusively political terms, inserting a warning that if anyone should 'take away al cyvylyte' that would 'bryng al to confusyon & tyranny' (8r), and equating 'gud cyvylyte' with 'polytyke ordur' (13r) and with pollycy (35r). Thus do Starkey's terms bend back on one another. But cyvylyte was also the goal of pollycy and consequently equivalent to 'quyetnes & hye [*ab.*] felycyte' (6r, 35v), which, of course, renders it a virtual synonym of commyn wele. For Starkey, the condition of being civilized was unavoidably political.

This is even clearer from his usage of the root 'cyvyle'. When it first appeared modifying 'ordur' Starkey coupled cyvyle to 'polytyke lyfe' (3r). Both adjectives could appear with 'lyfe' (6r), or polytyke could be left out and cyvyle used to modify lyfe and then coupled with ordur (7r). Almost every time cyvyle crops up, ordur is not far away (e.g., 7v, 13r, 29v, 33r, etc.). Starkey offered three explicit definitions of 'the cyvyle lyfe' in the course of the first fourteen folios, all of them subtly different. 'Lupset' posited first that it meant 'lyvyng togyddur in gud & polytyke ordur, one ever redy to dow gud to a nother, & as hyt were conspyryng togydur in *al vertue & [*ab.*] honesty' (7r), but when 'Pole' essayed to repeat this definition, he added that the

---

[21] G. Huppert, 'The idea of civilization in the sixteenth century', 760–4.
[22] *The Oxford English dictionary*, s.v. 'civility', I. 5 and 6, and II. 10.
[23] Huppert, 'Civilization', 764 and 767.

'conspyracy' had been '*stablyschyd by commyn assent [*ab.*]' (7v). Finally, 'Pole' defined the word in more or less the same way, as 'a polytyke ordur of a multytude conspyryng togyddur in vertue & honesty', but this time tacking on 'to the wych man by nature ys ordeynyd' (14r). In other words, cyvyle lyfe was a commyn wele, as Starkey occasionally made explicit (30v).

By contrast with the cyvyle complex, rude and its cognates were amongst Starkey's strongest terms of abuse. 'Rudenes' meant living 'lyke wylde bestys in the woodys wythout lawys & rulys of honesty', as well as following one's own fantasy (3v). A people 'wythout polyty' were rude, and 'untyllyd' or 'wast ground' was, too (8v, 46r). Once again, the escape from 'rudnes & uncomly lyfe' meant adopting 'some ordur & cyvylyte' (34r). Starkey varied the pitch of condemnation in the word, from speaking of 'grosse & rude pepul' (96r) or 'grete rudenesse & faute' (97r) to 'a gret rudenes & a barbarouse custume' (108r). Similarly, a pepul could be 'somewhat rude' and when Starkey wrote about the need to 'induce the rude pepul to [*ab.*] the trayn of vertue' (72r and 86v), he was not openly contemptuous.

As for Cicero and his Latin original, so for Starkey cyvylyte or the cyvyle lyfe was only possible in an urban setting. Starkey regularly wrote of 'cytes & townys' when describing England, but almost never of the countryside, and even used the word cuntrey for the whole island in a geographical sense infrequently (e.g., 4v, 6v, 7r). Once he so far forgot himself as to compare 'our cuntrey' with 'other cytes' but then replaced the latter with 'cuntreys' (108r). In an extended passage featuring 'cuntrey, cyte or towne', only cyty appeared alone (35v). Starkey would allow that civilization might be possible in 'castellys', too, but that was the limit (8r–v). The first thing men had done after escaping rudenes was to build 'cytes & townys' (34r). By the same token, when Starkey's repopulation plans bore fruit 'hyt schal be necessary, in placys deserte to byld mo cytes castellys & townys' (38v). He treated cyte and commynalty interchangeably (98r). Occasionally he noted the existence of 'vyllagys' (63r and 101r), but considered them only poor efforts at a 'good towne'. They definitely would not qualify as 'ornamentys' of the commyn wele like 'cytes castellys & townys' (107v). Starkey almost always restricted the application of his plans to urban areas. His civic humanism manifestly induced a powerful bias towards the *civitas*. This carried over into the way in which Starkey labelled inhabitants of England, calling all of them 'the multytude of pepul the nombur of cytyzyns' (29v). It apparently did not trouble Starkey that his compatriots were in fact all subjects. His reading of English circumstances through Italian lenses went further, as in the instance when he could not make up his mind whether to write 'rularys' or 'cytysyns' which he left undeleted beneath his second choice (44r). Starkey did not use the latter term with great regularity, but when he did, it always included all English-men, at least on the surface. Starkey's use of the same term to apply to 'cytyzyns of london' (104v), however, may mean that he intended (or at least could not escape) a more limited reference in the rest of his usages.

Starkey's other collective terms for denizens of the political arena include 'multytud(e)', 'cuntrey', 'pepul', and 'natyon', but only very rarely 'socyety'. After a flurry of use near the beginning of the Dialogue (three times on 7r–v), Starkey virtually ignored the last. Starkey usually employed the first of these as his most inclusive collective term, equating it, for example, with the 'pepul & hole commynalty' (35r), or, as we have seen, setting it as the foundation of a true commyn wele, as well as equating the 'prosperouse & most perfayt state of a multytud' with the commyn wele (36v). After a series of examples from the nobility and clergy, Starkey proposed to 'examyn the multytude in every ordur & degre', which appeared to include the two groups he had already discussed (50v). Similarly, he reduced the essence of his programme to the formula 'some by wysdome *& pollycy [*ab.] to kepe the *rest of the [*ab.] multytude in gud ordur & cyvylyte', and the insertion seems to indicate that Starkey wished to remove any possible ambiguity (51r). Starkey used multytude to identify the third of Aristotle's forms of rule, in distinction to that 'under a prynce' or 'commyn conseyl of certayn' (35v). Multytude could also mean simply 'so many' (e.g., 49r and 58v). Like commynalty, it apparently had no negative connotations.

Ordinary sixteenth-century usage would not serve Starkey in the case of 'cuntrey'.[24] In contrast to the more usual meaning of district or county, Starkey meant the word to apply to the whole of England, although some of his uses might shade toward the standard definition, especially in the coupling 'cuntrey & frendys' (e.g., 3v and 24r). Much more often, Starkey juggled cytes and natyonys and commynalty with cuntrey (3r, 20v, 29v, 30v, 45r, etc.). 'Pole' and 'Lupset' constantly referred to 'our cuntrey', which would have made no sense if Starkey had adopted the restricted meaning: Pole was born in Staffordshire, Lupset in London (e.g., 17v and 102v). Starkey also bent the bounds of ordinary language with cuntrey's near relatives 'pepul' and 'natyon'. He seems to have thought of pepul as virtually identical in meaning to cuntrey, leaving the two one above the other at one point (69r), and sometimes linking them (9r). Like multytude, pepul included all the members of a political society, and government by 'the hole pepul' could also signify Aristotle's *democratia* (34r, 35r, 31r). On the other hand, Starkey drew some measure of distinction between pepul and 'rularys', making the 'prudence & pollycy' of the latter responsible for maintaining the former (36r), and equating 'our pepul of englond' with the commyns (58v). Again, when Starkey bemoaned the impact of drinking on 'the pepul', he deleted the adjective commyn for stylistic reasons, since he had just written 'commyn

---

[24] But cf. J. H. Elliott, 'Revolution and continuity in early modern Europe', 47ff. for the expansion in meaning of the Latin equivalent *patria*.

tavernys' (61v). Nevertheless, Starkey did not restrict pepul to the lower orders only, as most of his contemporaries usually did. Finally, he also stretched the Latin original *natio* beyond its usual confines to an 'ethnic' or territorial group smaller than the population of a whole kingdom to make it synonymous with pepul (2v and 9r).

Man in the collective and in the individual had the same goal for Starkey, the pursuit of 'vertue', the end of the commyn wele. It was vertue 'wych to every man gyvyth felycyte & to every cuntrey hys true commyn wele' (40v). Starkey summed up his moral and political philosophy near the beginning of the Dialogue.

Thys ys the marke that every man *prudent & polytyke [*ab.*] ought to schote *at [*undel.* ',' *bel.* 'a'] fyrst to make hymself perfayte wythal vertues garnyschyng hys mynd, & then to commyn the same perfectyon to other, for lytyl avaylyth vertue that ys not publyschyd abrode to the profyt of other (5r).

Starkey insisted repeatedly that vertue could not be kept to oneself. Anyone who refused to commyn his vertue 'lyeth then unprofytabul to hys cuntrey' (e.g., 22r–v). Vertue was partly natural, and partly a matter of convention (8r, 9r, 11v), and it often had a 'physical' dimension in the sense of 'power' or 'ability' (22v and 23v). Vertue taught people how to use the worldly goods Starkey claimed were necessary, but it was still vertue alone which 'doth not only kepe man from mysery, but hyt doth also set hym in hye felycyte' (25v). Starkey linked vertue most often to honesty (e.g., 7v, 9r, 11v, 23v, etc.), in much the same way Robert Whittinton translated Cicero's *officium* by adding honesty. Beasts in the woods lacked 'rulys of honesty' (3v), and Starkey described the worst state of the commyn wele as 'one takyng plesure of a nother wythout regard of honesty' (7r). Unlike many medieval and contemporary writers, Starkey declined to list the vertues, probably because he thought that nature provided them in a self-evident fashion. In any event, living 'vertusely' meant living 'accordyng to hys [man's] natural dygnyte' (7r).

But 'dygnyte', like vertue, was not entirely natural, even though it almost always appears coupled to 'nature' especially in the phrase 'dygnyte of [or 'and'] the nature of man' (34r, 35r, 36v, 38v, etc.). In other places, nature and dygnyte were parallelled, and both led to felycyte (28v), as might be expected: 'suche end & perfectyon ... by the provydence of god ys [*ab.*] ordeynyd to the excellent nature & dygnyte of man' (42v). This may sound as if dignity was evenly distributed, like the rest of man's 'excellent nature', but the substitution of 'nature & dygnyte' for 'nobylyte' (95v) immediately shows that was not the case. Likewise, although the 'dygnyte of al the cytyzyns' demanded 'dystrybutyng to every man accordyng to hys [*aft. del.* '&'] vertue & dygnyte such thyngys as be dyvydyd among the cytyzyns', Starkey clearly envisioned an unequal sharing of the pie (100r). Again, 'commyn offycys of authoryte & dygnyte' meant 'al byschoprykys & al hye offyce of dygnyte', and 'offyce' could even stand as a replacement for dygnyte (110v–111r, 113r). But the restricted social scope of both dygnyte and vertue emerges most clearly from a tag which smacks of the classroom. 'When vertue ys not rewardyd worthyly [ab.] then hyt rebellyth sturdyly [ab.]'. (Starkey must have forgotten the rhyming couplet at first.) The only solution, of course, was to ensure that 'men be regardyd accordyng to theyr dygnyte' (111r). Starkey was thinking only of those eligible for office in the first place. Their dygnyte was of a higher order than that of the rest of the cytyzyns.

Ultimately, all virtue derived from nature, and Starkey assigned a central causative role to nature in establishing civil society.

Thes vertues & other lyke wherby man of nature meke gentyl & ful of humanyte ys inclynyd & sterryd to cyvyle ordur & lovyng cumpany wyth honeste behavyour both toward god & man, are by the powar of nature in the hart of man rotyd & plantyd. (9v)

Nature may have been the engine, but it was no more morally neutral than its instrument, the 'hart', which was both the 'fountayn of al natural powarys' (including 'al *wyt reson & [ab.] sens felyng') which it 'mynystryth ... wyth dew ordur to al other [parts of the body]' (31r), and also the locus of conspiracy against 'the dygnyte of vertue & nature of man' (12v), as of 'love of ryches of thys world' (27v). Starkey's faculty psychology dictated that the heart be the seat of the 'affectys', even if it also gave rise to 'reson', the means of reining them in (35v). Reson functioned in the same way in both macrocosm and microcosm, since it was also 'the only hede & rular of reemys by the ordur of nature' (67r). Together with nature, reson was the ultimate standard of ordur and rule (24r and 56r). As the Dialogue wore on, Starkey made reson less of an autonomous force, finally calling it a 'sparkyl of *the godly & [ab.] eternal reson' (94v).

Earlier Starkey had leaned heavily on 'ryght reson' alone (10v, 19r), and much of the time nature had stood by itself, too, or at least come prior in order of time to God's action. Starkey's apostrophe to 'cyvylyte so natural to man' and 'most agreabul to reson & nature' left God out of the equation altogether (7v). Frequently Starkey proposed to 'take nature for our exampul' (94r). It had, after all, provided 'the mater' of 'thys polytyke body' (94v). But shortly after these two passages, Starkey changed his mind and suddenly decried 'nature, whose instyncte only by specyal grace we may overcome' (96r), while man was reduced from the king of the beasts to a creature who 'by nature ys so frayle *& corrupt [ab.]' (102r). This change heralds Starkey's increasing concern with religion, but it was not entirely discordant with the rest of the Dialogue. Starkey had frequently linked nature with 'god', but the latter appeared as a sort of sleeping partner, as when Starkey had 'Pole' argue that Christians surely considered their polity 'most agreabul to reson & nature as a thyng confyrmyd by goddys own dyvynyte' (7v). And unlike nature, 'god' never appeared as an independent actor. Sometimes, however, Starkey reversed the order of things and attributed priority to 'the provydence of god' which determined the end of 'the excellent nature & dygnyte of man' (42v), and had established man as the ruler of the earth (8r). 'Lupset' at one point maintained that some facets of human existence 'commyth by the provydence of god, wych by no wyt nor pollycy of man may be amendyd' (59r), and 'Pole' finally conceded that one of these was that princes alone could implement remedies for problems (87r). Part of the reason 'Pole' could accept Henry despite his objections to monarchy was that he had been provided by the 'provydence of god' (104r).

Nevertheless, until the final section of the work nature had the upper hand, especially because it alone bound men to 'offyce & duty' or 'offyce & authoryte', which those who qualified were obligated to exercise (6r, 7v, 57r). When they did not, they wrecked the commyn wele. 'Authoryte' lay at the heart of Starkey's political system. Some of Starkey's language may have been rooted in Roman or civil law, although most of these terms could have come from a number of other sources, including scripture. For example, those with the authoryte to make laws enjoyed 'domynyon' over the rest of the people (11v), and authoryte once appeared in tandem with 'jurysdycyon' (124r). But Starkey did not rely on such terms nor did he probably use authoryte to translate *auctoritas*, since his English word rarely had the mainly moral denotation of its Latin cognate. Some such overtones appear in the frequent coupling of authoryte and dygnyte (e.g., 22r, 40r, 72r, etc.), but Starkey was usually more blunt in linking authoryte (and dygnyte) to 'ryches ... & wordly abundaunce' (24r) or to 'wordly prosperyte' (40r). Phrases like 'hye authoryte & rule' (16r; cf. 101v) and 'frank lyberty & hye authoryte' (34v) begin to reveal the meaning of the word, but the marked association with 'powar' says most.

In one place Starkey treated authoryte and powar as equivalents, substituting the latter for the former (104v). In another, powar constituted the final element in the triad of authoryte and dygnyte (72r). While 'royal powar & pryncely authoryte' was probably a case of rhetorical expansion (65r), one of Starkey's discussions of monarchy offers the clearest instance of the connection of authoryte and powar. 'Lupset' objected to 'Pole' that 'you alow the state of a prynce, & wold not but that we schold be governyd therby, & yet you wyl not gyve hym the authoryte of a prynce ... you must also gyve hym the powar perteynyng to the majesty of the same' (67v–68r). Then again, powar needed authoryte to be legitimate (81v and 119r), although it was also possible for a prince to take advantage of the powers granted to him by parliament in order to usurp an 'authorysyd tyranny' (109v). To avoid this, Starkey maintained that 'the lawys ... must have chefe authoryte, they must rule & governe the state' (109v).

This sounds very much as if Starkey espoused a modern theory of sovereignty, even if he did so in heavily Aristotelian language. So Quentin Skinner argued by implication when he put Starkey once again ahead of his time, in this case because he used the word state in the modern sense of constitutional order. The situation is more complex.[25] Skinner admitted that Starkey used state in a sense 'hovering' between the older meaning of 'estate' or 'condition' and the 'self-conscious' modern one, but two of the examples of the latter Skinner cited closely parallel two of the former (35r and 31v). State as 'estate' is by no means rare: that seems to be the sense of the word in combination with 'degre' (23r, 50r, 62v), although some of these uses carry at least overtones of 'status' in the sense of position or standing. State in the related meaning of condition occurs very frequently (21r, 22v, 24v, 36v), and Starkey made the meaning explicit when he substituted 'dysposytyon' for state (37v). That is also its sense in phrases like the 'state of chrystundome', but when Starkey continued by paralleling 'other kynd of pollycy' to 'other statys of polytyke pepul' (39r) or when he followed Aristotle to argue that 'thys commyn wele determyth to hyt no partycular state, wych by polytyke men have byn devysyd & reducyd to iij' (38r) Starkey's meaning began to fade in the direction of constitution. Thus it would seem that when he substituted state for rule in the combination 'governance & state' that he was groping for yet another extension of English vocabulary (44r).

When discussing the government of England, whether actual or ideal, Starkey did not use state in such a way. The 'state of a prynce' clearly means 'estate', while in the phrase 'hedys & rularys ... [who] maynteyne they state *stablyschyd in the cuntrey [*ab.*]' (38r–v) state must mean condition or, perhaps, status quo. Starkey employed these two senses together when writing about the 'state of pryncys wych by theyr regal powar & pryncely authoryte have jugyd al thyngys perteynyng to the state of our reame' (65r–v). Consequently, when Starkey wrote 'he or they wych have authoryte apon the hole state' or 'pryncys & rularys of the state' (31v), he most likely meant those in charge of maintaining the condition of the country, as he did when he set 'conserve the hole state' parallel to 'conservaterys of the commyn wele' (123v). Similarly, despite the connection of commyn state to pollycy, the former meant 'hole state [condition] of the commynalty' which follows it very shortly in one place (104v). Finally, when Starkey wrote that the king's

[25] Q. Skinner, *Foundations of modern political thought*, II, *The reformation*, 357. Philip Corrigan and Derek Sayer have explicitly followed Skinner in *The great arch: English state formation as cultural revolution*, 45. They cite Starkey's usage as a key piece of evidence that '"the State" first came to be spoken of impersonally, as the repository of political loyalty, precisely in the 1530s'.

council should 'represent the hole state commynly' he was not thinking far in advance of the sixteenth century, since 'the hole *body of the pepul wythout [*ab.*] parlyament' was his translation for 'hole state commynly' (110r). Thus there is probably an overtone of the historiographical notion of the 'political nation' in Starkey's connection of 'commynalty & polytyke state' to mean those who had a part in politics (31v), but much less of any idea of constitutional order.

Starkey's state was run by a conciliar government made up of those 'wych have authoryte & rule', who might regulate the prince's actions through a system of councils (101v–102r), at the same time as they created 'thys bande of rekenyng *before the conseyl of hyar authoryte' (105r) to keep lesser officials in line. The role of the greatest of these councils – parliament – and the extent of its authoryte is more obscure than may at first appear.[26] These councils exercised authoryte originally delegated to them by parliament, even when it was not in session (104v), just as the permanently established cardinals had the authoryte of the general council, which had also given the pope his authoryte (118v). Starkey described the pope 'as hed *appoyntyd by commyn authoryte', which must mean the council. This suggests that when he used the last phrase to refer to secular matters, he meant parliament. Such seems to be the sense of 'Pole's' argument that if the English settled for hereditary succession, 'then to hym [the prince] must be joynyd a counsele *by commyn authoryte [*ab.*], not such as he wyl, but such as by the most parte of the parlyament schal be [*ab.*] jugyd to be wyse & mete therunto' (104v). While Starkey here seemed to assign parliament a major role in bringing about his reform of the prince, the equation of it with 'commyn authoryte' was an afterthought. Every use of commyn authoryte is inserted, especially when Starkey assigned parliament the oversight of the nobility (101r and 119v). Perhaps these changes are a function of Starkey's realization that his programme as originally written did not take sufficient account of English conditions. Hence these modifications may have been part of the revision Starkey undertook after his first attempt to enter royal service failed.

Not all of Starkey's references to parliament are added, but he refers to the institution no more than a dozen times in the whole Dialogue. It usually appeared together with either 'conseyl' or 'commyn conseyllys' and sometimes both (17r, 45r, 66v, 110r). Unfortunately, Starkey spent no time

[26] J. A. Guy, 'The king's council and political participation', in Fox and Guy, *Henrician age*, 140–2, argues flatly that 'Starkey approached counsel in an hereditary monarchy from the perspective of public authority as enshrined in Parliament'. Cf. also Fox, 'Interpreting English humanism', 26, where he claims that Starkey proposed 'parliamentary sovereignty', and K. W. Beckmann, 'Staatstheorie und Kirchenpolitik im Werke des englischen Humanisten Thomas Starkey', 95–6, where he alleged that Starkey's idea of parliament represented 'eine entscheidende Schritt in Richtung auf die Neuzeit'. G. R. Elton made a similar point when he asserted that Starkey made 'casual references ... to Parliament as the obvious constitutionalist element in the English state'. *The body of the whole realm*, 23.

describing the nature of parliament, and aside from giving advice, passing laws (67r), and inadvertently facilitating princely tyranny (109v), we get little idea of what he thought it could do, except if we assume that the whole of his programme was to pass through it on the analogy of several of his plans for the nobility. Nevertheless, Starkey left no doubt that parliament had some connection to his councils designed to check the prince, but the relation between parliament and the rest of the kingdom is much more obscure, and can only be understood once the shape of Starkey's programme is clear.

At the moment it is not. Although a majority of historians regards English humanism as an aristocratic phenomenon, many of those same historians join another substantial majority which treats Thomas Starkey as an exception, at least for his politics. Instead of belonging in the early sixteenth century, Starkey has usually been seen as a sort of displaced Roundhead, at very least the first modern liberal or, most recently, 'a "humanist" in the broader, anachronistic, modern sense'. Fox further maintains that Starkey was exceptional also for his resistance to having England 'governed by a hereditary elite'.[27] Even Fritz Caspari, who argued vigorously that Starkey deserved a place amongst the common rout of English humanists, accepted the single most powerful argument for Starkey's peculiarity, and those who have followed Caspari more recently continue to insist on how 'radical' Starkey was.[28]

This is especially true of Skinner's interpretation. Skinner placed Starkey in the tradition of northern humanism, while underlining his radicalism. Skinner labelled the Dialogue 'one of the major treatises [an unfortunate genre designation] of humanist political thought to be produced in sixteenth-century England', but not all of his description of northern humanism applies to Starkey's work.[29] According to Skinner, most northern humanists could only import from Italy whatever they could understand, which made it impossible for them to pick up either the ideal of *libertas* or the republican system which was designed to preserve it.[30] Nevertheless, Skinner argued that the northern humanists stood in the same tradition as their Italian predecessors, whether because they adopted identical literary genres, or because they continued to aspire to positions as political advisers (for which their understanding of the past especially fitted them), or because they dealt with the same problems (especially the conflict between *otium* and *negotium*) (213–20).

---

[27] Fox, 'English humanism', 48 and 'Interpreting English humanism', 26 for Starkey's resistance to having England 'governed by a hereditary elite'.

[28] F. L. Baumer offered the most compelling case for an anachronistic Starkey. 'Thomas Starkey and Marsilius of Padua'. Caspari accepted it in *Humanism and the social order in Tudor England*, 114. For the nearly general acceptance, see below chapt. 5, note 2.

[29] *Foundations*, II, 100.

[30] Q. Skinner, *Foundations of modern political thought*, I, *The renaissance*, 200.

Much of the rest of Skinner's analysis has a disembodied quality, especially because it takes off from the premise that the 'radical humanists' including Starkey were interested only in reform of the commonwealth, not in promoting 'the special interests of the ruling classes' (215). In the case of Starkey, these two are not necessarily distinct goals. Nevertheless, Skinner was surely correct to connect the northerners and Starkey to the main argument offered by earlier humanist social critics: individual and factional self-interest posed the greatest danger to the commonwealth (222). But Skinner also maintained that sixteenth-century humanists, like their forebears, put forward a 'basic demand ... not so much for a reform of institutions, but rather for a change of heart' (220). For this to apply to Starkey, a great deal of weight must be placed on that 'not so much'. Part of the problem with this argument is that it gets caught up in another of Skinner's more specific points about Starkey which cannot be sustained. Skinner argued that Starkey set out, as a radical humanist, to appeal to the 'whole body of citizens' for moral renewal, offering 'a particularly vivid statement' of 'the traditional humanist claim' that virtue could eliminate faction (236). This is true only in part, and is in fact a subsidiary argument to Starkey's main point that institutions – his councils – would suppress ambition and sedition. Ferguson came closer to getting Starkey's position right when he argued that civic humanists, including those in England, thought of 'counsel in an institutional rather than a personal context', as did Starkey.[31] Those institutions, like Starkey's whole programme, were aimed at the nobility, as we shall see. Thus Starkey did not have to neutralize the 'subversive implications' of the 'potentially radical theory' that virtue, not wealth and birth qualified one for leadership by an appeal to hierarchy, as Skinner thought.[32] He simply blended the two through a system designed to ensure that virtue was the preserve of the natural rulers. There is no need to be surprised that he should do so (240). Starkey, in this as in most other things, imported the latest Italian thought to underpin a traditional English political system.

Starkey formed his programme on the commonplace metaphor of the body politic, but he gave it a distinctly hierarchical impress.[33] The end of the commonwealth was ordur, put into effect by rulers (94r, 29v, 33r, 100r). 'From the pryncys & rularys of the state commyth al lawys ordur & pollycy, al justyce vertue & honesty' (31v). Alas they, the head of the commonwealth, were its most diseased part, because rulers had neglected their responsibilities (7v). Nevertheless, any cure of England's ills depended on their reform. Only great and wise men could act as physicians to the realm and guarantee the

[31] A. B. Ferguson, *The articulate citizen and the English renaissance*, 148–9, 328.
[32] Skinner, *Foundations*, I, 236–8.
[33] P. Archambault's 'The analogy of the "body" in renaissance political thought' stands out above the rest of the vast literature on this metaphor.

success of the rest of Starkey's plans (37r, 45r–v, 112v and 116v). In addition to the ambition of many great men, Starkey excoriated the negligence of others who fled their duty rather than use their wisdom to restrain the multitude as leaders had done at the beginning of society (7v). Someone at the top had to take the blame for England's faults.

As at many crucial points, Starkey refused to specify exactly whom he meant. Sometimes his vocabulary betrays distinctions between the nobles and the gentry (e.g., 62r, 73v, 84v), but on other occasions he listed 'the gentyl-man, ye lordys & pryncys' as the same thing (58r), or even more clearly referred to 'gentylmen, lordys * & others of the nobylyte [*ab*.]' (51v; cf. 108r and 96v), and once substituted 'nobul' for 'gentyl' (50r). There was likewise no clear line between princes and nobility (e.g., 97r). In this, Starkey conformed to contemporary usage, which also refused to establish any clear categories amongst all those above the ignoble.[34] All the same, Starkey began and ended with the nobility, and hinged his entire programme on their complete monopoly of studying and practising law (115r–6v). This aspect of Starkey's programme provides the strongest evidence that he assimilated the gentry to the aristocrats and meant to treat them as a single class. The gentry would have to come up, not the high nobility down. If Starkey's proposals had gone into effect, and if the gentry were a separate order from the nobility, then Starkey's own intention to become a lawyer would have been pointless. Starkey nevertheless let neither group escape serious criticism, but the nobility posed the single most serious obstacle to the reform of the commyn wele. Instead of abandoning them, Starkey proposed to reeducate them. Once his programme had been put into effect it would make the nobility 'worthy of the name wych we now unworthyly gyve unto them commynly [*ab*.], then they [*ab*.] schold be nobullys in dede' (113r). Implementing this programme would lead to Plato's true commonwealth, or at least to good Christian doctrine. With such heads there would be no need for further particular remedies (116v). Starkey left no doubt that those heads were nobles, born and (properly) bred.

The specifics of Starkey's programme would have given the nobility a monopoly, both of law and of social distinction. Rather than leaving law open to commoners born in poverty as continental countries did, England would allow only nobles who had learned the discipline of the commonwealth to be lawyers (116v). When speaking of practitioners of law, Starkey referred to the gentry, but he confined instruction in Roman law – which England should receive in place of the barbarous common law – to the nobility. Caspari made one of his greatest errors on this point. He discussed Starkey's educational provisions in great detail, but he misunderstood them, primarily because of his dogged effort to make Starkey fit the thesis that the

---

[34] K. B. McFarlane, *The nobility of later medieval England*, 6–8 and G. W. Bernard, *The power of the early Tudor nobility*, 212.

political target of all English humanists was the gentry (2). Thus Caspari completely distorted Starkey's argument by claiming that Starkey meant to write that 'not only poor men but also noble men' should learn Roman law (126–7). Caspari got some of Starkey's system right, for example its two-tiered structure in which the universities served to educate clergy (who could apparently be commoners) and separate new schools would train the nobility (128). Nevertheless, he was wrong to think that a university-educated man could still aspire to rise into the ranks of Starkey's governors. Caspari noted Starkey's explicit prohibition against any but nobles practising law, but took Starkey's earlier call for examinations of candidates 'to be priests, clerks and learned in the law' to indicate that Starkey placed no restrictions on those who might be lawyers. This is certainly a mistake. Given the context it is most likely that Starkey referred to canon lawyers (128; fol. 100v). Caspari compounded this incorrect argument by discovering a spurious 'silence' in Starkey's text. According to him, Starkey failed to explain how to deal with unworthy nobles or talented commoners because he 'probably felt that such problems would take care of themselves'. Thereby Caspari completely overlooked Starkey's clear claim that his institutional design for the education of the nobility would make certain that they were fit for their position (128).[35]

Starkey handled the nobility in a similarly élitist way when he came to their economic and social status. He argued in general that virtue by itself could not lead to the commonwealth's highest felicity. That required wealth, and disposable wealth anyway was restricted to the upper class of nobility and gentry. As 'Lupset' noted in one place, 'the most parte of mankynd ... can not attayn to wordly ryches' (26r). In these two cases Starkey amalgamated the nobility and the gentry into a single economic class, those wealthy enough to be able to dispense justice impartially, but he could also draw a sharp economic distinction between them. Primogeniture and entail were to be restricted to the nobility, specifically in order to keep them separate from the gentry (72r–4r).[36] Starkey also proposed to protect noble property by doing away with wardship, the first reform he mentioned after finishing with the prince (72v and 112r). Likewise, choice ecclesiastical preferments were to be reserved to 'yong gentylmen', probably as a means to provide for second sons of great families, a major problem according to Starkey (112v). Starkey also insisted that no member of the nobility or gentry should be allowed to build above his station – not all of them could be princes (62v). On a lesser but still

---

[35] Caspari is not the only guilty party on this head. Joyce Youings offered a very similar misreading in *Sixteenth century England*, 120, but she corrected most of the mistake with a more careful interpretation of Starkey's views on 122.

[36] This is another point on which Starkey came much closer to current designs than has been realized. A similar measure was debated in the Parliament of 1529, and may have been meant to guarantee support for the peerage, exactly as Starkey intended. S. E. Lehmberg, *The reformation parliament, 1529–1536*, 94–5.

significant level, only the nobility as 'men of powar' were to have wine (99r). All together, these measures would ensure that the lords would be set above the commons, all of whom came out more or less equal in social status (74v).

These stringent economic measures underpinned a political system which would have left virtually all power in the hands of the high nobility. No one doubts that Starkey was not fond of monarchy, but the reasons for his dislike have not been understood. Monarchy suited only a people content to live in retirement. This Starkey would never have allowed, since it would have meant abandoning the civil life. His appeal for the establishment of a 'myxte state' in place of a monarchy seems to demand consideration for the views of the lower orders, but Starkey's typology of constitutions quickly dissolved into a thinly concealed preference for 'the rule of a commyn counseyl' which fitted a people 'desyrouse of frank lyberty & hye authoryte' (34v). Like his friends Contarini and Giannotti, Starkey was thinking of aristocratic rule, not democratic. Starkey's phrasing is almost identical to Tolomeo da Lucca's assertion that Aristotle thought 'those who are of virile spirit and brave heart ... cannot be governed by any other regime than the *principatus politicus*, including in this, aristocracy'.[37]

Starkey pursued two different ends for his new governmental system. On the one hand, he posited an almost quietist ideal for the majority. The 'ende of al lawys & polytyke rule ys to kepe the cytyzyns in unyte & peace' (69r). On the other and when speaking of the higher orders, he struggled to preserve the civic humanist ideal of liberty, with which he did more than toy.[38] Its social referent determined his attitude to the word: neither lower classes nor prince deserved liberty. If either got it, that would destroy the commyn wele. The problem of princely tyranny, which would inevitably result if he were allowed to rule at liberty, was the greatest possible evil and anything but a divine punishment (104r and 65r). Starkey called it a 'frencey' in the head (meaning all officers including the prince), and put it down as the chief cause of all the commyn wele's problems (55r–v). Princes bore the brunt of Starkey's criticisms, especially if they came to power through hereditary succession. Election of the ruler could remedy the problem, but Starkey also put forward a complicated scheme for limiting a hereditary monarch's exercise of his authority. These two solutions functioned almost as alternatives, since Starkey argued that the dangers of succession made safeguards necessary, but election would remove those threats. He must have meant his ideas about choosing a prince seriously enough, but may well have intended them in part as a foil to intensify the attractiveness of his conciliar option.

Up to a point, the common council of parliament had a major role in

---

[37] Tolomeo da Lucca, *De regimine principum*, 76. English translation (together with discussion) from N. Rubinstein, 'Marsilius of Padua and Italian political thought of his time', 52.

[38] Skinner, *Foundations*, I, 235.

Starkey's scheme to restrain the power of the prince (104r, 55r–v, 65r–v). Originally, Starkey wished Henry's successor to be chosen 'by electyon of the commyn voyce of parlyament'. After he abandoned this suggestion, he proposed instead that the prince's 'prerogatyfe' should be transferred to 'the commyn counseyl of the reame & parlyamente assemblyd', in order to prevent the king from undoing parliamentary decrees by 'placardys' (66v).[39] Most of the time, however, the 'grete parlyament' would not be in session. Starkey proposed that it should meet only 'at the electyon of our prynce, or els for some other grete urgent cause' (104v). Therefore, its authority 'schold ever be remeynyng' at London in the hands of a council which 'schold be redy to remedy al ... causys & represse al sedycyonys, & defend the lyberty of the hole body of the pepul'.

At this point parliament dropped out of the picture, unless the London council saw fit to convene it in an emergency (104v). Starkey spent very little time on parliament, partly because he assimilated it so thoroughly to the *consiglio maggiore*, which did a great deal of talking, but left real power in the hands of smaller councils. Similarly, the members of the *consiglio* were coopted, not elected in the way members of parliament were, which helps to explain why Starkey gave no consideration to how parliament 'represented' England.[40] He may once again have applied Italian political thought to England, since the most up-to-date hybrid Florentine and Venetian thinking about the Venetian constitution saw the *consiglio* as the guarantee of equality and liberty, and hence of leadership by the *ottimati*.[41] Parliament also failed to interest Starkey because he turned his attention elsewhere. Starkey instead imported limits on the *doge*'s authority, and transformed Venice's system of councils into a restraint on the royal prerogative, intended to make the office of prince as unattractive as that of *doge* (111v). Venetian models marked these councils less strongly than Starkey's elective monarchy, probably because here he had potent if strange English precedents on which to draw. Then again, his Venetian lenses may have distorted his vision sufficiently to cause him to overlook the existing king's council. His lack of practical experience of governing also betrayed him here, since he paid no

---

[39] 'Placardys' has usually been taken to mean proclamations here, but Starkey may have intended it in the sense of letters patent. Cf. *LP*, IV:3, 6467, Wolsey to Henry VIII, referring to the king's 'letters of placard' to attach a ship and its cargo, and John Heron's financial memorandum book recording a placard to Bishop Seaver of Carlisle, meaning a letter patent demanding some of Seaver's records. BL Add. MS 21480, fol. 167v. The original is in E101/414/16, fol. 134v in the PRO. Many thanks to Mark R. Horowitz for assistance with this item.

[40] Giuseppe Maranini, *La costituzione di Venezia*, II, 35–7.

[41] J. G. A. Pocock, *The Machiavellian moment: Florentine political thought and the atlantic republican tradition*, 281 discusses Guicciardini and Giannotti, and R. Pecchioli covers the blending of Florentine and Venetian ideas in *Dal 'mito' di Venezia all' 'ideologia americana'*, 56ff., esp. 69–70 for Guicciardini and Giannotti.

attention to the functioning or staff of his councils, and failed to allow for a figure like Thomas Cromwell, expert manipulator of councils.[42]

The first of Starkey's two councils, the permanent one at London, consisted of four of 'the gretyst & ancyent lordys of the temperalty [*ab.*]', two bishops (London and Canterbury), four judges and four citizens of London who were left to keep an eye on the king and his council and review all diplomatic actions. Most important, the London council chose the king's 'propur' council, whose advice bound the monarch. It contained two bishops, four lords and four 'of the best lernyd & polytyke men expert [*ab. del.* 'lernyd'] in the lawys both sprytual & temporal'. Together they averted sedition by distributing offices and forcing all inferior magistrates to do their duty (104v–5r). These two councils were heavily aristocratic bodies. Under Starkey's plan to restrict legal education to the nobility, the king's council would probably contain nothing but nobles, and the majority of the London council (four lords and four judges) would be aristocrats, too.

At a remote extension, this system rested on consent, as Starkey's forays into English history demonstrated. At some unspecified time, 'the hole commyns' had granted princely authority, but various kings beginning with William the Conqueror had usurped power (67v). Here as elsewhere, Starkey very quickly abandoned consent, and turned the system over to the nobility. He did not introduce the usual defence offered by consent theory and argue that the commons – or anybody – had the power to depose an errant prince. (He did observe in another place that it was 'in mannys powar ... hym that ys a tyranne so to depose', but Starkey there argued only in the abstract [103v].) Instead he told the story of how, because of royal abuses, 'our old aunceturys' had established the constable 'to conturpaise the authoryte of the prynce' and to avoid tyranny. Whenever that had threatened, the constable could assemble parliament. Starkey played down consent to a degree unusual amongst those who proposed to restrain royal power.[43] The historical argument just cited marks the only time Starkey gave consent an explicitly political meaning. More often he assigned the commons a subordinate role as

---

[42] Thus Ferguson came perhaps the closest to deciphering Starkey's theory. Although Ferguson began with a gross overstatement, claiming that Starkey thought that 'responsibility lies ultimately with the people', he quickly qualified that by restricting Starkey's attention to 'the governing classes, specifically those represented in Parliament'. *Articulate citizen*, 326. Ferguson then built on this promising beginning by noting that the relation between Starkey's parliament and his councils 'reduc[ed] the problem of government once more to that of good counsel ... in consonance with a tradition deeply imbedded in medieval thought'. *Ibid.*, 327–8. Thus Ferguson recognized parliament's limited role, and placed Starkey's ideas into the proper tradition, but failed to realize the implication of these two points for Starkey's politics. Beckmann, 'Staatstheorie', 91–2, also understood the relation of Starkey's ideas to his Venetian experience, suggesting that parliament stood in for the *Gran consiglio* (=*consiglio maggiore*) and Starkey's little parliament for the Senate.

[43] For the more usual state of affairs, see F. Oakley, '*Legitimation by consent*'.

the support of the princes and lords, but with no mention of the latter depending on the consent of the former (36r). The commons had no part in legislation: 'lawys are made *for* the pepul' and serve to 'conteyne the pepul in gud ordur & rule' (72r, emphasis added).

Even when describing the origin of civility, the *locus classicus* for consensual theories of government, Starkey managed to reproduce most of Cicero's theory, but without even the moderate concessions to consent Cicero had offered.[44] Society had appeared when certain wise men persuaded the rest to submit to their rule – Starkey never mentioned a covenant between them. The object of this new arrangement was to direct the multitude to virtue and honesty. As society became more refined, the wise and politic men devised increasingly more perfect laws, by which men 'were brought' from rudeness to civility (34r). When defining the cyvyle lyfe, 'Pole' modified 'Lupset's' original description into 'a conspyracy in honesty & vertue *stablyschyd by commyn assent' (7v), but the mere fact that Starkey had to add consent here, while he did not bother in any of his other numerous discussions of the same point indicates how unimportant the idea was to him. Hence it is not surprising that Starkey failed to consider any mechanism by which popular consent might operate.

Instead, Starkey proposed to resurrect the constable, to act as viceroy in exactly the way his historical predecessors had. Starkey recognized that the office had recently been suppressed because of an excessive concentration of power in the hands of one man, but he nevertheless intended to make the constable the head of the London council, along with three other nobles, all of whom held office by hereditary tenure: the earl marshal, the Steward, and the Chamberlain. Caspari erred once more in his treatment of these councils as a result of his interpretation of Starkey's educational plans. They, like the practice of law, would, according to Caspari, have been open to the talented. Nobles would make up only part of them, and professionals would outnumber them. Caspari again had to read Starkey's mind to sustain this case, this time claiming that 'he cannot have expected that they [the members] would all be noblemen or perhaps even gentlemen by birth, but he certainly hoped [*sic*!] that the noble lords in both councils would be properly qualified by the right education'.[45] Thus when Starkey laid down that the constable as head together with his council as body 'schold represent the hole body of the pepul *wythout parlyament and commyn counseyl', he both proposed to replace parliament with an almost entirely aristocratic institution (a 'lytle parlyament') for most purposes, and signalled his bias clearly. In common with nearly all his medieval predecessors, Starkey must have meant that the constable's council represented the pepul (the rest of England) because it

---

[44] Ferguson, *Articulate citizen*, 379.   [45] Caspari, *Humanism*, 129.

offered the 'best' picture (representation) of it, a body of the wise and powerful best represented England's *identitas* (110v).[46]

Representation is an exceedingly difficult term to define, and up until twenty years ago, hardly anyone had tried. Since then, Giuseppe Alberigo has insisted that the meaning of this key term must be derived from its context.[47] This, alas, Starkey's text does not offer. Therefore his meaning will have to depend on the probabilities of various usages in his environment. Hasso Hofmann, the author of the most thorough survey of ideas of representation, calls *repraesentatio identitatis* the standard medieval meaning. For particular, limited actions, the council 'is' the community. This sort of representation did not depend on election, especially because a complete picture rested on principles of value which were anything but majoritarian. The wise and the powerful almost always 'represented' the community most accurately, as is clear from the constant mediation of *repraesentatio identitatis* through the schema of head and body, which of course Starkey used as the basis of his entire work. The great fourteenth-century jurist Bartolo developed this idea into *concilium repraesentat mentem populi*, that is, the leaders acted for the people, for example by electing officers, who could nonetheless also be called representatives of the people.[48] This formulation has striking affinities to Starkey's.

The chief competitor of *repraesentatio identitatis* was proctorial representation, and, although Hofmann considers only Sir Thomas Smith and Richard Hooker, he finds both these sorts of representation – proctorial and pictorial – current in England from the fourteenth century on.[49] Proctorial representation is a major thread in the development of medieval ideas about parliamentary institutions: those who attended them might indeed be elected, but they had only the legal authority of proctors, a *plena potestas* which would allow them to accede in the place of their electors to whatever the ruler wished.[50] The English examples cited by S. B. Chrimes have this sense.[51] Hofmann amplifies Gaines Post to argue that in this sense of *personam alicuius repraesentare* (or more commonly *gerere*) the relation between principal and proctor had nothing to do with a consensus of wills between them, nor with any abstract sense of attributing the actions of the representative to the represented. This static concept of representation was distinct from that of 'acting as' the principal which could become representation as 'the crystallization of a multitude in the actions of a part selected by whatever means'.[52]

---

[46] Guy calls Starkey's system of council's 'representative', but without considering what that word meant to Starkey, nor how Starkey designed the councils to supersede parliament. 'King's council', 140.

[47] Giuseppe Alberigo, 'Il movimento conciliare (XIV–XV sec.) nella ricerca storica recente', 934.

[48] Hasso Hofmann, *Repräsentation*, 213–15 and 219–20.

[49] Ibid., 338–41.

[50] Gaines Post, '*Plena potestas* and consent in medieval assemblies'.

[51] S. B. Chrimes, *English constitutional ideas in the fifteenth century*, 76–9, 352.

[52] Hofmann, *Repräsentation*, 165, 215, 211.

But as Hofmann's choice of 'crystallization' should immediately indicate, the relation between representative and represented (or council and community) is not reversible (as it is in more modern senses), nor very clearly thought out. Hofmann's conclusion about English usage together with Starkey's staunchly 'conservative' conciliarism suggests that he could not have gone beyond these limits, say in the more 'democratic' direction of a John of Segovia or other theorists of the Council of Basel.

Yet when Starkey delivered his final case for the king's council he appeared to argue that virtue deserved reward, regardless of its possessor's social status, and thereby to open his government to the talented. Considering how much trouble the terms gave him and how fuzzy Starkey left the line, if any, between nobility and gentry, it may have been with a sigh of relief that he noted at the end of the Dialogue that he had managed to avoid discussing the problem of true nobility (128v). Nevertheless, Starkey's assurance that his proposals for the equal distribution of offices would remove 'the occasyon most chefe of al sedycyon' provides a clue about those who caused the problem and opens a case against Starkey's having shared Richard Morison's belief in partial meritocracy.[53] Starkey produced no unequivocal definition of 'sedycyon', any more than he did of any of his other terms, but this passage seems an obvious restatement of one on the previous folio where Starkey worried about getting rid of 'any dangerouse sedycyon betwyx the pryncys of our reame * & hys nobylyte [ab.]'. Similarly, competition for the throne could produce sedycyon, which was one of the reasons Starkey finally settled for hereditary succession. He apparently regarded sedycyon as at least very often the preserve of the nobility. It had touched one noble in particular, as 'Lupset' reminded 'Pole' – Pole himself, the same man 'Lupset' thought the example of his noble ancestors should inspire, a point Starkey emphasized by inserting the adjective (117v, 110r, 105r; and 69v, 1v [?]). Thus it would seem that the distribution of offices designed to remedy sedycyon might have been confined to those whose competition chiefly caused it.

Michael Mendle offers a different interpretation of Starkey's councils. He argues that far from trying to restrain the king in order to prepare a place for a revived high nobility, Starkey meant to give Henry virtually complete control of the new system. According to Mendle, the London or constable's council was 'largely composed of men who owed their membership to an appointment to office by the king', including the four great officers of state. These councils could not have represented the three estates because their members had not been elected.[54] Mendle therefore accuses Starkey of paying lip service to the ideal of the mixed state, using it as a cover for 'a bureaucrat's idea of

---

[53] Fox, 'Interpreting English humanism', 26 overstates Morison's position. Cf. T. F. Mayer, 'Thomas Starkey's aristocratic reform programme', 458–9.

[54] Guy, 'King's council', 142 maintains likewise that Starkey thought in terms of the estates.

Utopia'.[55] Starkey's ideas of representation and consent seem to suggest that Mendle is correct, but Mendle misunderstands the nature of Starkey's constitutional ideas. First, it is difficult to see how Mendle arrived at the conclusion that Starkey's councillors were under Henry's thumb. None of the four great offices of state was Henry's to dispose as he saw fit; all of them were hereditary.[56] Perhaps Mendle drew on a confused interpretation of the difficulties of the last holder of the constableship, the third Duke of Buckingham, who engaged in protracted litigation in an ultimately futile effort to secure the office. Buckingham won his suit, but Henry responded by allowing the office to lapse.[57] Mendle overlooks Starkey's rationale for the king's own council, over which Mendle argues tendentiously that the king had almost as direct control, despite Starkey's insistence that he should have nothing whatever to do with choosing it. This council existed to ensure that the distribution of offices, including bishoprics, did not rest in the king's hands (110v). If Mendle misinterprets the principle of selection Starkey used to create his councils, he also distorts how Starkey thought they represented England by suggesting that only election could produce representatives. But in the proper sense of *repraesentatio identitatis*, who better to embody the rest of the realm than great aristocrats, clergy, judges and citizens of its most 'representative' city, London? These were certainly the wise and powerful. Expecting representation to have any necessary connection to election is a gross anachronism.

Finally, Mendle is right that Starkey's 'myxte state' masked (and obscured) another sort of constitutional reality, but there is no reason to question Starkey's commitment to this favourite humanist device.[58] The difficulty in understanding the term arises because humanists used a newer vocabulary to describe the constitution which had prevailed in most of western Europe since the early twelfth century, which Brian Tierney calls 'divided sovereignty'.[59] The balance of authority tipped constantly back and forth between king, lords, and various representative institutions in secular government, or pope, cardinals and councils in the church, but the first two parties in both spheres almost always kept the upper hand. Starkey thought in the same terms, and tried to cut a classical garment to medieval dimensions.

[55] M. Mendle, *Dangerous positions: mixed government, the estates of the realm, and the making of the answer to the XIX propositions*, 45.

[56] H. Miller, *Henry VIII and the English nobility*, chapter 6, esp. 165–8. Cf. also David Starkey, 'The lords of the council: aristocracy, ideology and the formation of the Tudor privy council', for further clarification.

[57] B. J. Harris, *Edward Stafford, third duke of Buckingham*, 170–1 offers the best treatment of Buckingham's suit and its aftermath.

[58] Most scholarship agrees with Mendle that the concept of the mixed state was of little importance in England before the seventeenth century. Donald Hanson is typical in recognizing this vocabulary in the writings of sixteenth-century Englishmen including Starkey, while considering it of small consequence. *From kingdom to commonwealth: the development of civic consciousness in English political thought*, 248.

[59] Brian Tierney, '"Divided sovereignty" at Constance', 254 and 256.

Thus despite the difficulties posed by Starkey's highly rhetorical approach, convoluted writing, word play and competing motives and intentions, the major thrust of his political programme has finally come out. It will have a familiar ring to twentieth-century readers. To adopt a perhaps incautious simile and one that cannot extend far, Starkey's remedy for the deficiencies of England's traditional rulers resembles that adopted by various sorts of successful modern revolutionaries: reeducation in special institutions. These may not have qualified as labour camps – Starkey's discipline was intellectual, not physical – and the compulsory retraining he would have applied to the high nobility was not designed to make them accept a new system but to fit them to run it, once they had been rehabilitated. Nevertheless, Starkey was quite as serious about his programme and quite as eager to see it implemented as any Mao. But the meaning of 'revolution' in the sixteenth century mirrors the fundamental difference between Starkey and modern reformers. As revolution to him meant returning whence one began, so Starkey intended to resuscitate a ruling class in decline, not replace it with a new order. To that end, he drew willingly even enthusiastically on just about any materials which he thought he could turn to his purpose. This chapter has examined his resources of language. The following one emphasizes Starkey's aristocratic leanings by locating his ideas in several classical and 'medieval' traditions and comparing them to those of some of his near contemporaries.

5

The Dialogue in classical and 'medieval' tradition

Instead of building up a context around Thomas Starkey largely by means of recovering personal contacts, this chapter documents how Starkey appropriated several 'traditions of discourse' (in Andrew Lockyer's sense) which go beyond the proximate inspiration and limitation which Starkey's immediate environment provided, his relation to an ideological context of aristocratic political thought, in other words. This is not an exercise in uncovering Starkey's 'sources'. In addition to the severe limits on the explanatory power of source-hunting, Starkey's eclecticism renders it especially unrewarding. Nevertheless, some of the materials with which Starkey apparently worked can at least be plausibly isolated in his experience. For example, we know Starkey read Aristotle on politics at Magdalen, even though, unlike Cicero, we cannot point to a particular person who probably tutored Starkey. Again, he almost certainly studied Aristotle's ideas in more depth along with Plato's in Italy. Unfortunately, some of the most important facets of Starkey's thinking only suggest points of contact with similar bodies of thought. All the same, there can be little doubt that Starkey came in touch with English traditions of the power and position of the nobility, which coalesced with Starkey's oligarchical civic humanism to produce the main thrust of his political programme. A *prima-facie* case points to Reginald Pole as Starkey's political mentor, but the evidence to support this supposition comes from much later in Pole's life.

Before Starkey can be placed in any new traditions, he must be disconnected from an extraordinarily persistent but fundamentally wrong-headed old one. The argument which locates Starkey in a line descending from Marsilio of Padua has proved durable and widely accepted. F. L. Baumer, its originator, put forward the fundamental premise that Starkey's ideas were so peculiar in the context of early sixteenth-century England, where absolutism and not constitutional monarchy was the dominant pattern, that Starkey must have found his ideas in some equally unusual source.[1] Neither late medieval political thinkers like Fortescue nor Starkey's patron Pole could have concocted such outlandish ideas (190). Since no source in Starkey's environment offered such radical notions, Baumer argued bluntly that 'the reason why Starkey was such a revolutionary in political thought … was because of the lasting effect a study of Marsilius of Padua must have had on him', and went further to label Marsilio as 'the main source' of Starkey's political thinking (191 and 205). Starkey took from Marsilio more than other Henricians like Thomas Cranmer, for Starkey adopted virtually the whole of the first *dictio* of the *Defensor pacis* as the groundwork for a democratic theory of constitutional government (192).

Baumer identified pronounced similarities between Marsilio and Starkey on the score of both approach and content. In some ways, Baumer depended more heavily on the first count. He noted that both began with a definition of the ideal state and then proceeded to discuss abuses of it. This was damning enough, but the 'resemblances begin to look suspicious' when they clinched this part of the argument by citing Aristotle. Baumer conceded that Starkey 'doubtless' knew the *Politics* directly, but he still read them through the 'medium' of the *Defensor*. Similarly, both Starkey and Marsilio followed a historical approach in their criticism of the papacy, and, when pointing out the faults in secular government, both wrote in an 'eminently realistic and utilitarian' fashion (192–3).

At this point, Baumer shifted to an analysis of the content of Marsilio's and Starkey's ideas. Their suggestion that kings be elected was 'most practical' for Marsilio, 'more practicable' to Starkey, and both thought kings were established by 'human ordinance', not divine. Both rested their case for election on the naturalness of the state and its progressive evolution, an argument which is again handled very similarly by both, including the citation of Aristotle (194). Likewise, Starkey's definition of the commonwealth resembles both Marsilio's and Aristotle's, and it led him to an 'analogous … fundamental distinction between the good ruler and the tyrant'. Provided the ruler acts for the common good, according to both Marsilio and Starkey, then the particular form of government makes little difference. When Starkey turned to a discussion of types of constitutions, he 'practically copies' Marsilio's definitions of monarchy, aristocracy and *politia* (195–6). Starkey followed Marsilio in both his proposed remedies for tyranny, arguing first that the monarch must be elected and subject to deposition, and second, that in order to

---

[1] F. L. Baumer, 'Thomas Starkey and Marsilius of Padua', 188–9, 205. K. W. Beckmann, in 'Staatstheorie und Kirchenpolitik im Werke des englischen Humanisten Thomas Starkey', 109–10 raised some fundamental doubts about Starkey's alleged dependence on Marsilio, but still accepted Baumer's conclusion and most of the parallels he drew between Starkey and Marsilio.

guarantee that the king would obey the law, conciliar checks must hedge his power (196–7, 199). While admitting that Marsilio had followed Aristotle's *Nichomachean ethics* in making his case for the supremacy of law, and more damagingly that Starkey and Marsilio differed over its source, Baumer continued to maintain that Starkey's system of restraints 'resembles to an amazing degree' the 'conciliar theory' of *dictio* II. Even if the two dealt with different problems, they once again shared the same method. Just as a general council had to approve Marsilio's pope, so parliament had to elect Starkey's prince. Both pope and monarch needed an assigned council of advisers without whom they could not act. Final authority in both cases lay with either the general council or Starkey's council of sixteen [*sic*]. Baumer hesitated to push his analogy too far, but still insisted that the 'similarity is, to say the least, striking'. So much for Starkey's Dialogue and the *Defensor*. Baumer extended his argument to cover the *Exhortation* as well without materially affecting his case. Simply put, Starkey took over Marsilio's 'democratic principles' wholesale (199–200).

The strength of Baumer's case induced later scholars to accept it almost without quibble. Until very recently, the only major modification to it came from W. Gordon Zeeveld, and it applied only to Baumer's reading of the *Exhortation*.[2] This universal acceptance is the more curious in that Baumer's general view of the Henrician political system as absolutist has been almost completely demolished. Even G. R. Elton, the man most responsible for the destruction of Baumer's broader case, nonetheless accepted the Marsilian Starkey, and indeed found Starkey's sometime patron Thomas Cromwell a follower of Marsilio.[3] Elton also obliquely accepted Baumer's contention that many of Starkey's ideas were peculiar, calling those parts of Starkey's position which Baumer had labelled most specifically 'Marsilian' 'shades of the provisions of Oxford'.[4] Harry S. Stout agreed entirely with Baumer, but without giving full credit to him. Stout made Starkey a central figure in his attempt to demonstrate the Henricians' dependence on Marsilio. According

---

[2] All the following took over Baumer's argument, although not always by name: W. Hudson, *John Ponet*, 168n; C. Morris, *Political thought in England. Tyndale to Hooker*, 54; G. B. Parks, *The English traveller to Italy*, I, 484; F. Caspari, *Humanism and the social order in Tudor England*, 119; A. B. Ferguson, *The articulate citizen and the English renaissance*, 174–5 and 247–8; J. K. McConica, *English humanists and reformation politics*, 167; J. P. Dolan, *History of the reformation*, 293; N. M. Égretier in her edition of Reginald Pole, *Défense de l'unité de l'église*, 108n and 122; B. J. Verkamp, *The indifferent mean: adiaphorism in the English reformation*, 143; S. K. Christie, 'Richard Morison', 18; D. G. Newcombe, '"Due order & reasonabul mean"', 17, 28, 62ff.; C. Condren, *The status and appraisal of classic texts*, 265; and A. G. Dickens and J. M. Tonkin with K. Powell, *The reformation in historical thought*, 60.

[3] G. R. Elton, 'Reform by statute: Thomas Starkey's '*Dialogue*' and Thomas Cromwell's policy' and 'The political creed of Thomas Cromwell'. Cf. also Q. Skinner, *Foundations of modern political thought*, II, *The reformation*, 86.

[4] Elton, '*Dialogue*', 181.

to Stout, Starkey's legal theory, which Baumer had not traced to Marsilio, also derived from the *Defensor*, for Starkey, like Marsilio, argued on the basis of a distinction between the 'material' and 'formal' elements of the law that 'the legitimacy of a law was determined not by whether it was just or honorable, but by whether or not the law could be supported by coercion'.[5] As Baumer had, Stout emphasized that Starkey's notion of election and his thinking about the *legislator* came from Marsilio (313). Finally, Starkey also borrowed his fervent commitment to unity, but along with it came Marsilio's 'republicanism'. The king 'became the people's servant' (314).

Baumer's interpretation of Starkey did not face serious challenge until 1977. Even then much the same oddity cropped up in Gregorio Piaia's attitude to Baumer as in Elton's. Although Piaia has been amongst those arguing most forcefully that Marsilio was no kind of democrat, he yet maintained that most of Baumer's analysis of Starkey's thought 'does not leave any space for modifications'.[6] Baumer's case exercised such an influence over Piaia that he inadvertently reproduced without acknowledgement Baumer's flat statement that Starkey read Aristotle through the *tramite* of Marsilio (414). All the same, much of Piaia's subtle case puts severe dents in Baumer's and Stout's position. Piaia accepted Elton's attack on Baumer for taking Starkey out of context and making him a revolutionary, calling the latter an 'excessive and deforming emphasis' (204–5). Correctly, if too quietly, Piaia suggested that Starkey could have found precedent for his conciliar checks on the ruler in the institutions of Venice, as well as in Marsilio (201 and 202n). As had Baumer but without dismissing the contrast, Piaia underlined the major difference in legal theory between Starkey and Marsilio: natural law as standard vs. 'a sort of positivism', an objection which Zeeveld on Starkey's adiaphorism enhanced (203–4). At bottom, however, Piaia found mostly value in and even pushed the first half of Baumer's approach by amplifying the parallels between Marsilio and Starkey on the score of method, extending his own earlier argument that Marsilio's 'extremism' lay there, not in the content of the *Defensor*.[7]

Two basic problems vitiate Baumer's case. Both are finally a function of his approach to context, but his handling of Starkey's and Marsilio's language should take priority over the difficulties in his choice of general context. As Baumer's misreadings and misinterpretations add up, they will point to the need for new consideration of the broader implications of his argument.

---

[5] H. S. Stout, 'Marsilius of Padua and the Henrician reformation', 311. Alistair Fox makes a very similar case for Starkey's 'radical political positivism', which clearly descends from Baumer and Stout. 'English humanism and the body politic', in A. Fox and J. A. Guy, *Reassessing the Henrician age*, 49.

[6] G. Piaia, *Marsilio da Padova nella riforma e nella controriforma*, 203, and 'Democrazia e totalitarismo in Marsilio da Padova', 374–6 for the analysis of Marsilio.

[7] *Marsilio*, 197n and '"Antiqui", "moderni" e "via moderna" in Marsilio da Padova', 342–3.

Almost wherever one picks up Baumer's case, problems of terminology appear. They are particularly glaring in some of Baumer's central contentions. Baumer typically maintained that Starkey imitated Marsilio's very precise phrases, but in ways which left no obvious reminiscence of their putative origin. For example, Baumer claimed that Starkey's notion that kings were humanly established rested on Marsilio's assertion that the 'people' were the *pars principans* and the 'holder of sovereignty'.[8] Yet Starkey never used either of these distinctively Marsilian terms, and all of his machinery for restraining royal power had no obvious links to anything other than the high nobility. Baumer's attempt to extend this argument to cover Starkey and Marsilio on election founders on the difficulty that unfit electors most concerned Marsilio, while Starkey ignored that problem and left unclear who, corrupt or otherwise, should choose the king.[9] Again, Baumer asserted that Starkey and Marsilio said 'practically the same thing' on the score of deposing an unfit ruler. Marsilio's theory that the *legislator humanus* could dispense with the *pars principans* supposedly lurked behind Starkey's bland statement that 'thys ys in mannys powar, to electe & chose hym that ys both wyse and just, and make hym a prynce, and hym that ys a tyranne so to depose'.[10] One might attempt to salvage Baumer's case by arguing that Starkey's terms should not be expected to resemble Marsilio's because of Starkey's objection to Marsilio's 'rude' style, but the fact remains that his terms do in fact look like Aristotle's, especially on points where Marsilio departs from his alleged master.

Baumer admitted that Starkey and Marsilio differed in their theory of law, even if he compressed a wide range of medieval thinking about natural law into a single position.[11] Piaia emphasized that this distinction was more important than Baumer allowed, but he did not take the point far enough. Baumer missed a key element in Marsilio's thought which was almost completely lacking from Starkey's. Both the law and the whole of civil society rested on the consent of the whole body of citizens, according to Marsilio.[12] As we have seen, Starkey almost never mentioned consent, and the concept was of practically no importance. Despite his inclinations, Starkey did not join the tradition descending from Stoicism which saw society as consensual because it had been founded by popular decision in the golden age.[13] Instead Starkey followed the rigorously aristocratic myth. Society had appeared when certain wise men persuaded the rest to submit to their rule – Starkey

---

[8] Baumer, 'Starkey', 194.
[9] T. F. Mayer, 'Thomas Starkey's aristocratic reform programme', 449.
[10] Baumer, 'Starkey', 199 and SP 1/90, fol. 103v.
[11] *Ibid.*, 199.
[12] Marsilio of Padua, *Defensor pacis*, I. 8 (ed. C. W. Previté-Orton, 28).
[13] M. d'Addio, *L'idea del contratto sociale dai sofisti alla riforma e il 'De principatu' di Mario Salamonio*.

never mentioned a covenant between them.[14] Marsilio, for his part, followed Aristotle almost verbatim on the transition from rule by elders to civil society, and both accounts are much different from Starkey's. Marsilio did not explain how better laws came about, for example, which meant that the prudent and politic men upon whom Starkey relied figured not at all in Marsilio's version.[15] Thus Starkey and Marsilio differed fundamentally because for the former the political body (the multitude) was to be kept in order by laws administered by rulers, laws which came from 'princes & rulers of the state'. The laws governed like reason, and reason was certainly not a part nor a product of the multitude. For Marsilio, the defining characteristic of the ideal temperate government was the consent of its citizens.[16]

Consent occasionally figured in Aristotle's political theory, but not in any important way.[17] While Marsilio isolated consent as the constitutive element of any *polis*, Aristotle had maintained that perfection or self-sufficiency set a *polis* off from other types of government.[18] Marsilio here distanced himself from Aristotle and set out to redefine Aristotle's basic political vocabulary.[19] Consequently, their definition of the citizen and of the citizens' political power varied substantially, too. According to Marsilio, all the inhabitants of a city were citizens and collectively as a *universitas* they possessed something very like a modern notion of sovereignty. Aristotle, on the other hand, had restricted citizenship to those who were both free and equal before the fact of becoming citizens, that is, those who possessed some measure of political power in their own right, or the members of the aristocracy. Their collective power then was simply the highest among the number of competing authorities, but they did not possess absolute sovereignty.[20] Put in terms of vocabulary, Aristotle distinguished the *polis* from the *politeia*. The former meant a body of citizens who possessed the latter, a constitution.[21] Marsilio instead identified the two, with the end in view of reducing their legitimacy to the element of consent. Starkey's usage does not come very close to either Aristotle or Marsilio, but by rejecting Marsilio's restrictive definition of *politeia* as necessarily founded on consent, Starkey remained within the broader confines of Aristotle's descriptive definition. Starkey offered no equivalent for *polis*, preferring instead to rely on renderings of *civitas*, and 'pollycy' served both for constitution and political wisdom.

Once more, Baumer obscured major differences in how these two

[14] T. A. Brady, jun., *Ruling class, regime and reformation at Strassbourg 1520–1555*, 18.
[15] *Defensor*, I. 3 (pp. 9–11).
[16] E. Berti, 'Il "regnum" di Marsilio tra la "polis" aristotelica e lo "stato" moderno', 173.
[17] A. Gewirth, *Marsilius of Padua and medieval political philosophy*, 221, 241–2.
[18] Berti, 'Marsilio', 174.   [19] *Ibid.*, 166.   [20] *Ibid.*, 174–5.   [21] *Ibid.*, 167.

approached Aristotle by arguing that both believed in the progressive development of the state and its naturalness. Both these points are true, as far as they go. As we have just seen, the former does almost nothing to connect Starkey and Marsilio, and the second papers over yet another major difference. Marsilio was a much more rigorous (and more Aristotelian) naturalist. The *civitas* was an animal by nature.[22] For Starkey, although civil society was also natural, civil life meant following the law of nature, a quite different thing.[23] Starkey and Marsilio converged on Aristotle again when discussing and defining types of constitutions, and both agreed that the precise form of the government was a matter of indifference, but this time Starkey adhered more closely to Aristotle by maintaining that the government had to fit the nature of the people who lived under it, while Marsilio once again insisted that any government was acceptable provided only that it rested on the consent of its citizens.

This catalogue of precise variations between Marsilio and Starkey amounts almost to the destruction of Baumer's case, especially by the standard of usage. Their terms are almost never similar, and usually quite different. Piaia's modification of Baumer stressing Marsilio's method could still save the phenomenon of Starkey's dependence on him. If by the *idealogizzazione* of Aristotle, Piaia meant to say that Marsilio departed from his predecessors by creating a practical, political programme, then Starkey did the same thing. This twist to the argument for Starkey's 'realism' probably does not explain much, especially if we consider that Starkey did not accept what Piaia calls the essence of Marsilio's new ideology – the emancipation of the secular *pars principans* from clerical control, which opened the *via moderna* in political thought by laicizing power.[24] Instead, by the end of his Dialogue and thence forward, Starkey decided the clergy had a key role to play in the commonwealth, even if they exercised their influence by different means from secular authorities. Marsilio, like Starkey, was a priest, but unlike Starkey he chose to exercise his vocation in secular political pursuits. Starkey became a preacher, a very odd thing for a convinced secularist to do.

What Alan Gewirth calls the 'Romanist' interpretation of Marsilio might yet save the thesis of a Marsilian Starkey. According to Georges de Lagarde and Jeanine Quillet, Marsilio was a defender of the emperor, not a republican. Consequently, all his protestations in favour of consent in *dictio* I fade into insignificance. If this interpretation of Marsilio were accepted, it would have the added advantage of helping to explain how Starkey could apply an allegedly 'civic' thesis to a kingdom – Marsilio had already showed him

---

[22] *Defensor*, I. 3.   [23] Gewirth, *Marsilius*, 55.   [24] Piaia, '"Antiqui"', 342–4.

how.[25] Another variation on this thesis argues that *dictio* I of the *Defensor* was an exercise in pure political science, or in creating an abstract theory of civil society, applicable under any circumstances.[26] Alas, as Gewirth demonstrated in his critique, the Romanists must be wrong. The people were to participate in all stages of law-making, or at least to elect representatives to initiate the process, while retaining the right to comment upon their findings and adopt the final version of a statute.[27] No means exist to reduce Marsilio's emphasis on consent, which remains the single most important obstacle in the way of those who would make Starkey his epigone. As for the suggestion that Marsilio meant his work in the abstract, Nicolai Rubinstein effectively demonstrated Marsilio's close dependence on the world of the Italian communes and of Padua in particular.[28]

A major reevaluation of Marsilio since Baumer wrote is partly to blame for the apparent weakness of his argument, but Baumer himself inadvertently laid his finger on the root difficulty. Even if he had demonstrated pronounced similarities between Starkey and Marsilio, by the 1530s they were 'the common coinage of the time'.[29] Although Baumer meant this judgment to apply only to the tidbits borrowed from Marsilio in Starkey's letters to Pole, it applies equally well to much of the rest of Marsilio's alleged 'influence'. Frederick Copleston's imprecisely worded judgment that Marsilio's 'spirit' rather than the specifics of his case exercised an appeal over the long run neatly isolates the difficulty in pinning down borrowings from him.[30] 'False positives' in tracking Marsilio's influence caused by his and his alleged successors' place in a common Aristotelian tradition no doubt produce part of this indistinctness. A great deal of work has been done on the place of Aristotle's thought in the Renaissance and the late middle ages, but not much of it has been directed to the impact of his political thinking.[31] Nevertheless, enough evidence has come up to suggest that civic humanists and Thomists at least still made plenty of room for Aristotle.[32]

[25] J. G. A. Pocock explained how civic humanism could spread to England, despite its different political circumstances from those of Italy. *The Machiavellian moment: Florentine political thought and the atlantic republican tradition*, 335ff.
[26] Piero Di Vona argued most strenuously for the former interpretation in his *I principi del defensor pacis*, while Conal Condren best represents the latter theory. 'Democracy and the *Defensor pacis*: on the English language tradition of Marsilian interpretation', 311–12.
[27] A. Gewirth, 'Republicanism and absolutism in the thought of Marsilius of Padua', 36, 40–1.
[28] N. Rubinstein, 'Marsilius of Padua and Italian political thought of his time', and 'Marsilio da Padova e il pensiero politico italiano del Trecento'.
[29] Baumer, 'Marsilius', 201.
[30] F. C. Copleston, *A history of philosophy*, III:1, 192.
[31] C. B. Schmitt produced much of the best work. For one of his last statements of the problem see *Aristotle and the Renaissance*.
[32] For the Thomists, see especially M. Wilks, *The problem of sovereignty in the later middle ages* and various works of M. Grabmann, including 'Die mittelalterliche Kommentare zur Politik des Aristoteles'.

Starkey and Marsilio certainly did. Everything Starkey allegedly found in Marsilio probably came directly from Aristotle, to whose language, concepts and even in part manner of preceding Starkey's Dialogue adhered closely. When Cromwell asked Starkey for an exposition of Aristotle's political ideas as a specimen of Starkey's wares, he responded enthusiastically, although not quite in the way Cromwell had wished (see chapt. 7). Rather than point constantly to parallels between Starkey and Aristotle, suffice it to say at the outset that every point considered is one on which Starkey agreed with Aristotle.

For Aristotle, politics consisted of ethics. Anyone who studied them should aim 'to make his fellow citizens good and obedient to the laws'. The good required knowledge of the soul, Aristotle's starting point in the *Nichomachean ethics*.[33] His argument there coalesced on most points with his discussion in the *Politics*. Happiness – 'activity in accordance with virtue' – was the highest good, and depended on self-sufficiency, which could be achieved only in a group.[34] Aristotle stressed the *vita activa*, dismissing the contemplative life as a counsel of perfection.[35] Since happiness required constant activity, it could not be complete unless supported by sufficient external goods.[36] They were necessary in order to overcome impediments to perfect happiness.[37] Aristotle admitted that fortune could play a role here, but the happy man could avoid misery by relying on virtue, even if misfortune prevented him from achieving the highest degree of happiness.[38] If a man succeeded in combining the highest degree of virtue with wealth, that would make him worthy of greater honour than the merely virtuous man.[39]

Then again, too many goods were as dangerous as too few. Virtue aimed at a mean.[40] Aristotle repeated these points in his *Politics*, pointing out the absolute advantages of property to the pursuit of virtue, but he developed this point further, arguing that 'the best way of life is one which consists in a mean, and a mean attainable by every individual'.[41] Therefore, property-holding had to be restrained, because those with a middling amount were most likely to listen to reason, and least likely to fall prey to ambition. A political principle followed from this. A political order had to consist of 'a

---

[33] Aristotle, *Ethica nicomachea*, 328 (I. 13. 1102a). Beckmann, 'Staatstheorie', 55, correctly pointed out that Aristotelian political theory undergirded the whole of the Dialogue, and also suggested that Starkey absorbed a good deal of Thomist thought as well (57 and 65). This may be, but Beckmann's case is impressionistic, and it makes as much sense to suggest that Starkey went directly to the source.

[34] *Ibid.*, 317 (I. 7. 1097b), 319 (1098a), 532 (X. 7. 1177a) and 320 (I. 8. 1099a).

[35] *Ibid.*, 532–7 (X. 7–8. 1177a–1179a).　　　[36] *Ibid.*, 322 (I. 8. 1099b).

[37] *Ibid.*, 467 (VII. 13. 1153b).　　　[38] *Ibid.*, 325–6 (I. 10. 1101a).

[39] *Ibid.*, 385 (IV. 3. 1124a).　　　[40] *Ibid.*, 340 (II. 6. 1107a).

[41] E. Barker, trans., intro. and notes, *The politics of Aristotle*, 313 (VII. 13. 7. 1332a), quotation on 180 (IV. 11. 3. 1295a).

society of equals and peers'.[42] Starkey may not have followed Aristotle to the letter on the economic basis of the best political order, but he certainly adopted Aristotle's corollary. Those who moderated their passion for acquisition and developed their character and mind instead would achieve felicity.[43] Again, Aristotle emphasized that felicity depended on proper action, while drawing a political corollary from his maxim.[44] Different routes to felicity produced different constitutions.[45]

Before he came to consider the varieties of constitutions in the *Politics*, Aristotle established principles of law and justice in the *Ethics*. In a sense, he argued, all law was just, but poor framing meant some laws communicated justice less effectively.[46] Political justice, justice which did not require legislative enactment, functioned according to both a society's degree of self-sufficiency and its measure of equality. Part of political justice was natural, and part legal. Legal justice covered behaviour which had originally been indifferent or morally neutral, but which a law had made so no longer. In most cases, legal justice still regulated relations between unequal men. This variety of political justice was mutable, even though only one justice was naturally best.[47] (Aristotle's explication of the difference between the two and of the principle of *epieikeia*, a means of moderating the strictness of the law, may well have helped to inspire Starkey's interest in the related notion of adiaphora.) Because of the uncertainties of legal justice, the political thinker had to pay attention to pleasure and pain, in order to use them as means to the end of virtue.[48] Good behaviour was a matter of training, and that required 'a sort of reason and right order, provided this has force'. In other words, the law needed teeth in order to induce men to observe its reasonable content.[49] A tyrant ruling in his own interest could not avoid committing injustice, so that Aristotle concluded that the 'rational principle' not the man must rule.[50]

Aristotle built his system in the *Politics* on this bedrock. All men would try to follow some idea of the good, and that would lead them to become dissatisfied with earlier versions of their law. Nevertheless, only habit could induce obedience. Hence the necessity of a political system.[51] The good was justice, which now became that which 'tends to promote the common interest', but this once again was a matter for the law to drum into citizens.[52] The problem was, which political system best promoted justice? Aristotle

---

[42] *Ibid.*, 181 (IV. 11. 8. 1295b).
[43] *Ibid.*, 280 (VII. 1. 6. 1323b).
[44] *Ibid.*, 288 (VII. 4. 3. 1325a).
[45] *Ibid.*, 299 (VII. 8. 5. 1328b).
[46] *Ethica*, 399 (V. 1. 1129b).
[47] *Ibid.*, 411–13 (V. 6. 1134a–V. 7. 1135a).
[48] *Ibid.*, 463 (VII. 11. 1152b).
[49] *Ibid.*, 539 (X. 9. 1180a).
[50] *Ibid.*, 412 (V. 6. 1134a).
[51] *Politics*, 72–3 (II. 8. 21. 1269a).
[52] *Ibid.*, 129 (III. 12. 1. 1282b) and 119 (III. 9. 8. 1280b).

considered monarchy, aristocracy and democracy before hitting on 'polity', which not only meant constitution generically but a specific form which Aristotle also called political rule.[53] This double usage is identical to Starkey's handling of the ubiquitous complex of words around 'pollycy', as are Aristotle's and Starkey's conclusions about the best form of government.

In the *Politics*, constitution meant 'an organization of offices in a state, by which the method of their distribution is fixed, the sovereign authority is determined, and the nature of the end to be pursued by the association and all its members is prescribed'.[54] But at the same time, the 'civic body' not only held sovereignty, it was also the 'polity (or constitution) itself'.[55] In order to describe its varieties, Aristotle turned to the categories of the one, the few and the many.[56] He had decided in the *Ethics* that monarchy was the best form of government, and he continued to argue that this was the variety of rule by a single person which considered the common interest. Now he nevertheless raised objections to monarchy.[57] Instead, Aristotle suggested that the whole people could 'become something in the nature of a single person', thereby not only contributing to the body politic image, but also explaining how the *polis* could conduce to the end of a self-sufficient and perfect existence.[58] Aristotle granted that an utterly superior man could rightfully be king, while still likening absolute kingship to rule over the pre-political organization of a household.[59]

Doubts still tugged at Aristotle's grudging acceptance of monarchy. Although he proposed that if a monarch were necessary he should be both elected and provided with a council, he ultimately pronounced in favour of the rule of law. Pointing to Sparta, Aristotle argued that 'each new king should be appointed for his personal conduct and character' in order to assure that 'insignificant persons' could not damage the state.[60] The office of Admiral in Sparta (a pronounced analogue of Starkey's constable) also came in for criticism. As 'a sort of second kingship, set up as a counter-poise to the kings' it caused 'civic discord'.[61] Attributing sovereignty to the law would solve the problem.[62] Better yet, the government should rest in the hands of 'a number of persons who are all good men', or an aristocracy.[63] Aristotle repeated that kings should be elected, but again reached the conclusion that

---

[53] G. Bien, *Grundlegung der politischen Philosophie bei Aristoteles*, 317 and 322.
[54] *Politics*, 156 (IV. 1. 9. 1289a).   [55] *Ibid.*, 110 (III. 6. 1. 1278b).
[56] *Ibid.*, 114 (III. 7. 2–4. 1279a).
[57] *Ethica*, 485–6 (VIII. 10. 1160a–b) and *Politics*, 114 (III. 7. 3. 1278b), 117 (III. 9. 2. 1280a).
[58] *Ibid.*, 123 (III. 11. 1281b); cf. IV. 4. 7ff. 1290bff.).
[59] *Ibid.*, 136 (III. 13. 25. 1284b) and 140 (III. 14. 15. 1285b).
[60] *Ibid.*, 78 (II. 9. 29. 1271a) and 84 (II. 11. 4. 1273a).   [61] *Ibid.*, 79 (II. 9. 33. 1271a).
[62] *Ibid.*, 127 (III. 11. 19. 1282b).   [63] *Ibid.*, 143 (III. 15. 10. 1286b).

the interests of equal justice demanded rotation of offices, and hence the supremacy of the law which governed their distribution. The law trained officers to decide according to its principles and also allowed improvements drawn from experience. Anyone trained in the law acquired good judgment and by implication an equal claim to an office. The law was the equivalent of reason, but reason free from all passion.[64] Just as reason ruled an individual man, so it should rule the state. Identical means served to promote goodness in both.[65]

A mixed constitution best assured political virtues. It existed in two possible varieties. 'Polity' blended rich and poor, oligarchy and democracy.[66] 'Aristocracy' was a more perfect form because it added merit to the free birth and wealth which polity united.[67] Nevertheless, Aristotle devoted much more attention to polity. Its strength derived from the fact that no part of the state would favour a new constitution.[68] The 'deliberative element' should be sovereign over war and peace, the making of laws, judgments involving life or property and the distribution and regulation of offices.[69] Its membership was restricted, as in an oligarchy. Only some of the citizens could decide on all matters.[70] Both polity and aristocracy probably came under the head of constitutions which involed rule over one's equals, or 'a knowledge of rule over free men from both points of view', ruler and ruled.[71]

But dangers could spring from the root of this very equality. It was apparently also the best citizens who could legitimately cause most trouble. At least the major kind of sedition Aristotle considered arose from competition among those 'pre-eminent in merit' and their 'passion for equality', although he did concede that the well-born might also be justified in rebelling.[72] Sedition might also arise for other reasons, of which 'a disproportionate increase in some part of the state' posed the most serious threat. A special guard had to be kept against sedition among the 'notables'. An appeal to the corporate metaphor reinforced the point.[73] Aristotle argued that the downfall of both aristocracy and polity came as a result of some injustice in their constitutions, 'a failure to combine different elements properly', while disputes within the royal family or the monarch's effort to rule tyrannically destroyed monarchy, which now became a species of aristocracy.[74] Restraining the royal prerogative in order to prevent the king from losing the willing obedience of his subjects would solve the latter.[75]

---

[64] *Ibid.*, 145–6 (III. 16. 3ff. 1287aff.).   [65] *Ibid.*, 152 (III. 18. 1. 1288b).

[66] *Ibid.*, 175 (IV. 8. 3. 1293b) and cf. Bien, *Grundlegung*, 325.

[67] *Ibid.*, 176 (IV. 8. 9. 1294a).   [68] *Ibid.*, 178 (IV. 9. 10. 1294b).

[69] *Ibid.*, 189 (IV. 15. 3. 1298a).   [70] *Ibid.*, 191 (IV. 14. 8. 1298a).

[71] *Ibid.*, 105 (III. 4. 14. 1277b).   [72] *Ibid.*, 204–5 (V. 1. 6ff. 1301af.).

[73] *Ibid.*, 209 (V. 3. 6. 1302b) and 226 (V. 8. 9. 1308a).

[74] *Ibid.*, 222 (V. 7. 5. 1307a), 241 (V. 10. 36. 1313a) and 235 (V. 10. 1. 1310b).

[75] *Ibid.*, 243 (V. 11. 1. 1313a).

The biological metaphor underlying Aristotle's treatise also appealed to Starkey. For both, the state was something at least partly natural, because it arose ultimately from a biological impulse to sexual union between a man and a woman.[76] The state, like an individual, could only reach its fullest perfection through self-sufficiency, but achieving that goal still depended on biology first and foremost.[77] The first factor in a state was population, and, in order to secure a sufficient number of people, marriage regulation became necessary.[78] From that basis, Aristotle went on to enumerate some of the rest of the necessary elements of the state, highlighting food, crafts, arms, property, public worship and justice. Converting these necessities into political terms, Aristotle concluded that a state had to contain farmers, craftsmen, a military, a propertied class, priests, and a deliberative body.[79] Elsewhere Aristotle provided another list of the necessities of a state, which included wealth, free birth, a 'temper of justice', and a 'martial habit'. The first pair of these was the minimum required of any state, while the second would guarantee a good life.[80] Again, the first pair made up half of Aristotle's definition of the 'quality' which 'quantity' (i.e., numbers) had to balance in any successful constitution. It is of great interest that the second two elements in quality were 'culture and nobility of descent'.[81]

These two schemata provided the outline of Starkey's Dialogue. All he had to do to apply it to England was to go a little beyond Aristotle by equating a military, propertied class with the deliberative body, which, of course, Aristotle did himself when describing aristocracy. Starkey began by explicitly following Aristotle's advice to study how to combine action and contemplation (SP 1/90, fol. 4v). If the business of the commonwealth were directed to living in tranquillity, it would attain its natural perfection (4v–5r). Starkey insisted a little more than Aristotle that the chief virtue was transmitting one's qualities to others, but their basic outlook was clearly one (6v). Starkey gave 'Lupset' a whole catalogue of natural virtues which underlay the commonwealth, but still maintained that they needed man's help in the form of civil law, which could vary according to circumstances (10v). Although Starkey made more of natural law than Aristotle had, they agreed that civil ordinance rested on nature (13r). Starkey proposed in effect to follow the same 'processe wyth ordur' as Aristotle had in the *Politics*: he would begin with the best form of government, compare the state of England to it, isolate the causes of England's problems, and conclude with remedies (17r–v).

In good humanist form, Starkey tried hard to reconcile Aristotle and Plato, but again like his fellow humanists, when he hit an ethical problem at the

[76] *Ibid.*, 3 (I. 1. 2. 1252a).   [77] *Ibid.*, 95 (III. 1. 12. 1275b) and 4 (I. 2. 4ff. 1252b).
[78] *Ibid.*, 290 (VII. 4. 4. 1326a) and 324 (VII. 16. 1ff. 1334b).
[79] *Ibid.*, 299 (VII. 8. 6ff. 1328b).
[80] *Ibid.*, 131 (III. 12. 8–9. 1283a).   [81] *Ibid.*, 185 (IV. 12. 1 and 2. 1296b).

outset, he wound up depending mainly on Aristotle's psychology to explain that ignorance was the root of the commonwealth's problems.[82] The ethical issue resolved, Starkey returned directly to Aristotle's methodological principle of treating the state as a human writ large (21r). Failure to regard the common interest was the fundamental problem, but the commonwealth also required all the necessities Aristotle had detailed. Although Starkey placed more emphasis on friendship for both individual and government than Aristotle had, Aristotle did argue that it would produce unanimity and expel faction.[83] Starkey here went a little beyond Aristotle in order to accommodate Greek political theory to the peculiar circumstances of an aristocratic patronage society like early sixteenth-century England. He may have had to bend over backwards to emphasize friendship because many Tudor people thought one could never trust friends.[84] Returning to Aristotle's agenda, Starkey began with health and riches. Virtue came only thereafter, even though it was most important (22v–23r). Starkey underscored the importance of wealth more than Aristotle had in order to expand Aristotle's point that happiness demanded both (25v–29r). Like Aristotle, Starkey recognized that fortune could take a hand in determining a man's wealth, but the truly virtuous man could overcome difficulties and could not be fully happy without prosperity. Starkey offered a consolation Aristotle could not: the person, no matter how virtuous, who could not overcome adversity on earth could still get his reward in heaven (41v). Starkey adhered so closely to Aristotle here that he not only rejected Plato's notion that the body was a prison, but also the 'doctryne of Chryst' on contempt of the present life (28v).

In the course of developing his basically Aristotelian corporate metaphor, Starkey accidentally approached Marsilio's image. The first requisite, the 'ground of the commyn wele', was 'a convenyent multytude', but Starkey did not originally pursue this point. Instead he turned to a consideration of the parts of the body politic, a section where he exercised his ingenuity in common with his numerous predecessors (30v). Despite the similarity of Marsilio's and Starkey's images, Starkey refused to use his to make the points Marsilio had. Both accorded priority to the heart, but Starkey's notion of who should be likened to it was much more restrictive. Where Marsilio wrote about 'the soul of the whole body of the citizens' acting through the heart, Starkey simply compared it to 'the pryncys & rularys of the state'. Once more, both agreed that the heart gave rise to the natural powers of the body

---

[82] SP 1/90, fols. 18v–20v. E. Garin, *Storia della filosofia italiana*, II, 748–9 discusses humanist syncretism.

[83] SP 1/90, fol. 22r; Aristotle, *Ethica*, 471 (VIII. 1. 1155a).

[84] For some overstated ideas about Tudor attitudes to friends, see L. B. Smith, *Treason in Tudor England: politics and paranoia*, especially chapter 2.

and the rulers or the citizens to the law, but the fundamental emphasis remained different.[85] For Starkey, the heads and rulers put the law into effect, while for Marsilio that fell to the whole body of citizens.

At the beginning of his consideration of the best constitution, the best form of the 'commyn wele', Starkey reproduced Aristotle's typology of governmental forms. This he tied to an Aristotelian notion of law as something which gradually achieved perfection as men constantly worked to improve it (34r). Any one of three constitutions could produce perfect laws, depending on the nature of the people who lived under it, but all alike had to aim at directing the 'hole commynalty' to virtue through 'polytyke rule, cyvyle ordur & juste [ab.] pollycy' (35r). In Starkey's hands, these forms of government quickly became types of 'complexyons', of which he preferred the 'sanguyne' rule of an elected prince (38r). This elected prince, of course, made Starkey's version of monarchy just as much an aristocracy as kingship had become in Aristotle's mind. As we have seen, the late-medieval Aristotelian Tolomeo da Lucca used language almost identical to Starkey's to describe Aristotle's theory of aristocracy. Baumer was wrong in thinking that Starkey was any kind of democrat, any more than Marsilio or Aristotle.

In addition to newer views of late-medieval Aristotelianism, rehabilitation of the rest of the alternative 'sources' for Starkey's ideas which Baumer considered but summarily discarded pull the rug from under him. The importance of Italian models to Starkey should be clear, and there is no reason to belabour the obvious point that the 'republican' atmosphere of Padua nurtured both Marsilio's and Starkey's ideas, the only difference between them being that Marsilio could still imagine working republican institutions, while Starkey could only learn about them in theory, or as transferred to the church. Again, significant elements of Marsilio's own context were still directly available to Starkey two hundred years later. For example, the *Dialogus inter militem et clericum* was printed in England in 1530. It sprang from the same circle of Philip the Fair's apologists as shaped Marsilio's ideas, and might almost have served as a blueprint for Cromwell's policy, even if its anti-clericalism and imperial language would have meant less to Starkey.[86]

If Starkey's relation to Marsilio's own context must remain hypothetical, his place in native English tradition deserves more attention.[87] In effect, Elton

---

[85] SP 1/90, fol. 31v and Marsilio, *Defensor*, I. xv. 6. (p.70). If Marsilio's usage is any indication, it would appear that the equation between the soul and civil law is not 'peculiar to English writers', as Newcombe suggests, although it is uncommon elsewhere; '"Due order and reasonabul mean"', 68.   [86] A. J. Perry, ed., *Dialogus inter militem et clericum.*

[87] Beckmann proposed a similar argument, but left it undeveloped. He suggested that *Magna carta* and the provisions of Oxford may have provided models for Starkey's constable, and asserted that Starkey's actual design derived from the Lancastrian privy council. 'Staatstheorie', 93–4.

was absolutely correct that Starkey's proposals looked like the barons' platforms. Even so, it is not always easy to pin down precisely where Starkey
looked for information about his predecessors. Some elements of his theory
have fairly pronounced parallels in existing sources, others do not. Perhaps
Starkey, despite all his humanist training, was no better at history than the
team which cobbled up one of the draft preambles to the Act in Restraint of
Appeals.[88] Nevertheless, Starkey meant his case to rest on a serious interpretation of England's past. He insisted, for example, that the abuse of hereditary
monarchy had been 'perceyvyd by our for fatherys days at dyverse & many
tymys' (68r; cf. 65v). Again, no matter how far-fetched a particular interpretation, early sixteenth-century Englishmen still alleged sources for their reading of history. Starkey could not have invented his portrait of the constable,
which he had allegedly derived from the behaviour of 'our old aunceturys'. If
it cannot be documented in public records, perhaps it rested on lost private
traditions, in this case descending through Edward Stafford, Duke of
Buckingham.

Pole was closely connected to Buckingham through the marriage of his
sister Ursula to Buckingham's heir which took place in 1519, shortly before
Henry Stafford was disgraced by his father's attainder.[89] Unlike many of
Buckingham's other marriage alliances, this one seems to have produced
reasonably cordial relations between Poles and Staffords.[90] When Buckingham went to the Tower in 1521, Pole's brothers Henry Lord Montagu and
Geoffrey accompanied him, though not by choice. Henry (or Wolsey) suspected Pole himself sufficiently for Henry to write to the Venetian Signory
warning it not to honour Pole too highly, lest he become as corrupt as his
brothers and relatives.[91] His mother, the Countess of Salisbury, also fell under
a cloud, but she was not forced to withdraw from court. Catherine protected
her, perhaps because she was just beginning her stint as the Princess Mary's
governess.[92] Not that Buckingham could have taught either Pole or Starkey
much about effective opposition. Both Barbara Harris and David Starkey
agree that in politics Buckingham was 'reactionary not innovative',
as Dr Starkey puts it.[93] Nevertheless, the furore Buckingham had raised over

[88] J. A. Guy, 'Thomas Cromwell and the intellectual origins of the Henrician revolution', in Fox
and Guy, *Henrician age*, especially 162–3.

[89] Henry Pole did not marry the daughter of the George Lord Bergavenny who was Buckingham's son-in-law, but rather of that Lord Bergavenny who married Margaret, daughter of Sir
Hugh Fenne. My thanks to Barbara J. Harris for correcting the mistake I made in 'Faction and
ideology: Thomas Starkey's *Dialogue*', 18.

[90] B. J. Harris, *Edward Stafford, third duke of Buckingham*, 61.

[91] *CSPV*, III, 204 (p. 120). Cf. *LP*, III:1, 1268.   [92] See her *DNB* entry.

[93] D. Starkey, *The reign of Henry VIII: personalities and politics*, 83, and Harris, *Buckingham*,
58 and 178, where she goes further and argues that Buckingham did not lead any 'coherent
aristocratic faction'.

the constableship coupled with his fall must have left echoes in both Pole's and Starkey's minds.

Other sources which could have caused trouble were apparently destroyed during Henry's reign, among them chronicles with inflammatory political content.[94] Many other chronicles to which Starkey probably had access, especially his fellow Cheshireman Ranulf Higden's *Polychronicon*, treat the upheavals of the thirteenth and fourteenth centuries cursorily.[95] It may be that the 'aristocratic' sources on which Starkey drew have simply disappeared. Nevertheless, we can document more than enough points of contact between Starkey and the late middle ages to obviate the necessity of any such speculation, and the balance of the evidence suggests that Pole catalysed Starkey's penchant for an aristocratic interpretation of English history and the English constitution.[96]

Pole has enjoyed enormous success in passing on his self-created image to historians. One element of his *persona* which he saw fit to downplay was his aristocratic behaviour and his sympathy with his fellow aristocrats. Nevertheless, Pole adhered to the traditions and attitudes of his order. Beginning at least with *De unitate*, Pole emphasized his Plantagenet descent, even if Cardinal Contarini recommended that Pole cut this passage.[97] Pole deduced that Henry's plans for the succession indicated that he intended to dispose of the nobility, and accused the king of holding the nobles in contempt.[98] Jean-Pierre Moreau judges that Pole's ideas of how to resist Henry from this point forward come closest to the plans of his fellow aristocrats.[99] Throughout his life Pole continued both to cling to his own ancestry and to defend the rest of the English nobility. In the course of his *apologia* to Protector Somerset, Pole highlighted his family's standing and how much it deserved royal

[94] In *A proper dyaloge betwene a gentillman and a husbandman* (c. 1530; ed. Edward Arber, 168), one of the speakers charged 'they destroyed cronicles not longe a gone ... for certeyne poyntes unreverently soundynge agaynst the kynges auncestrye as they say'. I owe this reference to the kindness of J. D. Alsop.

[95] John Bale recorded several MSS of Higden's work in Magdalen's library. *Index britanniae scriptorum*, ed. R. L. Poole and Mary Bateson, 489 and 492. John Taylor noted a total of five full and partial copies at present in the same place. *The universal chronicle of Ranulf Higden*, 157.

[96] Guy also suggests that Pole probably put Starkey in touch with some version of aristocratic political thinking. 'The king's council and political participation', in Fox and Guy, *Henrician age*, 141. Cf. Beckmann, 'Staatstheorie', 84, who overstated the case a little by claiming that 'Starkeys Kritik an den englischen Verhältnissen zeugt ganz deutlich, dass er in Opposition zur Tudor Monarchie steht'. His goal was the same as that of the *Adelsopposition*: reducing the king to *primus inter pares*. This last is undoubtedly true, but it took Starkey a while to translate the platform of the Dialogue into real opposition.

[97] T. F. Dunn, 'The development of the text of Pole's *De unitate ecclesiae*', 463.

[98] Reginald Pole, *Ad Henricum octavum Britanniae regem, pro ecclesiasticae unitatis defensione*, fols. LXXXIr and LXXXIIIr.

[99] J. -P. Moreau, *Rome ou l'Angleterre?*, 251.

favour.[100] In another letter written to the Marquess of Exeter's son Edward Courtenay after Mary's accession, Pole exalted in the new queen's justice which could be seen especially clearly in her decision to release Courtenay, 'the flower of the ancient nobility of England which its adversaries sought especially to destroy root and branch'. Pole reminded Courtenay that Henry Pole had been executed at the same time as Exeter, which created a natural tie between the two of them. Exeter had been the last noble to talk to Pole before the latter went into exile twenty years earlier. He had told Pole:

Lord cousin Pole, your departure from the realm at this present time shows in what a miserable state we find ourselves. It is to the universal shame of all us nobles, who allow you to absent yourself when we ought most to avail ourselves of your presence but being unable to find any other remedy for this, we pray God to find it himself.[101]

Pole obviously hoped to work his passage back to England by appealing to Courtenay's fellow-feeling and Pole's aristocratic pride is clear. He apparently made much of his royal blood in conversation with the imperial agent Martin de Çornoça in Venice, and Chapuys stressed his leading role in the White Rose, too.[102] Pole's first biographer, Ludovico Beccadelli recounted a brief summary of English faction struggles from the time of Edward III, highlighting both the role of the White Rose and Pole's royal descent.[103] Pole's close adviser Niccolò Ormanetto alleged that Pole explained the whole of the English Reformation from the fact that the bishops were neither nobles themselves nor allied to any of them. Indeed, according to Pole, John Fisher was the only member of the episcopate who was even a gentleman.[104] And Pole's grandfather, of course, was the notorious troublemaker the Duke of Clarence.

Pole proposed to restrain Henry in much more violent fashion than Starkey, whether by popular rebellion or outside intervention. Starkey instead went back to constitutional traditions of the late middle ages for some of the inspiration for his conciliar checks on royal authority. He hoped to tip the balance in the system of divided sovereignty back towards the nobility, who had held it until they fumbled it away during Henry VI's reign, and had often expressed their programmes in the language of the common weal.[105] The only thing 'radical' about Starkey's ideas was his attempt to revive an older system of government which had begun to decline from the accession of Henry VII. Their most remote roots probably go back to the reign of Edward II, and both

---

[100] Biblioteca marciana, Venice, MS Ital. X. 24 (6527), fol. 16v (*CSPV*, V, 575).

[101] *CSPV*, V, 806 (quoting the calendar summary, given in quotations in the original).

[102] *CSPSp*, V:1, 80 (Çornoça) and 109 (Chapuys).

[103] Ludovico Beccadelli, 'Vita del cardinale Reginaldo Polo', 278–9.

[104] Moreau, *Rome ou l'Angleterre?*, 142.

[105] B. Wilkinson, *Constitutional history of England in the fifteenth century*, 222 and *passim* for common weal language. C. Richmond, 'After McFarlane', surveys recent writing about the fifteenth century nobility, stressing its blundering, especially 47–8 and 57.

the Lancastrian opposition and a 'neutral' royal official. Starkey apparently combined the 'Tract on the steward' with the 'Modus tenendi parliamentum' to give him his theory of the constable and his council.[106]

According to the former, the steward's office required him to 'supervise and regulate below the king and immediately after the king all the kingdom of England and all the lesser ministers of the law and peace and war'. Any matters which came before the king's council but did not receive justice fell to the steward to remedy. He should force all officials to do their duty. The common good offered his overriding standard. If evil councillors threatened to subvert the king, the steward could associate the constable and a committee of twenty-five other magnates and members of the *communitas* of England with himself in order to preserve the kingdom. He and the committee could go so far as to raise war against the king's bad advisers *pro bono puplico*, if the king refused to stop listening to them.[107] As Bertie Wilkinson commented, the stewards always led the opposition to the king, who proposed instead to replace them with the constable.[108] For some reason, Starkey reversed these two offices. It seems likely that the celebrated troubles of the Duke of Buckingham inspired his confusion, or perhaps the high stewardship, which had been absorbed into the crown under Henry IV, was too nearly a red flag because of its 'impossibly viceregal pretensions'.[109]

It may also be that the form in which Starkey read the 'Modus' influenced his decision to substitute constable for steward. The 'B' recension of the 'Modus' was always bound together with the 'Tract on the constable and marshall'.[110] Even if neither constable nor marshal is painted in the colours of the steward, their titles were readily available to Starkey. The 'Modus' was once considered a political tract like the 'Steward', but it now appears to have been a manual for lawyers explaining the workings of parliament, even if it was probably written during the crisis of 1321.[111] There is no evidence that the tract ever figured in political controversy.[112] Instead, it offered the only source for the origin and nature of parliament available in the late middle ages. By the early sixteenth century its 'main era' had passed, but numerous copies attest to its popularity before that.[113] The earliest copy may have been

---

[106] At Dr Starkey's urging, I here revive a theory I had abandoned earlier because of difficulties in pinning down the connections between Starkey and his medieval predecessors. Some of those problems still remain.

[107] Quoted in L. W. V. Harcourt, *His grace the steward and the trial of peers*, 164–6.

[108] B . Wilkinson, *Constitutional history of medieval England, 1216–1399*, III, 362.

[109] D. Starkey, 'The lords of the council: aristocracy, ideology and the formation of the Tudor privy council', note 53.

[110] N. Pronay and J. Taylor, eds., *Parliamentary texts of the later middle ages*, 21.

[111] *Ibid.*, 6–7.   [112] *Ibid.*, 14.

[113] *Ibid.*, 49, 52, 203, 206. Dr Starkey has discovered another copy in the Isabella Stewart Gardner Museum in Boston. See 'Stewart serendipity: a missing text of the *Modus tenendi parliamentum*'.

compiled for Thomas Mowbray when he was earl marshal in the 1380s.[114]

The 'Modus' offered Starkey authoritative proof that a system like that envisaged in the 'Tract on the steward' had actually existed. In the event of 'discord between the king and some magnates, or perhaps between the magnates themselves' or of war or some difficult legal case over which the king and his council could not agree, then the steward, the constable and the marshal, or any two of them, elected twenty-five people 'from all the peers of the kingdom, that is to say two bishops & three proctors for all the clergy, two earls and three barons, five knights of the shires, five citizens & five burgesses'. These in turn could progressively reduce their number, even down to one until a decision was made.[115] According to the opening of the 'Modus', this system had existed from the time of Edward the Confessor.[116]

The precise mechanics described do not fit Starkey's system very closely, nor does the 'Modus's' general view of parliament which made the commons its constitutive element.[117] The committee of twenty-five was to guard against anything being done behind the commons' back and without their consent.[118] Nevertheless, the 'Modus' could have given Starkey some historical support for his scheme. Read in the light of other nearly contemporary proposals, it could become another sign of how much the nobility relied on councils. Even in the relatively stable reign of Edward III it was proposed in parliament that elected magnates should 'continually supervise the business of the king and of the realm'. They could hear legal cases held up in the courts and 'call to account all the ministers of the king'.[119] By the early fifteenth century, the magnates had achieved a commanding position, in part because of their role in Henry IV's seizure of the crown in 1399 and in part because of their prominence in notions of reform. It was to this age that Starkey looked for inspiration, hence his conservatism. Starkey's designs came even closer to Henry IV's own constitutional expedients, especially the king's appointment of both lords and citizens of London to his council.[120] The basic pattern of Lancastrian government by council had been established. All that remained to set the stage for the struggles over Henry VI was for an inner core of magnates to assert their right to dominate the council, which they did very quickly in opposition to Humphrey of Gloucester's moves in the late 1420s.

---

[114] *Parliamentary texts*, 18n and 20.   [115] *Ibid.*, 87 and 107.   [116] *Ibid.*, 103.

[117] *Ibid.*, 37. Cf. especially chapter xxiii, 'De auxilio regis', for the commons as defining element. For a different view – that both 'Modus' and Starkey reflected a 'representative ideal' and that Starkey borrowed from the 'Modus' – see Guy, 'King's council', 123 and 141.

[118] *Parliamentary texts*, 108.

[119] D. W. Hanson, *From kingdom to commonwealth: the development of civic consciousness in English political thought*, 170.

[120] Wilkinson, *Constitutional history of England in the fifteenth century*, 222–4 and cf. 237. Beckmann recognized the precedent of the 'Lancastrian constitution', but understood it as Stubbs had. Beckmann, 'Staatstheorie, 94.

Humphrey's enemies even went so far as to claim to exercise the full authority of the house of lords when that body was not in session.[121] Starkey could almost have drawn on the settlement of 1427 for his proposal that the London council exercise parliament's authority during the latter's absence. It survives in two copies, and its central contention was confirmed on the parliament roll of 1428.[122] This system disappeared after Henry VI's minority ended, but the precedent remained for Starkey.

Sir John Fortescue summarized Lancastrian ideas for reform of the government and perhaps put them into the form most accessible to Starkey; at least a number of fifteenth- and sixteenth-century manuscripts of the work survive.[123] Reviving an older argument, Lorenzo d'Avack claimed Fortescue's overriding influence on Starkey as a nearly sufficient explanation of Starkey's ideas.[124] Undoubtedly they both saw themselves at some point as spokesmen of reform parties and both proposed conciliar solutions to the English king's difficulties, but these differ considerably in detail and rationale. Most fundamentally, Fortescue insisted that the magnates be excluded from the council, because they were most interested in preventing reform.[125] Instead, twenty-four professionals should swamp four temporal and spiritual peers in a new council. The councillors were to take no fee from any but the king. They should coopt replacements, although the king could add four of each kind of lord every year. The great officers of state could attend, and the chancellor could preside. All difficult matters of 'pollycye' fell within their purview, including improvements in the law.[126] If the 'Example what good counseill helpith' is genuine, Fortescue drew on the same examples of Rome, Sparta and Athens which Starkey used, and also left no doubt that these councillors were intended to restrain the royal excesses which overly great dependence on 'private Counselloures' had produced. But Stanley Chrimes doubted the authenticity of this work and observed that otherwise Fortescue's reforms had the effect of strengthening the executive, the last thing on Starkey's

---

[121] Wilkinson, *Constitutional history of England in the fifteenth century*, 222 and 229.
[122] *Ibid.*, 248, and cf. Hanson, *Civic consciousness*, 186 and S. B. Chrimes, *English constitutional ideas in the fifteenth century*, 36, 148–50.
[123] For the manuscripts, see C. Plummer's edition of Sir John Fortescue, *The governance of England*, 87–93. Five of the ten probably date from Starkey's time or earlier. C. A. J. Skeel ignored this problem in 'The influence of the writings of Sir John Fortescue'.
[124] L. d'Avack, 'La teoria della monarchia mista nell'Inghilterra del cinquecento e seicento', 582–4. J. W. Allen first pointed to some connection between Fortescue and Starkey. *A history of political thought in the sixteenth century*, 151, and Baumer also floated such a prospect, 'Marsilius', 190. David Starkey makes a somewhat similar case by placing Fortescue and Starkey in the same relation to their respective reforming parties. 'Public debate and public policy: the course of reform, 1440–1540', unpublished paper. I am grateful to Dr Starkey for letting me see a copy.
[125] Fortescue, *Governance*, 145–6.   [126] *Ibid.*, 148.

mind.[127] Fortescue was still very much in the tradition of mirrors of princes: bad advice was the problem, not royal tyranny. True, both Fortescue and Starkey argued that a conciliar system would restore the commonwealth to health and England to greatness, but the widespread diffusion of similar ideas makes this a doubtful argument to rely upon. As in the case of Starkey and his Italian friends, it seems more likely that a common environment and common constitutional tradition explain the similarities between Fortescue and Starkey better than a hypothesis of direct influence.

The suggestion that Starkey owed something to Fortescue or to late medieval aristocratic tradition in general goes against the prevailing interpretation of him as an anomaly in an age when most social critics attributed a 'divine right' to the nobility, as J. W. Allen put it.[128] George Bernard agrees with Allen's general assessment, but goes beyond him by noting that even those critical of the nobility wound up offering 'vigorous justifications' of it.[129] Although Starkey does not figure in Bernard's impressionistic survey of early Tudor public opinion, the same was true of him. Starkey was no hostile critic of the nobility like Thomas More. A comparison with Edmund Dudley, a man often labelled the last exponent of purely medieval political thinking in England, and with John Skelton, usually portrayed as a rock-ribbed conservative, offers the best measure of Starkey's position. Many of the particulars of Dudley's *Tree of Commonwealth* recur in Starkey's *Dialogue*, despite the superficially much more conservative appearance of Dudley's work. In fact, Dudley is the more 'modern' of the two in his exaltation of the power of the prince at the expense of the nobility. Nevertheless, Dudley analysed the problems of the nobility in exactly the same way as Starkey, and proposed the same solution, even if in less detail and to newer political ends. Although Skelton's case is more difficult, much the same is true of him.

Dudley made some of the same proposals as Fortescue about restraining the magnates' influence, but he still came back to the basic proposition that example of superiors held the commonwealth together.[130] Dudley often wrote in this moralistic fashion, but could be as 'realistic' as Starkey about the role of poverty as the mother of all vice, especially discord. Nevertheless, like Starkey Dudley insisted that concord rested on the static basis of 'a good agreement and conformytie emongest the people or the inhabitauntes of a realme, Citie, towne or fellowship, and every man to be content to do his dewtie in thoffice, rome, or condision that he is sett in, And not to maling or disdaine any other' (40). This, of course, is conventional enough, as was Dudley's plea for indifferent justice from the king, but he continued much as

---

[127] *Ibid.*, 348. John Fortescue, *De laudibus legum Anglie*, ed. S. B. Chrimes, lxxvii and Chrimes, *Constitutional ideas*, 331.
[128] Allen, *Political thought*, 137.
[129] G. W. Bernard, *The power of the early Tudor nobility*, 185.
[130] Edmund Dudley, *The tree of commonwealth*, ed. D. M. Brodie, 34–5 and cf. 42.

Starkey did by arguing that 'the Prince must specially see yt the nobles of his realme be not at variance one with an other ... For if men be at ther owne liberties therin beware the Prince in a while' (41). Dudley, of course, emphasized the danger to the prince, rather than to the commonwealth as Starkey would have.

Dudley placed the burden of establishing concord on the 'chivalrie' of England, which included everyone from 'other gentlemen by office or authoritie' on up (44). They, like the rest of Englishmen, had to live 'after the honour and degre yt god and his prince hath callid hym unto', neither envying their superiors nor contemning those below them. Acceptance of their lot would fit the nobility to assist the prince in guarding both church and 'commynaltie' (45). Good education would ensure that the nobility deserved (and could maintain) its position, while other measures would preserve the nobility's standing above the lower orders, exactly as Starkey argued.

For be you suer it is not Honorable blood and great possession, or riche apparell, yt makyth a man honorable, Hym self being of unhonorable condicions; and the more honorable in blood yt he is the more noble in condicions he ought to be ... Therefore, you noble men, for the better contynewaunce of your Blood in honor sett your childeren in youth ... to the lerning of vertue and conning, and at the lest bring them up in honor and vertue.

Dudley continued with the harsh judgment that 'the noble men and gentlemen of England be the worst brought up ... of any realme of christendom', but this did not make him an opponent of aristocracy, any more than it did Starkey (44–5).

Far from it. Dudley intended to guard its position in the same fashion Starkey did, by preventing the lower orders from aping the nobility (46). Englishmen could not 'take and pull from this tree at libertie', but only so much as they needed and the commons had to work for its living (53 and 55). It should realize that the equal distribution of virtue did not entail that riches were evenly divided. To clinch the case, Dudley appealed to the macrocosm and the order God had fixed by grace between 'hym self and Angell, and betwene Angell and Angell; and by reason betwene the Angell and man, and betwene man and man, man and beest'. Reason was unequally distributed, and those who had more of it were most fit to rule (90). But in the end Dudley was less conservative than Starkey, since he aimed to exalt the prince over the nobility by arguing, for example, that all the 'honorable dignitie' of the nobility and gentry was at the disposal of the king. They should not 'presume to take it of ther owne auctorite' (57).

The accepted line on Skelton makes him, like Dudley, a defender of strong monarchy, but in contrast to Dudley an equally staunch partisan of the existing nobility. According to K. B. McFarlane's interpretation of the relations between king and magnates in the late middle ages, this is only what one might expect. The nobility wanted a strong monarch in order to relieve them of the burdens of governing and keep the pump of favours well primed.[131] But Skelton did not think about aristocracy that simply. Perhaps because of the blinkers imposed by outmoded historiographical categories, most critics have missed Skelton's insistence that the nobilty had to earn back its rightful place, that it as much as the king bore responsibility for England's slide to wrack and ruin.[132] The means, as for Starkey and Dudley, was education. Granted, Skelton came to distrust the sort of humanist learning Starkey advocated, but their vision of the problem and their suggested remedy were otherwise at one. Even those interpreters who have done most to make Skelton's message simultaneously quietist and universal (and hence reduce its political import in context) have had to admit that Skelton was at bottom an activist, albeit usually a disappointed one.[133] Skelton and Starkey also shared much the same attitude to the church, even if Skelton defended its privileges more quickly. Fundamentally, the (noble) prelates had failed to set a proper example, especially through regular preaching. Skelton's reputation as a dyed-in-the-wool archconservative may be a little unfair. A comparison of Starkey and Skelton is particularly apt because Starkey could not have expected his readers to overlook the pronounced parallels between his diagnosis of the 'frencey' in the head of the commonwealth and Skelton's strident insistence on exactly the same problem. And, of course, in both cases the cause was autocratic rule. Starkey had no better an opinion of Wolsey than Skelton.

Skelton's critical stance *vis-à-vis* the nobility comes out even in his early 'Upon the Dolorous Dethe ... of the Mooste Honorable Erle of Northumberlande'. The poem is a paean to Northumberland's noble virtue, a tirade against the commoners who murdered him and an equally bitter recrimination against his noble retainers who failed in their responsibility to defend their lord. The fourth Earl of Northumberland had been the commons' 'moste singlar goode lord', 'So noble a man, so valiaunt lorde and knyght / Fulfilled with honour', whose household contained large numbers of gentry as menial servants, but Skelton blamed the latter first for their master's death.[134] True, the commons had risen against their 'naturall lord' (line 54), but only after Northumberland's 'awne servauntis of trust' had run away

---

131 K. B. McFarlane, *The nobility of later medieval England*, 120–1.
132 This is especially true of S. E. Fish's interpretation, which depended on a framework which opposed the centralizing efforts of Wolsey and the middle class against aristocratic conservatism. This amounts almost to a New Critical reading. S. E. Fish, *John Skelton's poetry*, especially 127. It is also true even of David Bevington's analysis, who finds simply that 'Skelton's political values were those of the old nobility', a conclusion based on analysis of 'Magnyfycence'. D. Bevington, *Tudor drama and politics*, 55.
133 Fish, *Skelton's poetry*, 173–6.
134 I cite by line number(s) throughout from the edition of J. Scattergood, *John Skelton: the complete English poems*. The reference here is lines 25–35.

(lines 36–42). Skelton repeated that refrain throughout the remainder of the poem. Northumberland had tried to defend the 'welle concernyng of all the hole lande', for which cause the commons killed him, 'But had his nobillmen donn well that day / Ye had not ben hable to have saide hym nay' (lines 64–70). Again, 'the nobelnes of the northe' (Northumberland) had stood up to the commons single-handedly,

> Trustinge in noble men that wer with hym there;
> Bot all they fled from hym for falsehode or fere
> Barons, knightis, squyers, one and alle,
> ... Turnd ther backis and let ther master fall,
> Of whos lyfe they countede not a fly. (lines 85–95)

Skelton's world may have turned on natural aristocrats, but it still contained a large number of nobles who failed to measure up.

In this early poem Skelton suggested no remedy other than penance by these traitors and their heirs (lines 183–9). Nor did he go beyond fairly conventional advice to the nobility in his play 'Magnyfycence', which ended with the equally conventional and quietist moral 'For the welthe of this worlde can not indure' (line 2558). Nevertheless, Skelton had by then spent 2500 odd lines elaborating on his text:

> But yf prudence be proved with sad cyrcumspeccyon,
> Welthe myght be wonne and made to the lure,
> Yf noblenesse were aquayntyd with sober dyreccyon.
> But wyll hath reason so under subjeccyon,
> And so dysordereth this worlde all,
> That welthe and felicite is passynge small. (lines 16–21)

Skelton's identification of felicity with material wealth (cf. the contrast between 'prosperyte and welthe' [line 140] and 'poverte and nede' [line 153]) combined with his sharp criticism of the behaviour of nobles in squandering both wilfully recall Starkey. Likewise, the worst thing for a lord was to 'use free lyberte' (line 1598). The nobility mistook wanton spending for the liberality they should exercise wisely (lines 2117ff.). Skelton apparently intended to give them a lesson in self-control, reason (and measure) over will.

'Magnyfycence' may well have been played before Henry at a time when Skelton, whatever his original reservations about the life of a courtier, still enjoyed royal favour.[135] By the early 1520s that had changed and Skelton began to write increasingly savage attacks on Wolsey's ascendancy, which also incorporated more and more shrill barbs against the nobility for letting Wolsey get away with his usurpation. 'Speke, Parott' was the first of these poems, and the most difficult to interpret. Whatever the ins and outs of Skelton's poetic art, his critical attitude to the nobility seems clear. Rule by

[135] *Ibid.*, 433–4.

one man alone posed the central problem (lines 329–34), but after further consideration, Parott heated up his rhetoric.

> Frantiknes dothe rule and all thyng commaunde;
> Wylfulnes and Braynles now rule all the raye.
> Agayne Frentike Frensey there dar no man say nay,
> For Frantiknes and Wylfulnes and Braynles ensembyll,
> The nebbis of a lyon they make to trete and trembyll.   (lines 420–4)

As Stanley Fish well described, it took Parott a while to work up the courage to blast Wolsey like that, but once the opportunity arose, he did not waste it.[136] The remainder of the poem catalogued at length the sorry state of England. Undoubtedly A. R. Heiserman correctly placed these lines in a long tradition of 'complaint against the times', but this interpretation obscures the specific content of Skelton's diatribe and reduces its political significance.[137] It is no exaggeration to say that Skelton's polemic lists almost exactly the chief grievances Starkey pointed to in his Dialogue. Skelton began by lamenting 'So many morall maters, and so lytell usyd', but quickly passed to more tangible complaints.

> So prodigall expence, and so shamfull reconyng;
> So gorgyous garmentes, and so muche wrechydnese,
> So myche portlye pride, with pursys penyles.[138]   (lines 458–60)

If this was not aimed at the nobility (as it may well have been), the next section on the state of politics most assuredly took them to task.

> So myche poletyke pratyng, and so lytell stondythe in stede;
> So lytell secretnese, and so myche grete councell;
> So manye bolde barons, there hertes as dull as lede;
> So many nobyll bodyes, undyr on dawys hedd.   (lines 464–8)

The nobles also may have come in for criticism later for 'So myche bely-joye, and so wastefull banketyng' and 'So many howgye howsys byldying and so small howse-holdyng' (lines 492 and 494).[139] Next came the common weal.

> So many complayntes, and so smalle redresse;
> … So myche losse of merchaundyse, and so remedyles;
> So lytell care for the commynweal, and so myche nede.   (lines 470–3)

Then came the legal system. 'So many thevys hangyd, and thevys neverthelesse; So myche presonment, for matyrs not worth a hawe', in addition to many worthless laws and too harsh punishments (lines 477–83). Skelton also noted 'So many vacabondes, so many beggers bolde', but rather than treating

---

[136] Fish, *Skelton's poetry*, 167–71.   [137] A. R. Heiserman, *Skelton and satire*, 168–89.
[138] Cf. Starkey's catalogue of grievances against the nobles in SP 1/90, fol. 84v.
[139] Scattergood (*Poems*, 464) thinks these both may refer to Wolsey.

this problem systematically as Starkey or More would have, Skelton apparently blamed it on 'cheryte so colde' (lines 498–500). There were differences of approach between Skelton and Starkey.

After 'Speke, Parott' Skelton had one more constructive step to take. In 'Collyn Clout' he once again raised the heat of his language against Wolsey, but now he had a solution to suggest. To better a situation 'where the prelates be / Come of lowe degre' (lines 585–6) it was necessary that

> Ye bysshoppes of estates [which may mean noblemen]
> Shulde open the brode gates
> For your spiritual charge,
> And com forthe at large,
> Lyke lanternes of lyght,
> In the peoples syght,
> In pulpyttes authentyke,
> For the wele publyke'.[140]   (lines 690–7)

Wolsey not merely overawed the church; he did the same thing with the nobility. Skelton suggested a similar solution. Whereas he had merely berated the nobles for their foolishness in the past, now he told them to get an education. Addressing Wolsey directly, Skelton observed fairly calmly

> For the lordes temporall,
> Theyr rule is very small,
> Almoost nothynge at all.
> Men say howe ye appalle
> The noble bloode royall
> In ernest and in game.[141]
> Ye are the lesse to blame,
> For lordes of noble bloode,
> Yf they well understode
> Howe connynge myght them avaunce,
> They wolde pype you another daunce.
> But noble men borne,
> To lerne they have scorne,
> But hunte and blowe an horne,
> Lepe over lakes and dykes,
> Set nothynge by polytykes.   (lines 608–23)

Starkey put these points no more strongly.

Skelton could express his disapprobation of the present nobility even more forcefully, though. 'Collyn Clout' again ended on a quietist note, but 'Why Come Ye Nat to Courte?', Skelton's most obvious attack on Wolsey, did not, even if it may have sputtered out in one last helpless expletive 'A daucock ye

---

[140] See Scattergood's gloss on 'estate' here, but his case is not entirely convincing. This problem highlights the need for a comprehensive study of early Tudor political vocabulary.

[141] Scattergood suggested that these lines may refer to Buckingham. Skelton called Buckingham's daughter his patron. Harris, *Buckingham*, 48.

be, and so shal be styl!' Instead, it opened with what John Scattergood calls 'a generalized indictment of the nobility'.[142] As Skelton put it bluntly later on, 'Our nobles are gone' (line 922). At the beginning of the poem, Skelton berated the nobility for, well, behaving like 'medieval' boors. They were too quick to take offence, too prodigal, too haughty, too stupid, too credulous, too easily deluded (lines 1–28). Worse, they were too timid.

> Our barons be so bolde,
> Into a mouse hole they wolde
> Rynne away and crepe;
> ... For drede of the mastyve cur,
> For drede of the bochers dogge
> Wold wyrry them lyke an hogge.[143]   (lines 292–9)

Instead, they let Wolsey's 'ierarchy / Of frantycke frenesy' take its course (lines 185–6). This led Skelton to his most explicit statement of political principle, and one which accords exactly with Starkey's basic credo.

> It is a nyce reconynge
> To put all the governynge,
> All the rule of this lande,
> Into one mannys hande;
> One wyse mannys hede
> May stande somwhat in stede.
> But the wyttys of the many wyse
> Moche better can devyse
> By theyr cyrcumspection,
> And theyr sad dyrection,
> To cause the commune weale
> Longe to endure in heale.   (lines 760–71)

Skelton was a poet, not a politician. Nor did he have Starkey's advantages of education and broad experience. Consequently, his hopes were dashed much more resoundingly than Starkey's ever were (at least until Skelton's reconciliation with Wolsey), but Skelton and Starkey intended nearly identical things. If Skelton was a conservative, then so was Starkey. Undoubtedly they differed over the means to reform the aristocracy, and Alistair Fox argues convincingly that this disagreement reveals that Skelton was no humanist.[144] The distinction between Skelton and Starkey should not be minimized, but it extends no further than literary matters. In some of the

---

[142] *Poems*, 482.

[143] Fish read these two passages against one another in order to give 'retroactive irony' to the first apparently 'open call to action' and thus concluded that the poem was only a piece of 'personal spite'. *Skelton's poetry*, 212, 217, 211. Whatever value this may have as a literary interpretation, Fish's criticism does not affect the reading of Skelton's disappointment in the nobility offered here.

[144] Alistair Fox, 'Facts and fallacies: interpreting English humanism', in Fox and Guy, *Henrician age*, 13–14.

same ways as Skelton, Dudley was more conservative than Starkey, but again not in politics. Dudley urged the nobility to humble itself before the prince, while Starkey designed a system which would reduce him to at best *primus inter pares*. Starkey came much closer to the aristocratic line of the 'Tract on the steward' than to the system portrayed in the 'Modus', which depended to a greater or lesser degree on the consent of the commons. Starkey's importation of the language of civic humanism obscured, but could not obliterate, his dependence on an interpretation of English constitutional history like that offered by the magnates, and one at least congenial to Starkey's patron Pole. English tradition and oligarchical humanism went hand in hand, Donato Giannotti's *maestro de' cavalieri* and the barons' aspirations.

Thus the main lines of Starkey's programme finally emerge, partly from his own words, and partly from setting his words in two broader contexts, two long traditions of discourse. Starkey's political thought was aristocratic *tout court* and in particular designed to preserve the position of the high nobility. Given the enormous strength of aristocratic ideals and their huge appeal to all other social groups, it would be very surprising if Starkey had managed to escape their pull.[145] G. E. Mingay put the position of the nobility after the middle ages bluntly and with particular relevance to Starkey. 'Of course the great lords continued to fulfil a role of social preeminence ... The lesser gentry, in particular, have always looked to the nobility for leadership and recognition.'[146] Mingay does not explain why that should have been, but T. A. Brady does. Brady draws on J. H. Elliott's construct of 'corporate or national constitutionalism' which was 'essentially the preserve of the dominant social and vocational groups in the state'.[147] Just as the object of corporate constitutionalism was to provide a static description of a hierarchy of communities which could be passed on to posterity intact, so the aim of all aristocratic political behaviour was 'collective survival'.[148] This inherently aristocratic ideal appealed especially to the lowest stratum of the ruling class, which Brady calls 'the dominated fraction of a dominant class'. They were 'just those persons to whom the regime of control, regulation, discipline, and corporate consciousness ... meant the most'. This static ideal offered them both protection from the lower orders and 'substantial independence' within the ruling order.[149]

Brady meant his model to apply to the ruling class of a city, but it works equally well to explain why Thomas Starkey, a member of the lesser gentry, should have espoused aristocratic ideals with particular passion, including

---

[145] Bernard, *Nobility*, 192, and cf. L. Stone and J. C. Fawtier Stone, *An open elite? England 1540–1880*, 408–19.

[146] G. E. Mingay, *The gentry: the rise and fall of a ruling class,* 30.

[147] J. H. Elliott, 'Revolution and continuity in early modern Europe', 48. Brady, *Strassbourg*, 16.

[148] Elliott, 'Revolution', 49 and Brady, *Strassbourg*, 45.

[149] Brady, *Strassbourg*, 16 and 269.

his precocious use of the mixed state. He may well have employed the concept much as James Harrington did in order to protect the nobility and gentry from the monarch above them and the lower orders beneath.[150] Starkey's family uneasily straddled the gap between mere parish gentry and county gentry. His immediate relatives probably came much closer to the former, but they had once aspired to something more, and other of Starkey's near relations still did. As a younger son of a family of doubtful status, Starkey would thus have felt the possibility of being 'declassed' particularly strongly. His resentment against his difficult position prevented him from embracing the nobility as easily as Sir Thomas Elyot, for example, the only son and heir of his well-placed father, but the necessity of establishing personal and social identity drove Starkey to embrace the only ideal available. It cannot be an accident that Starkey attached himself to Pole and tried to lead his patron to implement a programme designed to preserve and legitimate noble dominance. As Lawrence Stone observes, whether the sort of paternalism Starkey advocated represents 'benevolent or oppressive behaviour depends upon the eye of the beholder'.[151] Stone declines to try to tease these two possibilities apart, but Starkey's thinking clearly mirrored their potential for conflict. Starkey resolved this tension by proposing a complete overhaul of the existing nobility in such a way as to preserve a place for both his patron and himself. In the longer run, however, it appears that the strain was too much for Starkey and helped to drive him in the direction of religion.

[150] C. Hill, 'James Harrington and the people', 306. Hill's analysis is disputed, especially by J. G. A. Pocock, *The ancient constitution and the feudal law*, chapter 6, esp. 129.
[151] Stone, *Open elite?*, 415.

6

An English 'spirituale'

When Reginald Pole left England for the third time in early 1532, Starkey went with him. Because his Dialogue had failed to persuade Pole to continue in Henry VIII's service, Starkey had already decided to abandon Pole's employ. It may be that Starkey acted on that resolution before he left England, but found few openings for fundamental thinkers with no practical experience. Someone may have advised him to equip himself with the tools for such service, or Starkey may have figured out the Henrician *cursus honorum* for himself. Starkey's Dialogue now became a piece of career planning, reflecting his decision to spend the time between about mid-1532 and the last half of 1534 studying civil law in Avignon and Padua. The increasingly Platonist line of the last part of the Dialogue together with Starkey's more overt interest in Pauline Christianity probably sprang from his effort to follow Pole's religious evolution and to adapt civic humanism to the confines of the court. By the time Starkey completed the work, he already doubted the career of a courtier and had laid out an alternative plan, despite continuing to study the law. Perhaps, as he frequently did, Starkey meant to leave himself options. He had demonstrated his skills as a rhetorician in the service of a largely secular reform, but he could convert those tools to Christian oratory without difficulty. After all, he needed only to move from one aristocratic institution to another, following a time-honoured path for younger sons. Starkey's stay in Avignon in close proximity to Pole's friend Jacopo Sadoleto, a strong Platonist and former papal courtier, no doubt helped to steer Starkey's thinking, even if Starkey backed away from Sadoleto's religious views. All the while, Starkey's breach with Pole widened, which probably helped to reinforce his desire to cut out a level of patronage between himself and the king.

The strain of conforming his behaviour to the expectations of a patron with whom he increasingly disagreed probably helped to push Starkey further in his religious evolution. When he rejoined Pole in Padua after about a year in Avignon, he continued his study of law in the foremost school in Europe, expanded his circle of friends amongst humanists and philosophers, and struggled with the eddying religious currents around Pole. Whatever their disagreements over politics, Pole was rapidly becoming a force in the circles of Italian Evangelism, and Starkey shared many of its beliefs, first and foremost, the irreducible core of justification by faith. According to Barry Collett, Evangelical soteriology hovered between two positions: salvation by gradual illumination and salvation by restoration. Those who believed the former thought they could help themselves, while the latter rejected works.[1] Starkey slowly moved from the first opinion to the second, probably following the example set by his friend Jan van Kampen (Johannes Campensis), one of the principal influences on Evangelical theology and scriptural interpretation. Starkey announced his arrival by adopting Kampen's language of the *beneficium mortis Christi*, even if the term is not a certain talisman of an Evangelical, and Starkey usually truncated it to merely 'benefit'.[2] Kampen had just published his commentary on two of Paul's letters, and he may well have directed the principal part of Starkey's studies of the Bible. Finally, Starkey proposed changes in the church like the administrative reform Gasparo Contarini espoused, and planned to put his beliefs into action through the recommended means of preaching. His legal training also reinforced not only his religious leanings, but also his conciliarism. In short, Starkey blended the third element found in many Venetian and Paduan humanists – religion – with the two he had already developed – republicanism and 'literary' humanism (or humanism in the narrow sense of philological method) – to complete his conversion into perhaps the most highly Italianate Englishman of his generation. Luigi Firpo was on the right track in using Starkey's Dialogue to shed light on the attitudes of Pole's friends, while Philip Hughes cast his net too narrowly but still in the right part of the ocean in suggesting that Starkey may have drawn on the reforms issuing from the Benedictine monastery of Santa Giustina in Venice. Wilhelm Schenk, on the other hand, missed the mark altogether by severing any ties between Starkey's plans and his Italian context.[3]

In January 1532 Pole left England after securing Henry's permission to study abroad.[4] His reasons for leaving are as obscure as most of the rest of his biography. Eustace Chapuys reported that Pole had threatened Henry with an appearance in parliament, and the king had immediately capitulated.[5] In one of the prefaces to *De unitate* written in the late 1530s, Pole claimed that

---

[1] B. Collett, *Italian Benedictine scholars and the reformation*, 15 and 26.

[2] Paolo Simoncelli uses the phrase as a badge of party allegiance (*Evangelismo italiano del cinquecento. Questione religiosa e nicodemismo politico*), but Collett demonstrates that it cropped up frequently amongst his non-Evangelical Benedictines.

[3] L. Firpo, *Appunti e testi per la storia dell'antimachiavellismo*, 68; P. Hughes, *The reformation in England*, I, 105; and W. Schenk, *Reginald Pole*, 44.

[4] *Ibid.*, 29.   [5] *LP*, V, 737.

he had fled to Venice in order to avoid the dangers and contentions in England.[6] Nearly twenty years later in a letter to King Edward, Pole claimed that he had escaped to Venice 'as into the safest harbor'.[7] This retrospective interpretation grew up along with Pole's stories about his doings in Paris, and should therefore receive cautious treatment. It is worth trying to determine Pole's motives, because they may have underlain the beginning of Starkey's estrangement from him. Alas, no reliable external evidence for them exists. Schenk quite correctly doubted Chapuys's story, even if he could have made a stronger argument.[8] As dean of Wimborne Minster, Pole had a seat in convocation, which met concurrently with parliament, but no right to speak in parliament itself. Perhaps if Chapuys meant convocation, Pole had indeed ceased to acquiesce in the Headship he had accepted in February 1531 and was prepared to make the reservations he had expressed in his 'divorce opinion' public. Others in Pole's and Starkey's circle trod cautiously just after they left, perhaps because they knew Pole's attitude might cause trouble. Edward Wotton wrote to Pole in Avignon in July 1532 with the news of Thomas Abell's attack on Cranmer's defence of the divorce, but added 'I would get it or send it to you ... but it is not commonly abroad, nor I dare not be so curious about getting it.'[9]

It is unlikely that Starkey ever shared Pole's opinion or Wotton's caution. Starkey intensely wished to enter royal service, and while Pole made for Venice, Starkey threw himself into acquiring a legal education under Gianfrancesco Sannazari, called della Ripa. Della Ripa specialized in marriage law among other things. How and when Starkey came to study with him in Avignon makes a complicated story. Pole may not have spent any time there nor did he stay long at nearby Carpentras with his friend Sadoleto. He left in early September and had arrived in Padua before 26 October.[10] Pole's short visit disappointed Sadoleto, who wrote to Starkey saying that he would have been glad if Pole could have stayed some months.[11] Starkey must have arrived with Pole sometime before Wotton's letter, but whether Starkey stayed with his patron in Carpentras or lodged alone in Avignon is unclear, as is how long he remained. In another letter of 3 December Sadoleto told Pole that *Thomas*

---

[6] *ERP*, I, 68.   [7] *ERP*, IV, 314.   [8] Schenk, *Pole*, 30.

[9] Marie Hallé, *Reginald Pole*, 89. For Abell's attack, see now V. M. Murphy, 'The debate over Henry VIII's first divorce: an analysis of the contemporary treatises', 243–50. Wotton was right about the delicacy of the situation. Abell's work even stirred Thomas Cromwell for the only time to take an interest in the pamphlets about Henry's marriage, *ibid.*, 250.

[10] Ludovico Beccadelli claimed that Pole stayed less than a year in Avignon, because of his health. 'Vita del cardinale Reginaldo Polo', 287. Two letters from Sadoleto announced Pole's anticipated departure in early September. *ERP*, I, 274–5 and Jacopo Sadoleto, *Opera quae exstant omnia*, II, 146. Pole thanked Sadoleto for his hospitality in a letter of 26 October. *ERP*, I, 397.

[11] BL Harl. 6989, fol. 38r.

tuus ad me Avenione scripsisset. The editors of *Letters and papers* translated this as 'your man Thomas wrote to me from Avignon', but *Avenione* may be a locative, in which case Starkey had written from Padua or Venice to Sadoleto at Avignon, on behalf of the indisposed Pole, whose ill health Starkey's letter reported.[12] Similarly, Sadoleto's letter to Pole of 15 July 1533 does not provide unequivocal evidence that Starkey had left Avignon, as W. Gordon Zeeveld thought. Sadoleto noted the receipt of letters '*a Thoma tuo* ... a man very worthy of your [Pole's] familiarity, and the studies to which he turns every day'.[13] Sadoleto may have drawn on personal knowledge of Starkey's industry, but he still said nothing about where Starkey was applying himself so diligently.

In fact, Starkey must have been in Padua. Just six days after Sadoleto's letter, Starkey wrote to his Avignonese friend Jerome Lopis to report that he and Pole were still studying, Starkey the civil law 'which pleases me exceedingly'.[14] But had Starkey begun his legal training before that? A long tradition based on Andras Dudith's adaptation of Ludovico Beccadelli's biography of Pole avers that both he and Pole did. Beccadelli did not make such a claim, nor did Dudith. He merely noted that the study of both civil and canon law, as well as of the liberal arts, flourished at Avignon at the time of Pole's visit.[15] Pole's second Jesuit biographer, Athanasius Zimmermann, embroidered on this considerably, but without citing either Dudith or Beccadelli. He observed that 'the famous legal teacher Alciato had founded a school here' and that 'its chief representative, G. F. de Ripa' was a 'qualified teacher and fatherly friend' to Pole.[16] Marie Hallé followed Zimmermann, although she called della Ripa only a 'worthy successor to Alciates [*sic*]'.[17] Zimmermann's imagined episode passed into F. W. Maitland's *English law and the renaissance*, although Maitland took an agnostic position about whether Pole had ever seriously studied civil law, and deleted the more extreme fabrications of Zimmermann's account.[18] By the time this tale had gone through Zeeveld's hands, both Starkey and Pole had become 'enthusiastic civilians' under the instruction of 'Ripa', who was then 'directing a renaissance of the *Corpus iuris civilis*', whatever that might mean.[19]

Most of this accumulated interpretation can be cleared away. In addition to the letter to Lopis, another from the Scot Florence Voluzene to Starkey together with one from Sadoleto establish Starkey's residence in Avignon and

---

[12] *ERP*, I, 402 and *LP*, V, 1665.

[13] W. G. Zeeveld, *Foundations of Tudor policy*, 85 and 87, and *ERP*, I, 407–8.

[14] Harl. 6989, fol. 44r.   [15] Andras Dudith, *Vita Reginaldi Poli*, 10.

[16] A. Zimmermann, *Kardinal Pole, sein Leben und seine Schriften*, 51.

[17] Hallé, *Pole*, 92.

[18] F. W. Maitland, *English law and the renaissance*, 6.

[19] Zeeveld, *Foundations*, 80 and 79.

Carpentras, and a relatively safe inference suggests that he must have studied law there. In the autumn of 1535 Voluzene wrote to thank Starkey for his recommendation of Carpentras and Sadoleto.[20] Starkey's high opinion of Sadoleto gave rise to the bishop's effusive thanks to Starkey in October 1534.[21] Working backward from letters addressed to Starkey soon after his return to England which called him a doctor of both laws (*iuris utriusque doctor*), we can infer that he must have begun his education in them at Avignon. No matter where he studied law, Starkey could not have put in anything even close to the ten years required for a double doctorate, but Sir Thomas Smith claimed his degree on the basis of only a few months in Padua about a decade later.[22] As at Oxford, dispensation for shorter terms of study was common, especially for those who had degrees in other faculties.[23] Starkey's draft letter to Lopis seems to offer evidence on both sides of the question. Lopis's brother took a law degree with della Ripa and the faculty in Avignon greatly interested him, but Starkey neither referred to it nor wrote that he was continuing his studies. On the other hand, when Starkey announced the death of Franceschino di Corte (Curzio) to Lopis, he knew enough about competing schools of interpretation to add that this was 'to the great grief of those who embrace the doctrine of Bartolo'.[24] Starkey certainly thought the law important. Quite apart from his proposal to receive Roman law in England, he also counselled an unknown correspondent in Pole's household (George Lily?) to study it. Most of this letter of advice is badly mutilated, but Starkey's selling point 'you see besides what fruit [there is] in the civil law in the face of this our tempest' stands out.[25]

One other piece of evidence may link Starkey and della Ripa. It comes from another badly damaged letter, addressed to Pole in London. It bears no contemporary indication of authorship, but a note in a later hand claims one 'Heinr. Dereino Olasco' wrote it on 28 October 1535.[26] The date must be an error. The writer may well not have known that Pole was in Venice then, but his report that 'Monsignore de Ripa' had returned to Pavia could not have

---

[20] BL Nero B VI, fol. 20r.   [21] Harl. 6989, fol. 38r.

[22] M. Dewar, *Sir Thomas Smith*, 21.

[23] Lucia Rossetti, *L'università di Padova*, 25 and Helmut Coing, 'Die juristische Fakultät und ihr Lehrprogramm', in *Handbuch der Quellen und Literaturen der neueren europäischen Privatrechtsgeschichte*, 72.

[24] Harl. 6989, fol. 44r. Lopis was a physician – he signed his letter to Starkey *physicus* – and not a law student as Zeeveld thought (*Foundations*, 87). For him see M. Ascheri, *Gianfrancesco Sannazari della Ripa (1480c.–1535)*, 93 and A. Hartmann, ed., *Die Amerbach Korrespondenz*, II, 1429, 1178, 1192, 1218 and 1238. Hartmann could discover no more information about Lopis than that his family was probably Jewish. In 1524 Lopis expressed interest in Thomas Linacre's edition of Galen which Boniface Amerbach apparently saw through the press (no. 981).

[25] BL Vitellius B XIV, fol. 40r.   [26] *Ibid.*, fol. 142r.

been news, especially since della Ripa had died in March of that year.[27] Nevertheless, the inclusion of this item suggests that the writer thought that news of della Ripa would further his strenuous efforts to curry favour with Pole. Pole and della Ripa could only have met at Avignon, because della Ripa had lived there almost constantly since 1519. The very last line of this letter offers a tantalizing link between the writer and Starkey. He asked *e mi ci rachomandiamo* [along with his brother] *el simile a* and just enough of the next two words can be deciphered to suggest that they are 'Thomas Starkey'.[28]

In any case, della Ripa would have been about Starkey's only choice of professor in Avignon.[29] Della Ripa had studied with di Corte at Pavia, as well as two other leading jurists, Filippo Decio and Giason del Maino. According to the legal historian Tommaso Diplovatazio, he had also studied under Andrea Botigella at Padua at the same time as Marco Mantova, who was probably one of Starkey's teachers in Padua, but Mario Ascheri doubts this.[30] After finishing his education at Pavia, della Ripa substituted for del Maino there for three years until 1512.[31] The university of Avignon called him in 1517, after Decio had turned it down. He drew a lower salary than that offered Andrea Alciato, but della Ripa had a guarantee of payment in case the plague disrupted classes, as happened frequently.[32] Unlike Alciato, he was hired to lecture *cum apparatu italico*. Students liked this method and one of them compared della Ripa's knowledge of the law favourably with Alciato's.[33]

Alciato would become the founder of the school of historical juris-

---

[27] Ascheri, *Della Ripa*, 83 and 86.

[28] The author of this greeting remains a mystery. His choice of Italian indicates that he either did not know Latin or, perhaps, that he was an Italian chauvinist. The letter's obsequious tone probably rules out the latter and may also exclude the most likely candidate for its author, Jan Laski's (à Lasco's) brother Hieroslaus (*Op. Ep. Er.*, VI, 1622). All the same, the author's apparent middle name may be a corruption or a misunderstanding by the annotator of *de regno*, so that it should be translated not as a middle name followed by a surname, but as 'of the kingdom of Olasco', or in other words a Pole. Perhaps Pole may have known the author only through Laski, whom Erasmus had recommended to Pole when they were both in Padua in October 1525 (*ibid.*, 1627). At any rate, Jan could certainly have been the author's brother who would want to be remembered to Pole. Perhaps the signature was an elaborate private joke. Even if this identification is accepted, it does not help much to tie Pole to della Ripa. Next to nothing is known of Hieroslaus. The similarly named Hieronimo Lascho (or de Lasko) was in England as Jan Zapolski's representative in 1527, when Wolsey gave him the Italian title 'Segnior', but he died in 1532 (SP 1/42, fol. 215r [*LP*, IV, 3883] and *CSPV*, IV, 771).

[29] E. de Teule, *Chronologie des docteurs en droit civil de l'université d'Avignon* does not list Starkey. De Teule probably used the mid-seventeenth-century list of doctorates in the Archives départmentales de Vaucluse, F. 36, fol. 33r. There seems to be no work currently going forward on students at Avignon in the sixteenth century, and nothing in print aside from de Teule. I am grateful to Gerard Giordanengo for much help on this point.

[30] Ascheri, *Della Ripa*, 19 and note.

[31] *Ibid.*, 20.   [32] *Ibid.*, 27–8.   [33] *Ibid.*, 30–1.

prudence, the so-called *mos gallicus*, which attacked what it saw as the hide-bound dependence on scholastic method of the *mos italicus*. Recently, the depth of the opposition between these two approaches has come in for critical analysis, and Donald Kelley demonstrates that both regarded the law as the queen of the disciplines and especially of moral philosophy. Alciato and della Ripa might have approached their materials differently, but what mattered for both was content, not mainly the eloquence (or lack thereof) which had so interested an amateur legist like Lorenzo Valla. Instead of a fight to the death, the contest between the two *mores* was part of the larger connection between scholastic and humanist method, and both varieties of interpretation co-existed throughout the Renaissance, as they did in other disciplines.[34] The coalescence of law and the humanities went back to the 'pre-humanists' around Lovato Lovati. If nothing else, both depended on rhetoric, as Agricola clearly saw.[35] Gerhard Immel said much the same thing as Kelley when he identified della Ripa as part of a transitional generation between *mos italicus* and humanist jurisprudence.[36] Della Ripa's training under del Maino fitted him ideally to play such a role. Although a Bartolist to the tips of his fingers, del Maino had launched the quest – which has got very little farther – for an accurate text of Bartolo.[37] Del Maino's example must have rubbed off on della Ripa, who sometimes referred to the results of the philological method in his lectures.[38] Della Ripa's student Boniface Amerbach became one of the leaders of the 'humanist' school, but he was also one of those who rated his master 'perhaps superior in the law' to Alciato and second only to Decio among the Italians, as well as praising his *grammaticem interpretatum*.[39] Thus Starkey would have seen no discrepancy between his allegiance to *humanitas* and the study of civil law. Nor would his republican sympathies have prevented him from learning from the law of the emperors. In fact, as the brothers Carlyle and J. W. Allen long ago recognized and as Quentin Skinner has emphasized more recently, Roman law was inherently civic, and its civil law descendant contributed a great deal to republican thought.[40] As Kelley

---

[34] D. R. Kelley, '*Vera philosophia*: the philosophical significance of renaissance jurisprudence', 268. See also Kelley, 'Civil science in the renaissance: jurisprudence Italian style', 777ff.

[35] J. M. Headley, 'Gattinara, Erasmus and the imperial configuration of humanism', 64–5.

[36] Review of Ascheri, *Della Ripa*, 487.

[37] F. Calasso, 'Bartolo', 664.

[38] Ascheri, *Della Ripa*, 98–9, 101.

[39] *Amerbach Korrespondenz*, II, 743 (an especially impressive testimonial, since Amerbach directed it to the violently partisan humanist jurist Ulrich Zasius) and III, 1015 (to 'Rufus').

[40] Virtually every time the Carlyles touched on civilian political thought in their great *A history of medieval political theory in the west* they emphasized its 'populist' potentiality or actuality. They continued that approach when considering the sixteenth century in their final volume. J. W. Allen, *A history of political thought in the sixteenth century*, 281 pointed out the complexity of the civil law impact on its sixteenth-century 'votaries'. For a similar argument, see now Q. Skinner, *Foundations of modern political thought*, II, *The reformation*, especially 124ff.

points out, by the sixteenth century, both methods of interpreting the law rested on its civic nature.[41] The humanists merely reinforced a dimension which their fifteenth-century Bartolist predecessors had occasionally played down, although Bartolo himself, writing in the great age of the Italian communes, had never done so.[42]

Della Ripa kept his opinions about current secular politics largely to himself, but he had no such hesitations about teaching the ecclesiastical analogue of republicanism, conciliarism. Although primarily a civilian, he made plain his corporate view of the ecclesiastical headship in his commentary on the Decretals rubric *de constitutionibus*. The same theory crops up repeatedly in della Ripa's *responsa* on the Decretals. In one of these della Ripa made clear that he drew much of his theory from Francesco Zabarella's corporatism, and in another he paraphrased Zabarella's famous ministerial theory of papal power by describing the pope's relation to the law *tanquam minister Dei non tanquam dominus*.[43] Della Ripa attacked the 'common opinion' that the pope could legislate without the cardinals, insisting 'I understand ... the apostolic see to consist in pope and cardinals.'[44] Later della Ripa went further and wrote that the *ecclesia* meant more than the pope, 'because the cardinals make up the Roman church. And indeed, if we want to know truly, the Roman church is made up of all the faithful, because the church established on the rock is one.'[45] Authority spread a little lower in the church for della Ripa than for Starkey. To della Ripa, 'the bishops represent the apostles and have succeeded to their place' and they have power equal to the pope's. Needless to say, in things of the faith 'the pope cannot determine anything without the consent of the general council', but della Ripa also thought that since the pontiff could make mistakes about belief, 'the pope can err besides in the rest which do not concern the faith, whence he cannot act without the council in which no error has been found'.[46] Finally, although the pope could declare positive law without taking advice, he ought not and, of course, he could not act alone in any difficult case involving divine or natural law, Starkey's point in his 'divorce opinion'.[47]

Della Ripa also spent much time criticizing the argument which made

[41] Kelley, '*Vera philosophia*', 270.
[42] Q. Skinner, *The foundations of modern political thought*, I, *The renaissance*, 61ff., and W. Ullmann, '*De Bartoli sententia: concilium repraesentat mentem populi*', 705–34.
[43] G. F. della Ripa, *Responsa in quinque libros decretalium*, fols. 8v and 17r. See also 4r and 45r.
[44] G. F. della Ripa, *In primum decretalium librum commentarium*, in *Opera omnia*, V, fol. 3v after no. 15.
[45] *Ibid.*, no. 18.
[46] *Ibid.*, fol. 4r, after no. 19; near the end of col. 1; and col. 2.
[47] *Ibid.*, no. 21 and col. 2 near the middle.

Christ's grant of jurisdiction peculiar to Peter. He clinched his case with corporation theory. Allow that Peter were the head of the apostles, della Ripa wrote, it would still not follow that he could settle hard cases alone, because (1) a head presupposes a body, and (2) 'the keys and the power to legislate were given to his brothers commonly'.[48] A modified passage in Starkey's Dialogue may clinch della Ripa's impact. Starkey concluded his argument against the collection of first fruits by maintaining that 'the defence of the church perteyneth not to the pope *& hys see [*ab.*], but rather to the *emperour & other [*ab.*] chrystun pryncys'.[49] Both these changes came from the civil law, and the second incorporated the famous doctrine of *rex in regno suo imperator est*, which Starkey nowhere else adopted.

As one might anticipate from della Ripa's constitutional ideas, he could criticize the papacy harshly. For instance, in his tract on the plague he complained that 'today the pontiffs are involved in temporal business because they have no concern for spiritual'. This worldliness set a bad example for their subjects, as did nepotism through which 'flesh and blood, not the Holy Spirit, reveals itself to the pontiffs'.[50] Ascheri sums up della Ripa's attitude by suggesting that his religion conformed 'to the fundamental nucleus of Erasmian teaching', as slippery as this definition may be.[51] Della Ripa may have communicated his opinions to his student and colleague Jean Montaigne, who wrote to Amerbach in 1527 asking him what he knew about the sack of Rome. Montaigne had received incredible reports about the amazement and 'stupor' of the pope, cardinals and all the Roman clergy. 'Our priests here', he continued, 'do not stop, they do not amend, they fear nothing, they are no more cautious because of the danger of others. I do not know whether God will repay them in another world. I will certainly marvel if they do not receive their reward here.'[52]

Such attitudes may help to account for della Ripa's friendship with Sadoleto, who became an open advocate of reform just after Starkey's visit. Even though the intellectual climate of Avignon did not impress Sadoleto, he conceded that his people were well educated in the law.[53] Sadoleto and della Ripa were closer than this oblique comment indicates. Their friendship, perhaps originally founded on della Ripa's consulting work for the diocese, went back further than 1521 when Ascheri thinks that Sadoleto may have worked to secure his friend's promotion as count palatine.[54] In 1527 della Ripa reciprocated by dedicating his *Interpretationes et responsa* to Sadoleto,

---

[48] *Ibid.*, col. 1. [49] SP 1/90, fol. 83r (Burton, 120). [50] Ascheri, *Della Ripa*, 50n.
[51] *Ibid.*, 51.
[52] *Amerbach Korrespondenz*, III, 1199. [53] R. M. Douglas, *Jacopo Sadoleto*, 258 n. 65.
[54] Ascheri, *Della Ripa*, 39.

and received warm thanks.[55] Della Ripa may have helped to relieve some of Sadoleto's 'chronic nostalgia' for his intellectual friends in Italy, especially those in Pietro Bembo's circle.[56]

While Starkey was in Avignon, Sadoleto finished his *De liberis recte instituendis*, which impressed Starkey enough that he simply abandoned his discussion of the same topic in his Dialogue and cited Sadoleto's book. Sadoleto's attempt to lecture afresh on Paul's epistle to the Romans during Starkey's stay would not have had as much appeal to the bishop's English friend.[57] Neither its determinedly 'classical' philosophy of man, nor its politics fitted Starkey's outlook. Even in *De liberis*, virtue came from knowledge, and perfection was possible without reference to faith. Proper study would produce resemblance to God.[58] Sadoleto followed philological method in his exegesis, as had Colet (more or less), but he diverged from Colet's soteriology from the beginning.[59] As had Starkey in the opening section of his Dialogue, Sadoleto emphasized the coalescence between the divine and the human. As usual, that required Sadoleto to concentrate on reason and denigrate matter. The incarnation had infused divine reason into human flesh, but only the former really mattered, only it was *virtus*.[60] The body stood 'to the spirit as the person is, which, since it conceals an extraneous and alien form, does not allow the interior, the true man to be known' (21). Human justice could aspire to imitate divine by subjecting the passions (26). 'Whoever conforms themselves to God in true faith … with the grace of God … the *similitudo* of the highest God, and of his justice, and goodness will illuminate' (28).

As that passage makes clear, human effort was independent from God and preceded grace. Sadoleto spelled that out explicitly a little later when he wrote 'first, the faith of the believers provokes the justice of God' (29). This 'double justification' could lead men through the example of God to 'what God himself is. They will become such, who study to commit themselves to God through faith and the Gospel' (31). Thus Sadoleto accorded priority to human action, to free will, and to inherent justice. Sadoleto may have set out to steer a new course between Pelagius and Augustine, but he wound up following 'a twisting path which veered far closer to Pelagius than Augustine'.[61] Plato inspired Sadoleto's view of man and salvation, and Sadoleto followed him in choosing the contemplative life, as his stress on reason reveals.[62]

Starkey would not have accepted Sadoleto's ideal, nor the politics which

---

[55] *Ibid.*, 67 and Sadoleto, *Opera*, 105–6.
[56] Douglas, *Sadoleto*, 64. For examples of this nostalgia, see Sadoleto, *Opera*, 106 and 108.
[57] *Amerbach Korrespondenz*, IV, 1624, 1541, 1766.   [58] Douglas, *Sadoleto*, 76.
[59] *Ibid.*, 48 and 81.   [60] *In epistolam ad Romanos commentariorum*, 18.
[61] Douglas, *Sadoleto*, 81, 82, 85.   [62] *Ibid.*, 75, 80, 58–9.

followed from it. Nevertheless, Sadoleto's good Platonist approach resembled Starkey's, both beginning to discuss the ills of society by an appeal to the organic analogy of the body politic. Like Starkey, Sadoleto most feared the ambitious man, but Sadoleto drew the opposite conclusion about how to prevent him from corrupting the rest of the *societas* (277). The order established by God depended on obedience to all powers, even if not all princes were beneficial.

For many have come to power through crimes and wicked deeds, and in power they turn profligate besides, because they have got possession badly. What then? Ought we to be subject to a bad prince? We ought by all means, so long as we bear his insolence patiently, rather than obeying that man eagerly. Even if the prince is not upright, yet all power is holy. (307)

This sort of quietism would have been distasteful enough to Starkey, even if Sadoleto had not used it as the basis for an argument in favour of papal authority (308). Sadoleto concluded his treatise on politics with the standard argument that princes were ministers of God, on whom all justice and order depended. Sadoleto interpreted Paul's injunction to obey princes 'non solum propter iram, sed etiam propter conscientiam' to mean either that Christians must act in such a way

that we avoid evil arising from the anger of the king we hold in contempt, or that we may be partakers of virtue and good morals which we follow, not as if forced as unwilling resisters, but as thoroughly convinced that public utility is established in the prince, we submit willingly and with a free spirit to them. (311)

Sadoleto may have employed much of the vocabulary familiar to Starkey, but to nothing like a civic humanist end. Nevertheless, Starkey may have begun his scriptural studies with Sadoleto, whose autodidactic exegesis resembled Starkey's own.

The mere fact that Starkey chose to stay in Avignon with Sadoleto instead of continuing on to Padua with Pole is significant enough, but when the depth of the differences between Starkey and the bishop is added in, then more than a suggestion of an estrangement between Pole and Starkey results. Pole's very different reaction to *De liberis*, together with Starkey's divorce opinion reflect a growing disagreement between them. Pole used his judgment of *De liberis* as eloquent but theologically lacking to initiate a long dispute with Sadoleto over the latter's religious failings, which the two friends left unresolved. No sooner did they drop that dispute than Pole and Sadoleto plunged into another over whether their friend Lazzaro Bonamico should become a theologian (see below). Much of Pole's new religion rubbed off on Starkey once they were reunited in Padua, but Starkey refused to let Pole deter him from the *vita activa*. As part of his second major effort to attract royal favour by the presentation of the Dialogue, Starkey wrote a 'divorce opinion' while he was in Avignon, which might almost have been intended to counter the dire domestic repercussions predicted by Pole perhaps two years earlier.

As Thomas Cranmer summarized the argument, Pole had stressed that the divorce would lead to upheaval at home by making the people who 'now do begyn to hate priests ... hate moche more learned men and the name of lernyng', at the same time as it would trigger a renewal of dynastic wars arising from 'dyversyte of tytles'.[63] Pole's concern with the standing of learned men like himself, combined with his stress on the succession neatly summarizes the groundwork of Starkey's Dialogue, and highlights the close connection between Pole's actions and Starkey's reactions. Changing his focus to international affairs, Pole continued that both the pope and the emperor would be bound to take a hand. The former could not grant a divorce, unless he wished to go against his predecessors, diminish his power to an unprecedented degree, and set a dangerous example for sedition in Portugal. (Its king had married two sisters in succession.) As for the emperor, the French king could not counterbalance him even if one overlooked notorious Gallic perfidy. No matter what Francis did, the emperor could 'put this realme into gret damage and ruyne' merely by prohibiting trade with Flanders and Spain (678). Pole offered this analysis out of a concern for Henry's honour, in terms which evoked no protest from Cranmer.

Nevertheless, Pole bluntly washed his hands of the divorce and refused to continue to be 'a doar therin, and a setter forwarde thereof' (675). Thus Starkey felt it was incumbent on him both to neutralize Pole's opinion, which he knew, and also thereby to offer himself in Pole's stead.[64] Starkey's opinion took a very different tack from Pole's, one consistent with his criticism of papal dispensation in the Dialogue. Virtually identical legal theory underlay both works. Human and civil law derived from natural law, which Starkey distinguished from the law which right reason 'established ought to be preserved among humanly and civilly ordered peoples everywhere'.[65] Apparently this was a circumlocution for divine law, phrased in terms Sadoleto would have recognized. The Levitical law prohibiting marriage to a dead brother's wife fell into the second category, hence the pope could not dispense from it. One man could not alter what right reason laid down as universally binding. So far Starkey agreed with many of Henry's legal partisans, but he went further. Right reason must also correct the pope's usurped authority, a 'plague which has infected the world with a thousand sorts of evils' and

[63] John Strype, *Thomas Cranmer*, II, 678 and 676.   [64] BL Cleopatra E VI, fol. 376r.
[65] SP 1/75, fol. 230v.

become the destruction of 'all Christian and true civil life' (231r). This is stronger language than any in the Dialogue, where Starkey never blamed the pope's abuse of authority for any more than destroying the church. Next Starkey introduced a favourite argument. The root cause of papal usurpation lay in princes, who had for too long attributed excessive authority to the pope, and made his authority almost equal to God's (232r). Starkey's principal solution struck one of the most consistent notes in his political harmonium. Henry should appeal to a general council. Imitating ancient practice, it alone could provide judges competent to deal with matters of divine law (233r). Starkey repeated his argument in the Dialogue that the pope ought not to consider weighty matters without the cardinals, but he apparently thought Henry's case too important even for collegial determination (232r). An appeal to a council would secure equity for Henry, avoid future 'inconveniences', and 'satisfy your britannic people' (233v–234r).

Nothing came of Starkey's second attempt to gain notice, as G. R. Elton demonstrated.[66] No option remained but to go on acquiring the tools necessary to emulate Henry's jacks-of-all-trades like John Tregonwell. Unfortunately, Starkey could not continue to study with della Ripa, whom the Duke of Milan recalled to Pavia in August 1533. The order had been reported as early as March, but neither Sadoleto's efforts with the pope nor the laments of della Ripa's students had any effect.[67] Deprived of probably the only professor still in residence in Avignon, Starkey had no choice but to seek out Pole in Padua.

From at least the time of John Tiptoft, study in Padua had offered the key to a diplomatic career in England.[68] Starkey may yet have gone reluctantly, but he could hardly have done better for a law school. According to its eminent historian Biagio Brugi, Padua was then in its *secolo d'oro*.[69] Despite its reputation as a citadel of Bartolism, humanists praised the Paduan faculty and sent their sons to study there. Vigle Zwichem van Aytta, a protégé of Erasmus and student of Alciato at Avignon (though before Starkey arrived), wrote to Erasmus in January 1532 saying that 'the professors of civil law satisfy me abundantly, for by great diligence and contention, they advance the studies of their hearers'.[70] To his friend Hector Hoxvinius Vigle exulted about his appointment as lecturer, since 'these Italians are more clever and

---

[66] Zeeveld supposed that Starkey parlayed his divorce opinion into government service before 1534, but G. R. Elton destroyed that oddly documented notion. *Reform and renewal: Thomas Cromwell and the common weal*, 47.

[67] Ascheri, *Della Ripa*, 83–4, 86, 96, and *Amerbach Korrespondenz*, IV, 1789, p. 245.

[68] Dewar, *Smith*, 24.

[69] B. Brugi, 'L'università dei giuristi in Padova nel Cinquecento', 2.

[70] *Op. Ep. Er.*, IX, 2994.

excellent in treating' the law than their French or Belgian counterparts.[71] Vigle liked Padua so well that he tried to secure this post permanently, without success. This rankled so much that four years later Vigle still recalled his 'failure against [Gaspar] Malmignazio, my one time antagonist [reader *in concurrens*]' which had made him 'more patient to the suffering of injuries'.[72] Vigle's master Alciato himself claimed to be eager to come to Padua over the course of fifteen years, but he was probably merely trying to extort offers he could use to have his salary boosted.[73] Nevertheless, Alciato recommended Padua to Amerbach, who later sent his own son there, as did his friend Ulrich Zasius.[74] Starkey's friend Niccolò Leonico, dean of humanists in Padua, wrote to Pole shortly before the latter arrived informing him that 'the law schools are carried on well', in contrast to the teaching of philosophy.[75] Vigle was just one of many northern Europeans attracted to Padua.[76] He moved in the same circles as Starkey, but he had left before Starkey arrived.[77]

In theory, Starkey had to meet stringent academic requirements. Students heard five lectures daily, and junior faculty had to give as many as three.[78] The statutes of 1432 dictated ten years' study for a doctorate in both laws.[79] Even an MA had to put in an additional six or seven years.[80] By 1550, the basic requirements had not changed, but they were probably no longer enforced.[81] Certainly lectures had shrunk from the statutory two hours to forty-five minutes, and students regularly paid scribes to take notes for them.[82] Likewise, the rigorous sounding oral examination leading to the doctorate may have become largely *pro forma*, since masters and students rarely got into disputes.[83]

Students had a good deal of power at Padua, and one of their most

---

[71] C. P. Hoynck van Papendrecht, *Analecta ad historiam scissi Belgii potissimum attirentia*, II, 146.

[72] *Ibid.*, III, 16. For Vigle's time in Padua, see also the recent account by F. Postma, *Viglius van Aytta als Humanist en Diplomaat*, 35ff.

[73] Brugi, 'Giuristi', 77–9.

[74] F. Dupuigrenet-Desrousilles, 'L'università di Padova dal 1405 al concilio di Trento', 634 and Brugi, 'Giuristi', 33 and 35.

[75] Biblioteca apostolica vaticana, Rossiana 997, fol. 55v. Cf. A. Gasquet, *Cardinal Pole and his early friends*, 115.

[76] Brugi, 'Giuristi', 38–9 and P. J. van Kessel, 'The denominational pluriformity of the German nation at Padua', 256–76.

[77] R. Stintzing, *Geschichte der deutschen Rechtswissenschaft*, I, 92.

[78] Dupuigrenet-Desrousilles, 'L'università', 631.

[79] F. C. von Savigny, *Geschichte des römischen Rechts im Mittelalter*, III, 287.

[80] H. Rashdall, *The universities of Europe in the middle ages*, ed. F. M. Powicke and A. B. Emden, I, 221.

[81] Savigny, *Geschichte*, 298–9 and Coing, 'Lehrprogramm', 78.

[82] Savigny, *Geschichte*, 299 and Hoynck, *Analecta*, I, 94.

[83] Brugi, 'Giuristi', 19 and 55.

important rights was choice of professor.[84] They picked one principal professor or at most two or three, who 'promoted' them for their degree, although other faculties took part in the various examinations of candidates.[85] As so often at critical points in Starkey's career, damaged records prevent the discovery of whom he selected. Aside from his presence as a witness at Wotton's MD exam in 1525, the university archives contain no trace of Starkey.[86] Nonetheless, the range of possibilities is limited, and boils down to three: Gianantonio Rossi, Mariano Socini and Marco Mantova Benavides. Rossi is least likely, in part because he was di Corte's protégé. His surviving works, mostly technical comments on single points of the law, offer no parallels with Starkey's concerns. Guido Panziroli, one of the first great legal historians and a Paduan alumnus, offered two other objections to Rossi. 'He was a man of great memory, but less penetrating learning, and tremendously arrogant, used to dealing intemperately with his colleagues.' He carried on 'ambitious contentions' with another candidate for Starkey's principal professor, Socini, even while Socini was still a junior lecturer.[87]

Socini looks like a better possibility. He came from a distinguished family of jurists, but his name has since become more famous for the theological vagaries of his son Lelio and nephew Fausto. Socini senior fell foul of the Inquisition in 1554 after he had moved to Bologna, which may mean that he earlier belonged to the tradition of heresy in the Paduan law school among both faculty and students.[88] Socini came to Padua in 1525 and succeeded to the most important chair in 1531. His lectures immediately proved popular, but professional opinion did not rate Socini's teaching very highly.[89] Although the amount of material in Socini's lectures impressed Vigle, Socini presented it so unmethodically that he 'leads us back to the original chaos'.[90] Panziroli faulted Socini's poor memory which meant that 'often he was forced to teach from a written text, and rarely was able to respond *ex tempore*'.[91] Panziroli may have erred this time. One of Socini's humanist students praised him both for his elegant Latin and for not reading his lectures.[92] Socini also had lively literary interests in the *volgare* and participated in the meetings of the academy of *gl'Infiammati* shortly before his call

---

[84] *Ibid.*, 24–5, 11.   [85] E. Martellozzo Forin, ed., *Acta graduum academicorum*, I, *passim*.

[86] It is difficult to say why Richard Morison, who definitely studied in Padua, never mentioned the law school in his voluminous correspondence with Starkey. But then George Lily never did, either.

[87] Guido Panziroli, *De claris legum interpretibus*, ed. Ottavio Panziroli, 346.

[88] A. Stella, 'Tradizione razionalistica patavina e radicalismo spiritualistico nel XVI secolo', 275–302 for the tradition and 281 for Socini.

[89] J. A. Tedeschi, 'Notes toward a genealogy of the Sozzini family', 292 and Stella, 'Tradizione', 281. For Socini's famous grandfather, see P. Nardi, *Mariano Socini*.

[90] *Amerbach Korrespondenz*, 1655.   [91] Panziroli, *De claris*, 342.

[92] G. Cianflone, *Giano Teseo Casopero*, 51.

to Bologna in 1542.[93] This all suggests some common ground with Starkey. In addition, Socini's reputation in the early 1530s had reached the English, who tried to procure his services in the divorce proceedings.[94] He was thought to favour Henry's side, enough so to worry the imperial ambassador to Venice. Socini's true opinion differed from English expectations. He may have written for Henry at one point, but his published *consilium* favoured Catherine, despite its ostensible neutrality.[95]

Socini's interests have already given the lie to Vigle's canard that the Paduan legists were 'unacquainted with more humane literature'.[96] As we have seen, Mantova fitted that generalization even less well. Humanist pursuits did not detract from Mantova's prodigious output of legal works or reduce his roster of students, some of whom thanked him for their education in *buone lettere*.[97] In addition to literary aspirations similar to Starkey's, only Mantova among the Paduan jurists had a certain link to Pole and his circle, on top of a record of partisanship to Henry, conciliarist ideas, and religious sympathies like Pole's which supported his conciliarism. All these tip the balance of probability in favour of Mantova as Starkey's master.

Mantova recalled having known Pole during the latter's student days in Padua in a letter of 1555, asking the then cardinal to favour Mantova's nephew Giovanni.[98] The mere fact of the request must point to some degree of familiarity between Mantova and Pole, and Mantova claimed 'che io conversava alle volte colla felice memoria del [Christophorus] longolio suo servitore nella casa del Rocabonella' (the palace in which Pole lived during his second stay in Padua). Cristoforo Madruzzo, cardinal bishop of Trent and one of Pole's closest political allies during the council held in his see, was among Mantova's best students, and never began a letter to his master without an expression of gratitude.[99] Mantova referred to both Madruzzo and Bembo as his patrons in the dedication of *Observationes legalium*.[100] Mantova was even closer to Bembo than this presentation suggests. At about the same time, Bembo's high hopes for a cardinalate had been dashed once again, and he chose to confide his disappointment to Mantova.[101] In fact, one of Pole's few Venetian and Paduan friends with whom Mantova cannot be

[93] Tedeschi, 'Genealogy', 296.   [94] *LP*, V, 586.
[95] *CSPSp*, IV:1, p. 547. For the *consilium*, see E. Surtz, *Henry VIII's great matter in Italy*, I, 272.
[96] *Op. Ep. Er.*, IX, 2994.
[97] For a short roster of Mantova's more important students, see T. F. Mayer, 'Marco Mantova: a bronze age conciliarist', 406, and for thanks from one of his students, Mayer, 'Marco Mantova and the Paduan religious crisis of the early sixteenth century', 44.
[98] Biblioteca marciana, Venice, MS Ital. X 91 (6606), fol. 34r.
[99] Robbins Law Library, University of California, Berkeley, MS 63, no. 2, 6–10.
[100] Marco Mantova Benavides, *Observationes legalium libri X*, 198.
[101] R. H. Terpening, 'Pietro Bembo and the cardinalate: unpublished letters to Marco Mantova', 75–86.

directly connected is Gasparo Contarini. Mantova tried to arrange an audience with Contarini shortly after the latter became a cardinal in 1535, but that is the only trace of a relationship in Mantova's massive correspondence.[102] Nevertheless, it strains belief to conclude that they did not at least know one another. They moved in exactly the same circles, and both numbered the della Torre brothers of Verona amongst their closest friends. Both brothers studied under Mantova, and another of his students offered Mantova a long eulogy when Antonio della Torre died in 1553.[103] As far as the circumstantial evidence of personal relations can go, the likelihood is strong that Starkey studied with Mantova. Furthermore, like Socini, Mantova involved himself in Henry's divorce. The Paduan legist offered the king a favourable opinion on it, which earned him a dressing-down from the Signory. The uproar suggests that Englishmen in Padua must at least have heard of him. Nicholas Harpsfield still knew of Mantova's *consilium* twenty-five years later and considered it highly incendiary.[104] It seems likely that Pole told his close collaborator Harpsfield about Mantova's work.

Unlike Starkey, Mantova did not ground his opinion on an appeal to a council, but he nevertheless espoused conciliarist ideas elsewhere. Perhaps more important, Mantova relied even more heavily than della Ripa on Zabarella's ideas, which had founded the long tradition of Paduan conciliarism.[105] Starkey once more had an opportunity to go *ad fontes* to a man whose thought ran parallel to Jean Gerson's on every point of interest to him. Mantova's own conciliarist ideas are more muted, but unmistakable all the same. They have been almost entirely overlooked, but by Francis Oakley's criteria, Mantova qualifies as at least two-thirds a conciliarist. We do not definitely know that Mantova held conciliarist ideas in the early 1530s. He first published such views in his *Dialogus de concilio* of 1541, although he began the work three or four years earlier and two of Mantova's motives for writing *De concilio* long antedated the work.[106] His deep concern for the state of the institutional church and desire for an intensely personal religion sprang from spiritual struggles in the early 1520s.[107] And Mantova probably acquired much of the support for his conciliar arguments earlier as a student in the school of Zabarella, Nicholas of Cusa and Panormitanus.

In Mantova's dialogue, his character usually affected to be an unreconstructed hierocrat, but his interlocutor Roberto drove an entering wedge into

---

102 Robbins MS 63, no. 157, Luigi Quirini-Mantova, 29 May 1535.
103 *Ibid.*, nos. 42 and 43 and F. Dittrich, *Gasparo Contarini*, 204.
104 Surtz, *Great matter*, 298ff.
105 Francis Oakley pointed out the strong parallels between d'Ailly and Zabarella, and they extend to Gerson. *The political thought of Pierre d'Ailly*, 128.
106 Mayer, 'Bronze age conciliarist', 390. 107 Mayer, 'Religious crisis', 51–3.

Mantova's emphasis on the pope's authority by raising the problem of protecting the faith which alone justified.[108] Little by little Roberto persuaded Mantova to accept not only that it was dangerous to rely on a single man's judgment, but also that all the apostles shared power equally with Peter, and consequently that the cardinals had an important place in the church. Like Zabarella, Mantova argued that they were an indispensable part of a council and that outside of one the cardinals controlled the pope by their advice. He could only transact problematic business by the cardinals' counsel. Both Mantova and Zabarella appealed to corporation theory to explain how the cardinals formed part of the same body as the pope. Mantova also accepted Zabarella's description of a general council as one in which the pope and all the bishops represented the whole church symbolically, standing in for 'a general collection of the assembling faithful'. Mantova usually spelled out his case less thoroughly than Zabarella had, but he certainly drew on the latter's *Tractatus de schismate*.[109] Mantova worked hard at spreading conciliarist ideas: it seems likely that some of his students would have heard of them, perhaps including Starkey.[110] Mantova, in keeping with the attitude of the legal faculty generally, was also strongly anti-clerical.[111]

As his views on justification by faith and the necessity of collegiate church governance (together with his literary output, detailed in chapter 2) indicate, Mantova was an Evangelical and thus very likely an important example to Starkey's religious beliefs as well as his politics. And indeed, during this second visit, Starkey developed the rest of the nebulous complex of Evangelical ideas, including justification by faith. Just what Starkey believed is as difficult to establish as is usually the case with Evangelicals. Delio Cantimori, the dean of historians of the reform in Italy, long ago put his finger on the problem in defining this group: it grew out of individual psychological experience and doctrinal positions therefore meant comparatively little to its members.[112] Most attempts to generalize about Evangelical beliefs have encountered difficulties, including even Cantimori's own argument that trust

---

[108] The man Mantova chose as the other speaker in his *De concilio* may further link Starkey to Mantova and to conciliarist ideas. Roberto Maggio was originally secretary to the nuncio to Venice Altobello Alveroldi. When Alveroldi died in 1531, however, Maggio filled in for him during the time when Pole's friend Pier Paolo Vergerio began his career as a papal diplomat with a mission to Venice. A. J. Schutte, *Pier Paolo Vergerio*, 51; see also F. C. Church, *The Italian reformers, 1534–1564*, 72. Maggio remained in Venice at least until Girolamo Aleandro was appointed nuncio in 1533. Whether Maggio held conciliarist views like his friend Mantova's is unknown, but he was understandably enthusiastic about *De concilio* after it appeared. Mayer, 'Bronze age conciliarist', 407–8.

[109] *Ibid.*, 396–402.   [110] *Ibid.*, 406–7, and 'Religious crisis', 57.

[111] M. Roberti, 'Il collegio padovano dei dottori giuridici nel secolo XVI', 229–33, seconded *completamente* by Brugi, 'Giuristi', 56n. For Mantova's attitude, see Mayer, 'Religious crisis', 49–50.

[112] D. Cantimori, *Eretici italiani del cinquecento*, 24–5.

in a general council characterized the *spirituali*.[113] Well as this works in Mantova's case, it will probably not hold water for most of his fellow believers. Despite difficulties in summarizing such a diverse group, Elizabeth Gleason blends four major points into a subtly nuanced characterization of mature Evangelical belief. Justification by faith, its most important theological tenet, arose in part from *paulinismo preluterano*, but the broils of the Reformation enhanced it. Most Evangelicals stressed the necessity of some reform of the church, and many proposed to achieve that through an overhaul of institutions, as well as through reaching the people by preaching. Literary efforts provided another major outlet for the Evangelicals. Gleason overlooks only Evangelism's social roots in the nobility.[114]

The depth of the controversy over the nature of Evangelism makes it exceedingly dangerous to propose that its scope may have extended outside Italy in the person of Starkey, but the ambiguity of Starkey's thought could serve as a paradigm of the Evangelicals' 'shape of development'.[115] Whatever Starkey's long-buried predilections induced by Colet, it would be too much of a coincidence if he had passed through the crucible of Evangelism and come out holding to its central beliefs without having absorbed at least proximate inspiration from his experience in Padua. With his usual eclecticism and ecumenism, Starkey managed to blend major tenets of both the crudely defined wings of the Evangelicals, probably largely because of his friendship with van Kampen. The Evangelicals divided according to their attitude to reform, and in particular how actively they should involve themselves in its pursuit. Contarini, who stressed institutional reform and the *vita activa*, marked one end of the continuum. Pole fell somewhere in between, but closer to the quietist terminus represented by Flaminio and Kampen.[116] Once again, there is no need to determine which way the lines of 'influence' ran between Contarini's circle and Starkey. Suffice it to say that a common environment nurtured similar ideas, including many of the same specific reforms.

In the early 1530s none of the divisions within the party of reformers which would prove crucial by the end of the decade and especially after Regensburg were yet readily discernible, making it easy for Starkey to draw on ideas from many of its members and perhaps contribute some of his own. Pole and

---

[113] D. Cantimori, 'Submission and conformity: "nicodemism" and the expectations of a conciliar solution to the religious question'. Dermot Fenlon made a similar case in *Heresy and obedience in Tridentine Italy*, 18.

[114] E. G. Gleason, 'On the nature of sixteenth-century Italian evangelism: scholarship, 1953–1978', 25. For Evangelism's place in the 'aristocratization' of the Italian church, see L. Donvito, 'La "religione cittadina" e le nuove prospettive sul cinquecento religioso italiano', 440 and 460.

[115] I owe this point to Prof. Gleason's comment on my 'Thomas Starkey, an English *spirituale*', Sixteenth Century Studies Conference, St Louis, 1986.

[116] Massimo Firpo described the range of experience covered by the label Evangelical, but did not include Kampen. Review of Marcantonio Flaminio, *Lettere*, ed. A. Pastore, 656.

Contarini's friends (if not yet Contarini himself) saw eye to eye and even Gianpietro Caraffa, who would become notorious as Pope Paul IV for his fervour in persecuting Evangelicals, could aspire to leadership of the movement. Pole eagerly anticipated meeting Caraffa, who may even have induced Pole's turn to religion.[117] Some members of Pole's household in Padua would join Caraffa's new order of the Theatines, which he had moved to Venice in the 1520s. At the time, 'Theatine' was synonymous with 'reformer', and Caraffa attracted all the *spirituali* in Venice to him. For the moment, he and they shared many of the same objectives.[118] Starkey testified to the unity of this group by bracketing Caraffa and Contarini when advising Pole to whom he should turn while thinking about the divorce.[119] He may also have owed some of his notions about fitting church music to the strictly unadorned 'Theatine style', which would later be in use in Pole's household.[120]

   Starkey's earlier experience in Italy together with his renewed exposure to Colet prepared him to regard Contarini's notions of reform and Kampen's religious ideas favourably. In the first part of his Dialogue Starkey treated the church in tandem with his plans for civil society in the way a Venetian would have. As Starkey had in the case of secular politics, he began with the head. He faulted the spirituality first for accepting the authority 'gyven to the hede [the pope] or els by many yerys usurpyd apon us tyrannycally' of dispensation from all laws of God and man.[121] Starkey made 'Lupset' raise the same objection he had made to 'Pole's' original attempt to limit royal authority: a single head must 'moderate & tempur the straytenes of the law, orels we schold have veray oft general connsellys' (81r). A conciliar and oligarchical solution to papal pretensions paralleled Starkey's remedy for secular tyranny, 'for as the prynce by prorogatyve & pryvylege brekyth the ordur of the lawys & the knot of al cyvylyte, so doth the pope ... usurpyng authoryte of dyspensatyon apon al the lawys by general counseyl decred, wythout communyng wyth hys counseyl of Cardynallys'. Difficult cases touching the 'welth of Crystundome' required consultation, because the cardinals exercised the authority of the general council. If the pope failed to seek their advice, he assumed a 'certayn clokyd tyranny under the pretext of relygyon' (118r–v). Neither pope nor cardinals had any power to dispense from general laws made by the church (81r). Starkey left the pope with much the same circumscribed powers as he did the king, except that the pope's headship depended more explicitly on the general council than the prince's did on parliament (118v). Divine institution of the papacy mattered little to Starkey. He conceded Peter only the power of absolution, which he appeared to distinguish

[117] Fenlon, *Heresy*, 29.   [118] Simoncelli, *Evangelismo*, 47–9.
[119] Cleop. E VI, fol. 376r, and see chapter 7.   [120] *ERP*, II, civ.
[121] SP 1/90, fols. 80v, 67r, 82r.

explicitly from the pope's jurisdictional authority. Starkey put forward a personal opinion that 'the authoryte gyven to sayn petur was nothyng of that sort, wych now adays the popys usurpe, but hyt was only to declayre penytent hartys contryte for their syn to be absolvyd from the faut therof & that hyt schuld be no more imputyd to them', and then continued immediately '& as for the dyspensatyon of lawys...' (81r–v).

Starkey's idea of reform rested on a hierarchical view of the church. Its heads had to reorder themselves into examples for the people. One of their principal duties was to be preaching which became a vital component in Starkey's more egalitarian soteriology. It was necessary first to prepare the people to benefit from preaching by 'certayn ordynance':

how be hyt the pryncypal cause lyth only in god, he must forme & lyght theyr hartys wyth hys grace, or els the prechyng can take lytyl effect, but the gudnes of god ys such that, al men what so ever they be wych by prayar & by humylyte make themselfe apte to receyve thys lyght & grace schal be by & by partetakers therof [*ab.*], he [God] ys not acceptor personarum, but even as the lyght of the sone schynyth in al bryght bodys wych of theyr nature be clere & bryght, so dothe thys grace & celestyal lyght comunycat hyt selfe by the gudnes of god to al hartys & myndys wych wyl wyth dylygence *& ardent affect [*ab.*] lovyngly desyre hyt. (126r)

This idea of salvation made up part of the new tack Starkey adopted near the end of the Dialogue.[122] Originally Starkey's notion was barely Christian, and was entirely a matter of human ability to follow the dictates of reason (6r, 13r, 13v). Later, Starkey had 'Pole' espouse a purely Coletian line. All goodness came from the Holy Spirit which illuminated human hearts and minds if believers wished it strongly enough (93v). Still as for Colet, this meant following nature through right reason to a pure civil society (94r and 95r). A little later, 'Pole' assured 'Lupset' that all good came from God, although providence required human assistance (102v). Reason would still learn to dominate bodily affects (103r). Only near the very conclusion did 'Pole' turn to Paul and propose to follow 'a nother way'. Starkey cast his Paul in Colet's neo-platonic, illuminationist mould. Diligent preparation was required 'to attayne thys celestyal doctryne, wych ys not inspyryd in to neclygent hartys, but only to such as by grete study have purgyd ther myndys from al wordly affectys'. All the same, salvation depended on 'perfayt fayth & sure trust' in God's promises, and came 'only of god & may not be by the powar of man'. Starkey aimed for a middle course between those who thought they could gain heaven simply by wishing for it, and those 'wych by theyr owne natural powar thynke themselfys abul to optayne & deserve such precyouse gyfte' (123r).

Starkey suggested Erasmus as the best spiritual guide at the end of the

---

[122] A. Fox, 'English humanism and the body politic', in A. Fox and J. A. Guy, *Reassessing the Henrician age*, 49 misses this change of direction.

Dialogue, but his model could as easily have been Contarini. Preaching counted as a vital element to him and his friends. Contarini tried to regulate it in typically Venetian fashion in order to control controversy among the common people.[123] One of Pole's earliest Italian friends, Gianmatteo Giberti, bishop of Verona launched a major campaign to improve preaching in his diocese just after Starkey wrote.[124] Many more similarities link Contarini's and Starkey's platforms. The nature of Contarini's reform emerges clearly from the *Consilium de emendanda ecclesia*, produced by a commission of cardinals (including Pole and Caraffa) in 1537. In many ways similar to its predecessor the *Libellus ad Leonem* X of Contarini's friends Querini and Giustiniani, the *Consilium* too 'bears a heavy Venetian imprint'. Luigi Donvito meant that judgment as a criticism, to emphasize that patrician reform confined itself to 'arid prescriptiveness'.[125] Paolo Simoncelli seconded Donvito on Contarini's 'conservative paternalism', but like Donvito he derided Contarini's taste for 'political' solutions, without regard for their theological coherence.[126] One may dispute the intrusions of moral judgments, but these analyses capture the essence of the *Consilium* nonetheless and underline how close Starkey came to its spirit and many of its particulars. Contarini, like Starkey, disagreed with Colet's contention that the basic evil in the church was the interference of secular princes. For them, abuse of papal power loomed much larger. Contarini and his commission shaped their proposals around the organic metaphor of a diseased body. The root of its problems lay in the pope, who had become accustomed to having his word taken for law. Flatterers had convinced him that he was 'the lord of all benefices'.[127] Basing itself on Aristotle, the commission adopted the fundamental premise that all laws must be obeyed, and the pope must therefore restrain his propensity to grant dispensations. 'No more pernicious custom can be introduced into the Christian commonwealth than the failure to observe the laws' (87). The cardinals should be compelled to reside in Rome, so that 'besides discharging their duties, [they] would enhance the grandeur of your court' (93). It was also suggested that the cardinals receive an equal income from the pope, so that they would not have to depend on the favour of secular rulers and could speak their minds freely. The framers of the *Consilium* trod cautiously here, but a corporate oligarchical view of the headship of the church lurks behind their soothing of the papal ego. They could write bluntly when necessary. Above all, they warned the pope that he must not use the laws of the church for financial gain, especially through the abuse of

---

[123] Simoncelli, *Evangelismo*, 79–80.   [124] A. Prosperi, *G. M. Giberti*, 235.

[125] Donvito, 'Religione cittadina', 451 and 442–3.   [126] Simoncelli, *Evangelismo*, 71–80.

[127] I use E. G. Gleason's translation in *Reform thought in sixteenth century Italy*, 86. The original is in B. J. Kidd, ed., *Documents illustrative of the continental reformation*, 307–18.

sacramental absolution (95). Unfit clergy posed one of the most serious problems in the overhaul of papal government. Like Caraffa, this commission placed the weight of reform on the bishops, who were to control ordination of priests, reside in their sees, hold no more than one benefice with cure of souls, and be responsible for the discipline of all residents of the diocese, including monks and nuns (88–93). The universities were to control their reading and strive to turn out properly trained clergy (95).

It needs no emphasis that Starkey followed the same basic line as this commission as well as advocating many of its particular reforms, but it should be underlined that Contarini consistently approached the power of the papacy in exactly the manner Starkey did. As Philip McNair concluded, Contarini favoured papal absolutism in religious matters and opposed it in political. As Contarini wrote to the pope in 1529, 'your holiness must set in the forefront of your responsibilities the welfare of the true church, which consists in the peace of Christendom, and allow the interests of temporal states to fall for a time into the background'.[128] Contarini attacked papal absolutism because it forced rational creatures to submit to the arbitrary wishes of a monarch. That conflicted with both the laws of Christ and of nature, which mandated human freedom.[129] All the same, for Contarini 'the problem of papal power did not exist'. That is, he did not dispute the papacy's exclusive claims to authority descending from Peter, from whom all other bishops derived their power.[130] Contarini also accepted most of the other usual arguments in favour of papal monarchy, because the unity of the church demanded a single head.[131] Still, Contarini did not flatly deny the value of councils, and at least once or twice sought precedents in them for his reforms.[132] After all, the church was the community of all Christians.[133]

Despite his agreement with Contarini, Starkey had one more step to take in tandem with Pole to complete his own religious evolution. As his new line at the end of the Dialogue indicates, Starkey had begun to drift in the direction of Evangelical soteriology. In the early 1530s reform did not yet much interest Pole. Instead, he wrestled for his salvation. He had already undertaken the theological and biblical studies which would bring him to the point in December 1535 when John Friar reported to Starkey that Pole 'is undergoing a great change, exchanging man for God'.[134] One of the midwives to Pole's rebirth was van Kampen, who arrived in Padua in May 1534 and entered

---

[128] P. McNair, *Peter Martyr in Italy*, 12–13.   [129] Schenk, *Pole*, 53.
[130] E. G. Gleason, 'Cardinal Gasparo Contarini (1483–1542) and the beginning of catholic reform', 76.
[131] Dittrich, *Contarini*, 300–2 and Gleason, 'Contarini', 73–5.
[132] Dittrich, *Contarini*, 339 and 91.
[133] *Regesten und Briefe des Cardinals Gasparo Contarini*, 43.
[134] *LP*, IX, 917 (quoting the calendar summary).

Pole's household just about the time Starkey left it in October.[135] These two became very close, despite the short time they could have known each other in Padua, as two letters from Kampen attest.[136] Perhaps they had already met in Louvain, where Kampen first studied theology, before turning to Hebrew which he taught from 1521 until the end of the 1520s.[137] For a time he entered the service of John Dantiscus, a Polish noble and bishop. During a trip back to Poland, Dantiscus paid for the printing of Kampen's paraphrase of Psalms, and Kampen wrote a short commentary on Romans. The *Paraphrasis* proved popular, and an English translation appeared quickly from Berthelet's press in 1535.[138]

Kampen made his way to Venice by using his *Commentariolus* on Romans (printed in 1534 in Cracow and in 1535 in Venice) to attract the favour of Girolamo Aleandro, the papal nuncio. Aleandro treated Kampen meanly, and Kampen soon wrote to a friend 'I am sorry to have defiled my book by his infamous name' and called the nuncio 'a man in whom there is nothing except perhaps an empty head'.[139] The announcement of Aleandro's appointment as legate to the Empire triggered Kampen's second outburst and indicates another reason Kampen disliked Aleandro, aside from frustrated ambition. From early in his career Kampen had designed his studies with the reclamation of at least Philip Melanchthon in mind. Kampen called Melanchthon the most learned and best intentioned of the reformers, and used his *Commentariolus* to respond 'modestly' to Melanchthon's own exposition of Romans.[140] In fact, Kampen never mentioned Melanchthon by name, and his other challenges to Luther's right-hand man were exceedingly mild by sixteenth-century standards. Kampen dismissed the chief conservative controversialists of the Empire as 'men whom I know would rather three new Luthers existed than to have a care for one of them here'.[141]

Kampen not only pushed Starkey further towards salvation by restoration rather than illumination, but he also offered his friend a new vocabulary to

---

[135] H. de Vocht, *History of the foundation and rise of the collegium trilingue lovaniense*, I, 200 and 202.

[136] Nero B VI, fol. 173r (16 July 1535; *LP*, VIII, 883) and Harl. 6989, fol. 53r (16 August 1535; *LP*, IX, 104).

[137] De Vocht, *Collegium trilingue*, I, 503–4 and II, 102.

[138] *Ibid.*, III, 191 and 193.　　　[139] *Ibid.*, 201.

[140] For Kampen's concern to recover Melanchthon, see H. de Vocht, *John Dantiscus and his Netherlandish friends, passim*. Elsewhere de Vocht called it 'the ultimate purpose of his [Kampen's] life'. *Collegium trilingue*, III, 157. Jan van Kampen, *Commentariolus in duas divi Pauli epistolas*, sig. Aiiv. This work is extremely rare. No major libraries in Venice, Paris or London have a copy. With the exception of the Biblioteca universitaria, Padua which holds a copy of the Venetian edition, the only copy I have located is in the Biblioteca Narodnowa, Warsaw. I am therefore most grateful to Prof. Dr Lech Szczucki for providing me with a microfilm.

[141] De Vocht, *Dantiscus*, 292–3.

express the means of justification, the *beneficium Christi*. Simoncelli attri-
butes 'a role of the first order' to Kampen's *Commentariolus* in the creation of
Evangelism, because it offered 'a scientific definition of the expression *beneficio di Christo* for the first time in Italy'.[142] The term *beneficium Christi*
occurs repeatedly in Kampen's work to mean 'the removal of sins' and
justification which makes Christian behaviour possible (sig. Bv). These two
most concerned Kampen (Aiiiv). He resolved the dispute between those who
stressed faith and those who emphasized works by drawing a distinction
between works before and after justification. No good works were possible
without faith, and although those done after one had faith did not save,
either, they could augment the believer's measure of justice through obedience to the spiritual law (Bvbv and Ciiv). Nevertheless, the *beneficium Christi*
first had to liberate the sinner from the 'accusation of the [old] law'. Christ
had satisfied its impossible demands for all (Bvav). In a pithy phrase Kampen
wrote that 'justification happens through faith in Christ, that is the benefit of
Christ, which we gain through faith, not by works' (Bvbr).

Kampen used language familiar to Starkey to refine his concept. *Virtus*
came from God by the benefit of Christ, without regard to the recipient (Br;
cf. Ciiv). The difficulty in transmitting *virtus* lay in the oppression of *mens &
ratio* by the 'wantonness' of the flesh, which obscured men's *intellectum*
(Biiir). Nevertheless, none of its efforts could produce good works without
faith (Bvbv). Nothing came from human *dignitas* (Bvcr). Most men succumbed to the war between flesh and spirit, choosing to follow the 'affect' of
the flesh and withdraw from the spirit (Diiiiv). After justification, however,
'we shall walk with the spirit, that is, we follow reason' (Diir). This led to
sanctification, but unlike Sadoleto (or Starkey at an earlier stage) Kampen
said next to nothing about how man became god-like. Human failings
interested him much more. Kampen occasionally used political terms, including the 'tyranny' of sin, or 'civil' justice, but he ignored the biblical
proof-text on civil obligation, Romans 13:1–5, and generally displayed next
to no interest in political matters. Nor did Paul's heavy use of organic imagery
intrigue Kampen, who merely observed that Christians were members of one
body, and each had different gifts (Eiiv).

---

[142] Simoncelli, *Evangelismo*, 66. Simoncelli makes more of Melanchthon's impact on Kampen
than Kampen himself acknowledged. Simoncelli argues that Melanchthon had revived this
'typically Pauline' term and made it the centre of his Christology and ethics by the time of his
Loci communes of 1535 (*ibid.*, 68; for similar arguments see Salvatore Caponetto's comment
on his edition of Benedetto da Mantova, *Il 'beneficio di Cristo'*, 471–2 and J. C. Nieto, *Juan
de Valdes and the origins of the Spanish and Italian reformation*, 319n). If this doctrinal
genealogy behind Kampen's work is accepted, it reveals a great irony in the interpretation of
Starkey's thought. Zeeveld will turn out to be correct about the importance of Melanchthon
to Starkey, but for all the wrong reasons. See T. F. Mayer, 'Starkey and Melanchthon on
adiaphora: a critique of W. Gordon Zeeveld'.

Starkey adopted Kampen's views in some brief sermon notes on the *bene-ficium mortis Christi* which liberated human nature through grace and led to eternal life.[143] These notes are very faded, and the paraphrase offered here rests on a probable reconstruction. Starkey scrawled them on the dorse of a letter from Edmund Harvel, but its date of 18 June 1531 means very little about when Starkey drafted his sermon. Almost all of Starkey's surviving in-letters come from after he returned to England, with perhaps one other exception, a 'love' letter.[144] It may be that Starkey saved that letter because it had particular emotional significance, and preserved this one because it taxed him with threatening to withdraw from the service of the commonwealth, the worst misdeed of which he could conceive. Later he recycled it for the sermon fragment which held special religious importance.

Kampen took only the first step in the diffusion of Evangelism. By writing in Latin he restricted his audience to the upper classes and he never showed interest in the common people.[145] This difference between Starkey and Kampen over tactics (and implicitly the necessity of institutional reform) reinforces the evidence of Starkey's disagreements with Pole that Pole's circle was anything but religiously homogeneous. Beccadelli recognized distinc-tions of religious attitudes in Padua by dividing Pole's acquaintance in two. The first sort were 'outstanding men, whose custom he [Pole] much used', a group which included Bembo, Gabriele, Marcantonio de Genova, Benedetto Lampridio and Bonamico. The last three were also certainly Starkey's inti-mates, but he shared none of the friends on Beccadelli's second list of more pious men to whom Pole was especially close: Cosmo Gherio, bishop of Fano; 'Marco the monk of Cremona' (probably Mario Armellini, another Pauline scholar); and Pole's very close friend, Alvise Priuli.[146] Recently, Simoncelli has argued convincingly that Bembo belongs in the ranks of the *spirituali*, but none of the other friends Starkey and Pole shared would qualify.[147]

De Genova, for example, dominated the Aristotelian philosophers of Padua in the middle of the sixteenth century in the same way Pomponazzi had in its opening years.[148] He spent his entire life in Padua, taking doctorates in both arts and medicine in 1512.[149] Beginning five years later, he moved

---

[143] Nero B VI, fol. 169v.

[144] Herrtage printed this letter in *Starkey's life*, lxviii–lxix. The original is in SP 1/85, fol. 1 (*LP*, VII, 901). Aside from being written in fractured French (not Franglais, but Fritalian), which might mean it dates from Starkey's sojourns in either Paris or Avignon, the letter contains no clues about when it was written.

[145] Simoncelli, *Evangelismo*, 69 and Gleason, 'Contarini', 25.

[146] Beccadelli, 'Vita', 287–8. De Genova, Lampridio and Bonamico enquired after Starkey through Henry Cole in 1536. SP 1/102, fol. 157r and Nero B VI, fol. 175r. See Fenlon, *Heresy*, 31 for Marco's identity.

[147] Paolo Simoncelli, 'Pietro Bembo e l'evangelismo italiano'.   [148] McNair, *Martyr*, 110–11.

[149] For this and what follows, see the capsule biography in C. Lohr, 'Renaissance Latin Aristotle commentaries', 726.

steadily through the ranks until he arrived at the first ordinary chair of philosophy in 1531. Until 1542 he held it *in concurrens* with Vincenzo Maggi, but thereafter it was de Genova's alone, a signal mark of Venetian respect. Like Mantova, de Genova went some way to blend humanist philological methods into his essentially scholastic approach to philosophy. He claimed that everything in the barbarous Latin translations of Averroes could be found in the more elegant Greek of the Aristotelians he preferred, Theophrastus, Themistius and especially Simplicius.[150] Paolo Manuzio, a member of the famous family of humanist printers (and probably an Evangelical), claimed that there was 'no more learned interpreter of Aristotle' than his master de Genova.[151] Another of de Genova's students went on to become professor of humanities at Padua.[152] Surviving notes of de Genova's lectures do not give much indication of what he had in common with Starkey, although Starkey doubtless refined his notion of method in conversations with the foremost contemporary member of the school of Padua, and de Genova was every bit as eclectic as Starkey.[153] De Genova's ideas of good definition had some points in common with Leonico's. Any complete definition had to embrace both matter and form, unlike those offered by dialecticians which rested on the latter alone.[154] He also emphasized the functional side of definitions, declaring that if an object did not do what its definition said it did, it should be called something else (78r). Elsewhere, de Genova argued that definitions from principles would provide real definitions of real parts. Adding those real, essential parts together by demonstration would produce a final definition, or the species of the object.[155] Therefore, perhaps the most useful theory de Genova offered Starkey was that nothing distinguished between the methods of *divisio* and *compositio*. In other words, de Genova adhered to the resoluto–compositive method (28r). Despite his Aristotelian loyalty, when de Genova occasionally employed political analogies, he turned to Plato. Even prudent rulers needed more than experience of ruling for their perfection. They, like all men, could grasp the eternal through their *mens* or *intellectus*.[156] Richard Morison also studied at least indirectly with de Genova, who was apparently also close to Mantova.[157]

---

[150] B. Nardi, *Saggi sull'aristotelismo padovano dal secolo XIV al XVI*, 342. T. Gregory selected passages from de Genova emphasizing his borrowings from Simplicius in *Grande antologia filosofica*, VI, *Il pensiero della rinascenza e della riforma*, 742–63.

[151] Nardi, *Saggi*, 387. Simoncelli discussed Manuzio's religious leanings in *Il caso Reginald Pole*, 41 and 240.

[152] Nardi, *Saggi*, 394.   [153] *Ibid.*, 343 for de Genova's eclecticism.

[154] Biblioteca apostolica vaticana, Vat. lat. 4705 (608), fols. 52r–53r. This, like the next two MSS cited, is a set of student notes, although none comes from the time of Starkey's stay.

[155] Vat. lat. 4704, fols. 27r–v, 28v, 29r (cf. 4705, 31v).   [156] Vat. lat. 4707, fol. 2v.

[157] Letter from Morison to Starkey, SP 1/95, fol. 102r (*LP*, IX, 103; 16 August 1535), reporting that he was reading Aristotle with his friend 'Poloni', who was probably de Genova's student Giuseppe (*Acta graduum academicorum*, I, no. 2188), promoted 16 October 1535. For de Genova and Mantova, see Robbins MS 63, no. 76, Alessandro Tyberino to Mantova, 10 April 1543).

Lampridio, once called de Genova's 'most dear brother', is a more obscure figure, as Antonio Santosuosso justly observed.[158] His surname appears to have been Alfeo or Alfeno and he came from Cremona.[159] Lampridio made his career as an educator and scholar of the text of Cicero, parts of which he edited during Starkey's final visit to Padua.[160] At various times he headed Leo X's Greek school in Rome, taught Beccadelli and Giovanni della Casa in the same language at Padua in the 1520s and finally, in 1536, went to Mantua as tutor to Francesco Gonzaga, whose brother Ercole (a cardinal and a remote ally of Pole) he had been asked to instruct in 1522.[161] Bembo sent his son to the duke's court to study under Lampridio, who impressed Bembo.[162] Much of the evidence for Lampridio's career comes from his correspondence with the famous Florentine republican and humanist Pier Vettori, through whom he apparently also knew Donato Giannotti.[163] Lampridio and Bonamico were living in Pole's household in October 1535.[164] Nothing whatever is known of either Lampridio's political or religious opinions.

Starkey may have known a little more about Bonamico's politics, and according to most historians, Bonamico's religion matched Pole's and Contarini's.[165] This is probably not true. As evidence, Rino Avesani cited Bonamico's fulsome congratulations to Contarini when the latter became a cardinal, and Bonamico certainly sounded enthusiastic.

What indeed has been done since the memory of men more illustrious for the commendation of the pontiffs, or more apt or wiser for restoring religion from such difficulties, than to desire men of virtue, who can and wish to give an example of Christian behaviour in natural disposition, learning, the handling of affairs, but above all of life?[166]

But when Pole returned to Padua in 1532, he made strenuous efforts to persuade Sadoleto to help him save Bonamico from his merely grammatical pursuits. The tactics Pole used on Bonamico reveal the depth of his divergence from Starkey. Religious studies came first, and Bonamico's continued immersion in Pomponazzi and the rhetoricians had to be stopped. Bonamico had to see that he would be better off concentrating on the kind of philosophy which 'deals with the precepts of life ... [rather] than remaining among the orators and poets, repeating the precepts for forming an oration from Cicero,

---

[158] *Ibid.*, no. 149 (Egidio Cathani-Mantova [1540]) and A. Santosuosso, 'Pier Vettori e Benedetto Lampridio', 155.
[159] F. Arisi, *Cremona literata*, II, 96.   [160] Santosuosso, 'Lampridio', 158 and 167.
[161] Arisi, *Cremona*, 95 and Santosuosso, 'Lampridio', 156–7.
[162] V. Cian, *Un decennio della vita di M. Pietro Bembo (1521–1531)*, 119 and Antonio Giganti da Fossombrone, 'Vita di Monsignor Lodovico Beccadelli', 6n.
[163] Santosuosso, 'Lampridio', 163.
[164] Nero B VII, fol. 111v (Bernardino Sandro to Starkey).
[165] R. Avesani, 'Bonamico, Lazaro', *DBI* and E. L. Hirsh, 'George Lily', 3 and xxi.
[166] Dittrich, *Regesten*, no. 255, 76.

or of tilling a field from Vergil'.[167] Bonamico, however, relied on Sadoleto's support to resist Pole's efforts to make him a theologian.[168] Had he become one, his views would have been strongly at odds with the Pyrrhonist Pole, anyway, since Bonamico believed in the rationality of the universe.[169] He and Pole differed over how to meet the current crisis in the church, too. Bonamico recommended the contemplation of the classics as a panacea for religious broils, even if he may have shared some of Pole's relatively tolerant attitude to Protestantism. The violently anti-papal Jakob Ziegler stayed with Bonamico in Padua, only a little while before Martin Bucer made strenuous efforts to attract him to Strassburg, and Bonamico's student and Ziegler's friend Julius Pflug was the same sort of moderate as Kampen.[170]

Most of Starkey's more humble friends in Pole's household eventually followed their master's religious bent, but the situation was still very much in flux in 1533 and 1534. George Lily, for instance, would accompany Pole to Rome in 1536 and end his life as Pole's chaplain under Mary I.[171] At this earlier time, however, he devoted himself to studying civil law, probably on Starkey's advice. He also pursued languages under Giovanni Battista Egnazio and Bonamico, as the son of the grammarian William Lily would almost have had to have done.[172] Like Starkey and Pole, Lily may have been a Magdalen man, but if so he matriculated after they left.[173] Somewhere he came to know their close friend Thomas Lupset well.[174] Bernardino Sandro also stayed with Pole, and took part in his legation which was designed to stir up trouble for Henry in 1537.[175] He entered Pole's service by 1528, when he appears in Starkey's expense ledger of Pole's trip to Paris.[176] Various domestic duties fell to Sandro's lot, and he also worked as a copyist and corrector of the press.[177] Finally, Henry Cole would spend the last twenty years of his life in the Tower, in no small part in recompense for his uncharitable sermon justifying

---

[167] *ERP*, I, 411–13.   [168] Sadoleto, *Opera*, I, 112.

[169] Stella, 'Tradizione razionalistica', 280 and Giuseppe Marangoni, 'Lazzaro Bonamico e lo studio padovano nella prima metà del cinquecento', II, 307.

[170] K. Schottenloher, *Jakob Ziegler aus Landau an der Isar*, 115 and 102, and H. Jedin in *Lexikon für Theologie und Kirche, s.n. Pflug*.

[171] Zeeveld, *Foundations*, 117 and 238.

[172] Nero B VI, fols. 165v–166r for Lily's curriculum (Lily to Starkey, 22 April [1535]). G. A. Andrich listed Lily in his *De natione anglica & scota iuristarum universitatis patavinae*, 130.

[173] A. B. Emden accepted G. B. Parks's statement in *The English traveller to Italy*, I, 488, but admitted that Parks's evidence was 'unknown'. *A biographical register of the university of Oxford A.D. 1501 to 1540*, 357. Lily does not appear in W. D. Macray's thorough *A register of the members of St Mary Magdalen college, Oxford*.

[174] J. A. Gee, *Thomas Lupset*, 11.

[175] 'A diet for Henry VIII: the failure of Reginald Pole's 1537 legation', 314.

[176] SP 1/55, fol. 194v (?).

[177] Schenk, *Pole*, 35 for Sandro's household responsibilities. For his work as a scribe see E. Lobel, 'Cardinal Pole's manuscripts', 98–9; Prosperi, *Giberti*, 229; and two letters to Starkey (Nero B VII, fols. 111v and 125r).

Cranmer's burning. For the moment, he joined Lily and Morison in the legal faculty at Padua, and upon his return to England may have authored a draft treatise on the power of general councils. He was not formally in Pole's household, but rather in the service of Dr William Knight.[178]

The odd man out amongst Starkey's friends in Padua was Morison.[179] As far as can be discerned, Morison distinguished himself before his return to England in 1536 chiefly by his irrepressible importunity. Almost all of the vast number of his surviving letters, whether to Starkey or anyone else, beg assistance, usually financial. Morison nevertheless had a noble end in mind – he intended to emulate Starkey and secure a post in England. Unlike Starkey, it does not appear that Morison ever approached Henry directly. This may be a function of their different social backgrounds or Starkey's greater experience with the high and mighty, but it may also reflect religious views. Instead of trying Henry, Morison went to Cromwell, patron of the 'forward' party in religion, although at first with little more success than Starkey had with the king. On the surface, Morison tried much the same tack as Starkey did. He used heavily civic humanist vocabulary, and he offered Cromwell all manner of vague bromides about reform and how to conduct it.[180] But once Morison succeeded in convincing Cromwell to give him a try, his career rapidly outdistanced Starkey's. If nothing else, Morison's presence on the fringes of Pole's circle is yet another testimony to its heterogeneity.

With the exception of Morison, Starkey probably stood at the pole furthest removed from his patron. He still moved in Pole's circle, but the 'influence' of the more congenial Contarini deformed the path of Starkey's orbit. It may even be that Pole and Starkey no longer lived under the same roof by the time Starkey left Padua. At least Starkey thought he had to explain to Pole why he had left Italy in his first letter from England, although that may have been for domestic consumption. The many letters between them to which Starkey also referred indicate that they must have been separated at various times.[181] It is harder to determine whether the apparent separation immediately before Starkey returned to England arose from Pole's preference for Venice, while Starkey's studies tied him to Padua, or whether it was a sign of their deepening estrangement. Depending on his audience, Starkey sometimes claimed he had gone home because of arguments with Pole. On other occasions, he

---

[178] *DNB*; P. A. Sawada, 'Two anonymous Tudor treatises on the general council', 210; and *LP*, XII:2, 40 for his connection to Knight.

[179] Two recent dissertations shed little light on this period of Morison's career. Neither C. R. Bonini, 'Richard Morison, humanist and reformer under Henry VIII', nor S. K. Christie, 'Richard Morison: an analysis of his life and work', dug into Morison's years in Padua. D. S. Berkowitz's life in his *Humanist scholarship and public order* is entirely derivative and contains errors, especially on the score of relations between Starkey and Morison.

[180] See in particular his letter from Padua of 27 October 1534 on how Cromwell should handle the commonweal. Nero B VI, fols. 151r–152r (*LP*, VII, 1318).

[181] Harl. 283, fol. 131r (15 February 1535).

offered to produce witnesses to substantiate his claim that Pole agreed with him about one of the key points at issue, the human origin of papal power (see the next chapter). Whatever his motive for returning home, Starkey did so with every expectation of continued success, having completed an education which fitted him to join the Henrician intellectual élite.

7

'Homo politicus et regalis'

Thomas Starkey returned to England sometime before 13 December 1534 in order to make good his once abortive plan of entering royal service.[1] By coincidence Starkey's career may almost serve as a barometer of the desperate struggle between Thomas Cromwell and the court conservatives.[2] His relative prominence means a new embarrassment of evidence, or at least wildly disproportionate coverage of about two years of Starkey's life. When Starkey returned home he hoped to inspire a broadly based reform movement, just as he had in the Dialogue, and probably cared little who executed his policies. He also did not worry a great deal about what role fell to him, although his principal goal would appear to have been preaching. It seems that he looked to both Cromwell (probably because of the minister's well-known interest in intellectuals) and the conservatives, and both would disappoint him. Starkey approached Cromwell almost immediately, but only after he returned home, in contrast to Richard Morison who inundated the Secretary with requests for assistance from Italy. Starkey may already have been trying to distance himself from the nobility, probably largely because of his disappointment in

[1] BL Nero B VII, fol. 106r (*LP*, VIII, 132), Edmund Harvel acknowledging Starkey's letters from London of 13 and 20 December, which reported his safe arrival, and Thomas Starkey, *Exhortation*, sig. 45v.

[2] For this, I follow the sketches in D. Starkey, *The reign of Henry VIII: personalities and politics*, 108–18, and J. A. Guy, 'Privy council: revolution or evolution?', in C. Coleman and D. Starkey, eds., *Revolution reassessed*, 77–80 and the fuller account in E. W. Ives, *Anne Boleyn*, chapters 15–17 and pp. 414–18. See also R. M. Warnicke, 'The fall of Anne Boleyn: a reassessment', and 'Sexual heresy at the court of Henry VIII'. The precise variations between the main accounts of D. Starkey, Ives and Warnicke do not matter a great deal to Starkey's fate, nor does any of them depart all that much from G. R. Elton's brief treatment in *Reform and reformation. England 1509–1558*, 250–3. Warnicke on the one hand and Starkey and Ives on the other differ mainly about when control over the plotting against Anne shifted from the court conservatives to Thomas Cromwell, and whether or not the minister acted at Henry's behest. Warnicke argues that the coup had begun already in January 1536 after Anne's second miscarriage, while both Ives and Starkey have Cromwell responding only in late April to an opening created by Anne herself. All agree on the threat to Cromwell's career posed by the manoeuvreings to replace Anne. In her most recent contribution, Warnicke suggests that the witchcraft charges against Anne should be taken much more seriously than they have been, and that early Tudor attitudes to aberrant sexuality help to explain her fate.

Pole. In any case, he did not turn to Pole's friends for patronage, even while living in the Countess of Salisbury's London town house in Dowgate.

Starkey's credentials impressed Cromwell, who quickly recruited him. At first, Starkey served as an intelligencer for Italy, assiduously soliciting the latest news from his wide range of correspondents in and around Pole's household in Padua and Venice. In return, he received a royal chaplaincy and soon came to act as a junior minister to Cromwell with portfolio for defending the new religious order both by engaging learned men in controversy and also by setting an example of preaching to the common people. In mid-1536 the auguries for Starkey's reform programme looked better than they had since 1532. The faction struggle which overthrew Anne seemed to promise the old nobility its chance, and Cromwell and Starkey were then still on good terms. Starkey, for his part, tried to accommodate his *Exhortation* to Cromwell's wishes. Despite his disillusionment with the nobility's potential for reform, Starkey may still have dusted off his Dialogue as a more explicit manifesto, after trying out some of its relatively innocuous sections on Cromwell. The honeymoon ended just a little later in the summer of 1536 when Starkey's preaching and, secondarily, his failure to induce Pole to accept the divorce led to his temporary disgrace. Very much the same fate befell the other members of the Marian party. At roughly the same time, Starkey seized his last chance to launch his programme by tendering the king a policy brief on the dissolution of the monasteries and the sensitive issue of the succession. Nevertheless, Starkey successfully defended himself, and a lucrative benefice in London rewarded his efforts. Yet he never again had Cromwell's confidence, as the opposite vectors of his and Morison's careers demonstrate. The superficial resemblance of his religious language to Cromwell's evaporated under the strain of the minister's demand for a 'protestant' or 'radical' commitment which the Italian Evangelical Starkey could not make. Nor, despite the bitter recriminations of some of his letters to Pole, would Starkey abandon his loyalty to his erstwhile patron. Throughout the efforts to bring Pole to book after *De unitate*, Starkey did his best to warn the cardinal of the moves afoot against him and remained in close touch with Pole's family, especially his brother Sir Geoffrey.

In the short space of about two years Starkey moved from aspirant for Cromwell's favour, through a period as one of the Secretary's tame intellectuals, to adherence to the conservative opposition. His last move was probably as much a matter of coincidence of goals, as of principle. Starkey, always the high-minded reformer with the interest of the whole body politic at heart, only reluctantly stooped to faction politics. The full implications of his detachment from Cromwell did not sink in until later in 1537. In the process of his political education, Starkey clung to his civic humanism, even if its activist and aristocratic component became increasingly muted. At least a residue of anti-monarchical feeling complicated Starkey's attempt to reach Henry directly. Whether Cromwell or common people, the audience of many of Starkey's later writings dictated heavy emphasis on obedience and consequently less attention to the active exercise of virtue.[3] Finally, Starkey ran out of political options. His turn to religion partly accounted for and partly helped to remedy his political failure. A more intense awareness of human weakness, frequently expressed in Pauline language, would by itself have affected Starkey's activism, but in combination first with Cromwell's demands and then with political disappointment, it finally led Starkey to renew his Stoic bent to contemn human existence. No other course but increasing withdrawal remained open to him.

G. R. Elton's account of Starkey's recruitment improves greatly on earlier efforts, but Cromwell's motives in employing Starkey as well as a few points of chronology need closer attention. S. J. Herrtage's suggestion that Starkey's *Exhortation* first caught Cromwell's eye, as well as the ridiculous assertion that he had been taken on much earlier to spy on Pole have been disposed of.[4] Nevertheless, George Parks's view that Starkey's close ties with Pole and abilities as a propagandist recommended him to Cromwell remains representative, and Elton is correct only up to a point that Starkey's 'What ys pollycye aftur the sentence of Arystotyl' showed Cromwell that Starkey could 'write the sort of thing that was required in propaganda pamphlets'. Parks's interpretation violates chronology, and both his and Elton's tell only part of the story and impose the modern overtones of 'propaganda' on the early sixteenth century.[5] They produce especially severe distortion in Starkey's case.

Shortly after his homecoming, Starkey approached Cromwell, who proved to be too busy to see Starkey during audience time. Therefore his suitor, a 'straunger & almost unknowne', wrote Cromwell two letters. As he had in the Dialogue, Starkey pinned his hopes on secular advancement, and expressed them in much the same language as he had used two or three years earlier. If Cromwell would help him, Starkey wrote, 'I schal ever juge that by you I have optaynyd a grete perte of my felycyte', and service to his prince would have the same effect. Starkey assured Cromwell that he hoped to enter government service only because he saw the king 'so sett to the restytutyon of

---

[3] Brendan Bradshaw distorts the nature of the relation between Cromwell and Starkey, but gets the content of their discussions right in 'The Tudor commonwealth: reform and revision', 469.

[4] G. R. Elton, *Reform and renewal: Thomas Cromwell and the commonweal*, 50ff. discusses the events leading up to the *Exhortation*, correcting, *inter alia*, S.J. Herrtage, *Starkey's life*, lxvi. M. Hallé, *Reginald Pole*, 67 and 135, and A. Zimmermann, *Kardinal Pole, sein Leben und seine Schriften*, 72 stated the case for Starkey as planted spy most strongly.

[5] G. B. Parks, *The English traveller to Italy*, I, 484; Elton, *Reform and renewal*, 49; and cf. Q. Skinner, *Foundations of modern political thought*, II, *The reformation*, 101 and W. Schenk, *Reginald Pole*, 62. The unfortunate connotations of propaganda could be avoided by the adoption of the sixteenth century term 'controversy'.

the trewe commyn wele'.[6] In his second letter, Starkey offered a résumé of his qualifications, which concentrated on his political skills. First, he had spent most of his youth in Oxford, studying philosophy and Latin and Greek. Then he had gone to Italy to acquire knowledge of nature. Next came Bible study,

aftur the wych, bycause my purpos then was to lyve in a polytyke lyfe, I set myselfe now thes last yerys past to the knowlege of the cyvyle law, that I myght therby make a more stabyl and sure jugement of the polytyke ordur & custumys usyd amonge us here in here [sic] cuntrey.[7]

Starkey first offered himself as one of Cromwell's jacks-of-all-trades, a man like Edward Legh or John Tregonwell, who had also been trained in civil law. Cromwell probably originally accepted Starkey's advertisement because of his recruit's ties to Italy. Cromwell kept a sharp eye out for Englishmen either at home or abroad who could assist in the gathering of foreign news. This was scarcely an innovation, even in England, but improved intelligence-gathering nonetheless coincides with Cromwell's approach to the levers of power.[8] In the period immediately before Cromwell's arrival, almost none of the voluminous correspondence of John Stokesley and Richard Croke contains any intelligence, regardless of the intended recipients. Croke and Stokesley may at least have had an excuse in the pressing business of the divorce, but neither of the contemporary resident English agents in Rome and Venice, Geronimo Ghinucci and Giovanni Casale, reported any political information worth knowing. By contrast, Cromwell's letters abound with requests for, and offers of, political news. In May 1531 Cromwell asked Stephen Vaughan to provide him with detailed information about the Low Countries, and Vaughan usually complied, despite his much greater interest in forwarding the careers of various English protestant exiles.[9] In July of the same year Thomas Winter thought he could ingratiate himself with Cromwell by offering to write about events in Italy once in a while.[10] Agostino d'Agostini, an Italian physician whom Cranmer may have directed to Cromwell, sent in a steady stream of reports, offering intelligence combined with increasingly abject begging.[11] Sir Clement West, who had been deposed as Turcopolier of the Order of St John of Jerusalem, pestered Cromwell incessantly for help, always adding the latest news from Malta.[12] More's friend Antonio Bonvisi

---

[6] SP 1/89, fol. 175v, and BL Harleian 283, fol. 130r. As D. G. Newcombe notes, Starkey had contacts in royal service, especially Edward Foxe, but there is no evidence that he used them. '"Due order & reasonabul mean"', 20.

[7] Harl. 283, fol. 129v.

[8] For the usual situation, see G. Mattingly, *Renaissance diplomacy*, chapter 11, especially 96–9, and F. M. G. Higham, 'A note on the pre-Tudor secretary', 365.

[9] *LP*, V, 248 and see Elton, *Reform and renewal*, 38–46 for Vaughan.   [10] *LP*, V, 338.

[11] *LP*, V, 888, 1027, 1413, 1422, 1657, 1667; VI, 22, 156, 261. Cranmer and Agostini had been in Regensburg together in 1532.

[12] *LP*, VII, 326, 651, 1100, 459; VIII, 1155; and IX, 920.

sent a half dozen letters on Italian affairs from Lyons in the spring of 1536, while Antonio Vivaldi kept Cromwell posted from Genoa.[13] When Thomas Legh visited Antwerp in February 1534, he thought Cromwell would want to know that no letters had come from Florence for six weeks.[14]

Doubtless Cromwell's experience in Italy had taught him to keep a close eye on the cockpit of Europe, and his apprenticeship to Wolsey reinforced the lesson. Perhaps faction struggles led him to go outside official channels for much of his information. Edmund Harvel may have obliquely indicated this in a letter of March 1535. He wrote that he did not need to write any news to Cromwell, since he would have it from the ambassadors, but then sent some anyway.[15] Cromwell may also not have trusted Peter Vannes, Henry VIII's Latin secretary, who ordinarily handled Ghinucci's and Casale's reports.[16] Vannes was another of Wolsey's protégés, for whom he had performed the same information-gathering task. When he went overseas himself in 1533 he sent his letters to Cromwell.[17] Nevertheless, he was not Cromwell's man and could not have been close to him. He became Dean of Salisbury in the year of Cromwell's fall.[18] Then again, perhaps Cromwell was simply fed up with the quality of the information English ambassadors sent in. However this may be, Cromwell certainly tried to develop his own sources of information and he concentrated in particular on Italy.

Starkey's correspondence supports the argument that Cromwell initially employed him as a high-powered clerk, even if he was posted to a vital department. Neither he nor any other humanist ordinarily filled his letters with news – Cicero had, after all, enjoined *brevitas* in the *narratio*.[19] Starkey's good friend Bernardino Sandro evidently regarded Starkey's request for news as unusual, yet almost immediately after Starkey's recruitment Sandro assured his friend that 'I am very desirous of saying new things, and I will willingly look to satisfy you in this to all my ability.'[20] For the most part, Sandro honoured his pledge. Harvel, who had been serving as an unofficial conduit for reports from Venice for years, began writing even more extensive and regular bulletins than Sandro, perhaps stimulated by the signs of Cromwell's favour about which Starkey often wrote.[21] Their correspondence breaks off at almost precisely the moment of Starkey's disgrace in mid-1536, and the newly arrived Morison stepped into Starkey's shoes.[22]

[13] *LP*, X, 368, 437, 442, 713, 714, 795 for Bonvisi, and 652 and 1130 for Vivaldi.
[14] *LP*, VII, 167.   [15] *LP*, VIII, 373.   [16] *LP*, VIII, 17, 91, 112, 1486; X, 632.
[17] *LP*, IV:2, 2202, decipher of a letter from Ghinucci to Wolsey, in Vannes's hand, and VI, 688 and 1399 for reports to Cromwell.
[18] *DNB*.
[19] Cicero, *De inventione*, ed. and trans. H. M. Hubbell, I. 20. 28., p. 59.
[20] BL Nero B VI, fol. 155r
[21] For some of Harvel's earlier bulletins, see *LP*, IV:5, 6620, 6694–6, 6702.
[22] Harvel's last surviving letter to Starkey bears the date of 15 June 1536 (*LP*, X, 1142), while his first to Morison comes from August (XI, 328).

Cromwell had a pressing incentive to recruit an Italian specialist just when Starkey turned up. The Venetians recalled Carlo Cappello in January 1535, and Starkey's stock would have gone up once it became clear that they would not replace their ambassador.[23] Already in 1531, Capello's appointment had spurred opposition for fear of arousing the emperor. Some Venetians also wanted nothing to do with the divorce.[24] After they pulled Cappello out four years later, the Signory left the post in the hands of secretaries until Domenico Bollani's appointment in 1547.[25] True, the *Serenissima* continued to send regular reports on the Turks to its representatives with instructions to pass them on to Henry, but the English could no longer rely on this channel, which now delivered a much more limited amount of information than it had once done.[26] When the English retaliated for Cappello's withdrawal by recalling Giovanni Casale on 17 March, the situation became critical.[27] Harvel did not succeed Casale until 1541. Thus official relations between England and Venice broke down for an interval of six years and Cromwell had to make do at first with Starkey, Morison and John Mason, with Harvel as their most reliable informant.[28]

Cromwell paid attention to other of Starkey's credentials and soon turned to him for a treatise on Aristotelian political science. 'What ys pollycye' resulted. But Starkey modified Cromwell's assignment to explain 'what thyng hyt ys aftur the sentence of arystotyl & the ancyent perypatetykys that commynly among them ys callyd pollycy' into a speech 'to the declaratyon wherof I have imagynyd & faynyd wyth myself a rude multytude & ignorant, desyryng to lyve in true pollycy to whome I dyrect my communycatyon'. It must be emphasized that Starkey changed Cromwell's request. In other words, Starkey picked up where he had left off at the end of the Dialogue and fell back on his skills as a Christian orator, a preacher.[29] Starkey's legal training may even have contributed to his new vocation, since the law schools especially emphasized the necessity of unifying theory and practice.[30] The rhetorical style of the Dialogue still marked 'What ys pollycye', but Starkey turned to the form of an oration for it and almost all the rest of his writing. It begins 'for by cause I have long observyd in you gud pepul an honest and a natural desyre of lyvyng togyddur' and Starkey went on to show them, as he

---

[23] *CSPV*, V, 31.   [24] *DBI*, s.n., 770.   [25] C. Cairns, *Domenico Bollani*, 29.

[26] *CSPV*, V, 148 (9 June 1537) noted a motion that the secretary in England should be written to, since he had not been for more than six months. Henry had to request a resumption of the reports, but when the Venetians began regular dispatches again in July they hoped to involve Henry in war against the Turks (*CSPV*, 151, and 159ff.).

[27] *CSPV*, V, 38.   [28] For Mason's involvement, see *LP*, X, 687.

[29] A. B. Ferguson was thus wrong to observe that Starkey gave 'only formal and belated respect to the value of preaching'. *The articulate citizen and the English renaissance*, 343–4.

[30] D. R. Kelley, '*Vera philosophia*: the philosophical significance of renaissance jurisprudence', 274.

concluded, 'now gud pepul ... how you may turne thys wordly pollycy ... by sure fayth & perfayt charyte in to chrystyan lyfe & spyrytual'.[31] He couched his *Exhortation* in exactly the same form, although it admittedly runs a bit long for delivery.

The content of 'What ys pollycye' also would have appealed to Cromwell. Starkey shaped it on a psychology identical to that in the Dialogue. Humans were born to 'cyvyle ordur & natural honesty', as their building of 'gudly castellys cytes & townys' made manifest (182r). (Starkey still made no room for the vast majority of Englishmen who lived outside urban areas.) Bad education and laziness stunted the 'sedys nature hath so plantyd in the hart of man' and the 'vycyouse affectys' he allowed to grow up prevented him from reaching 'hys natural perfectyon & due felycyte' (182v). This situation continued until wise men made laws which forced the rest to virtue. Their sagacity made policy the bridle of the multitude, even as reason was in an individual, and turned the mass of people into 'the polytyke body by pollycy rulyd' (183r). The corporate analogy again described this aggregation of men, even if Starkey truncated his elaborate treatment in the Dialogue (185r).

From the origin of civil society Starkey passed to a discussion of various forms of government. Different polities fit different sorts of people. The rule of a prince best suited those people most accustomed to it, 'beyng not ambycyouse of hye authoryte but in pryvate lyfe content to lyve quyatly'. A common council was proper to those 'beyng of grete currage & hye stomake ... brought up in franke lyberty' (183v–184r). As always, Starkey's ambivalence about the word liberty makes it hard to say whether he continued to recommend the latter. He certainly insisted that the precise sort of government did not matter, provided the rulers 'ever refer & dyrect al theyr conseylys actys & dedys, to the commyn wele of the hole commynalty' (184v). If they did not, civility was destroyed and tyranny introduced. Starkey's survey of constitutional forms carefully avoided any inkling of the radical proposals of the Dialogue and even the comparatively innocuous observation that there were three basic types of government – by prince, council or people – was toned down on its second appearance to just the first two (184v).

Self-serving motives might explain why Starkey concealed his former leanings, but his openness about his new religious views suggests that he had at least developed a large measure of sincere doubt about his earlier political ideas, enough to approach Cromwell without them. Then again, ambiguity might almost have been Starkey's watchword and he may not have known himself which course he meant to pursue. Even though Cromwell therefore learned much more about Starkey's religion than about his politics, he and

[31] SP 1/89, fols. 182r and 186v.

Starkey apparently still misunderstood one another. Starkey may have dropped the political line of his Dialogue, but he faithfully reproduced the religious views in its final section. Starkey now insisted that policy was merely a means to the end of good religious observance and described a Christian polity in which only 'perfayt workys groundyd in chrystyan fayth & charytabul' counted towards salvation, while 'dedys wych wythout fayth were downe in vanyte' did not. Similarly, Starkey assured his hearers that 'you schal undowtydly trustyng to the promysys of god surely by hys mere benefyte & mercy injoy everlastyng lyfe in immortalyte' (186v). Cromwell apparently read this *spirituale* language as protestant. Again, whatever Cromwell may have thought about Marsilio's ideas, Starkey's coupling of the two polities provides one of the best arguments against his reliance on Marsilio, for whom church and civil society were to be kept rigorously apart.

Cromwell's misinterpretation probably accounts as much as any of Starkey's other qualifications for his most momentous assignment, the Pole desk. Of course, Starkey's long friendship with Pole and extensive Italian experience as well as current contacts also helped to fit him for the task. Starkey did not seek the job and, as Elton observed, it 'can hardly be described as the service to the commonwealth' Starkey had in mind.[32] Nevertheless, Cromwell may very well have begun to look for the sort of men on whom he came to rely from 1536 forward, those who shared his religious beliefs. If some reality lies behind Pole's famous story of his interview with Cromwell in 1531, and if Cromwell knew of Pole's white paper on the divorce as his fellow Boleyn ally Thomas Cranmer did, then he may already have decided that Pole would have to be dealt with. Cromwell may well have appreciated the inflexibility of Pole's intellect and have deduced that he could best undo Pole in early 1535 by persuading him to give his true opinion of the divorce.[33] Hence the medium of Starkey, a friend, but one on whom Cromwell thought he could also rely for ideological reasons.

Cromwell as the villain of the piece alters the standard interpretation of the conflict between Henry and Pole, which rests largely on Pole's own account. A full-dress treatment of this complicated *pas-de-deux* would be out of place here, but in light of Pole's success in creating a *persona* and propagating his

---

[32] Elton, *Reform and renewal*, 49.
[33] Starkey, *Henry VIII*, 120 probably emphasizes Cromwell's ruthlessness too much. Guy argues that Cromwell's radicalism was much more pronounced after 1537, but there are certainly clear signs of it before that, especially in the restructuring of the privy council in 1536 when Cromwell went head to head with the religious conservatives who dominated the emergency council. 'Privy council', 79. Elton obliquely suggested an interpretation of the relations between Pole and Cromwell much like mine when he described the man of the world Cromwell twitting the prig Pole. *The Tudor revolution in government*, 7.

side of the story, historians would be well advised to swallow his version with a large grain of salt.[34] If we follow the order of events, rather than reading them backwards as Pole did, no evidence appears of a concerted design on Henry's part to entrap Pole or even force him to swallow the official line. On the contrary. Henry repeatedly allowed his protégé to go his own way, ignoring the reasonable expectation that the crown might have some service from a man whose education it had underwritten. Likewise, there is no reason to doubt Pole's desire to be left to his studies, nor his frequent protestations of loyalty and regard for Henry's welfare. Alas, a large matter of principle came between these two strong-willed, even pig-headed men, but Pole handled a pen much more adeptly than Henry or most of the king's supporters. Pole's fluency distorts not only the tale of his breach with Henry, but also Starkey's career in royal service. The overwhelming importance of the struggle between king and cousin has overshadowed everything else Starkey did, but probably neither he nor Cromwell nor Henry saw his service exclusively in that light. Nor did Starkey totter uncertainly on a tightrope stretched between Henry and Pole. Instead, he and Pole and a large group of Pole's friends occupied what Lacey Baldwin Smith dubbed the 'intermediate middle ground'.[35]

Starkey's third assignment offered him the chance to fulfil the hopes of the *Dialogue* and induce Pole to adopt his proper office (and, of course, benefit Starkey's career). Starkey consequently approached the task with enthusiasm, but also with caution. Perhaps Pole's repeated refusals to follow Starkey's plans had reduced Starkey's expectations, or the involvement of other people in this correspondence may have induced circumspection (or enthusiasm, for that matter). Starkey's first letter to Pole, dated 15 February, survives in two drafts and others in the series bear corrections in other hands. The presence of an encomium of Cromwell in the revised Harl. MS 283, but not in the Cleopatra E VI original, may give a clue to the director of that second pen, if not to its owner (132r/368r). Starkey began 'I most hertely commend me un to you', a much more cordial greeting than any of the subsequent missives bore, but pulled no punches. He immediately informed Pole that his letter concerned 'the hole ordur of your lyfe here … in thys our cuntrey among your natural loverys & frendys'. Cromwell had by now secured Starkey's entry into royal service and Henry had already sounded Starkey about Pole's opinion on the divorce. Starkey had waffled, telling Henry that he could speak for Pole only about 'such thyngys as I knowe manyfest and true'. Pole's habitual silence kept his opinion about divorce and papal authority hidden

---

[34] P. S. Donaldson develops a subtle appreciation of Pole's self-fashioning in 'Machiavelli, antichrist, and the reformation: prophetic typology in Reginald Pole's *De unitate* and *Apologia ad Carolum quintum*', and for Pole's successful diffusion of one episode directly relevant here, see T. F. Mayer, 'Reginald Pole in Paolo Giovio's *Descriptio*: a strategy for reconversion'.

[35] L. B. Smith, *Tudor prelates and politics, 1536–1558*, 175.

from Starkey (Harl. 283, 131r). Lest the point be missed, Starkey later insisted that he had no idea what Pole thought 'by cause syth our last deperture owt of our cuntrey lytyl communycatyon concernyng thes materys hathe byn betwyx us had' (132r). Proclaiming his ignorance would not have been the best way for Starkey to trade on his relationship with Pole, had he tried that.

Starkey laid out many of the basic themes of the correspondence in its first number. He reminded Pole that 'you owe your educatyon to God' and more to the point 'hys gracys lyberalyte'. Cromwell had told Starkey to remind Pole of his preferment and his family. The king had ordered Starkey to write because he did not want Pole to waste his virtues in a strange country (131v). When Starkey got around to reasoning with Pole about Henry's two questions, he kept it short. On the one hand, the Levitical law justifying the divorce was 'rotyd in the law of nature', and 'by general conseyl hyt hath byn many tymys declaryd & authorysyd'. On the other, the 'abusyd authoryte of the pope' had very slight support. It had arisen 'by patyence of pryncys, simplycyte of pepul, & ambycyouse avaryce of hys predecessorys', and had gradually 'growen to thys intollerabul iniquyte'. Starkey concluded with another historical argument, familiar from the Dialogue. Laws remained in force 'untyl such tyme that to hys hyghnes, & to hys most wyse conseyl *hyt schal appere expedyent [ab.] them to abrogate, & other to substytute by commyn assent more agreabul to thys tyme, and to the nature of our men & also to our hole cuntrey more convenyent' (132r). Originally this had read that statutes did not need to be altered 'tyl tyl [del.] hyt schal ['otherwyse' del.] appere to hys gracys wysedome & most nobul conseyl by authoryte of perlyament them to abrogate & other to substitute by commyn assent' (Cleop E VI, 368v). The draft emphasized the role of parliament more clearly and both passages made much more of consent, but otherwise either of these passages could have come from the Dialogue in their reliance on king and council. Whoever dictated Starkey's revisions here caught a glimpse of his radical conservatism, but one which could almost be explained away as a rhetorical slip.

Perhaps even without waiting for a reply from Pole, Starkey launched a more complete argument in favour of divorce and supremacy. Someone had remembered Pole's 1531 'book' and had become worried that Pole would write that sort of thing again. Therefore Starkey told him bluntly that Henry wanted only his judgment on the two questions: 'you schold leve your prudent & wytty pollycy tyll you be requyryd'. Starkey supported his case in favour of the divorce and against the pope's power to dispense in much the same way as he had in his first letter, but he placed more weight on a conciliarist argument by writing that the pope could not 'dyspense wyth law made in general conseyl' because the power to do that had never been transferred from council to pope. Nor should one man have the authority to meddle with a general precept of natural law, 'convenyent for the conservatyon of the cyvyle & polytyke lyfe unyversally & convenyent to the dygnyte of the nature of man'. Turning to the primacy, Starkey adduced seven arguments against it. Christ rebuked his disciples when they squabbled over precedence. While Paul confessed only Christ as head of the church, he recognized numerous civil and political heads. The book of Acts contained no trace of Peter's alleged superiority, nor would the four patriarchs have admitted it. Papal pretensions had produced the schism with the Greek church, Paul had refused to bow to Peter's will and, finally, Antioch had as good a claim to supremacy as Rome, since Peter had been its bishop, too (375r). Starkey concluded by warning Pole once again to stick to Henry's orders and leave policy alone (375v). Starkey admitted that he had seen Pole's earlier opinion and that its portrait of disaster had scared him. Nevertheless, Starkey put the best construction on it, reassuring Pole that the whole thing rested on scripture and that he knew that Pole had not meant to be arrogant. This admission and Starkey's positive evaluation of Pole's work make nonsense of the traditional view of Starkey desperately waving Pole's match away from Henry's touch hole. After all, Starkey's interpretation of Pole's 1531 opinion comes very close to that once held by the archbishop of Canterbury. On the other hand, Starkey's closing recommendation to Pole to 'dyrect your knolege yf you see nede by mastur gaspero [Contarini] the byschope of chete [Caraffa] wyth other such men of lernyng & jugement' really does signal distant religious danger (376r).

Thus by early 1535 Starkey had begun all three of his assignments. His reward may not have satisfied him. Either that, or Pole kept the news to himself. Harvel did not hear of Starkey's advancement until almost three months after Starkey's first letter to Pole, despite urging Starkey to write more often.[36] Starkey's office is unclear. It has been usual to assert that his one and only position was a royal chaplaincy, which he received in exchange for corresponding with Pole. If Richard Pate's undated letter congratulating Starkey that his return had restored his health came soon afterwards, then the chaplaincy did indeed nearly coincide with the beginning of Starkey's letters to Pole.[37] Otherwise, the only evidence for that appointment comes from two letters of 1536: one from Philip Hoby dated 23 April; and Pole's covering

[36] Nero B VII, fol. 116r, 7 April 1535. Harvel's first letter in this series is Nero B VI, fol. 159r, misdated in *LP*, X, 223 to 1536. Harvel wrote that 'the pope or after your maner the busshop of Rome hath lately given sentens ayenst the Duke of Urbin that the duchye of Camarin doth not pertayne to him' which must refer either to the deposition and excommunication of the duke of Urbino on 17 February or to the interdict placed on the latter duchy between 13 and 18 March, more likely the former. See L. von Pastor, *The history of the popes, from the close of the middle ages*, XI, 304–6.

[37] *LP*, VIII, 785.

letter for *De unitate* of 26 May. Neither gives any indication of how long Starkey had been a chaplain.[38] In early 1535 Starkey was 'in the kingis familye', as Harvel put it.[39] Starkey's new post failed to impress Harvel, too. Whatever it was, Harvel told Starkey he was still waiting to hear of 'your preferment wiche can not (I hope) be long differid'. Starkey may not have boasted of his job, but he did of Henry's favour and even more of his friendship with Cromwell. Virtually every one of his letters to Harvel contained a report of how well Cromwell thought of Harvel, and some explicitly noted that Starkey was 'somoche frendid by mr secretarye', as Harvel paraphrased.[40] Starkey's prospects looked bright.

The progress of the negotiations with Pole and the reports on Pole's writing forwarded to Starkey by his agents in Italy did nothing to dim them.[41] Harvel, who shared some of Starkey's anti-clericalism, sent Starkey no less then three letters in April 1535.[42] Already in the second of them responding to a letter Starkey had written a week after his first letter to Pole, Harvel assured Starkey that Pole was eager to return to England and to satisfy the king. Harvel spoke the same language as Starkey and his masters, intoning solemnly that Pole's 'vertu awght rather to be spent in his natiff cuntre, then her to perpetually to be [*sic*] spent *in umbra*'. For his part, Harvel promised 'I will not cesse to exhort him to follow some other kind of liff than to consume his perpetual liff in letters, & that the kingis grace, his contre and his frendes may somtime have his work.'[43] Toward the end of the month Harvel wrote confidently that Pole's book would be 'a monument of his witte and vertu', and that when Pole should return to England 'his practise schalbe convertid to some other matters agayn his frendes and kinnismen wil stime him as his vertu deservith'. Harvel expected that Pole would return in the coming September.[44]

These reports were not the only cause for optimism. Other members of Pole's household fulsomely celebrated Starkey's entry to royal service in the same civic humanist language which Starkey used.[45] George Lily in particular heaped praise on Starkey not only 'comuni civium causa' but for his own part. We should, he wrote, all be pleased 'quod si tales in rep. viri, qualis estu, summis honoribus semel florere ceperint'. It was fitting that the best and most prudent should have authority in the commonwealth, as well as honours.

---

[38] SP 1/103, fol. 162r and SP 1/104, fol. 55r (*LP*, X, 719 and 974.1).
[39] Nero B VII, fol. 116r, 7 April 1535.   [40] *Ibid.*, fol. 121r, 21 April 1535.
[41] Starkey's friends reported to him regularly, if not always by the usual monthly post from Venice. For it see Harvel's letter of 7 April above, and for Starkey's use of *tabellarius iste communis* George Lily-Starkey (Nero B VI, 158r and 163r, September and October 1535).
[42] In his first letter to Starkey Harvel observed laconically 'I percayve by yor writing that prestis are put to greate charge sondrye wais. wherby the fruttis of the crowne shalbe increasid not meanely'. Harvel did not object. Nero B VII, fol. 116r.
[43] *Ibid.*, fol. 122r, 12 April.   [44] *Ibid.*, fol. 121r, 21 April.
[45] For example, Sandro in Nero B VI, fol. 155r, 13 April.

Needless to say, Lily hoped to catch Starkey's coat-tails, ending his letter by assuring Starkey that he had always planned to follow him, and hoping fervently that Starkey would retain his good opinion of him. Lily aspired to the 'virtutis et gloriae laudem' which Starkey's expectation that he could contribute to the 'comuni utilitati, et patriae' had aroused. He hoped to succeed through 'the good will of the gods' and, as an afterthought, by studying the 'veteres jurisconsulti'. This is all rather overdone, even by humanist standards, but the paean Lily delivered to Britain might have delighted Starkey at the prospect of recruiting such a client.

And so I seem to see that day when the name of our Britain, in these our times (as I hope), by the examples of most famous and most seminal (?) men, and by the talents of the most learned, famous not less for their merit, will now have been most famous in all places and among all people, as that of that old Roman city and empire which until now had filled up their world and ours also.[46]

E. L. Hirsh erred badly when he wrote that Lily was already discouraged, because he could tell which way things were going in England.[47] Hindsight sees particularly dimly here.[48]

Probably sometime in April, Cromwell found other work for Starkey, using him to persuade Richard Reynolds to accept the supremacy. Starkey probably knew Reynolds from his earlier retreat at Sheen with Pole; Starkey may have been 'uncomfortable' with the monks's execution.[49] There is no evidence of Starkey's attitude at the time, but some of his comments in private two years later express oblique disapproval. Starkey did not report how he argued with the monk, but whatever he said did not please Henry, who found it insufficiently scriptural.[50] At about the same time Starkey must have written Pole a third letter, now missing. Early in May, Harvel wrote noting a letter from Starkey to Pole of 12 April, but the next one extant answered Pole's letters to John Walker of the same date and of 22 April to Starkey, both of

[46] *Ibid.*, fols. 165r–6r, 22 April.   [47] E. L. Hirsh, 'George Lily', 4 and xx.

[48] The continued contacts between Morison and the notorious Harry Phillips document the degree of openness in the religious climate in 1535 and most of 1536. Morison wrote Phillips about the progress of his *Lamentation* in October 1536, more than a year after Phillips had betrayed Tyndale in Antwerp (SP 1/113, fol. 212r; *LP*, XI, 1482). Phillips would later pursue a most checkered career, including involvement in one of the more bizarre plots to do in Pole, all the while secretly cooperating with the cardinal. Perhaps similarly straitened circumstances led Morison to sympathize with Phillips, who had apparently been disowned by his family for earlier malfeasance. See T. F. Mayer, 'A diet for Henry VIII: the failure of Reginald Pole's 1537 legation', 320–1.

[49] Starkey reported his activity in an undated letter to Pole, Nero B VI, fol. 373v. Starkey's attitude to Reynolds' death is suggested by Newcombe, '"Due order & reasonabul mean"', 23–4.

[50] SP 1/92, fol. 59v where Starkey recalled Henry's disapproval.

which arrived at different times on 16 May. Starkey must have been reasonably intimate with Walker; Harvel had commended himself to Walker early in April.[51] Pole's letter to Walker finally acknowledged receipt of the king's command, probably in the form of Starkey's two earlier letters, but Starkey accepted Pole's excuse that they had unaccountably gone by way of Florence.[52]

Starkey could not afford such tolerance when it came to Cromwell's orders. Now he further instructed Pole to send at least a synopsis of his opinion to Cromwell (372r). Starkey devoted the bulk of this letter to further attacks on papal supremacy, calling Jerome to support his case that the papacy's 'superyoryte' arose in the first place only 'in remedium scismatis', and arguing again that only the 'patyence of pryncys *et tacito quodam christiam [sic] populi consensu*' had allowed the primacy to grow, little by little, into 'the gretyst brake ... to al chrystyan cyvylyte' (372v). Starkey fired a new salvo by calling the pope the root of all sedition, and hoping that Christian princes would not be brought to fight over his position again (372v). The matter of the monks' defiance of the Act of Supremacy also bulked large. Pole could earn an honourable reception in England by spreading an accurate account of the Carthusians' superstition which had caused them to commit suicide, rather than submit (373r). Henry's supremacy, passed in parliament, had been accepted 'wyth one consent' and the monks alone had been 'dysobedyent to the pryncely authoryte' (373r–v). Starkey concluded with some advice from Cromwell and then added a postscript from Cromwell's ally Sir Edward Baynton. Cromwell brandished a stick in favour of the active life, and Baynton offered a carrot on Henry's behalf.

maystur baynton also ... your old lovar & frende [to] *whome the kyngys plesure ys not unknowen [ab.] aftur most harty commendatyons, apon hys behalfe wyllyd me thys to wryte to you, that you schold wel consydur how the kyngys hyghnes most gracyously serchyth & ever hath done, a convenyent mean to set you in such case, that he myght accordyng to the fame of your vertues & merytys, handyl & intrete you.

Baynton also reminded Pole how much Henry wanted Pole's opinion, even though it could make no difference (374r).

This postscript may reinforce the argument that Cromwell was out to ensnare Pole. Baynton was a relative of Pole's, but, of greater importance, Anne's vice-chamberlain and a pronounced evangelical. A few months before this letter he had secured the presentation of the reformer William Barlow to the living of Bisham, near the Countess of Salisbury's mansion house.[53] William Latymer's biography of Anne described Baynton debating

[51] Nero B VII, fol. 123r. For Harvel and Walker, see *ibid.*, 116r.
[52] BL Cleopatra E VI, fols. 372r and 374r.   [53] M. Dowling, 'Anne Boleyn and reform', 32.

scripture with the Queen over supper and defending Hugh Latimer and his parishioners.[54] The bishop's *Remains* contain two letters from him to Baynton, both of 1531. The first thanked Baynton for letting Latimer know 'who be grieved with me and what behooveth me to do, in case I must needs come up', defended Thomas Bilney, and closed by asking Baynton to pray for Latimer. The second letter irrascibly answered further criticism of Latimer's preaching, which Baynton's friends had offered.[55] Baynton's role in 1535 takes on heightened significance in light of his close cooperation with Cromwell in the 1536 coup against Anne. Perhaps Cromwell was already plotting the double manoeuvre which allowed him to use the court conservatives' animus against Anne to destroy her and them both.[56]

John Russell's patronage of Harvel, in tandem with Cromwell and at nearly the time of Baynton's and Cromwell's communication with Pole, supports this theory. In June, Harvel asked Starkey to greet Russell profusely and promised to write to him soon.[57] Russell, who disliked Anne profoundly and apparently thought she had thwarted his career, helped to engineer the *putsch* against her. A protégé of Wolsey's, Russell had moved in Cromwell's circle since 1525.[58] Cromwell seems to have been coordinating the campaign for Pole on a broad scale.

Harvel's optimism about the outcome of Cromwell's efforts continued. In the letter just cited he wrote Starkey that Pole would certainly please Henry, 'for his mind is aswel disposid as can be imaginid without any doublenes'. Pole still needed more time to compose his opinion, though. Recurrent trouble with his eyes was part of the problem, as Starkey learned from Sandro.[59] Whatever Pole thought, Harvel approved of recent events in England. Starkey had asked him about the Italian reaction to the executions, and Harvel replied 'al venice was in grete murmuracion to her it. and spake long time of the bessines to my grete displesure for the infaming of owr nacion'.[60] Starkey also welcomed current religious developments in Italy, especially the election of Contarini to the college of cardinals. Sandro told him of the celebration the Signory put on, but objected to it as 'much greater than pertains to any holy man'.[61] Contarini deserved his reputation for virtue, thought Starkey, but his fourth letter to Pole continued in a vein reminiscent of Marco Mantova's attitude to the cardinals.

---

[54] Bodleian MS Dan C 42, fols. 13–28. My thanks to Dr Dowling for this reference.
[55] G. E. Corrie, ed., *Sermons and remains of Hugh Latimer*, II, 332, 330 and 334 for the first letter, and 336–48 for the second.
[56] E. W. Ives, 'Faction at the court of Henry VIII: the fall of Anne Boleyn', 176. Ives incorrectly identified Baynton as a conservative.
[57] Nero B VII, fol. 107r.   [58] D. Willen, *John Russell, first earl of Bedford*, 23 and 25.
[59] Nero B VII, fol. 109r (*LP*, VIII, 875 dated this 15 June).
[60] *Ibid.*, fol. 107v.   [61] *Ibid.*, fol. 109r.

I thynke he schal more rather gyve & adde honowre to the ordur, then therof to take any ornament, and yf I had sure confydence in hys dyvyne nature & as you say angelyent, I wold some what feare lest by thys dygnyte he schold also conceyve the nature of a cardynal, of whom ther I have hard many tymys sayd that wyth the hatte wyl remayne never, nother honowre nor yet honesty.

Nevertheless, Starkey conceded that 'he by hys synguler vertue [*ab.*] may be peraventure, a mean to restore to that ordur some dygnyte'. This retreat from the importance Starkey had accorded the cardinals in the Dialogue may have been another small accommodation to the official line, or Starkey may simply have carried through his distinction between political and doctrinal matters. The cardinals may have failed at the latter, but that did not necessarily reduce their competence in the former. Or perhaps Starkey's rejection of the papacy's political authority, combined with his souring attitude to the nobility, may have made the cardinals unnecessary, too. Not even Contarini had much chance of restoring unity to Christendom,

yf he were pope, as I conjecture truly he schortly schalbe. Of thys I have no expectatyon at al, for that unyte is now to open & playn that men ... schal never in our days desyre hyt to be restoryd agayne aftur that sorte ... to thys I suppose not only the nature angelycal of mastur gaspero ys not suffycyent, but the angellys of hevyn, yf they schold come to preach that superyoryte [*ab.*] agayn, of many I thynke they schold scaresely be hard.[62]

Starkey added more encouragement to Pole to write quickly, weigh scripture 'leying a perte al authoryte of man', and 'put asyde al such *preiudicia* as by custume & tyme in sympul myndys be reputyd of grete weyght' (369r). Starkey repeated an attack on long-established customs, which he originally essayed in his Dialogue, and then added a new one which would reappear in the *Exhortation*. Those who resisted the new order in England failed to understand that all politic things, including custom, steadily deteriorated, and that 'chrystys doctryne determyth no one kynd of pollycy, but in al statys may be stablyschyd and groundyd'. Here for the first and only time Starkey referred to Marsilio, 'whome I take though he were in style rude, yet to be of a grete jugement, & wel to set out thys mater', that is, the relations between secular and religious authority (369v). Starkey seemed to think that Pole had never heard of Marsilio. If not, this suggests that Starkey had not previously, either. Otherwise, Marsilio's ideas would surely have come up during Starkey's conversations with Pole about just this subject.[63]

The angelical Contarini and his friend Pole had already set a course which rendered all Starkey's efforts worthless. Pole may even have approached the

---

[62] Cleop. E VI, fol. 369r–v.

[63] K. W. Beckmann also noted that this letter probably meant that Starkey had previously not known Marsilio. 'Staatstheorie und Kirchenpolitik im Werke des englischen Humanisten Thomas Starkey', 108.

emperor before he received Starkey's first letter.[64] At any event, in June Contarini definitely wrote to the emperor asking for protection for Pole.[65] Pole's potential very much interested Eustace Chapuys and perhaps even Charles himself.[66] Starkey and Cromwell were oblivious to these manoeuvres. Cromwell's much vaunted spy network, if it existed, would have suffered a serious breakdown.

Starkey calmly spent the summer writing his *Exhortation*, taking breaks strolling in Antonio Bonvisi's garden.[67] Starkey probably began to write on his own initiative, but with encouragement from Cromwell, which 'What ys pollycye' may have engendered. Both Cromwell's evangelical bent and Henry's objections to Starkey's reasoning with Reynolds probably helped to reinforce Starkey's increasing concern with religion. He described the course of his studies in the *Exhortation* in such a way as to emphasize his scriptural learning, not his legal training as he had in his job applications to Cromwell. Not only that, but he now asserted that Bible study had motivated his return to England. As he had read, Starkey had begun to think about the discrepancy between the state of worldly policy and pure Christianity, and that had led him to realize that 'common religion' needed reforming. When he saw the pope's supremacy uprooted in England, he rejoiced that reform had begun and proposed to chip in.[68] He offered an unstable blend of Colet and Kampen which first raised Cromwell's suspicions of Starkey's religion.

Two letters to Cromwell probably reflect the course of Starkey's writing. One reads like a prospectus, and the other reacted to Cromwell's criticism of

[64] On 6 February, Charles wrote his ambassador in London, Eustace Chapuys that he was expecting a message from someone named 'Reynard' (as the calendar summary has it) who lived near Venice. *CSPSp*, V:1, 133. 1535 must be the correct year. Chapuys was also to find out how to protect Catherine and Mary if Charles came to the aid of the 'malcontents'. The reference to Catherine rules out 1536, since Charles must have heard of her death on 9 January, as it does 1537, when writing about 'malcontents' would make much better sense.

[65] Contarini assured Charles that Pole 'thinks of nothing save doing some act by which God and the whole of Christendom may be benefited'. Pole's deed would certainly be non-violent, since 'he considers martyrdom the greatest boon that can be obtained in this world', and had 'resolved to help the king and his kingdom, not indeed by force of arms, not by promoting troubles in his own country, but merely by ways of peace and persuasion'. A member of Pole's suite, the bearer of this letter, would give the emperor Pole's precise plans by word of mouth. *CSPSp*, V:1, 172. P. de Gazangos's summary (quoted here) lacked any explicit appeal for Charles's protection, but both F. Dittrich and W. F. Hook include it in their reading of the letter, so Gazangos's abstract may be defective. F. Dittrich, *Regesten und Briefe des Cardinals Gasparo Contarini*, 76–7 and W. F. Hook, *Lives of the archbishops of Canterbury*, VIII, 72.

[66] As early as 1533 and again in 1534, Chapuys suggested attracting Pole to the emperor in case an opportunity for an invasion arose. *CSPSp*, V:1 109 (citing his earlier report). Chapuys's second letter about Pole responded to a request from the emperor for confirmation of a report from the Spanish consul in Venice, Martin de Çornoça. Çornoça had offered his expertise in English affairs and sent a detailed description of Pole's value. *Ibid.*, 80.

[67] Florence Voluzene to Starkey, Nero B VI, fol. 20r (*LP*, IX, 867; 21 November [1535]).

[68] *Exhortation*, sig. 44r–45v.

Starkey's efforts. In the first letter, Starkey told Cromwell that their last conversation had inspired him to write up his 'fancy & opynyon' about points Cromwell had raised.[69] The two polities reappeared, or 'ii dyverse fascyons of passyng thys pylgrymage the one cyvyle polytyke & wordly, the other, hevenly spiritual & godly' (179v). The description of the civil life could have come from the Dialogue, but as the image of pilgrimage indicates, that of the spiritual life already pointed to the much more pronounced religiosity of the *Exhortation*. At this point, Starkey continued to draw heavily on Colet. Human reason could not attain knowledge of the heavenly polity, so that it must be subdued and replaced by reliance on faith.

Fayth must be hys gyde, fayth must be hys ye, fayth must schow hym al the mysterys therin, fayth must lay the groundys in thys kynd of lyfe as nature dyd in the other.

Faith together with love and charity 'governe & lede the man made spiritual'. Starkey continued in such Pauline language, arguing that 'faythful love & charytabul faythe' would bring man to his 'sure felycyte', and to 'true lyberty' by freeing him from the 'bondage of the old man'. Consequently, even on earth, man could live 'lyke a chryst, lyke a god, lyke reson hyt selfe'.

This discussion served to prepare a religious case for civil obedience. Although these two lives might appear 'dyverse & almost contrary', in fact 'the cyvyle & polytyke ordur must be observyd, as the ground & foundatyon of the spiritual & hevenly conversatyon', 'to that wych by nature ys more excellent' (180r). Starkey adduced the Germans as an example of people who had not taken this truth to heart, just as he would in the *Exhortation*, and then came to the point. The pope's abused authority was 'pernycyouse to al chrystyan cyvylyte', and it was therefore proper for 'our prynce to be only hed polytyke of thys hys commynalty'. Going further, Starkey claimed that all ecclesiastical arrangements depended on 'mere pollycy', including the sacraments. They, however, as 'the chefe bandys & knottys, wherby the polytyke lyfe ys couplyd wythe the spiritual' could not be lightly altered 'wythout the ruyne & manyfest subversyon as wel of the cyvyle lyfe & polytyke, as of the spyrytual & veray catholyke' (180v). Starkey closed by asking Cromwell for his opinion and promised to follow whatever the Secretary might think. This was politic and pious, but not quite true.

Before Starkey finished the *Exhortation* in late summer, he submitted his 'lytyl oracyon' to Cromwell for final approval. Cromwell objected to it because, as Starkey put it, 'thys mean ys not put out at large, wych you require' (177r). Starkey expressed doubt whether he could satisfy Cromwell, 'for thys mean in al thyng ys a strange stryng, hard to stryke apon & wysely to touch'. Fortunately, his audience did not need a thorough discussion. 'To the pepul thys pertycular mean fully to prosecute I thynk hyt schold not nede, to

[69] Both letters are in SP 1/89, but in reverse order.

whome you know obedyence ys more necessary to thyngys decred by commyn authoryte, then scrupulouse knolege'. Therefore, Starkey could leave them to the sum of Christian faith in the Nicene Creed (177v). Recycling the conclusion of his Dialogue recast into Kampen's language of benefit and faith, Starkey continued that common people everywhere should obey meekly 'wyth sure fayth & expectatyon of ever lastyng lyfe here aftur to be had, by the mere benefyte of god, who to us trustyng in hym hath made such promys of hys benefyte'. As before, such religiously grounded obedience was 'the most sure knot ... of al chrystyan cyvylyte' (178r). Anybody who refused to submit, acting either out of superstition or 'arrogant opynyon' (i.e., too aggressively protestant religion) was not worthy to live in the commonwealth. Since Henry knew that, and God would doubtless inspire him to find means to solve the realm's difficulties, Starkey could content himself with persuading the 'scrupulose sorte' to abandon their opposition to 'thys alteratyon of pollycy' (178r–v). Starkey incorporated this material into the final draft of the work by rewriting its beginning and ending. He presented it to Henry in Bristol in early September.[70]

The *Exhortation* is not as complex a work as the Dialogue, but that has not meant correspondingly greater success for its interpreters. It has been called the cornerstone of the Anglican *via media*, especially because of Starkey's alleged introduction of the concept of adiaphora or things indifferent, and as a result it has attracted a fair amount of attention. It has, however, also been customary to treat the *Exhortation* and the Dialogue as if they form a seamless web.[71] They do not. Perhaps the biggest difference between the two works lies in their religious content. Instead of a few folios tacked on, as at the end of the Dialogue, Starkey's religion forms the basis of the *Exhortation*, even if it was not of the sort most students have imagined. A glance at Starkey's rhetorical strategy indicates another large gulf between his two major writings. Starkey's purpose in the latter was to justify the supremacy, to exalt Henry's power, not to bridle it severely as he had set out to do in the Dialogue. In the *Exhortation*, Starkey tried to fit his beliefs to the official line and retreated as far as he could from his aristocratic republicanism and

---

[70] Cf. SP 1/89, fol. 178r and *Exhortation*, sig. 7v on salvation by God's mere benefit; fol. 177v with sig. 7r–v, especially on the council of Nicea; and especially *ibid.* with sig. 83r on the mean, the latter following the former almost literally. For the presentation, see Starkey's preface to Henry, sig. aiiiv.

[71] The most recent published study to emphasize this aspect of the work is B. J. Verkamp, *The indifferent mean: adiaphorism in the English reformation to 1554*, 28–9, 41, 143, 157, 170–1. Newcombe has a useful chapter (IV) on Starkey's adiaphorism in his '"Due order & reasonabul mean"', although he overestimates Starkey's importance, partly because he misses the official promulgation of Starkey's position by Thomas Cranmer and others before the *Exhortation* was published. Newcombe (45–56) also continues the traditional conflation of Dialogue and *Exhortation*. Beckmann, 'Staatstheorie', 27, is the only exception to the tendency to make Dialogue and *Exhortation* fit the same bed, although he distinguished them only according to the polemical nature of the latter.

conciliarism. Nevertheless, Starkey neither provided an unqualified endorsement of the headship nor abandoned some of his more awkward ideas.

The prefatory letter sounds very much like the Dialogue, as Starkey solemnly told Henry that princes bore responsibility for 'the order & redresse of their commynalties' in order to bring them to 'suche quietnes & felicite as they are broughte forth into, by the goodness of god & nature' (aiiv). The opening pages of the text struck a different chord. Natural concord and unity were still the keynote, but the harmonics came from the divine providence singled out in the margin (1r–v). Starkey tackled the problem of theodicy head on, assuring his readers that even the worst human acts, the worst tyranny, declared the providence and governance of God (2v). God would turn even sedition and heresy in 'the Christen polycie' to 'the settyng forth of his true religion'. Or, should the pendulum swing all the way from superstition to irreligion, that would still serve God's purpose of bringing 'us at laste to the meane'.

Starkey's treatment of civil polity immediately marked the distance between Dialogue and *Exhortation*. He still described the civil life as he had earlier, but instead of a long disquisition on how to make it work, Starkey immediately passed on to the spiritual life 'bycause man is no aungell' (39r). In the Dialogue, this objection had served to inspire 'Pole', not bring the discussion screeching to a halt. Similarly, ruleship was still the linchpin of civil society, but 'Christis doctrine techeth [us] to treade [it] underfoote' as 'unstable and transitorye ... vyle by nature and of small dignitie' (49r [*recte* 51ar]). But this apparent condemnation led to an argument that while charity converted civil society into the spiritual life, without common policy Christianity would soon fall into confusion (40v). Thus Starkey returned to obedience, but now with a fully fledged religious justification for it, not merely a secular one. The law must be fulfilled out of love, not 'outwarde respecte' (41r).

As he did here, Starkey leaned heavily on Paul (often through the medium of Kampen) throughout the *Exhortation*, not only to support his arguments for obedience, but also for unity. The whole description of the two lives came from 'the doctrine of Poule' (40r). Paul was the best interpreter of the mystical body of Christ, which Starkey used as the foundation of Christian unity, to which end all laws should be directed, as Paul also wrote (12v). Perhaps even more important, Starkey claimed to derive his notion of soteriology from Paul. If faith were added to love, then man would come to 'sure felicitie' and 'true libertie' and live 'like a Christe, like a god in erth, and like reasone it selfe' (39v). This, wrote Starkey, was pure Christianity, albeit of a pronounced Stoic impress. Elsewhere, Starkey used words which sounded much more like Kampen.

The somme of Poules doctrine and the chiefe poynt therof ... stondeth ˙in this, to perswade us despisyng al thinges worldly and transitorie ... ever to loke up to them whiche be eternall ... and distrustinge oure owne power, workes, and dedes, as thinges by the whiche we can not ever lastynge lyfe deserve, put our hole truste and affyance in Christe, by whose only goodnesse we may attayne our salvation ... and lyke membres of one body coupled in spirituall unitie, by the mere benefyte of our heed, and his infinite goodness, at the laste attayne to our perfyte ende and felicitie. (57r)

Starkey also adopted Kampen's distinction between works before and after grace. If he could sometimes claim that salvation was 'not by our owne merites, but by the mere benefytte and only goodnesse of god', and explain carefully that 'almesse dede, with all other outwarde dedes of man, be not of them selfe sufficient to mans salvation', works were nonetheless necessary for salvation, since in performing them the Christian displayed trust in God's promises (80r). To make his distance from the 'hot radicals' crystal clear, Starkey fulminated:

A more pestilent opinion, & more pernicious to Christis doctrine was never I trowe amonge menne then this, to saye that faythe alone, without charitable workes, is sufficient to mans salvation.

Starkey called on Paul's authority again to close his discussion. According to the apostle (sounding like Kampen once again),

nother our fayth, be it never so great, nor yet our workes, be they never soo many ... can deserve our salvation, the which he [God] of his only goodnes hath promised to give us, if we beleve faythefully in hym, and truste in his promysse with faythefull harte, and in outwarde dede obey his commaundement. (81r)

This is the sort of complicated, nuanced formula that always appealed to Starkey.

As a doctor of theology, such reasoning was officially Starkey's preserve. Although ideally everyone else should believe his formula implicitly, they needed only to obey those in authority (84r). As in his letter to Cromwell, Starkey flatly stated that the Nicene Creed summed up everything the common people needed to know about Christianity (7r). Christians were subject to reason itself, Christ, and therefore should obey especially meekly, since even those people governed only by nature knew enough to respect the dominance of reason (5r–v). But Starkey did not argue in a completely quietist manner. Even if all subjects had to obey both common laws and prince according to divine law, that same law dictated that if worldly policy decreed anything contrary to God's word, 'it must be utterly abrogate and bodely disobeyed with al constancy. For suche barbarous tyranny may not be suffred in christen civilitie' (8v). Again, any law which broke spiritual unity should not be obeyed (40v). Starkey hurried on to take back most of these concessions. Private persons who refused to obey were almost *ipso facto* branded as seditious, and he never clarified who could resist (8v).

'Unlerned people and rude' should especially avoid troubling themselves about controversy over things indifferent (8r). Starkey here used a concept relatively new to English Reformation literature. Although he probably did not introduce it and certainly did not borrow it from Melanchthon, he nevertheless leaned heavily on it.[72] Everything not in itself either good or bad was indifferent or morally neutral and neither required nor prohibited by divine law. But rather than an invitation to Christian liberty, Starkey made this point the opening wedge of yet another argument in favour of obedience. Indifferent things were 'lefte to worldly polycie, wherof they take their ful authoritie' (6v). Passing to another of his purposes, Starkey drew on his experience with Reynolds to advise the scrupulous to be sure that their reservations did not rest on an indifferent thing (10r). Reynolds's superstitious objections led him to commit suicide gladly (26v).

Starkey devoted much attention to defining indifferent things and to condemning those on both sides who refused to see the same. His first list included such things as reading the Bible in the vernacular, clerical marriage, chantries, monasteries, papal pardons and holy days, all of which at least needed reform (43v). His final accounting of things allowable differed considerably. Only holy days made both rosters. Starkey thought them licit as an opportunity for prayer (79v). Apart from pilgrimage which was a part of penance, almost all of Starkey's indifferent customs involved prayer (77v). Calling on saints honoured Christ and indirectly communed with God (78v). Prayers for the dead again delighted Christ, even if they might not help either dead or living otherwise (79v). Despite the strictures he had placed on monasticism in the Dialogue, Starkey now argued that common authority had long accepted monasteries, and if they were rid of 'certayne ceremonyes' they would be most beneficial to good religion (75v). (Starkey also did not want his hearers to take a too conservative view of the institution, following Contarini in arguing that a merchant engaged in the world was as valuable to God as a monk in his cell [13].)[73] Scriptural support provided the touchstone of an indifferent thing, but some beliefs which lacked it might still be allowed, purgatory, for example. Since the ancient doctors affirmed its existence, that was enough for Starkey (76v–77r).

Starkey defended many ceremonies especially staunchly, for without them the weak would lose their faith and eventually the Gospel itself would vanish (28r, 73r). Similarly, traditions were not to be ruthlessly cast aside, especially

[72] T. F. Mayer, 'Starkey and Melanchthon on adiaphora: a critique of W. Gordon Zeeveld', corrects Zeeveld's almost universally accepted theory on both points. To the references in note 1 of that article, add Smith, *Tudor prelates*, 197; Ferguson, *Articulate citizen*, 221, even though he elsewhere argued that Starkey's adiaphorism grew out of a 'secular Aristotelian legal tradition', 176–8; S. K. Christie, 'Richard Morison', 20; and, obliquely, A. G. Dickens and J. M. Tonkin with K. Powell, *The reformation in historical thought*, 60. Skinner agreed that adiaphora was a Lutheran concept, developed by Melanchthon and 'imported' by Barnes; *Foundations*, II, 103.

[73] For Contarini, see G. Alberigo, 'Vita attiva e vita contemplativa in un'esperienza cristiana del XVI secolo', 188 and 196.

ones of long standing. Both ceremonies and traditions could induce the common people to remember 'the misteries of Christ' (43r). Starkey poured scorn on those arrogant men who derided all ceremonies, who 'covertly subverteth all good order and civilitie' (24v). Many of these critics were 'undiscrete preachers' (35v). Starkey no doubt felt that they abridged his chief professional competence. As in the Dialogue, the clergy remained largely responsible for the nature of the people, as rulers had been in Plato's republic (34r).

In addition to an argument for obedience, Starkey used adiaphora to explain political degeneration, in particular that of the papacy. Anything men instituted, including all indifferent or politic things, would 'in processe of tyme by littell and littell ever grow to injuste extremitie, in so moch that of necessitie they require prudent reformation' (22v). Papal primacy, a glaringly obvious indifferent thing, was no longer necessary or even desirable to spiritual unity, and bore an extra burden of blame for the world's decline from perfection (44v). The bulk of Starkey's argument rested on a history of the papacy, tracing it from its origin as a useful device through its usurpation, to its present degeneracy (47v). One by one Starkey destroyed papalist arguments, sometimes in devastating fashion, sometimes by breathtaking intellectual legerdemain. His first point falls into the latter category and reveals that Starkey studied biblical exegesis with someone far out of the mainstream. According to Starkey, his favourite interpreter Paul had said that the only thing prefigured in the law of the Old Testament was Christ, who swept away the Mosaic law (48r). This was an extremely radical position and it left Starkey with little more than some of the Anabaptists and Spiritualists for company, at least so far as the contemporary relevance of the Old Testament went. At one stroke, he destroyed a whole arsenal of papalist arguments of the sort advanced by Albert Pighe, which Starkey would brush aside a few years hence. Starkey gave patristic tradition equally short shrift. Whatever the Fathers said about the papacy was entirely beside the point (48v). The institution either was present in the Gospel or clearly deduced from it, or it had no legitimacy.

It had none. Christ had left the government of his church to secular rulers in an effort to draw his followers away from worldly ambition. He was its true head, and his disciples were 'to have in a maner contempt' of the world. When they squabbled over precedence, Christ rebuked them (49r). Starkey dilated on this argument for two pages, summing up that Christ 'never taught one poynt of worldely policie', considering it 'a thynge base and vyle compared to that doctrine whiche he ever taughte' (50v–51r). Next came a long criticism of the papacy's claim to foundation by Peter. Christ never conceded secular authority to any of the apostles, and the spiritual power to bind and loose which they received was spread equally among them (49 [*recte* 51]v). All had equally great sacramental powers, too (51v). This could not have been of much importance to Starkey, since he interpreted the power of the keys in a ministerial not a sacramental sense. When Christ told the apostles in Matthew 18:18 'what so ever ye loose in erthe, the same in heven shall be losed: and also what so ever you do there bynde, the same in heven shall be bounded also', he was talking about preaching, not confession and absolution as the usual interpretation ran (52r–v). Starkey took a few liberties with perhaps the most famous text in favour of the papacy's Petrine claims, the sixteenth verse of the same chapter of Matthew. He followed the standard medieval exegesis of the 'rock' in the passage to mean Peter's faith, not Peter himself, but added that Christ addressed him particularly because of his eloquence. When Peter answered, he spoke for all the apostles, whose faith had earned them Christ's favour (51r–v [*recte* 52 ar–v]).[74] Far from any special sign of favour, Christ's prayer for Peter in Luke 22:32 arose from Christ's knowledge of Peter's peculiar weakness (50r [*recte* 52br]). Lastly, Starkey disposed of John 21:15–17 in which Christ told Peter to feed his flock after three times asking Peter if he loved him, another principal prop of papal claims. Starkey interpreted this passage tropologically in line with his view of justification. An internal 'affect' – in this case, love – was worthless unless given external expression. Christ had said nothing about power, but was merely after an outward expression of Peter's love in order to give his followers an object lesson (50r [*recte* 52br]–53r).

Starkey turned next to the practice of the church in the rest of the New Testament, which he regarded as a better field for argument than the exegesis of controversial passages. Starkey's case turned on the claim that Peter never attended to any important business by himself. He only proposed the election of a replacement for Judas, who was elected by common consent, as were the seventy-two deacons. The other disciples dispatched them to preach the Gospel. The council of apostles resolved the dispute over circumcision, and James pronounced its decision. In any case, all the disciples were equal. Paul did not have Peter's instruction to preach, but he nevertheless corrected Peter at Antioch. The meeting of the apostles at Jerusalem was 'a leage, a confederacyon, and a socyetie, ye and as a companyon with hym [Peter] nothyng inferiour in power'. To clinch his case, Starkey produced the 'somme of Poules doctrine' quoted above: the compiler of the epitome of Christian belief never recognized any headship in Peter (54r–58r).

This situation continued throughout the early church, until pope Sylvester, during the reign of Constantine. Before his claim to superiority, congregations or at least local clergy elected bishops and Rome took no hand. Indeed, Rome lagged behind the other patriarchates in 'vertue and knowledge

---

[74] For medieval exegesis, see J. E. Bigane, III, *Faith, Christ or Peter: Matthew 16:18 in sixteenth century roman catholic exegesis*, chapter 1.

of Christis doctrine' because of imperial persecution. As this point indicates, Starkey saw the attitude of the Roman authorities as the key variable in the creation of Roman primacy. Princes initiated doctrinal consultation, including the early general councils (58v–60r). Once the council became an established institution, the emperors elevated the popes to lead it. Thereafter, they drew ever increasing authority from the emperors (62r–v). The popes knew a good thing when they saw it, took advantage of the naïve desire of secular rulers for unity, and arrogantly constructed their own superior position on that 'pretexte of a conveniencye, to the conservacyon of a certayne unitie' (63v and 61v). Starkey turned to reason for one last argument. Would not the Indians under Prester John, the Armenians and the Greeks all be damned for failing to recognize papal supremacy, if it were a thing necessary for salvation (60v–61r)? This point may speak poorly of Starkey's knowledge of the history of fifteenth-century councils, for at Florence both Greeks and Armenians did recognize the pope. Three years later he made a note on Pighe's use of Florence in exactly the opposite sense, but he gave no clue of what he intended to do with the reference. It might, therefore, have represented new information to Starkey. Then again, perhaps he did not consider this temporary *rapprochement* sufficiently important to make it worth ruining his cadence.

Once Starkey had identified the culprit, he returned to a favourite argument from the Dialogue in order to explain how to do away with the primacy. As he pointed out repeatedly in the course of his attack on it, local churches varied considerably in their customs. He said the same thing more formally when he asserted that Christ's doctrine

is as a cornerstone, agreinge to al polycie, and determyneth therin no certayne kynde at al, but as wel may the perfection of Christis doctrine be fulfilled in that state, where as be many heedes and dyvers polyticall, as there as is but one chiefe & principal.

Some things in the church were rooted in natural law, but 'common authoritie' established many other things which only 'the consent of the hole congregation' might alter (41r–v). The chain which linked spiritual and worldly government led Starkey to see even more similarities between the two than he had in the Dialogue. Now secular unity too rested on 'a concorde, agrement and a consent of all them whiche be in one polyce' (64v). This change from the Dialogue emphasizing consent could well have been dictated by Cromwell, in order to make it appear that his programme had wide popular support, or perhaps Starkey defined the 'hole congregation' by restricting it to only the upper reaches of the English church, as he did the political nation. Despite the close link between them, Starkey emphasized again that the spiritual unity dictated no particular sort of government, although this time he did a better job of reproducing the Aristotelian categories of constitutions. All that mattered was Christ's command to obey 'all kynd of policie' (65v).

All of this history and political science stood in the service of Starkey's polemic against papal primacy. After trotting out a lengthy agenda of grievances, running from dispensations to indulgences, Starkey insisted that none of these problems could be cleared up without acknowledging the diversity of Christendom. If that did not happen, it would be impossible to dispense justice and equity (67r). Pulling the threads of his case together, Starkey called papal primacy an indifferent thing, which automatically meant that it was established by common consent and could therefore be rejected without endangering anyone's salvation (68v–69r). Transferring most of the pope's power to princes would best allow for local differences. That is, Henry deserved the same sort of control over the church as the emperor Justinian had exercised (84r).

Thus Starkey legitimized an enormous increase in princely power, even at the cost of one of his own most cherished beliefs. True, Starkey nonetheless reverted to his favourite remedy for secular ills in order to explain how Henry acquired his new authority through election. As he rhetorically asked,

For what strangeness is this, a hole congregation and perfyte, as this is of our nation, to electe and chose theym a heed polytike with free libertye, whiche may with his highe wysedome directe and redresse all suche thynges as pertayne unto christian polycye? (83v)

But once such a ruler was elected, his position posed problems for Starkey's allegiance to conciliarism. General councils became an indifferent thing. The church had originally done without them for five hundred years (Starkey did not have a noticeably strong grasp of chronology), and when they had appeared their decrees were of no force until they were 'received' by secular authority and established by common consent. Starkey's argument that religious arrangements had been left to the secular power forced his hand. The decisions of councils therefore became no more than counsels until they were once again 'received' (9r–v). Starkey rigorously excluded things indifferent from the council's purview, but he did not retreat altogether from his usual staunch belief in the power of the council.[75] If traditions now lay in the hands of princes, the council kept the authority to interpret scripture, which it had from the beginning (69v, 73v, 10r). Starkey emphasized the distinction between the competence of prince and council several times. Only the latter

---

[75] Skinner is wrong to call Starkey's attitude to councils a last minute addition of a more conservative approach, rather than a modification of a central belief. *Foundations*, II, 105 and 123–4.

could interpret scripture, the ultimate authority (5v, 29r–v, 69v). (Starkey also left open the possibility that some other forms of secular government could have the same authority as the prince.) Nevertheless, Starkey repeated that the council's decrees were merely advisory until given coercive force by the prince. Only his command bound Christians under pain of damnation (69v).

F. L. Baumer extended his argument that Starkey depended heavily on Marsilio's ideas to embrace passages like these from the *Exhortation*. Simply put, Starkey took over Marsilio's 'democratic principles' wholesale. When Starkey wrote that decrees of a general council needed 'common authoritie' and 'common consent' to enforce them, he 'obviously' meant to refer to 'not only the will of the prince', but 'the common counsell of the realme' as well. In his whole treatment of the *ecclesia anglicana*, Starkey was equally 'obviously thinking of his master's words', although Baumer did not indicate which ones.[76] Even Starkey's argument about indifferent things and their establishment by the whole congregation Baumer thought 'reminiscent' of Marsilio.[77] Starkey's discussion of the early growth of papal power was 'eminently Marsilian'. Even if he and Marsilio handled parts of the case differently, they drew the same conclusions.[78] Like Marsilio, Starkey spun corollaries about the present jurisdiction and primacy of the pope from New Testament precedents. Originally, all the apostles were equal and settled questions of doctrine jointly, but, 'more striking still', Starkey adopted Marsilio's claim that Peter had been chief of the disciples only for the strength of his faith, and none of them had any coercive authority.[79] Nevertheless, Baumer recognized that Starkey did not toe the Marsilian line on the church altogether. He never adopted Marsilio's definition of the *ecclesia* as all the faithful, and also parted company with Marsilio over its poverty and, more fundamentally perhaps, on the role of general councils in holding the church together.[80]

This time around, parts of Baumer's case rest on firmer ground, but it still says less about Starkey's basic ideas than Baumer argued. For example, even if Starkey borrowed the notion that conciliar decrees needed secular legislative enforcement, that was only a temporary aberration in his thought, and very likely part of his effort to trim his ideas to Cromwell's demands.[81] Otherwise, the mechanics of Starkey's governmental machinery once again do not resemble Marsilio's. True, Marsilio thought the council might elect the pope and perhaps the cardinals, but the faithful human legislator had a much

---

[76] F. L. Baumer, 'Thomas Starkey and Marsilius of Padua', 200 and 204.
[77] *Ibid.*, 201.
[78] *Ibid.*, 202–3.
[79] *Ibid.*, 202.
[80] *Ibid.*, 204 and 202. Newcombe offers a similar, but less elaborate case and without citing Baumer; '"Due order & reasonabul mean"', 69–71.
[81] Marsilio of Padua, *Defensor pacis*, ed. C. W. Previté-Orton, D. II. xxi. 4, 329.

more important role, which Starkey never mentioned.[82] In short, Starkey's language and Marsilio's still had few points of contact, even after Starkey's explicit reference to Marsilio in his fourth letter to Pole. Starkey adopted none of the distinctive parts of Marsilio's theory.

Probably at the same time as Starkey first publicly demonstrated his skills as a preacher, he proposed to force the rest of the English clergy to follow his example. A draft proclamation in his hand and headed 'Of prechyng' begins 'For as much as al truthe … ought to be openyd & declaryd un to al faythful pepul' and ends by threatening any person who failed to abide by its provisions with charges of sedition.[83] Starkey's legal language leaves no doubt that he intended his draft not only to influence policy, as he did his letters to Cromwell, for example, but also to be policy. Preaching needed regulation because some passages of scripture were not immediately clear, 'wherin hyt ys not mete, that al men schold fantasye aftur theyr owne pleysure'. Therefore, preachers had to be prevented from departing 'at theyr owne lyberty, from the most commyn & of long tyme receyvyd interpretatyon therof, made by the auncyent doctorys of our relygyon, beyng approvyd'. In cases still left in doubt, clergymen were to conform 'unto the consent & laudabul custume of the church of england'. Starkey's appeal to consent is the best indication of when he wrote 'Of prechyng'. Such an argument should have embarrassed him after his initial critique of De unitate, in which he took the other side of the issue against Pole's excessive reliance on the consent of the church.

Just as Starkey completed his Exhortation and floated his first policy draft, disquieting signs from Italy appeared. Lily, Starkey's sometime protégé, wrote in early September that he had changed his mind about serving his country. Starkey had asked Lily to come home, and he admitted that was his fondest wish, the more so because of his father's example. Lily gave two excuses for remaining in Italy. First, he had to complete his studies, and second (and more worrisome to Starkey), Lily no longer saw a career open to the talents stretching away in front of him. Instead, he could only cast about for some means to escape 'the disturbances of so many things which now impend'. Joining the Theatines, Caraffa's order, or some similar group appeared to be the solution. Lily used religious language close to Starkey's but to somewhat different ends when he continued that everything depended on God's will and beneficium. Humans were stuck on earth and Lily could only

---

[82] Ibid., II. xxii. 9, 349 and A. Gewirth, Marsilius of Padua and medieval political philosophy, I, 285. Beckmann, 'Staatstheorie', 29–30, although conceding that Starkey's ecclesiastical constitution greatly resembled Marsilio's, ultimately rejected Baumer's argument, partly on grounds of chronology (assuming the Dialogue was written in 1533) and partly because of Starkey's experience in Venice and receptivity to native English traditions of aristocratic dominance.

[83] SP 1/100, fols. 130r and 130v.

hope that God would rescue 'our family' from its persecutors and bring a better day.[84] Lily carefully avoided explaining what he meant, and especially whom he had in mind as persecutors, which may make it appear that Hirsh was right that events in England upset him (158v). Another letter from Lily six weeks later dispels that interpretation. Lily acknowledged that he had resolved not to write to Starkey any more, not because he objected to anything at Starkey's end of their correspondence, but rather because domestic upheaval within Pole's household left him with insufficient time to write. Pole had moved to Venice and Lily had to attend him whenever Pole went out in public. Lily commiserated with Starkey about their mutual dependence on patrons which meant that neither could do what he wished, and what little free time they had must be given to study. Nevertheless, since Starkey had written in such *suavissimis verbis*, Lily would somehow hold up his end. He concluded with local news, including the arrival from Avignon of Marco Fortia, who may have been a friend of Starkey's, to study with Lazzaro Bonamico.[85]

John Friar passed on further news of friends and a glimpse into Starkey's connections in England. He addressed his letter to Starkey 'in the kyng his courte', which may mean that Starkey had lodgings there. Starkey had sent Friar news of his patron Edward Foxe's promotion to the episcopal bench and instructions from Foxe. Foxe may have used Starkey in this way because of their earlier relations in Paris, and Starkey seems to have tried to trade on that relationship. His friend Florence Voluzene also asked Starkey to greet Foxe for him at about the same time.[86] Friar wrote asking Starkey to give letters for Foxe to 'Chamberlain' who would know what to do with them. Unfortunately, this person seems to have been merely a courier of some sort, rather than either the only prominent member of the Chamberlain family, Sir Edward, then chamberlain of Catherine's household and resident in Kimbolton, or the Great Chamberlain, William Lord Sandys.[87] Chamberlain was 'not unknown' to Starkey and 'not seldom in the court'. Friar continued to use him to handle his communication with Foxe.[88]

By the same post as these letters from Lily and Friar, Starkey received

[84] Nero B VI, fol. 158r, 6 September 1535.   [85] *Ibid.*, fol. 163r–v (*LP*, IX, 673).
[86] Nero B VI, fol. 20r, where Voluzene referred to Foxe's promotion.
[87] Nero B VI, fol. 147r, 20 October [1535] (*LP*, IX, 648) and *LP*, IX, 1050 and 428 for Sir Edward. Sandys would have made a highly interesting contact for Starkey. He had contemplated active resistance along with Lord Darcy at the beginning of the year and remained very unhappy with Cromwell at least through 1537, so much so that he spent most of his time in retirement in Hampshire. *LP*, VIII, 48 (Chapuys–Charles V, 14 January 1535) reported Sandys's disaffection and politically induced ill health. Sandys would be in a key position during Cromwell's attempts against Pole in 1537 and may well have helped to torpedo them. He was captain of Guisnes, and treated one of the men set to spy on Pole as his personal servant (*LP*, XII: 2, 801).
[88] SP 1/99, fol. 124r, 1 December [1535] (*LP*, IX, 917).

another from Harvel, whose insistent wish to hear of Starkey's preferment must have become irritating. Harvel reported that Pole continued to write, but 'keepith it secret to himselff for after him he wold the king sholdbe the first reader of his worke'. Starkey had apparently sent word of his *Exhortation*, which Harvel was sure would be fine stuff, too. It seems that Henry may have demanded revisions in it, which Starkey took in hand before the work was finally printed early in 1536. In a postscript Harvel added that a general council would open shortly, news which Starkey probably welcomed in private, if not officially.[89]

Probably at the same time, Sandro posted Starkey up on the latest household news, as well as his work on an edition of Basil and some texts of Mark. Sandro likened Pole's house to a bandit's lair, where anyone could get food and drink. 'M. Gasparo' (probably Contarini) and 'M. Matthio' visited constantly after dinner, and 'M. Lazaro' (Bonamico) and 'M. [Benedetto] Lampridio', together with Piero Boemo and Alvise Priuli, lodged with Pole.[90] The latter had been with Pole for a month. Although Pole moved around constantly, Sandro's editorial work kept him in one place. Walker had given Sandro *un scuto dal hole* as a friend, which means he must have continued to travel back and forth between England and Italy.[91]

Early in December Harvel's regular letter noted that 'Master Pole is in vehement studye of writing *ut regi satisfaciat*'. John Mason had passed on news of Starkey including 'quod tu moliris aliquid egregii operis'. Harvel hoped shortly 'to see yor workes come to light & also prayse of men as pertaynith to both yor vertus'.[92] Towards the end of the month, both Starkey's potential clients Friar and Lily sent their gratitude, as well as news of a man who would shortly outstrip Starkey in Cromwell's favour, Morison. His circumstances were as poor as ever, but he still managed to join Lily for studies with Giovanni Battista Egnazio and 'Fausto'.[93] Starkey had sent Lily two letters asking about both Pole and Priuli. Lily reticently replied that Pole still had his old friends and habits, having added only the French ambassador (Pierre Danès). He was slightly more forthcoming about Priuli, whom he reported had accompanied Contarini to Rome. Sandro also begged Starkey's

---

[89] Nero B VI, fol. 139r (*LP*, IX, 1029, where this letter is dated 28 December, but it bears the date of 24 October 1535 in the MS; the postscript was written on the 28th. This addendum also included a puzzling report that Pier Paolo Vergerio was in Venice, but leaving immediately for Rome. In October 1535 Vergerio was in the Empire, as he had been for that entire year according to A. J. Schutte, *Pier Paolo Vergerio*, 271; she cites this letter with *LP*'s date on 96n.

[90] 'Piero Boemo' or Petrus Bechimius was among those urging Pole on during the final stages of the composition of *De unitate*. See Pole's letters to Priuli of 31 January and 8 February 1536. *ERP*, I, 430 and 431.

[91] Nero B VII, fol. 111v–r (mounted in volume backwards).   [92] *Ibid.*, fol. 120r.

[93] Nero B VI, fol. 167r (*LP*, IX, 1034). Hirsh identified the latter as Fausto da Longiano. 'Lily', 163. Friar's letter in Nero B VI, fol. 148r

favour, telling Starkey he would gladly send his Basil as a present, could he
but afford to. Sandro gave somewhat better value than Lily, informing
Starkey that Bembo had just sent them Sadoleto's 'Hortensius' in
manuscript.[94]

In the first three months of 1536 Pole completed *De unitate* and Starkey's
Exhortation arrived in Italy. This conjunction neatly highlights the counter-
point between their two careers. Harvel noted Pole's slow progress in letters
of 18 January and 5 February. In the former, yet another encomium of Pole's
work preceded Harvel's assurance that 'I dowt not but his writing shalbe both
grateful and also admirable to al vertuos men, and specially unto yow who
delitith of him somoche, as I am perswadid yow do.' Harvel also faithfully
passed on intelligence, despite Starkey's complaints about old news.[95] On 1
March Harvel claimed that Pole had almost finished and that Starkey had
'put us in grete expectation of your work ... for persuading [?] men to unite
and obedience'.[96] A letter from Henry Cole offered his services and passed on
requests from Bonamico, Lampridio and (Marcantonio) de Genova for news
of Starkey. It must have gratified Starkey with the thought of acquiring one
more client.[97] When a printed copy of the *Exhortation* appeared sometime in
March, both Harvel and Pole began to read it, but the latter still would not let
anyone see his manuscript until it had been 'substancilly overseen & correc-
tid'.[98] Lily concurred in Harvel's judgment of Pole's work, hoping that it
would be born to 'summam gloriam atque felicitatem' of both country and
posterity.[99] Pole finally finished his *magnum opus* on 24 March, and Harvel
reported its completion to Starkey on 2 April.[100] Sandro very likely had a
hand in copying the final part of the MS, although he wrote nothing about his
activity to Starkey.[101]

Then for two months nothing happened. Probably Pole's preparation of
the presentation copy for Henry took up this interval. Otherwise, there was
still no inkling of any serious trouble on the surface. Henry may then have
become suspicious that Starkey was leading him on by pretending that Pole
would satisfy the king, when Starkey knew perfectly well that would not

---

[94] *Ibid.*, fol. 118r.   [95] Nero B VII, fol. 114r, and also 119r for intelligence.

[96] *Ibid.*, fol. 130r.   [97] SP 1/102, fol. 157r, 3 March 1536.

[98] BL Vitellius B XIV, fol. 280r (*LP*, X, 600). A reference to the death of Ibrahim Pasha, vizier to
Suleiman the Magnificent, dates the letter. Ibrahim was assassinated on Suleiman's orders on
30 March. R. E. Dupuy and T. N. Dupuy, *The encyclopedia of military history*, 498. W. G.
Zeeveld, *Foundations of Tudor policy*, 149 misdated the assassination but probably still got
the letter's date right.

[99] Hirsh, 'Lily', 166, 19 March [1536].

[100] *ERP*, I, 445 and Nero B. VII, fol. 129r, 2 April 1536 (Harvel–Starkey).

[101] *ERP*, I, 447 where Pole reported that he had given the work to *librarium meum*. Sandro was
the only known copyist in Pole's employ.

happen. In an undated letter which must come after the close of Starkey's first round of correspondence with Pole and after he had moved back to Dowgate, Starkey begged Cromwell to reassure Henry that neither he nor Pole would ever dissimulate.[102] Nevertheless, the events in Pole's study, Morison's departure for England, and Harvel's shocking announcement that he wished to follow a quiet life and give up a worldly were straws in the wind.[103] But the change of weather hardly approached the sort of gale most historians have created around the arrival of *De unitate* and the sequel. Certainly Pole's violent diatribe against Henry and all his works did Starkey no good, but, in the context of the grand factional crisis manifested in Anne's fall, *De unitate* need not have done him any permanent damage. Nor did it. The evidence is complicated, but Pole's revelations caused only part of Starkey's problem in mid-1536, and the disgrace which it helped to induce proved temporary.

Pole dispatched *De unitate* to England on 27 May 1536, probably in the care of Michael Throckmorton.[104] It arrived on 14 June.[105] Once Pole decided to send his work, he acted in a great hurry. Lily had time to write Starkey only a few lines by the same bearer.[106] The English responded much more deliberately. Starkey was in the thick of the reading of *De unitate* and, for a time, in the fashioning of a response to it. Most of the evidence comes from a letter to Pole giving Starkey's initial reaction. It must date from sometime after the middle of August, since Starkey warned Pole not to go to Rome as Pole had written to Cuthbert Tunstall saying he intended to do so on the first of that month.[107] Starkey read *De unitate* a total of three times. First,

at such tyme as your boke was delyvyryd to the kyng ... I forgettyng not the offyce of frend, requyryd that your boke myght be commyttyd to the examynatyon of them wych bothe had lernyng to juge & wold wey the mater indyfferently, they wych I promys you was done, and to them I as your frend was joynyd also.

But Starkey was 'so amasyd & astonyd with the mater' that he could not form a solid opinion. 'Wherfore I obtaynyd your boke to over rede myselfe', once alone and then for a third time with Tunstall.[108] Starkey probably first read the book about the middle of July. At the opening of this letter, Starkey alleged tht he had decided never to write to Pole again before ever he saw *De unitate*, because even at the 'second retorne' of Pole's servant after he delivered the book, Pole had still sent no letters to Starkey. The round trip from Venice to London took about a month, so that Throckmorton could not have

---

[102] SP 1/92, fol. 60r.   [103] Harvel–Starkey, Nero B VII, fol. 124v, 26 May 1536.
[104] Herrtage, *Starkey's life*, xxxi printed Pole's cover letter, dated 27 May. The original is Cleop. E VI, fol. 347r (*LP*, X, 974.2). R. B. Merriman identified Throckmorton as the bearer. *Life and letters of Thomas Cromwell*, I, 203–4.
[105] *LP*, XI, 91.   [106] *LP*, X, 971.   [107] *LP*, XI, 210.   [108] Cleop. E VI, fol. 379v.

returned to England much before mid-July.[109] Starkey had also heard of Pole's invitation from the pope of 26 June to go to Rome and consult about the council, which pushes the letter further into late July.[110] Then again, Tunstall sent Pole the official response on 13 July; if Starkey's version of the first committee reading is correct, he and its other members must have set to work soon after *De unitate* arrived in order to leave him time to get through it twice more. Although Starkey may have had a chance to read *De unitate* alone, that did not make him an independent actor. Someone else carefully vetted the draft text of his letter to Pole. Unfortunately, the writer used a standard secretary script, but it shares some peculiarities with John Stokesley's hand and does not resemble that of the only other obvious candidate, Tunstall.[111] Stokesley served on the committee and cooperated with Tunstall in handling official negotiations with Pole after Starkey was removed from the centre.

Starkey's claim that the members of the committee 'lovyd you [Pole] intyerly' is no understatement.[112] Not only was Starkey made a member of this committee and the recently returned Morison its secretary, but Morison's abstract of *De unitate* glossed over many of its most inflammatory passages.[113] Even more, Tunstall sat on the committee in part at least because Pole asked for him.[114] Pole benefited greatly from the struggles within Henry's court, as he would again in the following year.[115] The English went out of their way to make the best of Pole's bombshell, and no wonder. As Starkey wrote to Pole, he was far from the only person who had expected great things from Pole, even if Starkey had gone a little further in boosting him than most others.[116] The powerful faction of court conservatives had a great deal invested in Pole, as did Henry himself. This group thought its moment had finally arrived in the downfall of Anne, which Starkey also regarded as a chance for a new beginning (382r). The conservatives probably hoped that Pole would play along and help them undo Cromwell.

Quite apart from this particular opportunity which Pole threatened to

---

[109] This calculation rests on the dispatch of *De unitate* on 27 May and its arrival in London on 14 June; Henry's letter to Venice, sent on 14 June and received the 30th; and Tunstall's letter to Pole, sent 13 July, arrived the 27th. This time is considerably faster than the average given by Pierre Sardella, as cited in F. Braudel, *The mediterranean and the mediterranean world in the age of Philip II*, I, 362.

[110] Cleop. E VI, fol. 383r and Hook, *Archbishops*, 99 and 101 for the pope's brief.

[111] My thanks to Dr Guy for suggesting Stokesley.

[112] Cleop. E VI, fol. 379v. Herrtage put the situation too mildly when he observed that 'all the committee seem to have been friends of Pole', *Starkey's life*, xxxiv.

[113] SP 1/104, 57r–61r. T. F. Dunn, 'The development of the text of Pole's *De unitate ecclesiae*', 457 noted that Morison managed to avoid mentioning any of Henry's crimes, on which Pole harped at length.

[114] Cleop. E VI, fol. 348v.   [115] For most of what follows, see Mayer, 'Diet for Henry VIII'.

[116] Cleop. E VI, fol. 381r.

waste, Starkey followed the general line of the campaign to reclaim Pole and taxed him with his 'wonderful ingratytude toward your prynce & cuntre' (381r). Starkey berated Pole for forgetting Henry's benefits, and especially 'how much you *above all other [*ab.*] are bounden to our prynce for your educatyon' (382r). In addition to his ungrateful behaviour, Pole's arguments surprised Starkey by their vulgarity. He had expected Pole to do better than 'the commyn sorte of men of weak capacyte' (383r). The problem, thought Starkey, was that Pole, who had once paid too much attention to 'wordly cyrcumstance', now gave it no heed at all (382r). Pole's case was not yet hopeless, however, and Starkey urged his friend to try again (382v). In order to help him see the truth, Starkey sent along a brief compendium of the central arguments in the *Exhortation*, some of them specially modified to counter Pole's invective.

Starkey began with his favourite Christian authority, Paul. According to him, Christian unity meant faith and charity in every sort of polity. Therefore, since England still kept both, it had not fallen from the same faith as Rome espoused (380r). Starkey repeated his theory of the two polities and used it to dismiss Roman primacy and to demonstrate that only the secular ruler had powers of coercion. This went beyond the position he had taken in the *Exhortation*, even if Starkey still thought it was not 'convenyent' for the offices of prince and bishop to be intermingled. Nevertheless, it was scarcely against divine law for a prince to oversee the commonwealth and see to it that his bishops did their duty (381r). Thus far Starkey had merely summarized his more or less life-long views, but when he came to Pole's argument about the *consensus ecclesiae*, he saw his chance to repudiate some of his 'trimming' in the *Exhortation*. Since Starkey had never considered broad consent of much importance, he had no difficulty accusing Pole of elevating the consent of the church above the authority of scripture. Pole's claim that long consent made customs necessary gave Starkey an opening to retort with one of his favourite arguments, that consent could only establish a human institution which could just as easily be altered as preserved (380r). While Starkey had once encouraged Pole to talk over his views with Contarini and Caraffa, he now cautioned him 'let not the advyse of Cardynal Contarene nor yet of the byschope of chete yf you have commynyd your censeytes [conceits] with them so wey wyth your stomake that you forget al humanyte, regardyng nether prynce cuntre nor frend' (383v).[117] Perhaps Starkey had begun to realize the political implications of Pole's religious position, and to see that his fellow Italian Evangelicals would never abandon the papacy.

A dawning awareness of this group's attitudes may also have lain behind Starkey's threats to Pole to deter him from publishing *De unitate* and going to

---

[117] Starkey here intuited the true situation. Contarini had read all of '*De unitate*' and approved most of it. Dunn, '*De unitate*', 456.

Rome. If he let his book be noised abroad, Pole would be 'one of the most extreme enymys bothe to the kyngys honowre to al your frendys & to our hole natyon, that ever was bred in our cuntre', and if he followed Contarini to Rome 'you schalbe notyd ... as sedycyouse a persone & mynystur as grete a breche to chrystun unyte as ever hathe done any other in our days' (383v). A political matter threatened to have a major impact on belief, which Starkey thought should never happen.[118]

All in all, a moderate appraisal and critique of an incendiary book. For the moment, the English knew nothing of Pole's continuing negotiations with the emperor, whom he had asked to invade England in a passage of *De unitate* which Pole cut from the copy he sent to England.[119] To judge from Starkey's career, Pole's many friends were still disinclined to expect the worst. Almost certainly Henry was in that number and even Cromwell probably decided to bide his time. On the traditional interpretation, Starkey's failure with Pole ended his career.[120] This is certainly not true over the long term, and most of the cloud over Starkey had lifted even by the end of the year. Starkey undoubtedly went through some uncomfortable moments, but the backlash against him over *De unitate* was only part of the reason behind his temporary disgrace in the summer of 1536. The best evidence for this case rests on chronology. Starkey's three letters detailing his difficulties all come from July, the first sometime after the 2nd when Cromwell became lord privy seal and the others from the 24th and 27th. Given the reconstruction of Starkey's involvement with *De unitate* offered above, it could not have produced disgrace as early as the beginning of July.

Two or three weeks later the situation had changed, but *De unitate* still was

---

[118] In a note at the foot of fol. 379v continued on 380v Starkey's editor added three points which Starkey did not pursue: Pole had relied too much on his eloquence, expecting to convert Henry by empty words; his 'slanderous oratyon' belied his claim to love Henry; and he had despised the consent of his country and of all learned men. The first would have made the professional rhetorician Starkey uncomfortable, and Starkey would not have liked the second, either. He never impugned Pole's motives, however much he criticized his actions.

[119] Dunn, '*De unitate*', 463. Even before Starkey replied, Pole had taken steps to render whatever the English did pointless. On 16 June he answered a letter from the emperor for the first time, after Çornoça had shown Pole an exchange of correspondence between himself and Charles. This had persuaded Pole that he owed it to his country to send a gentleman from his household 'who will verbally explain both my ideas in the matter and the means of executing my plan'. Its precise details do not survive, but Pole did urge the emperor to try peaceful means before proceeding to violence. *CSPSp*, V:2, 63 (quoting the summary). Charles did not reply until October and then he told Pole that any action would be contingent on the pope's attitude. *Ibid.*, 109. This might sound like the expected waffling from Charles V, but he was not above trying to influence Paul III's thinking, and he would do so on Pole's behalf later in the year.

[120] Elton, *Reform and renewal*, 55; Zeeveld, *Foundations*, 110 and 226; D. S. Berkowitz's introduction to *Humanist scholarship and public order*, 24; and L. Firpo, *Appunti e testi per la storia dell'antimachiavellismo*, 69.

not alone. Probably almost immediately after he finished reading *De unitate*, Starkey retired to his benefice in Holy Trinity, Bosham, Sussex. He heard quickly from Wriothesley that his choice had aroused suspicion in London because it put him close to the Countess of Salisbury's seat at Warblington, less than ten miles away.[121] Starkey also held livings at Great Mongeham, Kent, and in Pole's deanery of Wimborne Minster, but he probably chose Bosham because his vicar there was removable at will.[122] Nevertheless, his decision may also have raised eyebrows because of his nominal patron in the living and the man who actually presented him, John Veysey, Bishop of Exeter, and Robert Sherborne, Bishop of Chichester. Both had been implicated in John Fisher's opposition to the divorce in 1534.[123] Wriothesley's attempt to protect Starkey may again signal the depth of faction-fighting. Although allegedly Cromwell's man, Wriothesley opposed his patron's attack on the Pole family in revenge for Reginald's defection, telling Starkey that Sir Geoffrey Pole and 'other of his famylie must nott be made Cok-[neyes]'.[124] Wriothesley would turn on Cromwell very quickly at the latter's fall.

While Henry's marriages and other people's opinions of them helped to induce Starkey to withdraw from the court, his preaching caused greater problems, and his doubtful loyalty to the new Cromwellian order more serious ones yet. His first letter to Cromwell opened dramatically with a plaint to Cromwell – 'my lord your wordys have goone through my hart'. After much more of the same, Starkey challenged the lord privy seal to 'prove that I have dyssemblyd, but in one word wyth you or wyth the kyng' about Pole, but Starkey went on immediately about 'my prechyng' and asked Cromwell not to credit hearsay about it. The bulk of the letter defended Starkey against Cromwell's charge that 'I study a mean doctryne for my owne glory'. Instead, Starkey insisted that he had 'studyd to exhort & move men from such extremyte, wherby they are styrryd to flye the obedyence to the

---

121 *LP*, XI, 169.

122 W. Page, ed., *VCH Sussex*, II, 110 and *Valor ecclesiasticus*, I, 310. Starkey was sacrist of the collegiate chapel and holder of Fishbourne chantry. A John Starkey was amongst four prebendaries of Wimborne in the *Valor*, 274–5. Since this is also how Thomas was listed for Bosham when we have the evidence of Sherborne's register that he held the living and because Pole was dean at Wimborne, the entry there is almost certainly another error. Unfortunately, this interpretation cannot be confirmed from Cardinal Campeggio's episcopal register for Salisbury, and there do not seem to be any other sources which might contain supporting evidence. I am very grateful to K. H. Rogers, Wiltshire County Archivist, for much assistance on this point. If John and Thomas are the same person, Starkey held the richest prebend at £16 15s 8d Lily had one of the other three.

123 *LP*, VIII, 859.i. 32–3 and iv. 39. Sherborne had also been called to task for his preaching of the Supremacy (*ibid.*, 941), but neither bishop appears to have suffered any repercussions.

124 SP 1/138, fol. 215r. The precise meaning of Wriothesley's injunction is obscure, but its general purport seems clear enough.

kyngys lawys'.[125] Cromwell could only have meant to call Starkey a hypo-
crite, since he had both proposed the mean to Starkey in the first place, and
was just then launching a programme based upon it.[126]

Starkey's explanation worked rapidly. By the time of his second letter to
Cromwell just a few weeks later he had the assurance of both Cromwell (in
person) and Thomas Cranmer that the former was again 'my gud lord aftur
your wont & customyd maner'. Henry still worried Starkey, though. Starkey
could not understand why the king had not rewarded him for his efforts with
Pole, instead of becoming suspicious. Starkey pointed again to his labours in
the *Exhortation* 'to the inducyng of hys pepul, to theyr offyce & dewty
concernyng the obedyence of hys lawys'.[127] Starkey called Cromwell to attest
to the amount of effort he had put into reasoning with Pole, only to find
himself blamed for Pole's resistance. How could that be? Starkey wondered,
the more so because 'hyt was an occasyon taken, & not apon my behalf
gyven, for I never movyd the kyng nor yet you to the inserchyng of hys
jugement at any tyme'. Starkey reduced the somewhat limited impact of that
last point by another declaration of his ignorance of Pole's thinking (384v).
Starkey recalled that he had told Henry to his face that he accepted the
supremacy wholeheartedly, but continued that although Cromwell was still
suspicious of his ties to Pole, Starkey did not want the king to suspect any
dissimulation on his part. Shifting his aim from Pole to preaching, Starkey
adopted the theory that the best defence is a good offence, and advised
Cromwell to chose preachers like him who could wean the people from the
old beliefs slowly. Starkey protested his wholehearted commitment to Cromwell's and Henry's programme by claiming that they had inspired him to
begin his own preaching ministry when they had set out to establish true
religion by removing papal primacy with the consent of all the English clergy
(384v and 385v). Starkey's appeal to consent here is a little strange, given that
he had earlier thought little of it and that he had criticized Pole severely for
relying on it. It appears that Starkey used the idea in whatever fashion seemed
appropriate, another argument against its having meant much to him. Here
he used the same argument as had figured prominently in the *Exhortation*,
and probably for the same reason. Cromwell would like it. From Starkey's
exculpation, it seems that Cromwell and his informants charged him with
insufficient evangelical ardour. Whatever the sufferings which might befall

---

[125] SP 1/105, fol. 181r–v.

[126] Elton, *Reform and renewal*, 51 makes much of Cromwell's protection, although he does not
notice this later attack. For Cromwell's policy, see G. R. Elton, *Policy and police: the
enforcement of the reformation in the age of Thomas Cromwell*, 244–5 where he discusses
the royal circular of 7 January 1536 which made exactly the same points as Starkey's defence.
Well might Cromwell have felt obligated to protect Starkey, as Elton surmised in *Reform and
reformation*, 259. There is no direct evidence for such protection, and if Cromwell offered it,
he acted out of prudential motives, not ideologically inspired fellow-feeling.

[127] Cleop. E VI, fol. 384r.

him, Starkey assured Cromwell, he had resolved to meet them with the same two principles he propounded to the common people: contempt of this life and hope of a better; and charity, obedience and humility (385r).

Probably while in Bosham, Starkey tried yet another measure to regain favour and wrote to Henry. This letter has always been read as one of Starkey's most brazen gambles, but in fact it could almost have served as the manifesto of the similarly disgraced court conservatives who, like Starkey, expected to be restored. Starkey did not risk all on one bold throw – he merely slightly mistimed the release of the dice. It is easy to see why this letter impressed Elton.[128] Starkey addressed Henry forthrightly, proffering both a defence of his role in the Pole affair and an agenda for reform to head off further opposition. But as he often did after one set of his plans failed to pan out, Starkey simply put them out of his mind. He nearly dismissed his involvement with Pole, devoting only a few lines to it. Starkey assured Henry that he had never expected such disagreement, and passed on quickly to seize the opportunity of letting Henry know 'myn inward affect' about Pole's judgment.

This Starkey failed to do directly. Instead, the Starkey of the Dialogue reemerged, and he may even have brushed off his grand reform programme once again.[129] He referred to it in the *Exhortation*, as if he still meant to get it out, and his central discussion of the reformed king's council bore remarkable similarities to the description Henry sent the Pilgrims of Grace.[130] Nevertheless, it will not do to underestimate the dangers to Starkey and his allies which his proposals still posed. Whatever the resemblances in structure between his constitution and Tudor monarchy, the two were designed to serve the much different ends of government by aristocracy as against government by bureaucracy. Apparently, neither Starkey nor his allies saw this fundamental difference clearly, and both thought to take the opportunity offered in 1536. The short span from the appearance of the *Exhortation* in March to June or at latest July probably explains why the Dialogue never appeared in print during Starkey's lifetime.

The best palaeographical evidence for Starkey's attempt to revive his Dialogue is that small scribble in the margin of fol. 125r recommending Erasmus's *Ecclesiastes*. Although Starkey could have heard of this book before it was printed in September 1535, those who have taken this reference as a clue to the later history of his MS may yet be right. Such a reference was still at least demonstrably incautious. When Erasmus's 'boke of the prechar'

---

128 *Reform and renewal*, 52.
129 My critics, especially Dr Starkey, have convinced me to allow this possibility. It fits Starkey's circumstances ideally, but has very little support in the MS.
130 *Exhortation*, sig. 44v; D. Starkey, 'Public debate and public policy: the course of reform, 1440–1540', perhaps overstates how much impact Starkey's designs had on the privy council list, but they are certainly similar; cf. Elton, *Policy*, 200; and Guy, 'Privy council', 78.

first appeared, it was not well received in England. Erasmus attacked Henry in the prefatory epistle for the execution of More and Fisher, to the latter of whom Erasmus had intended to dedicate the work.[131] In early October 1535, Simon Heynes reported to Cromwell that Erasmus had written a book 'wherein he do sore inveie against the kynges Highnes for the deth of Mr. More'.[132] Whether or not Starkey knew of Heynes's intelligence, he could have had no doubt about Henry's attitude to criticism on this point after his correspondence with Pole. Nevertheless, Starkey remained unconcerned. He knew that the deaths of More and Fisher had shocked humanists throughout Europe. Even Morison had tried to advise Cromwell in 1534, after More's arrest, not to proceed to such extreme measures against dissidents – exile was much better.[133] Starkey probably saw nothing wrong with continued criticism, either from him or from Erasmus, and he raised the point directly with the king in his letter.

Pole may have disappointed Starkey's hopes for the moment, but the removal of 'that woman' offered another cause for optimism. Starkey asserted confidently that divine providence had led Henry to rid himself of Anne.[134] Anything done during her tenure was like a sore in a body which might appear sound, but was still weak. The people had accepted her as queen only because of the obedience they owed Henry. Now that she was gone, everything would improve (121r). Or at least it would if Henry paid attention to Starkey's suggestions, the first of which revealed his factional allegiance even more clearly than his opposition to Anne. Until such time as Henry should have children from his marriage to Jane Seymour, he should restore Mary. Starkey never named Mary and affected not to care whether she ever came to the throne, but the long encomium he gave her as 'the floure of al ladys, & the veray glas & image of al vertue & nobylyte', belied his pretended lack of interest. Mary's restoration, which Cromwell had supported just a little earlier, would 'stablysch the fyrst ground ... of al the rest of your actys, & of al reformatyon', etc., etc., by providing domestic tranquillity. Starkey repeated the point in his brief conclusion (121r and 140r).

Religious policy was uppermost in Starkey's mind. The mean took a while to emerge, as it had in the *Exhortation*, but a course between 'superstytyon' and 'the new fastyon' remained Starkey's object (135r–v). Nevertheless, he came down harder on the latter. Starkey unsparingly criticized the executions of 1535 which he had warned Henry would weaken his case, even though Starkey still argued that the monks and the others had committed suicide. Proper preaching interested Starkey much more, and he aimed all his blasts at

131 *Op. Ep. Er.*, XI, 3036, p. 192.
132 *LP*, IX, 521. Heynes was one of Cromwell's circle of religious radicals. See Dowling, 'Anne Boleyn', 38 and *Humanism in the age of Henry VIII*, 65, 93, 124.
133 Nero B VI, fol. 151r (*LP*, VII, 1318; 27 October [1534]).
134 SP 1/105, fols. 121r and 123r.

the radicals. Preachers must not expound the 'dark placys of scrypture aftur theyr owne fantasys', departing from the ancients and the 'consent & custume of the church' (123r).[135] Those who claimed that true religion had only just been revealed had caused a huge controversy. Their attacks on tradition and popishness 'had almost dryven away al vertue & holynes, they had almost sett your pepul at such lyberty from al old custumys & ceremonys, that they began, as hyt apperyd, lytyle to estyme other vertue or honestye'. Starkey had no stronger terms of abuse in his vocabulary. Naturally, contempt of heavenly felicity had followed and with it an end to the obedience which the preachers should have emphasized, and the introduction of 'lewd lyberty' (123v). Starkey proposed to reduce the amount of preaching drastically and ensure that only grave, learned men addressed the people. Experience proved that the best Christian living went hand in hand with the least preaching. Henry should have proceeded much more frequently on his own authority, rather than relying so much on the clergy to justify his actions; Starkey's appeal to their consent in the *Exhortation* must have been a tactical manoeuvre (136r–v). Instead, the clergy should lead by example (138v–9r). Starkey thought Henry had begun to order preaching, but much remained to be done (124r). In light of all the current noise, Starkey's hope that all Englishmen would accept the recently promulgated 'unyte of doctryne' 'wyth one consent' but without much persuasion is a monument to his disdain for the common people and would have rung hollow in Cromwell's ears (124r and 136r).

But Starkey's religious principles increasingly dictated such a stance. As he had in the *Exhortation*, Starkey relied on Paul's 'charytabul ordur in a commynwelth' to undergird his conservative insistence that 'in the church, the mystical body of chryst, ordur must be observyd, every membyr therin doyng his offyce & dewtye' (128v). The well-functioning 'chrystun commyn wele' still needed some traditional charitable deeds, for example, alms-giving and prayers for the dead (127v–8r). The corporate analogy made another appearance in Starkey's peroration, where he argued that all Englishmen, including bishops, were subject to their head. This rearguard but still anticlerical action took up only a small part of Starkey's discussion, perhaps because he knew Henry's own leanings well enough. The balance of this letter was designed to defend the religious conservatives against the charge of papistry launched against them by their enemies. Starkey's allies did not wish the restoration of the papacy, and Starkey explained why not, or tried to (124r).

As he had when allegedly fostering the mean, Starkey came down much further on the conservative side of the fence than the protestant. Papal

---

135 I will forebear to belabour the point, but here Starkey turned to his own advantage exactly the same argument about consent which he had earlier denied to Pole.

supremacy might have to go, but Starkey founded his argument against it on a case in favour of the general council. The pope's power had arisen originally because of its utility in running a council.

For as much as general counseyl of al chrystun natyonys, was jugyd of wyse men to be expedyent, both to redresse al commyn errorys and heresys, & also to stablysch a conformyte of manerys & unyte of chrystys doctryne in the unyversal church, hyt was thought also mete & convenyent, to determe & appoynt, one to be hede & chefe in the same, to ordur the counseyl. (132v–133r)

These purposes, of course, could adequately describe Starkey's own agenda. The second reason for the primacy was to prevent princes from making doctrinal errors. Starkey hurried on to write that popes had usurped too much of secular rulers' legitimate authority and brought the papacy to an intolerable and superstitious 'tyrannycal jurysdyctyon', but his discussion amounted to an oblique warning to Henry not to disregard the pope altogether (132v–134v). Starkey again attacked the *ex post facto* exegesis which sought support for the papacy once it had been established, and underscored the importance of separating scripture from human traditions (133v and 134v–135r). Starkey praised Henry as the first 'who by publyke authoryte, hath cast downe thys hedy powar of rome'. Nevertheless, he never suggested that the pope should not still preside over a council and act as its chief doctrinal authority.[136]

Starkey advised the king to cease to act unilaterally. The investigation of papal tyranny was a matter for a council, not for king-in-parliament as it had been in the *Exhortation*, and Starkey warned Henry that he would be very sorry to see him do anything which he could not justify before the whole church (134r, 138v, 139v). Needless to say, Starkey hoped to see a council shortly in order to restore concord and unity to Christendom, and expected Henry to play a leading role in convening one (139v; hope for council repeated twice).

One last matter worried Starkey, and it reveals the extent of his disappointment with attempts to make the nobility responsible to the ideal of the commonwealth. Starkey stole up on the problem of what to do with the spoils from the dissolution of the smaller monasteries, against which he inveighed fiercely, by lecturing Henry on the prince's obligation to liberality (125r and 127r).[137] If Henry refused that duty, he would destroy the commonwealth and foment sedition (142v and 133v–136r). This sounds like a conventional appeal to the prince to keep his nobles happy, and in part it was. Henry should apply the proceeds to the support of learned men and soldiers. The

---

[136] Starkey's attitude fits one of the dominant positions adopted by English catholics. J.-P. Moreau, *Rome ou l'Angleterre?*, 144.

[137] Ferguson pointed to this 'systematic and penetrating analysis' as some of his strongest evidence for Starkey's unique stature as social theorist. *Articulate citizen*, 241.

former were as necessary to good policy in peace as the latter were in war. Starkey underlined their equivalence by calling both professions noble, although he spelled out the social dimension of the warrior class more clearly, writing that 'I trust to see now many a nobul gentylman relevyd, by these actys, and exercysyng themselfys in al featys of armys' (125v).

Yet, as Starkey expanded on his plans, he proposed only that some monasteries be converted into schools for the clergy and that most of them be kept intact and leased to younger, married sons who would then remedy England's great lack of people (127v and 130v). These two solutions were connected, since Starkey largely blamed clerical chastity for the problem of underpopulation (129v and 130r). Starkey most feared that 'grete lordys & gentylmen of much possessyonys', who were to be the chief beneficiaries of his Dialogue, would come away with all the monastic property (130v). Thus education was still uppermost in Starkey's mind, but he no longer viewed its utility to the commonwealth in quite the same way, in part because he had developed a degree of hostility to the nobility. Now, rather than appealing to it to cure the ills of the commonwealth, Starkey turned to Henry to see to 'the commyn welth of your pore subyectys' (132v). Starkey couched his pitch in the same language of common (or now public) authority, but whereas in the Dialogue such words had covered an appeal to the nobility to restrain the prince, now the roles were reversed (126v–7r, 128v). He added insult and injury by formulating a legal justification for the dissolution in the shape of an argument that the supreme authority had always had the right to break men's wills if their original intention was not being fulfilled. Therefore, since the monasteries founded by past generations had fallen into decay, and the testators were dead or absent, they could be assumed to consent to Henry's revocation of their grants (128r and 126v).[138] Perhaps Starkey's anti-clericalism and anti-monastic attitude overpowered his aristocratic leanings for the moment, but disillusionment with Pole and with his brother nobles is a more likely explanation of why Starkey could demand the expropriation of institutions like the Pole family foundation of Bisham, where the Dialogue had been set.

Starkey's plain writing might have extended his disgrace. If so, this letter must have reached Henry after Starkey's partial recovery at the end of July. Probably word of Pole's journey to Rome put Starkey in further trouble later in the autumn after the first wave of the Pilgrimage of Grace had ended, that is in late October or early November.[139] At any rate, Starkey again had to defend himself to an unknown recipient against most of the same charges

---

[138] This is not only another most peculiar usage of consent, but marks Starkey's independence of mind once again. His fellow conservatives came to regard the legal attack on wills as part of the justification of the Pilgrimage. Moreau, *Rome ou l'Angleterre?*, 238.

[139] Starkey's reference to 'thy[s] pernycyous & devylysch sedycyon' and his hope that 'such plantys take among us no ferther rote' establishes the date of this letter. SP 1/105, fol. 48r. Pole announced his departure on 10 October. *ERP*, I, 483 (*LP*, XI, 654).

which he had already answered to Cromwell and Cranmer. The obvious bone of contention was Pole. Starkey began by asserting that he had frequently quarrelled with Pole until 'at the last, hyt bradde a certayn brakke in our frenschyp'. Starkey left Italy in part because of the rupture. Nevertheless, he had never had any inkling that Pole disagreed with his judgment of papal primacy as a matter of 'the consent & constytutyon of chrystun men, & not to be rootyd in goddys word expressely'. This point so concerned Starkey that he offered to produce witnesses in England who could confirm that Pole held the same opinion when Henry had first approached him through Starkey, but that the executions of More and Fisher had changed his mind (47r).

Starkey sprinkled popery and popishness liberally around his letter as part of a defence against accusations that he had helped to 'conteyne men in blyndnes & superstycyon', the same charge he had countered back in July. This time Starkey's assailants were clearly religious radicals. They had taken exception to his efforts to 'forge a certayn mean in goddys truthe & in hys worde, whereas non ys, f[or] ther ys but one truthe therin conteynyng no mean'. Starkey's use of adiaphora had also raised objections, and he defended it at length, in much the same terms as he had employed in the *Exhortation*, emphasizing the point that 'such thyngys may not of every pryvate man be condemnyd at lyberty, bycause they be not expressyd in goddys word clerely' (47v). Starkey insisted that he, like his opponents, strove for the 'pure truthe of relygyon'. He refused to see the desperation in his situation that most historians have, either because of his irrepressible optimism or perhaps because he knew better than they that he still had others in his corner, even if Cromwell were not. In any event, Starkey bluntly claimed that two acts of policy particularly disturbed other countries, although he named only the dissolution of the monasteries. As he had at least twice before, he urged their conversion into 'lytyl unyversytes, and ... as hyt were commyn scolys of lernyng & vertue to the ryght educatyon of youthe', without specifying of what social class or background, nor to what end they should be trained (48v).

Starkey probably misplaced the trust in Cromwell's continuing benevolence with which he closed this letter. Regardless of his suspicions, Cromwell had much less use for Starkey now, as a comparison of Starkey's very short '[An In]ductyon to Concord to the pepul of Englond' with Morison's three published tracts to the same end makes painfully obvious. Starkey mapped his oration on much the same lines as his *Exhortation*, beginning with divine providence and the goodness of the prince, but he emphasized the former who 'by hys only infynyte powar' had prevented bloodshed and the destruction of the realm.[140] Starkey praised Henry's moderation which had brought him 'by gentylnes & patyence to wyn you [the people of England] to your dewtye &

140 SP 6/9, p. 219.

obedyence, then by force & powar to destroy you wyth vengeance' (220). Probably Morison forestalled Starkey's writing with his *A Lamentation* and *Remedy for sedition*, but it may also be that Starkey could only just squeeze out three pages, possibly because of latent sympathy with the Pilgrims. His scheme of conciliar restraints on Henry's power was very similar to that proposed by the rebels, and he may have sympathized more with their religious conservatism than with Cromwell's protestant evangelicalism, although endorsing neither. Starkey certainly indulged in none of the invective against them which Morison produced so effortlessly. If anyone else saw Starkey's broadside, it probably would not have helped his bid for a second chance.

Thus by late 1536 it appeared that Starkey had managed to blot his copybook with both king and minister, although he displeased them for different reasons. While Henry suspected that Starkey had dissembled about Pole's attitude to the divorce and supremacy, that is about an essentially political issue, Cromwell charged Starkey with seditious preaching and constructing a religious justification for political changes out of concern for personal glory. Perhaps it is nearly impossible to separate the strands of politics and religion here, as it is to unknot the issue of 'king or minister?', but it still appears that Cromwell posed the more immediate threat to Starkey, given Starkey's decision to seek his fortune as a preacher. Certainly Cromwell's resolve to do down the court conservatives was much more deeply rooted in religious and political animosity than his somewhat desperate measures against Anne. And if the new story of the manoeuvres around *De unitate* offered here at least somewhat reduces the onus on Henry, the sequel in 1537 suggests that Cromwell was more interested in dealing with Pole – and by implication Starkey – than the king was.[141]

This segment of Starkey's life should not end on a note of unrelieved gloom. By another striking coincidence with Pole's career, Starkey received a valuable benefice by royal grant in December 1536 at nearly the time Pole became a cardinal. The mastership of the collegiate chapel of Corpus Christi in St Lawrence Pountney, London, brought authority over twelve chaplains, a seat in convocation, and a total income of £99 17s 11d.[142] It is tempting to suggest that the Marquess of Exeter may have had a hand in Starkey's promotion. He had once taken over the Duke of Buckingham's patronage of the living, only to surrender it to the king on Wolsey's demand.[143] Exeter's town house was in

---

[141] See my 'A diet for Henry VIII'.
[142] George Hennessy, ed., *Novum repertorium ecclesiasticum parochiale londinense*, 297 for details of the benefice and *LP*, IV:3, 6047 for its seat in convocation. The letter of appointment is in *LP*, XI, 1417 (29) and partially printed in Herrtage, *Starkey's life*, lxiii. The loss of most of the *Valor* for London makes it impossible to determine what Starkey's mastership alone brought him.
[143] SP 1/39, fol. 246r, Exeter–Wolsey, 21 October 1525 (*LP*, IV, 2576).

the parish and he may therefore have continued to take an interest in the incumbent of St Lawrence. Nevertheless it is more likely that Paul Withypoll helped most to deliver this benefice to Starkey. Withypoll also lived in this parish (his daughter was buried in St Lawrence and he requested burial there), he was one of Henry's particular favourites, and either a religious conservative, or a man of 'evangelical' beliefs similar to Starkey's. He has been suggested as the author of a proposal to forestall the Act in Restraint of Appeals by a grant of £200,000 to Henry if the king would submit his divorce to the judgment of a general council. If this identification is accurate, then he and Starkey would have had a major political belief in common, since that was exactly Starkey's plan at probably very nearly the same time. Starkey may well have come to know Withypoll in the first place through Thomas Lupset, who tutored Withypoll's son Edmund.[144] Starkey and Withypoll would serve together by royal command in early 1538. Perhaps this putative relationship even helps to explain some of the prominence Starkey accorded to representatives of London in his constitutional plans. In any case, his new living left Starkey with an income of perhaps £85. If not yet in the league of his friend Lupset, Starkey received considerably more than the average English clergyman.[145]

Perhaps Starkey finally succeeded in clearing himself of charges of complicity with Pole by producing the witnesses he had offered in October – Morison and Cole, the latter recently returned home.[146] Not that Starkey completely escaped suspicion. His last letter to Pole of 16 January 1537 survives in three drafts. Although no one else corrected any of them, Starkey noted Morison and Cole's testimony on the foot of one, which suggests that someone at least checked it.[147] Whoever he was, he had no animus against Pole. Starkey spent most of the letter trying to repair his ties to Pole. He apologized for his sharp tongue when he had rebuked Pole for going to Rome, reminded Pole how well they had known each other by chiding him for thinking that Starkey could have acted out of ambition, and closed 'Yourys

---

[144] For Withypoll, see Helen Miller's biography in S. T. Bindoff, ed., *The house of commons, 1509–1558*, III, 649–51. His daughter's epitaph is recorded in J. Stow, *Survey of London and Westminster*, II, 189. My thanks to S. E. Lehmberg for suggesting Withypoll's importance, and to Maria Dowling for letting me see a copy of her unpublished 'Education of men and women of the early Tudor merchant class: the Withypoll family of London'. She presents considerable circumstantial evidence for Withypoll's 'evangelical' leanings.

[145] Lupset enjoyed an annual income of £160 1s. 6d. J. A. Gee, *Thomas Lupset*, 116. Starkey would appear never to have held any cathedral living, at least he does not appear in the index volume of John Le Neve, *Fasti ecclesiae anglicanae 1300–1541*, *passim* and index, XII compiled by J. M. Horn.

[146] *LP*, XI, 402.3.   [147] Herrtage, *Starkey's life*, xxxviii.

yet I trust aftur the old maner'.[148] Starkey explained that the danger to Pole and his family had inspired his harsh tone, but if he now wrote to Pole two things 'frendly movyd', that did not mean Starkey thought Pole was any less at risk. Pole should not accept the cardinalate because he would increase the schism and disobey the dictates of love of country which certainly must still motivate him, as did 'the desyre of servyng your prynce'. The cardinals, Starkey repeated, had done little to advance the doctrine of Christ (377v). Pole should turn his back on Rome and come home, for Starkey was convinced that he would see a day when pure religion would be established there, however severe the upheavals of the moment (378r). Events quickly overtook this optimistic prognosis.[149]

One more failure with Pole did not abort Starkey's career entirely, any more than any of the earlier ones had. In fact, one of the last of Starkey's public appearances gave him a major venue in which to exercise his religious expertise. In March he was deputed at royal order along with one Leighton to confer with the bishops about the invocation of saints, purgatory, clerical celibacy and the doctrine of satisfaction as part of the run up to the Bishops' Book. This marked a rehabilitation for both men, since the order probably referred to Edward Leighton, who had got into trouble over his preaching in 1534.[150] Henry himself may well have intervened. On at least three of these points, excepting only the third, he probably would have preferred Starkey's views to the pronounced evangelism of the final formulations or to the probable views of his own chief minister.[151] Both W. G. Zeeveld and Joseph Block erred in seeing another sign of Cromwell's hand in this episode. They ignored the content of the mandate to Starkey and Leighton and assumed that Starkey was summoned to deliver his 'directive' (Zeeveld's word for Starkey's draft proclamation) on preaching. Block embroidered on Zeeveld's notion by claiming that the 'discourse' was 'authorized by the vicegerent in the name of

---

[148] Cleop. E VI, fols. 377r and 378r.

[149] SP 1/105, fol. 50r–2r (*LP*, XI, 74), a letter to Pole in Wriothesley's hand, is not from Starkey. Its cocky assurances that the writer could bring the king to dismiss *De unitate* as a rash work, invective against Pole and much shorter sentences all suggest Morison as the author. Passages such as 'are you not sorry to have wasted them [your virtues] in renting his honor / in defiling his name / in obscuring his memory', or 'But you must leave Rome / if you love England / you must forsake the bisshop therof if you woll wynne the king' are reminiscent of Morison's rhetorical cadences. It could even be that Wriothesley himself wrote the letter, especially because of its insistence that Henry was still favourably disposed to Pole, as Wriothesley himself probably was. SP 1/111, fol. 151r is another letter to Pole in Wriothesley's hand, dating from about the same time.

[150] *LP*, XII:1, 708 and Elton, *Policy*, 213 for Leighton. It is possible that this is the same conference to which Cromwell took Alexander Alesius after meeting him in the street. If so, Alesius makes no mention of either Starkey or Leighton in his account of John Stokesley's stupidity in *Of the word of God against the bishop of London*.

[151] J. J. Scarisbrick, *Henry VIII*, especially 405–8.

the King'.[152] It is also unlikely that Starkey wrote his draft so late. The upheavals of 1536–7 would have shaken even his confidence somewhat and probably have deterred him from offering such a straightforward programme in one of the areas which had caused him the most trouble.

[152] Zeeveld, *Foundations*, 226 and J. Block, 'Thomas Cromwell's patronage of preaching', 40. S. E. Lehmberg suggests that Starkey tried to influence policy even earlier with a draft bill (SP 1/89, fols. 25–41; printed by T. F. T. Plucknett in *Transactions of the royal historical society*, 4th ser., XIX [1936]) to establish a court of conservators of the common weal. *The reformation parliament*, 216. Lehmberg based his suggestion on Elton's 'Parliamentary drafts' in which Lehmberg claimed Elton fathered this bill on Starkey. He did not, identifying it instead as the work of 'a man closely associated with Latimer, Armstrong and Hales, whose chief interest lay in the law', 124. Given the author's great interest in having statutes put into 'our maternall Englishe tong', perhaps he may be identified even more with the circle around John Rastell and George Ferrers who made the Englishing of the common law their special project. However that may be, the bill contains nothing to suggest Starkey's authorship, save only the name of the officers of this court.

8

Writing for the drawer

The old story which sank Starkey into oblivion after he failed to bring Pole into the fold contains some truth – Starkey did disappear from near centre-stage in the last eighteen months or two years of his life. But he did not vanish, any more than all conservatives became reactionaries.[1] As J.-P. Moreau argues, English Catholics went through a major readjustment of attitudes between 1534 and 1539, as most came to accept the new order and only a few resisted. Starkey found himself suspended between these two positions.[2] Manuscript evidence, some of it known but unused and some of it unknown, shows how Starkey reacted to the fiasco of 1536–7. A set of notes on the Old Testament dated 14 October 1537, another batch of jottings on Albert Pighe's (Pighius) *Hierarchiae ecclesiasticae assertio* probably written in mid-1538, and, finally, the records of the investigation into the Exeter conspiracy, produce a much fuller portrait of the last period of Starkey's life than previously available. They reveal that Starkey followed the turn to religion which he had announced at the end of his Dialogue and pursued ever since he decided to become a preacher. This meant major changes in his political programme, most of them probably arising from his disappointment over the failure of both his and Pole's plans, but despite some apparently strong temptation, he refused to withdraw altogether. Starkey undoubtedly found himself in a difficult position. Although he retained Henry's favour – or at least thought he did – he had lost Cromwell's. There is no evidence that any of Pole's erstwhile supporters took up the slack. As Starkey found himself increasingly boxed in during his last few months, he turned to old Oxford connections for help. He died a natural death in remote Somerset just ahead of the executioner.

Both of Starkey's last writings present problems of interpretation, from their form, to his purposes and intentions. On their face two sets of rough notes, it is possible that Starkey meant them as paraphrases in the manner of

[1] Maria Dowling makes such an equivalence in 'Humanist support for Katherine of Aragon', 54–5.
[2] J.-P. Moreau, *Rome ou l'Angleterre?*, 23, 147, 163, 225.

247

those his friend Jan van Kampen wrote, albeit highly compressed ones. Then again, the first of these, BL MS Royal 7 C XVI, might be described as 'Notes to myself', or perhaps 'A journal of a conversion'.[3] That is, it may have been purely private. On the other hand, Starkey seems to have finished these observations, while he did not put the final touches to SP 1/141, the notes on Pighe. The jottings end with a series of conclusions designed 'to remove the foundation of [Pighe's] book', which seems to promise more, perhaps a full-dress refutation. The relation between both documents and their originals compounds the difficulty produced by uncertainty about their form and purpose, but Starkey's selection also presents certain advantages. Not only does it highlight the significance of those passages which Starkey considered worthwhile, but those he skipped can also produce information when handled cautiously.

The colophon of Royal 7 C XVI summarized the thrust of the document in a small piece of autobiography.

Just as once, a boy admiring the works of nature, I began curiously examining everything, so reading this book [the Old Testament] I turn to wondering at the works of God. After I had been held for a while by a certain stupor of mind, finally then having been encouraged in spirit (?) until I advanced, in order that as I learned at least religiously to worship mysteries not understood, so likewise I cherished in a most holy fashion those to which it is licit to penetrate. Certainly I have exerted myself in the hope that I may by Christ's protection win through to those more hidden. (226r)

The tone differs markedly from either of Starkey's earlier reports on the course of his studies, much of which he now denigrated. Different things concerned him now, especially human weakness and the necessity of leaving everything to inscrutable divine providence, sin and penance (as a means to avoid punishment), and escaping worldly thoughts and behaviour. Nevertheless, Starkey's view of psychology, law and politics, the nature of the church and the relations between secular and ecclesiastical power remained similar to his earliest positions. While Starkey had soft-pedalled most of the subversive potential of his political thinking in works designed for public consumption, and had never openly criticized Henry despite his strong reservations about monarchy, in late 1537 he privately singled out stories of tyrants which he thought applied peculiarly well to England, at least obliquely criticized the divorce and Henry's rationale for it, and probably

---

[3] This MS remained unknown because it was erroneously ascribed to Morison in *LP*, XII:2, 904, although it is clearly in Starkey's hand. This volume of the Royal MSS contains an odd lot of mainly theological tracts, described as 'mostly connected to Thomas Cromwell'. Starkey's immediately succeeds a list of criticisms of the Bishops' Book offered by Nicholas Heath, Richard Sampson, Thomas Cranmer and Christopher St Germain, and precedes a treatise purporting to show that Christians living in charity reached a more perfect state than Adam in paradise. G. F. Warner and J. P. Gilson, *British museum: catalogue of western manuscripts in the old royal and king's collections*.

continued to expect great things from Pole, even if he camouflaged all this more or less carefully under Old Testament stories.

Starkey's exegesis served him well to these ends. He could paraphrase the literal sense of a passage, but then insist that he intended only the 'spiritual' meaning. 'Mysteries' and allegories also interested Starkey. When Yahweh spoke to Moses from a cloud of dust, that meant he used 'obscure words, containing mysteries beneath allegories', which made interpreting them singularly difficult.[4] Wild beasts, woods and dead men all qualified as mysteries.[5] The law governing jealousy also had to be read allegorically.[6] Starkey proposed a few allegorical readings of his own, hazarding that the manna Yahweh gave the Israelites to eat meant that divine commands were not impossible to obey, that the seven people removed from Canaan represented the seven deadly sins, that the Queen of Sheba 'signifies perhaps the love and study of virtue, which wishes to embrace knowledge', and that Ruth 'can be a figure of the soul wandering to its true country, and pleasing itself in the pleasures of this world at first, but afterwards renouncing them'.[7]

This protective coloration worked only up to a point. It was still safe enough to write that 'the temple of the Lord is a mind pure of vices', but when Starkey underlined how Solomon's purity of mind fitted him and not the blood-stained David to build the Temple, then he came close to a comment on contemporary politics.[8] Starkey further subverted his own method by applying historical criticism, especially when writing about the prophets. Nebuchadnezzar, for example, was perfectly historical and led Starkey to assert out of context that 'to the understanding of the prophets, observe well the times and kings with which the prophets lived'.[9] Since he also claimed that Old Testament prophecies most assuredly covered his own times – 'what was said by the prophets to impious people always applies to the iniquities of our times' – the moral stood out. For their kings, read our kings.[10] Likewise, when Starkey asserted that the story of Samuel's killing of King Agag was 'moral', he prepared any audience to regard the tale as an object lesson for a modern prince.[11]

Starkey's exegesis cleared the way for political analysis, too, by helping him

---

[4] Royal 7 C XVI, fol. 212v, col. 2 (*Ex.* 19). In future references to this MS, I will cite the folio number (without folio designation)/col. number and biblical reference (when it can be determined) in parentheses.

[5] 223v/2.   [6] 213v/2 (Num. 6 [*recte* 5]:11–31).

[7] 212v/2 (Ex. 16), 214v/2 (Deut. 7), 219r/2 (I Kings 10:1–13), 217r/2 (Ruth 1).

[8] 219r/1 (I Kings 8), 219r/1 (I Kings 5), repeated on 220r/1 (I Chron. 29 [*recte*]), 220r/2 (I Chron. 23 [*recte* 22]).

[9] 219v/2 (II Kings 25). Starkey treated the genealogies at the beginning of *Chronicles* in the same way, explaining that the author 'narrates briefly the old histories according to the *rationem temporum*'. 220r/1 (I Chron. 14; actually chapters 1–14).

[10] Introductory comment to the prophetic books, 223r/2.   [11] 218r/1 (Sam. 15).

argue that the 'sense [of the Law] is something other than the letter imports'. Therefore, not only must it be understood 'spiritually', but it was itself 'spiritual', and held a 'hidden sense', a claim from which large religious consequences also followed.[12] Nonetheless, Starkey still held a theory of law like that in the Dialogue. Above all, even divine law required rewards and punishments to make people obey it.[13] Starkey constantly harped on both. His tune, however, had acquired a muted counter-melody. Although he regularly ignored the covenant between Yahweh and the Israelites, Starkey occasionally brought it up as yet another reason for obedience to the law.[14] If anything, this pact strengthened Starkey's conviction that law was not to be lightly tampered with. When commenting on both Maccabees, he emphasized how much resistance Antiochus Epiphanes met when he tried to force the Israelites to give up their old laws, and the sufferings they willingly endured to keep them. And Starkey no longer doubted whether to seek the best prince or the best monarchy. The story of Gideon showed him that 'not men but laws ought to be superior', and those laws had to be founded in equity.[15]

While Starkey had never played down obedience, he used it in these notes to reinforce an argument for a much more conservative approach to change than he had espoused in his Dialogue. It was a cardinal point of wisdom 'not to draw back easily from the fathers and old laws', and he warned his readers when writing about Antiochus to 'see how much the status of the commonwealth changes with danger and recedes from the statutes of its ancestors'.[16] External threats should not induce any modification of society, but neither should internal troubles. 'The *status rei publicae* must not be changed on account of errors and abuses' was a comment on Israel's clamour to Samuel for a king.[17] Starkey probably did not mean to take back much of his earlier platform, since he had never proposed any similarly fundamental change in the nature of England's government as Israel's from rule by holy men to monarchy, but he still struck a much more cautious pose here.

Starkey drew the expected corollary from his conservative stance and clung as tightly as ever to the notion of order. 'Order must be preserved above all, for it is one and the same how it is set up and so overthrown; apply this to laws and customs.'[18] The opposite of order was, of course, 'perpetual confusion', but Starkey observed this when reflecting on the evils of Babylon as described in Jeremiah 51, a chapter which prophesied destruction in return for idolatry,

12 214r/1 (Num. 19), 213v/1 (Lev. 26), 214v/1 (Deut. 4 [*recte* 5?]).
13 215r/2 (Deut. 28).　　　　14 224v/2 (Ezech. 16). Also mentioned on 216r/1 (Joshua 7).
15 225v/2–226r/1 *passim*, 216v/2 (Judges 8:22–4), 224v/2 (Ezech. 13).
16 222v/1 (Prov. 1:8–9?) and 225v/2 (I Maccabees 1).
17 217v/2 (Sam. 8).　　　　18 213v/1 (Num. 2).

but said nothing about order. Thus order received a heavier religious impress than earlier, but it also acquired more militant overtones. Starkey twice commented on passages in Numbers, praising their descriptions of order, but both originals concerned military order, whether the arrangement of an army, or how it pitched its camps.[19]

Neither greater reluctance to tamper with institutions, nor certainty that they and not men must rule, deterred Starkey from pursuing his favourite line of political analysis. 'The heaviest punishment of the commonwealth [was for? because of?] unsound prophets and princes.'[20] Starkey delivered the expected blasts against tyrants, but with a new twist.[21] Whereas he had previously argued that men had only themselves to blame for a bad prince, by 1537 evil princes, 'than which nothing is more pestilent', had become yet another divine punishment.[22] This reference is the more curious, because Starkey went out of his way to make the point. Ezekiel had merely included evil princes in a whole catalogue of human crimes and had not proposed them as a punishment. But in a complete reversal from the Dialogue, Starkey had come to think that God established both good and bad kings, although he displayed much less interest in the origin of civil society or kingship than he had in the Dialogue. For example, he noted the fate of the tyrant Abimelech, but not his election in place of the seventy elders.[23] Bad princes could both reward and cause sedition, still the most horrid fate of the commonwealth.[24] Starkey said much less about the good prince, but it would appear that his primary task was the care of the *potestatem coactivam*, which included the external forms of religion.[25] Starkey preserved some of his agenda for the good prince, suggesting that his 'dignity' lay in the size of his population.[26]

'As the prince, so the people.' 'Note how much evil and how much felicity from the prince.' 'How bad is Israel when there was no king.'[27] Starkey continued to believe in hierarchy. Left to their own devices, the people were certain to go astray, but without any hope that their sedition would succeed.[28] Those who murmured against Moses could not enter the promised land.[29] Nevertheless, Starkey once or twice admitted that the literal sense seemed to say that 'it is proper for the people of God to be freed from tyranny through

---

[19] 224v/1, 213v/2 (Num. 10:11–28), 214v/1 (Num. 33:53–55).
[20] 225r/2 (Hosea 9:7–9).
[21] E.g., 216r/2 (Jud. 1:5–7), 222r/1 (*Ps.* 9), 225v/1 (Micah 1–4).
[22] 224v/2 (Ezech. 22:6). [23] 222v/2 (Wis. 6:1–12) and 217r/1 (Jud. 9).
[24] E.g., 217r (Judges 9:1–7 and 12:25), 218v/2 (Sam. 19), 219v/2 (II Kings 17:21–23), 223r/2 (*Isa.* 3?).
[25] 220r/1 (I Chron. 16) and 219v/2 (II Kings18:1–8).
[26] 222v/1 (Prov. 14:28).
[27] 223r/1 (Ecclus. 10:2), 222v/2 (Eccl. 10:4–7), 217r/2 (Jud. 18:1?).
[28] 217r/1 (Jud. 17 [*recte* 18:1?]) and col. 2 (Jud. 20 [*recte* 19–21]).
[29] 213v/2 and 214r/1 (Num. 11:4–6 and 14:20–38).

force', although this was not the spiritual sense, and he noted that the people saved Saul's son Jonathan from his father's vengeance.[30] Starkey also observed that the Philistines had seized all the Israelites' arms and pointed out 'what this may signify': it made rebellion impossible.[31] He first commented on Exodus that princes were not always to be obeyed.[32] But just as Starkey had come to regard tyrants as divine punishments, ignoring the possibility that the nobility could bring them to heel as he had argued forcefully in the Dialogue, so here he failed to suggest the nobility as leaders of a revolt. In fact, they almost disappeared altogether from these notes. Starkey's disappointment in both the nobility and Henry was not so great as to force him into open opposition, but by the same token he could not flatly condemn those who might take matters into their own hands, perhaps even the Pilgrims.

Strictures on the shortcomings of princes notwithstanding, Starkey espoused an ecclesiology predicated on the secular power's jurisdictional superiority, while at the same time making dire threats against monarchs who dared to usurp the clergy's sacramental *officium*. Starkey lost no opportunity to assert that 'the king was above the priest' or that 'priests obeyed the commands of the king'.[33] This relation grew out of that between Moses and Aaron, on which Starkey spent a great deal of time.[34] Moses and David gave the Levites their *officium* and 'ordered' or 'constituted' the priesthood.[35] Kings were responsible for screening candidates for the priesthood and for handling temple revenues, if necessary.[36] They also 'sent preachers to teach the people'.[37] Moses was the archetype of how the ruler should treat the church, Saul of the evil ruler who interfered in *rebus sacris*. Despite the annointing which enrolled him in the ranks of the prophets and got him off to a good start as 'the best prince', Saul usurped the *officium* of the priest. That led to sedition and to his loss of the kingdom.[38] King Uzziah exemplified the same thing, despite, like Saul, having been very successful and pious at first.[39]

This is all clear-cut. Kings have jurisdictional authority over priests and reign in the external sphere, but they must not meddle in the sacramental realm. The theory became muddied when Starkey returned to his favourite conciliarist theme. On the one hand, he flatly stated that 'at the command of the king, priests assemble for Passover, therefore by the order of princes

---

[30] 216v/1 (Jud. 3:12–30) and 217v/2 (Sam. 14:24–45).   [31] 217v/2.
[32] 212v/1 (Ex. 1).   [33] 220v/1 (II Chron. 31) and 214r/2 (Num. 27:18–23).
[34] 212v–213r, *passim* (*Ex.* 4–28).
[35] 213v/1 (Num. 4), 220r/1 (I Chron. 24 [*recte* 23] and 26), 220r/2 (II Chron. 8:14–15), 213r/1 (Ex. 28).
[36] 219r–v (I Kings 13 [*recte* 12–13?] and II Kings 12:4–16).
[37] 220r/2 (II Chron. 16 [*recte* 17]:7–10 – royal officers and Levites sent to instruct in the law).
[38] 217v/2 (Sam. 10–13).
[39] 220v/1 (II Chron. 26:16–20).

pontiffs ought to assemble for a council in this tempest'.[40] A general council remained Starkey's remedy of choice, even after the official English condemnation of Mantua. But on the other hand, Starkey adduced the potent precedent of the apostles to note that princes apparently obeyed them, when they assembled in a general council. To further confuse the issue, Starkey added in the same place that 'recourse in controversies must always be had to the supreme priest *pro tem*'.[41] On balance it seems that Starkey still thought of the relation between princes and the whole teaching (and perhaps even jurisdictional) authority of the church as he had in 1536. The large problems in the papal office did not argue for its abolition provided the general council was recognized as the final authority over both king and pope. But Starkey once again did not see fit to spell out the constitution of the church in detail, except to note that 'Christ [is] the rock [which is] the foundation of the church, not Peter'.[42] He passed up the chance to dilate on the constitutional position of the general council when dealing with the seventy elders, a set of *loci* which frequently served as proof texts for conciliarist writers. Instead, he emphasized that the new elders had to be chosen because their predecessors' greed had barred the latter from entering Canaan.[43] Starkey would merely note the same passages without comment the following year when annotating Pighe's *Assertio*, despite Pighe's reliance on them as evidence for the superiority of a single head.

Starkey's defence of the clerical *officium* did not preclude strong criticism of the priestly estate. He hammered away at the dangers posed by negligent or lazy priests and almost never merely noted that a passage spelled out the duties of a good priest without also lambasting a poor one.[44] Bishops, the standard bearers of Starkey's earlier reform proposals, and others in authority in the Church were liable for the failures of the lower clergy.[45] By inference from a passage in Isaiah, Starkey maintained that a negligent bishop was like a dumb dog, adopting one of the sixteenth century's favourite metaphors for an ineffective clergyman.[46] The clergy certainly had to adhere to high standards, although exactly how high is difficult to tell. Naturally, a priest, like any good Christian, had to renounce all affects and 'earthly greediness', but the meaning of the latter is unclear. Starkey sometimes appeared to argue that the clergy should own no property. 'If it is bad and impedes the perfection of the Christian life to have possession, no Christians

---

[40] 220v/1 (II Chron. 30).   [41] 215r/1 (Deut. 17?).
[42] 223v/1 (Isa. 29 [*recte* 28]:16–17).   [43] 213v/2 (Num. 11:24–35).
[44] E.g., 213r/1, 217v/1 *passim*, 225r/1, 225v/1.
[45] 217v/1 (I Kings [*recte* Sam.] 3:12–18).   [46] 223v/2 (Isa. 56:9–12).

ought to possess, since they all are struggling toward the highest perfection.'[47] Likewise, he pointed out that the Levites had no inheritance when they entered the promised land, although they had previously been supported by tithes and would receive urban and suburban property later.[48] Starkey's claim that kings should handle temple monies would seem to support a case for evangelical poverty. If this interpretation is correct, Starkey had again changed his mind since the *Exhortation*, where he had merely argued for proper use of possessions, not absolute poverty.[49] If that was Starkey's point, he did not therefore think kings had free reign to 'despoil the Temple of the Lord', citing the story of Heliodorus's bout with an apparition when he tried to strip the Temple.[50] Propertied or not, Starkey observed that 'our priests are separated from the common people' and found a precedent once again in the Levites.[51] Separation did not mean clerical privileges impressed Starkey. He noted 'the immunity and liberty of priests among the Egyptians', the oppressors of the Hebrews, in a probable slap at current clerical claims to both.[52]

These notes suggest a psychological motive for some of Starkey's anticlericalism. Starkey apparently never managed to reconcile himself completely to his vow of chastity. His note on Wisdom 8 (?), 'chastity is a gift', was conventional enough, as were his references to various sorts of vows and 'what is the reason of vows, and what must be observed and what avoided'.[53] This last instance, however, concerned vows between men and women and fathers and daughters, as did those referred to in Judges 11:29–40. Starkey could have commented on many other Old Testament vows if he wished to consider them in the abstract, rather than using explicitly sexual ones as his text. Starkey also paid a good deal of attention to polygamy and concubinage, from that between fathers and daughters in Genesis 19 (a 'mystical' story) to 'Gideon and many others' to 'the old men [who] had many wives (from many passages of Scripture)'.[54] Three notes on Leviticus concern the uncleanness of seminal emissions.[55] From all this, it appears that the sexuality which had led young man Starkey to offer his love to a woman probably after he had become a priest still had not been harnessed, and that Starkey felt his vow of chastity as a burden.

So much for the major continuities in Royal 7 C XVI from Starkey's earlier

---

[47] 214r/2 (Num. 26).　　　[48] 214r/2 (Num. 26:62–5), *ibid.* (18:8), 214v/1 (35:1–8).

[49] *Exhortation*, 28v–29r.

[50] 226/1 (*II Macc.* 1 [now 3]). For this as the basis of a case against secular interference imported from Venice to England, see P. I. Kaufman, 'Polydore Vergil and the strange disappearance of Christopher Urswick', 81 and 83.

[51] 213v/1 (Num. 1).　　　[52] 212r/2.

[53] 222v/2, 214v/1 (Num. 29 [*recte* 30]), 213v/1, 217r/1 (Jud. 11:29–40).

[54] 212r/1, 217r/1, 217v/1.　　　　[55] 213r/2.

thinking. The most obvious difference is Starkey's constant hammering on the theme of punishment and penance. Many of the instances he singled out concerned rebellions or sedition as a punishment for idolatry.[56] In all these cases, however, penance could have averted divine vengeance. As Starkey put it when commenting on Ezekiel, 'anyone will be punished for his sins, but no one will be excluded from glory if only he does penance'.[57] Or again the similarly general comment 'note in Jeremiah and the rest of the prophets how punishments follow those who neglect divine precepts, and that penitents by the right and order of nature [are restored?] to the first state of felicity'.[58] Earlier Starkey had exhorted his reader to 'pay attention to how often, oblivious of the benefits of God, they [the Israelites] fell into idolatry, and then [were] called back through penance to health'.[59] His last comment on Job summarizes virtually the only thing Starkey could make out of the book: 'Penance led Job back to much greater felicity than he once had.'[60] He handled most of the minor prophets in the same way.[61]

Starkey's great concern with penance, while conventional enough up to a point, suggests that the direction of policy in the late thirties displeased him even more than it had earlier and that now, as then, he was willing to let his discontent be known, even if only in yet another unpublished work. One of Starkey's myriad comments on penance pointed in a more dangerous direction: 'Note how God always sustained someone for freeing the people where at the same time it did penance.'[62] This could be taken as a strictly historical comment, applicable strictly to the Old Testament, but Starkey's highly 'spiritual' exegetical method suggests that 'always' refers to his lifetime, too. In other places he explicitly drew the parallel: 'Penance saved Rehoboam for a while, just as it can us', and 'the discovery of the book of Deuteronomy incited Josiah to penance. Would that it were found again!'[63]

When Starkey reached the great prophetic books, he hammered at the theme of penance and its contemporary utility. We have already seen that he thought the prophets still spoke to his age and that he probably aimed many of the Old Testament's cautionary tales at Henry VIII. More than that, the

---

[56] E.g., 215r/1 (Deut. 27:11–26), 218v/1 (II Kings [*recte* Sam.] 15 and 16), 219r/2 (a marginal note and to III [*recte* I] Kings 11–13), 219v/1 (IV [*recte* II] Kings 17:7ff.), 220v/1 (II Chron. 24:17–26), 223v/1 (Isa. 19:1–15). This is only a small sample of such passages.

[57] This text indicates that 'do penance' is the correct translation of Starkey's *penitaverit*. The Vulgate has *egerit poenitentiam*. 224v/2 (Ezech. 18:20–23).

[58] 224r/2 (Jerem. 43?).   [59] 217r/1 (Jud. 10?).   [60] 221v/2.

[61] E.g., Hosea or Joel (225r/2).   [62] 216v/1 (Jud. 3:7–31).

[63] 220r/2 (II Chron. 12:6–13) and 219v/2 (IV[*recte* II] Kings 22:3–13). It is worth remembering that the Pilgrims had pointed to the example of Rehoboam, who provoked sedition by listening to young advisers. J. A. Guy, 'The king's council and political participation', in A. Fox and J. A. Guy, *Reassessing the Henrician age*, 122.

way in which Starkey read the prophetic books and the themes he singled out suggest that many of his comments referred to the epic struggle between Henry and Pole, and largely followed Pole's interpretation of that conflict as set out in the guise of his new prophetic *persona* in *De unitate*. Anyone who read both Pole's intemperate blast against the king and Starkey's notes could have been left in little doubt about where Starkey stood. Starkey used more subdued language, but he adopted exactly the same attitude to Henry as Pole had, as Starkey was perfectly well aware. Starkey wrote to Pole exactly as Pole wrote to Priuli. The whole work was about penance.[64]

The significance and danger of sedition, of which Pole had warned Henry as early as 1531, could hardly have escaped the king or any other sentient Englishman in the wake of the Pilgrimage, although many would not have agreed with Starkey's oblique suggestion that domestic rebellion and discontent punished idolatry. As threatening as that was, many of Starkey's other readings cut even closer to the bone. The punishment of kings who shed innocent blood menaced Henry directly. Pole had taken the king to task severely in *De unitate* for the deaths of More and Fisher. Starkey's capsule on 2 Kings 21 told most heavily. After a marginal heading 'Prophets' and a pointing hand, Starkey wrote 'God admonished kings [through] prophets, but they did not hear, whence they perished. Manasseh sinned and shed much innocent blood.' Starkey returned to Manasseh shortly after, making his crimes the cause of good King Josiah's death, even though this went further than the original text.[65] King Joab was also 'killed for the blood of the just'.[66] The prophet Ezechiel had predicted 'punishment for those who kill citizens without mercy'.[67]

Starkey stressed that kings who refused to listen to prophets got themselves into trouble, and that prophets should expect difficulties, too. In one of his few comments on Judith, he observed that 'Achior [was] sent into exile on account of having declared the truth', that is for having warned Holofernes not to attack Israel.[68] Did Starkey mean to refer to Pole's self-imposed exile from England? One of his four notes on Amos, all of which dealt with punishment for idolatry in one way or another, pointed out the 'punishment of those who hold prophets preaching the truth in contempt'.[69] Again, Starkey noted that the Babylonian Captivity followed from the Israelites' failure to obey the prophets, whose duty it was to recall the people to obedience.[70] And in a comment made out of sequence and, therefore, perhaps

[64] *ERP*, I, 441 and BL Cleop. E VI, 397v.
[65] 219v/2 (IV [*recte* II] Kings 21: esp. 10–16 and 23: esp. 25–7).
[66] 219r/2 (III [*recte* I] Kings 2).   [67] 224v/1 (Ezech. 11:6–8 and 14–21).
[68] 221v/1 (chapt. 6).   [69] 225r/2 (chapt. 5?).
[70] 219v/2 (IV [*recte* II] Kings 17: esp. 13 and 23).

of heightened significance, Starkey tagged the story of the prophet Jehu, who was 'killed because he admonished King Baasha about his sins'.[71]

The theme of kings and prophets cropped up most prominently in Starkey's extensive notes on the story of Saul and David, as did Starkey's heavy emphasis on the frailty of man. This passage requires extended analysis, especially since it may well be that Starkey meant his treatment as an allegory of the relation between Henry and Pole.[72] After first observing that God abandoned Saul to his troubles, Starkey immediately turned his Old Testament history lesson into a contemporary moral comment. David's harping, which calmed the possessed Saul, was needed once again. 'O, would that the divine harp might sound in our ears!' Starkey continued, 'note that Saul never conquered his enemies, unless David the prophet prophesied the same.' When fleeing from Saul, David tricked the priest Ahimelech into giving him consecrated bread in order to keep himself alive, but Saul then killed David's benefactor. Starkey elsewhere justified dissimulation in the service of the commonwealth, as he apparently meant to do here, and once adduced evidence that even God occasionally deceived an impious king or two.[73] The role of a courtier had not worn out entirely.

Starkey's attenuated narrative began to apply even more obviously to Pole and Henry when he noted 'that perpetual struggle between Saul and David born of the suspicion of the kingdom and jealousy'. Starkey apparently meant to say that Saul had doubted David's motives and pursued him in a preemptive strike. This barely disguised the bad feeling between the English royal cousins. Starkey may well have been thinking of Pole's legation in a similarly transparent way when he emphasized how often David could have killed Saul but had forborne, since he, at least, had no wish for revenge. Rather, Starkey called attention to 'how often David called Saul to penance and he never put it out of his mind', i.e., David never gave up hoping for Saul's conversion. A reference to the 'moderation' and moral of *De unitate*? Almost certainly.

Thus far Starkey leaned heavily on Pole's side, masking his former patron beneath the figure of David the prophet. Once David became king, however, Starkey apparently began to treat him as a stand-in for Henry. In any event, after Saul's death and David's accession Starkey inserted a comment that 'David fell into sedition and hatred and infinite evils on account of one sin. See, therefore, what one sin can [do], especially in a prince dear to God.' David's sin, of course, was the matrimonial offence of adultery with Bathsheba, compounded by the murder of her husband. Starkey quickly pointed out that 'the Lord removed David's most serious sin on account of his

---

[71] 219r/2 (III [*recte* I] Kings 16).   [72] 218r/1–v/1 (I Sam. 16–II Sam. 12).
[73] 221v/1 (Judith 10), one of his very first notes on 212r/1, 220r/2 (II Chron. 18 [*recte* 17]:4–8).

penance'. That was Starkey's interpretation, anyway, of the chapter recounting the birth of Solomon, which the text did not explicitly call a reward for David's repentance. Starkey again stretched a point in order to enhance its import when he introduced David's adultery. He claimed that it had come after David had conquered all his neighbours and was enjoying a spell of peace, whereas in fact the king succumbed to Bathsheba in the midst of a war. This blatant alteration of historical circumstances could well have been intended to square David's situation with Henry's.

The contemporary moral of David's adultery must have been crystal clear, especially in Starkey's modified version. If Henry had only taken Pole's exhortation to repent, God would have given him an heir. Starkey made the same point in other comments. Again riding roughshod over the literal sense, Starkey generalized wildly from the birth of Samuel that 'the sterile often obtain fruit from the Lord in sacred history'.[74] Similarly, while he skipped Leviticus on marriage with a brother's wife, Henry's favourite text, Starkey singled out the levirate in Ruth. 'Note the custom of substituting the seed of a dead man through the same family.'[75] Perhaps Starkey chose to discuss this custom in Ruth rather than Deuteronomy in order to defuse its emotional impact. This interpretation is certainly peculiar. Starkey usually either ignored Hebrew ceremonial law or treated its meaning morally. He may have meant to make a similar point when he commented (again inaccurately) that 'Moses's father married his cousin [instead of his aunt]'.[76] As if this were not enough, Starkey metaphorically assured Henry that he had nothing to worry about, even if he never got a male heir. Starkey rhapsodized on Deborah, 'a woman [who] was judge among the people, and ruled *optime*'. That last was an editorial comment, since the scriptural text made nothing special out of Deborah. Starkey had not abandoned his advocacy of the Princess Mary.

His support of Mary, and criticism of the divorce and Henry, together with continued anti-clericalism, are of a piece with the attitude of the old nobility as expressed, for example, in Darcy's anti-clerical outbursts of 1529 and open rebellion in the Pilgrimage.[77] Attacks on the church served to distance Starkey from Pole, and mark out his private *via media*. But both Pole and Starkey evaluated the course of policy since 1536 negatively, the former caustically and the latter cautiously, and both levelled their criticisms more or less in private. Nevertheless, if Starkey had found himself a platform (or perhaps he did, but no further record of his actual preaching survives after 1536) he would have launched almost as heavy an attack on England as Pole had. He inserted a set of notes for a sermon modelled on one in Isaiah, one of the books which apparently taught Pole how to behave like a prophet after he

---

[74] 217v/1 (I Kings [*recte* I Sam.]1).   [75] 217r/2 (c. 4:5–6).   [76] 212v/1 (Ex. 6).
[77] J. A. Guy, *The public career of Sir Thomas More*, appendix 2A, 206–7 for Darcy's 'memorandum'.

read it with Starkey's friend van Kampen.[78] The story of how God punished the Israelites by the 'tyranny' of Assyria inspired Starkey.[79] 'The beginning of the sermon' was 'how God warns us of the duties [*officij*] of Christians by famine with sickness and sedition, and yet we are blind'. Starkey continued that Englishmen should 'note the example of the Israelites and of the Assyrians whom divine vengeance used as a whip, until finally the branch is cast into the fire, and we, the whip of the clergy, but in the meantime we abuse the goodness of God'. Finally, 'and gather the burden of Babylon because of sins. Similarly, a future ruin to us and all cities [Starkey's pronounced urban bias crops up again] for similar sins. So he postulates the order of nature and of divine providence, and the prophets prove it.' Starkey packed an outline of his entire new outlook into this brief sketch. Our troubles are a divine punishment because we have gone too far in the attack on good religion. Providence will destroy us, just as it did Assyria and Babylon.

Starkey's thinking had changed strikingly since the early 1530s. Gone was his reliance on human powers, in both politics and religion. In fact, Starkey now declared full allegiance to Italian Evangelism in language remarkably like that which Pole had used two or three years earlier. Starkey still refused to give up on politics to the extent of the introvert Pole, but his view of salvation reduced the degree to which sinners could help themselves as sharply as Pole's did. As Pole did constantly, Starkey located the root of England's problems in human presumption, or, more specifically, in 'human prudence', and he prophesied 'woe to them who desert God and rely on their own powers'.[80] The story of Judith and Holofernes demonstrated that 'human powers must not be trusted, but only God'.[81] Not surprisingly, the looming threat of punishment and his profound awareness of human impotence altered Starkey's earlier optimistic assessment of human existence. Now he moaned that 'the life of man is subject to so many miseries and calamities', and instead of a triumphant progress to earthly felicity, it had become a *peregrinatio*.[82]

In place of men fashioned in the image of God, Starkey now saw sinners. He converted his psychology of virtues and vices into one of sins and salvation without too much difficulty. Nature endowed humans with vicious affects, which reason must still subdue.[83] Starkey retained his Stoic bent, speculating that the 'perpetual war between Joshua and Amalek [is] perhaps a figure of the fight between sense and reason'.[84] As this quotation makes clear, Starkey now saw the relation of virtue and vice as a much more equal

---

[78] P. S. Donaldson, 'Machiavelli, antichrist, and the reformation: prophetic typology in Reginald Pole's *De unitate* and *Apologia ad Carolum quintum*', 228, and D. Fenlon, *Heresy and obedience in Tridentine Italy*, 30.
[79] 223v/1 (Isa. 10:5–19).
[80] 223v/2 (Isa. 30:1–5). See also 211v/2 (I Kings [*recte* Sam.] 15), 212v/2 (Ex. 23).
[81] 221v/1 (Jud. 13).   [82] 223r/2 (Ecclus. 40:1–10) and 212r/2.
[83] 216v/1 (Jud. 3:1–16) and 212r/2.   [84] 212v/2 (Ex. 17).

struggle. Virtue was still the goal and natural virtue still existed, but Starkey emphasized with redoubled vigour the difficulty of achieving it.[85] He interpreted a proposal to blind all the adult males of Jabesh metaphorically to mean that 'we have two eyes, the left always fixed on earthly things, and the right looking up to heavenly, for the task is not only to look to the present, but rather to the future'.[86] Worldly thoughts now became the principal vice.[87] Elsewhere, Starkey castigated those 'who as wanderers enjoy the pleasures of this life, and who immerse themselves in those, forgetting [?] their dignity and exist contemning their future life'.[88]

Now the relative weight of the two incentives of praise of virtue and hope for a future life is reversed from what it was in the Dialogue as Starkey continued to import more vocabulary like Kampen's. Human dignity virtually disappeared from Starkey's lexicon. Felicity, which had usually meant earthly happiness in the Dialogue, came to mean a heavenly reward. 'The land of promise is the seat of virtue, in which at last felicity is displayed.'[89] But as Starkey's denigration of human strength has already shown, humans could not rely on their own powers. Starkey hammered away constantly at 'arrogance', or 'trusting in human powers'.[90] Arrogance had originally cost man Paradise, so Starkey proposed a new code of behaviour, based on 'mildness and humility, the foundation of all goods'.[91] Adopting Pauline language, Starkey cursed those who 'built Jericho' or 'put on the old man' and exhorted his readers instead to 'newness of life', which, however, came only from God, who 'gives a new heart and a new spirit to those who observe his commands', and do penance, of course.[92] Starkey frequently reminded himself of God's 'benefits' to men, and the providence which distributed them.[93]

Instead of human effort, divine providence governed everything which befell men. It was unfathomable, but not to be doubted.[94] Any who question providence or 'who attempt anything above their powers and outside their *officium*' would be punished.[95] Then again, 'when things are most desperate, then God helps the hopeless, as by the coming of Samson here'.[96] Reliance on

---

[85] E.g., 215r/2 (Deut. 32).   [86] 217v/2 (I Kings [*recte* Sam.] 11:1–4).
[87] 220r/2 (II Chron. 9:1–12). For other comments on worldly thoughts, see e.g., 212r/1 (Gen. 5), 212v/1 (Ex. 1 and 3), 223r/2 (Isa. 5:8–24), 223v/1 (Isa. 24), 223v/2 (Isa. 29), 224v/2 (Ezech. 20).
[88] 216v/2 (Jud. 7:1).   [89] 214v/2 (Deut. 11).   [90] 225r/2 (Hosea 7:8–12 or 8:8–10).
[91] 212r/1 (Gen. 2; Starkey's first note) and 222r/1 (*Ps.* 24?).
[92] 216r/1 (Jos. 6:26), 224r/1 (Jerem. 4), 225r/1 (Ezech. 36:26).
[93] 226r/2 (Hosea 11:1–6 and chapt. 12), 223v/2 (Isa. 44) and 224r/1 (Jerem. 2).
[94] 224r/2 (Jerem. 12:1) and 222v/1 (Eccl. 8:17).
[95] 218v/1 (II Sam. 6:6–8).   [96] 211r/1 (Jud. 13).

providence is another fundamental theme of Starkey's Old Testament notes. For example, Starkey read the whole of Psalms as underlining the nature of providence. Starkey tied providence to punishment by making it the pedagogue of virtue. As he paraphrased 2 Chronicles 12, 'God allows his people to be captured, that it might know the destruction of [i.e., caused by] its servitude ... that is he allows it to play in vices in order that it may finally understand the difference between virtue and vice.'[97] Curiously, some of the old Starkey still hung on in the new. Once, instead of writing about providence, Starkey mentioned 'the wonderful variety of fortune', meaning the casting of lots as a prelude to divine vengeance.[98]

Stress on human impotence and divine power stemmed from the new soteriology – justification by faith – Starkey had borrowed from Kampen. He stated flatly under the heading 'faith' the by now familiar refrain that 'from the story of Hezekiah, gather that you must not trust in your powers, but trust only in the Lord'.[99] As a remedy for disasters, Starkey recommended praying with faith.[100] Starkey repeated the conclusion of the Dialogue that 'they cannot hear to whom God does not give ears for hearing'.[101] When he compared 'works' to the 'promise', he stated succinctly that 'we will see heaven not by our own works, but by the promises of God'.[102] But Starkey had developed some confusion about the relation of works and grace. Sometimes he followed Kampen and argued that the works of the law could not avail to lead to felicity, or that providence paid no attention to 'external works' when it made the final judgment about salvation.[103] Likewise, he had developed some doubts about traditional means of salvation, stating bluntly in a note on 'purgatory' that 'works must not be hoped in after death'.[104]

Purgatory might have lost out, but Starkey preserved intercession by the saints, in the same passage from Tobit just cited.[105] At other times, works still had some value. Religious feasts, for example, were 'slave work[s]', of no value if done only in order to serve 'affects'.[106] Nevertheless, works done out of the proper intention could help in salvation. After the tag 'faith/charity [*charitas*]/ceremonies', Starkey opined that 'without faith and love [*amor*], all ceremonies are sordid in the sight of God'. Once again he added a dimension missing from his text in which Yahweh had rejected Israelite sacrifices because they were offered hypocritically, but nothing was said about either faith

---

[97] 220r/2.   [98] 221v/1 (Esther 9).   [99] 223v/2 (Isa. 37:21–32).
[100] 212v/1 (Ex. 2).   [101] 215r/2 (Deut. 29).   [102] 214v/2 (Deut. 9:1–6).
[103] 214r/1 (Num. 20:12) and 215r/2 (Deut. 34), 222v/2 (Prov. 8:10–14).
[104] 222v/2 (Eccl. 8:11–2?).
[105] 221r/2.   [106] 213v/1 (Lev. 23) and 214v/1 (Num. 28).

or love.[107] Or, put another way, 'so much must not be prayed from God if we persevere in our impieties, in which neither fasting nor alms-giving have any value, and he [Isaiah] teaches what true fasting is', that is, right action.[108] In a note on the deuterocanonical book Tobit, Starkey explicitly singled out a passage which assured him that 'almsgiving saves from death and purges every kind of sin'.[109] Starkey emphasized the point by another paraphrase immediately after this one, which treated the Tabernacle as something spiritual, but read the rest of the passage literally and put forward the duty of taking care of the poor and miserable. Or, in what would seem to be the final word, Starkey noted early on under the heading 'works' that 'this above all Moses taught: certain precepts and complete works. Therefore works are necessary, and are not impossible, as many [believe?].'[110] Starkey also preserved the necessary concomitant of works, free will.[111] Still, aside from free will, all of this may come closer than first appears to Kampen, who had distinguished between works done before and after justification, just as Starkey had once done. Although Starkey did not make this point explicitly, we might infer from his stress on human impotence that only divine intervention in the form of justification would make possible a *mens pura* and hence acceptable works. Kampen, too, had tried to steer a middle course between those who emphasized works and those who considered them entirely unnecessary. Perhaps this was Starkey's intention. At least, this is the most plausible interpretation of his cryptic comment on Ruth and the birth of David's grandfather Obed. 'Works: Ruth finally bears a son, Obed, for the soul full of virtue always bears fruit.'[112] Here we seem to have gone full circle back to the emphasis on virtue and human action of the Dialogue, but the original passage clearly stated that divine intervention produced Ruth's reward. As Kampen had, Starkey had changed the meaning of virtue sufficiently to make it a divine gift, rather than a product of human effort.

   Once salvation became a major issue, the Gospel also achieved prominence. Starkey occasionally drew a clear contrast between Gospel and law, for example, in a note on Hosea 6:6 headed 'Gospel'. 'He [Hosea] prefers the knowledge of God to all holocausts [sacrifices]. Therefore the Gospel must be read.'[113] More often, Starkey's taste for the spiritual sense blurred this

---

[107] 223r/2 (Isa. 1:11–16). It may be noted in passing that Starkey evinced no interest in the dispute over the meaning of charity and love in which Thomas More and William Tyndale engaged. He used *amor* and *charitas* interchangeably.

[108] 224r/1 (Isa. 58).   [109] 221r/2 (Tobit 12:8–15, esp. 9).   [110] 214v/1 (Num. 5).

[111] 216r/2 (Jos. 24:14–24), 217v/2 (I Kings [*recte* Sam.] 15, 223v/2 (Ecclus. 15:14, a passage which pointedly made men responsible for their own actions).

[112] 217r/2 (Ruth 4:13–17).   [113] 225r/2.

distinction. 'The law is not the letter, but spiritual, as Paul and Origen say.'[114] The citation of the allegorizing Origen is significant. Starkey interpreted the ceremonial law of the Hebrews 'spiritually' by claiming that it applied to everyone. 'The words of the law were not given to the Jews, but to all humankind.'[115] Likewise he further broke down the divide between law and Gospel by paralleling the two. 'The people did not understand the law until Joshua read it, so neither we the Gospel unless [by] Christ reading and teaching.'[116] Starkey, in common with many other exegetes, took Isaiah to contain a compendium of the gospel *in futuris*.[117] Finally, he reduced the one to the other in a pair of notes on Deuteronomy 13:7. 'All evangelical precepts can be found in the Old Testament' and 'the Gospel does not differ from the law in precepts, but they clearly lead commonly to the same road, because the holy law is obscure.'[118] The Gospel underpinned Starkey's new code of behaviour. 'The fruits of the Gospel [are] truly a most innocent life and full of humility.'[119] Finally, Starkey's notion of Gospel may explain how he reconciled belief in free will and in human depravity. In an early note on the 'word of God' he insisted that 'he must not do what seems right to himself, but the precept he has from God'.[120] No more here than in the Dialogue was the will free to corrupt itself. 'There is no evil in the *civitas* which the Lord does not do.'[121]

Starkey apparently drew experiential corollaries from his reading of the Old Testament. He commented on Jonah's 'vocation' that 'he who flees the call of the Lord is thrown into the sea, that is into a thousand empty thoughts and into the flood of evils'.[122] Starkey very likely thought of his own recent call to preaching. At any rate, he took the inability of the Hebrew people to follow Moses up the mountain to mean that 'ours must be ascended by the mysteries of the Gospel'.[123] Or again, 'Observe how the people had been prepared before it could hear the word of God, and that only Moses with Aaron climbed the mountain.'[124] Religious changes in England concerned Starkey, and he seems to have offered himself, albeit cautiously, to put things in order. The Gospel may have meant a new life, but Starkey stood foursquare for the 'old belief', and against those who tried to raise sedition 'about new doctrine which is not new'.[125] He was after 'true piety', which could never be learned from 'young men [who must not] be believed'.[126] These two

---

[114] 215r/1 (Deut. 14).   [115] 215r/2 (Deut. 29).   [116] 216r/1 (Jos. 8:32–5).
[117] 223v/2 (Isa. 34).   [118] 214v/2.   [119] 223r/2 (Isa. 2).
[120] 214v/2 (Deut. 12:8–11).   [121] 225r/2 (Amos 3?).   [122] 225v/1 (Jonah 1).
[123] 214v/1 (Num. 5).   [124] 212v/1 (Ex. 19).
[125] 224r/2 (Jerem. 6:16, only a tiny part of the chapter) and 216r/2 (Jos. 22).
[126] 224r/2 (Jerem. 7, which contains no reference to young men).

last references, combined with Starkey's staunch belief in justification by faith
and human weakness, indicate that he was still opposed to hot gospellers
while nevertheless defending a more Pauline Christianity in exactly the
fashion of Contarini.

In all this, including especially his indifference to dogmatic niceties, Starkey
expressed Italian Evangelical beliefs. No evidence shows that Starkey arrived
at his understanding of justification in the same way most of the Evangelicals
did. Contarini, Mantova, Pole, all went through experiences much like
Luther's more famous *Turmerlebnis*, and some kind of personal or more
public disaster served as an alembic in all three cases. This scenario would
certainly fit Starkey's life between the first appearance of religious concern
near the end of the Dialogue – including justification by faith – at nearly the
same time Pole began his quest, and the disappointments of 1536–7. Starkey's religion ultimately fitted him little better than his politics for life in
England. He did not therefore give up, despite discouragingly little opportunity. He found recorded official employment only twice between his consultation with the bishops in early 1537 and his death. In January 1538 he took
part in a commission to investigate a case of witchcraft in London. This was a
blue-ribbon panel. The other two members were Wriothesley, then head of
Cromwell's private office, and Paul Withypoll, Starkey's likely patron.[127]
Then, in March, Starkey received a twenty-shilling reward for preaching at
York Place.[128] Starkey's preaching had finally passed muster, but by comparison with the rewards falling to Starkey's friend Morison, this was very small
potatoes. Still, Starkey soldiered on. In the last months of his life he undertook an ambitious theological work, an attack on Pighe's *Assertio*.

Pole and Pighe were sometime allies. Just as Starkey completed his notes on
the Old Testament, Pole praised Pighe for two works he had sent, one of them
attacking Henry VIII's condemnation of the council of Mantua. It filled Pole
with admiration and he 'vehemently' approved it.[129] Pighe also tried to
ingratiate himself with other members of Pole's party, from Contarini to
Giovanni Cardinal Morone.[130] In addition to the threat posed by Pighe's

[127] *LP*, XIII:1, 41. G. R. Elton, *Policy and police: the enforcement of the reformation in the age of Thomas Cromwell*, 49 discusses this case. For Withypoll, see chapt. 7 above.

[128] *LP*, XIII:2, 1280, fol. 4b.

[129] *ERP*, II, 110. Pole repeated his praise a year later in the course of making excuses to Pighe for having failed to show the work to the pope. *Ibid.*, 116. Paul III finally read the book and by May 1539 Pole had passed the pope's reactions to Pighe. Pighe to Paul III, in W. Friedens-burg, 'Beiträge zum Briefwechsel der katholischen Gelehrten Deutschlands im Reforma-tionszeit', 114.

[130] F. Dittrich, *Regesten und Briefen des Cardinals Gasparo Contarini*, 294–5, and Friedens-burg, 'Briefwechsel', 123. In March 1540 Pighe approached their patron, the cardinal nephew Alessandro Farnese, for help in publishing his writings. Farnese responded a few days later asking Pighe to send his works, which Farnese would guard carefully, and expressing his love for Pighe. Friedensburg, 'Briefwechsel', 118–21.

factional allegiance, the English had reason to fear his powers as a contro-
versialist. Some of Pighe's more vituperative attacks are almost unprintable,
even by sixteenth-century standards. In his book against Henry, Pighe began
with the expected sort of abuse that the king's tract differed from the
Lutheran reaction to Mantua only in being dictated by the Devil, but moved
immediately to harp on Henry's 'singular bitterness', which had produced the
schism.[131] Pighe next launched the obligatory assault on Henry's sexual
proclivities, claiming that the king's uncontrollable libido had led him to take
up with a prostitute, Anne (781–2). But Pighe outdistanced his competitors
by singling out Anne's breasts as the cause of Henry's inebriation (795). Pighe
concluded that Henry, driven by his lust and that of a prostitute, had become
a worse persecutor of the church than Nero (783).

Even more worrisome to the English, Pighe had written both an attack on
the divorce and a vindication of the pope's judgment against it. This stirred
Cromwell and his agents to extraordinary counter-measures. They suborned
Pighe's chaplain into stealing the autograph of the latter work and bringing it
to England, where it seems to have disappeared. At least a search of all likely
titles in the State Papers at the Public Record Office and the British Library
did not yield anything written in Pighe's hand. John Hutton, English ambassador to the Regent of the Netherlands and the man who handled the final
phase of the response to Pole's legation, arranged to have his brother-in-law
shepherd both chaplain and MS to England. Pighe, undeterred, set out to
replace his purloined work.[132] He made a formidable opponent.

If Cromwell stood behind Starkey's assignment, he probably saw it as a
natural extension of Starkey's involvement with Pole. Thus Starkey's copy of
the *Assertio* may have reached him through official channels not long after it
was printed in March 1538 in Cologne.[133] This would suggest that Starkey's
theological expertise still attracted respect, and that he had once again
achieved a relatively important position. The campaign aimed at Pighe included another royal chaplain, John Leland, who composed his 'Antiphi-
larchia' at about the same time Starkey drafted his reply.[134] Starkey's career
would also have reconverged with that of Morison, who occupied himself
with Johannes Cochlaeus's polemics.[135] Then again, Starkey may have acquired his copy privately, perhaps from van Kampen. He must have known

---

[131] Albert Pighe, 'Adversus furiosissimum librum Henrici Angliae regis et senatus eius', ed. V. Schweitzer, 775.

[132] Friedensburg, 'Briefwechsel', 115 and 123. I am grateful to Virginia Murphy for assistance looking for Pighe's missing text. For Hutton's involvement, *LP*, XIII:1, 1469.

[133] H. Jedin, *Studien über die Schriftstellerartigkeit Albert Pigges*, 24.

[134] Gregorio Piaia treats Leland's work in *Marsilio da Padova nella riforma e nella controri-forma*, 187–93.

[135] S. K. Christie, 'Richard Morison', 43.

Pighe, since they were both born in the same city at about the same time and both studied under Adrian of Utrecht (later Pope Adrian VI) at Louvain.[136] In mid 1538 Kampen was probably in the right place to forward a copy of the *Assertio*. He died not far from Cologne in September 1538.[137] Kampen's limitless contempt for Catholic controversialists like Pighe could well have led him to keep track of one he knew personally, especially one who earlier in the same year had published an attack on the moderate Philip Melanchthon's comment on the calling of Mantua.[138]

Pinning down the auspices under which Starkey began his last work is only one of the difficulties in the way of interpreting it. The state of the MS, with its small hand and darkened or mutilated paper, has not helped merely establishing what Starkey wrote. Again, tracking Starkey's inspiration to Pighe's text has proven difficult. Most of Starkey's references to the Old Testament were fairly easy to locate, but that is often not the case here. (I have been unable to see a copy of the edition Starkey used, which compounds this difficulty, but judging from his errant references in his second to last work, this would probably not have helped much.) Starkey singled out only parts of Pighe's massive work, making even less of an effort to be comprehensive than he had in Royal 7 C XVI. It is unsurprising that these notes have never been studied. Nonetheless, as Starkey's death-bed work, they provide one last glimpse of how he thought as well as explicit clues to the provenance of some of his key ideas, together with the best measure of how little Marsilio interested him.

Starkey's first note picked up where he left off in October 1537 with the problem of justification, but he quickly turned to tradition and then to the main thrust of Pighe's work, ecclesiastical authority. After the marginal heading 'faith/spirit/church (?)' Starkey interpreted Pighe to mean that 'a pious *affectus* of mind cooperates to the receiving of faith and the spirit, indeed it is necessarily required to illuminate [the sinner?]'.[139] He then inserted in English 'the authoryte of the church ys the seale to scripture even as workys be to true faythe'. Although thus far Starkey may have agreed with Pighe, when Pighe went on to make a case for the overriding importance of ecclesiastical tradition, Starkey refused to follow. He first argued against Pighe that 'ecclesiastical traditions are not to be equated to holy and canonical scriptures' (191v/2). Starkey agreed with Pighe's distinction between

[136] Jedin, *Studien*, 48.
[137] A. J. van der Aa and G. D. J. Schotel, ed., *Biographisch wordenboek der Nederlanden, s.n.* H. de Vocht's account of Kampen in *History of the foundation and the rise of the collegium trilingue lovaniense* skips from June 1537 to his death.
[138] Jedin, *Studien*, 21–2 summarized the tract.
[139] SP 1/141, fol. 188r/1, referring to Albert Pighe, *Hierarchiae ecclesiasticae assertio*, IV, chapter 3. Hereafter cited by folio/column for Starkey's MS and book number and chapter for Pighe's work.

divine and human traditions which came very close to Starkey's own concept of adiaphora (188r/1). By and large, however, Starkey editorialized much less freely when commenting on Pighe than when reading the Old Testament, which usually makes it nearly impossible to tell what he thought about most of the arguments he noted down. Therefore this study will concentrate mainly on Starkey's proposed lines of counter-attack.

Starkey's long-standing attachment to a conciliarist, or at least non-monarchical, theory of the ecclesiastical constitution emerges immediately from them. He poured scorn on Pighe's claim that Christ had established papal primacy. The last of his five main rebuttals stated 'To remove the whole foundation [of this book] is to establish that Christ had established no certain order, but just as he established nothing in the law of nature, so neither in the Gospel, in which he wished men [?] of all lands everywhere to be restored to the first state in all sorts of polities' (191v/2 [no. 5]). Phrased more succinctly, 'No ecclesiastical polity was established by Christ, but he left this to the judgment of his church' (no. 2). 'Nor did it please Christ to establish his church by any political reason [i.e., with any particular form of government], but he seems to accommodate his doctrine in every polity' (191r/2, top).

This argument was nothing new to Starkey. Nevertheless, he approached Pighe's ideas cautiously. He originally objected obliquely to Pighe's attack on Marsilio that a single *principans*, but not one established by the multitude, was necessary to preserve unity. Starkey told himself to 'think whether one head on earth is necessary to containing the ecclesiastical polity, and whether Christ alone may not suffice'.[140] In a note to another long passage in which Pighe extolled the virtues of unity in any body, Starkey doubted Pighe's assertion that 'the church is a visible body whose unity is contained in a visible head', warning instead that 'if the church is an invisible [body], contained by a spiritual unity under one head, only Christ, all his demonstration falls to the ground. This, therefore, observe.'[141]

In the course of reading book VI of the *Assertio*, Starkey developed his objection to Pighe's case for an ecclesiastical monarchy, relying on the same model of government as he had recommended in the Dialogue. Starkey again observed that 'if it is true that this ecclesiastical monarchy was established by Christ, and not put in place by the church, all the rest which is deduced in this book is true', but if not, then Pighe's case would collapse (190r/1). Starkey singled out the 'problem' of how to make divided sovereignty work in the church. 'Since the unity of order is preached so many times in this book, to which it is necessary, as he says, to refer the whole multitude, how therefore

---

[140] 189v/2 (V, 10).   [141] *Ibid.* (V, 14).

will the *status* of the people stand, or of the *optimates* in which all is ruled by the votes of many and not of one?' Starkey wondered 'whether, perhaps, on that account he [illegible word] only these *status*, because the foundation of the commonwealth procedes from this distinction, but yet it is necessary that all practice, exercise and jurisdiction must be given to one'. Starkey ended with reservations not only about Pighe's conclusions, but about how he deduced them from his authorities. 'In this spot the places of Aristotle in the politics which he recites here must be more diligently examined' (190v/1).

Starkey again questioned Pighe's reading of Starkey's favourite Aristotle near the end of book VI, where Pighe tried to demolish three objections to his belief that the ecclesiastical community had no right to correct an errant pope. Starkey ignored the first and last of these, the natural law defence that a mad man had to be stripped of his sword (or the spiritual sword in the case of a pope who neglected the church), and one based on the organic analogy which claimed that Christ would never have left his church without a remedy for a putrid member which threatened to infect the whole body. Instead, he referred only to Pighe's version of Aristotle to the effect that

this especially pertains to a free community, that it can accuse its prince if he turns himself into a tyrant and further deprive and remove [him] where improvement should have been despaired of ... But the church is a free community. Therefore the correction of its prince pertains to it, and the deprivation of an incorrigible besides.

Starkey accepted the full force of Aristotle's case. 'In all human societies it is certain that the people has the authority of correcting human errors, in as much as they have been made by men', a rebuttal to Pighe's assertion that 'if governed by the holy spirit and on the foundation of Christ, the head and prince and first foundation of this ecclesiastical polity is subject in nothing to human correction, but only to divine', as Starkey summarized.[142]

Starkey did not refute Pighe's arguments singly and in total. Perhaps he thought he had already dealt sufficiently well with many of them in his *Exhortation*. In any case, Starkey merely noted most of Pighe's points, objecting strongly only to his claim that the church needed a visible head. He singled out Pighe's summary of his case for the primacy, which rested on three points: (1) Christ wished the church to be firmly established; (2) it depended on Old Testament precedents; and (3) it was necessary for the 'conserving of ecclesiastical discipline and unity'.[143] Starkey drew particular attention to two of Pighe's conclusions. Pighe had denied that 'the apostles were equal in authority', since Christ had established Peter to avoid leaving the church in Babylonian confusion (191r/1, no.2). Lastly, Starkey noted Pighe's historical

---

[142] 191r/1 (VI, 17).   [143] 190r/2 (VI, 11).

argument 'that from the time of the apostles to the Nicene council he [the pope] exercised the primacy'.

Pighe's exegetical support for his claims also did not interest Starkey much. After all, Starkey thought that forms of government, whether ecclesiastical or secular, varied according to circumstances, so that scriptural warrant for one kind or another could not count for much. Starkey skipped over altogether Pighe's interpretation of the key texts in support of papal primacy, despite Pighe's large contribution to the new exegesis of Matthew 18 which read *petram* as *Petrus*, and Starkey likewise merely noted that Pighe discussed the text 'dic ecclesiae', which had often been given an anti-papal sense.[144] Again, Starkey in one place flagged Pighe's attention to the Levites as evidence that the authority of a single head was needed to resolve doubtful matters, but passed over Pighe's much more extended treatment of them as model for the same point at the beginning of book VI.[145] On the other hand, Pighe read some of the Old Testament exactly as Starkey did. Both took the way the Israelites pitched their camps as a model for 'the ordered church', as Pighe called it.[146] Perhaps Starkey's own penchant for allegorical and metaphorical interpretation made him uncomfortable about criticizing Pighe's similar approach. Certainly partisanship did not concern Starkey. If he agreed with Pighe, he was unafraid to say so, exclaiming at one point 'Oh! how very clearly he exhorts to obedience', or in another observing that 'he paints the visible church excellently'.[147] Wherever Starkey's indifference sprang from, he expressed reservations about Pighe's exegesis only in his conclusion. Pighe's heavy reliance on ecclesiastical traditions and the 'sense and consent of the church' led Starkey to complain that 'his rule for the understanding of scripture seems to be uncertain', and to retort (as he had against Pole) that 'ecclesiastical traditions are not holy and equal to canonical scriptures'.[148] The mechanics of determining what was or was not an ecclesiastical tradition seem to have been the sticking point for Starkey. How many doctors' opinions counted and which ones? Worse, he was worried that ignorant people would know little more than that 'this multitude of Christ is the catholic church and [it] is illuminated by a divine, not a human, spirit' (191r/2).

Starkey did not show himself much more interested in the details of Pighe's arguments about the structure of the church. For example, he compressed the whole of Pighe's book VI, an eighty-folio refutation of conciliarist ideas, into one folio of his own text (although that represents almost a quarter of the total). Starkey did not declare himself forthrightly until he reached his conclusions and rudimentary sketch of a refutation. Apparently his forays into

---

[144] 188v/2 (III, 2 and 3) for Peter as the rock, and 190v/1 (VI, 13) for *dic ecclesie*.
[145] 189r/1.   [146] 188v/2 (III, 90).   [147] 189r/1 (IV, 1) and 189v/2 (V).
[148] 191r/2 and 191v/2.

scriptural interpretation in the *Exhortation* and the notes on the Old Testament had not weaned him from his basic interest in constitutional matters. At any rate, Starkey summarized Pighe's major points about the government of the church much more thoroughly and more fairly than he did any of the rest of Pighe's case. Five of Starkey's fifteen (actually seventeen) numbered conclusions were devoted to relations between pope and council. According to Starkey, the Dutch theologian had argued that general councils were 'mere human inventions, and therefore to be subject to the judgment of the head constituted by Christ'. The most important of the three sorts of councils, that which dealt with general cases, should be held 'by the sole heads of the church with few councillors'. Councils claimed general authority invalidly, since 'universal councils in no case can have any jurisdiction, nor have any power by divine law, which never had been delegated to it in any place by the church'. Thus, the councils had no warrant of any sort to compete with Christ's commands to Peter. Consequently, 'the decrees of Constance and Basel lack beginnings and foundations'. In short, 'universal councils are not legitimate nor of any authority unless in deciding by the authority of the head', that is, unless the pope had delegated some of his authority to the council. He alone had the right to call such an assembly.

Starkey replied directly to Pighe's ideas about papal supremacy in his fourth suggested rebuttal. 'Chastising and tempering the authority of the pope is by the judgment of the church and the general council, nor is he above it.' Pighe's case for papal inerrancy also drew a blunt rejection from Starkey. 'The supreme pontiff can err and very often has' (191v/2). Starkey here responded to two conclusions he had extracted from Pighe's text. First, the primate could not be a heretic, and second, if he were, he could not be deposed under any circumstances. Starkey noted that these two amounted to a paradox (191r/2).

The last major portion of Starkey's conclusions covered Pighe's ideas about relations between ecclesiastical and secular powers. Starkey opened with a criticism of what Pighe 'adduces against the *legislator humanus*, from which all authority of making laws and the form of the commonwealth seems to depend' (191r/2). Starkey then labelled Pighe's claim that the emperors and the kings of France and Britain have their authority from the pope another paradox, but he did not explain what he meant. Starkey continued by citing Pighe's claim that the empire rested on force until Constantine ceded it to the pope. After that, however, Charlemagne dealt with ecclesiastical affairs 'and took from the Roman pontiffs' (191v/1). Here Starkey probably meant to refer to the civil law doctrine that no emperor could diminish the authority he handed on to his successors. Pighe's treatment of ecclesiastical–secular relations attracted a good deal of Starkey's attention in other notes, too.

The retreat from some of the central concerns of his Dialogue occasionally cropped up in Starkey's comments on Pighe. For example, he merely cited in passing Pighe's bald assertion that 'the study of liberty is the fount of all evils', and agreed with Pighe that 'tyrants are not instituted by God' but 'he [God] uses them to the good of God the highest good' (189v/2). Nevertheless, Starkey gave much more explicit attention to politics in these notes than he had in his jottings of 1537. Thus Starkey made a number of major points against Pighe, most of them concerning the constitution of the church. First and most fundamental, Pighe's exegetical method was unreliable. Therefore Starkey could fairly easily demolish most of Pighe's case, nearly all of which rested on scripture. Second, Starkey rejected Pighe's argument in favour of the establishment of the papal primacy through Peter, insisting instead that Christ, the invisible head of the church, left no visible order for it. Third, since the church was a political community exactly like any other, it should have a 'mixed constitution', that 'sanguyn complexyon' which Starkey had recommended for the secular state, and as a free community it had the right to correct its ruler. In terms of the actual structure of the church, that meant that the pope was subordinate to a general council, especially since he could err and even fall into heresy. Starkey adhered as staunchly as ever to his conciliarist ideas. Finally, Pighe's notions about the *legislator humanus* and the form of the laws and the commonwealth were wrong, in large part because Pighe failed to separate secular and ecclesiastical jurisdiction. Whatever else Starkey still thought of his erstwhile patron, by rejecting Pighe's ecclesiology, he rejected Pole's.

Part of the reason for the difficulty in interpreting Starkey's notes on Pighe may arise from the trying circumstances under which Starkey wrote them. In the course of 1538 Cromwell continued to watch for an opening to avenge himself on Pole and his friends and they finally gave him his chance in the form of their plot known as the Exeter conspiracy. It began to unravel with the arrest of Sir Geoffrey Pole at just the time of Starkey's death in August. The full story of plot and counter-plot is much too complicated to be told here, but Starkey's prominence is hard to miss.[149] All of his warnings and helpful tips to the Pole family during Reginald's legation came out, as well as the activities of his servant on behalf of the worrisome John Helyar. Geoffrey Pole's interrogators focused on Starkey in both his second and third examinations in early November, displaying particular interest in Starkey's breach of security when he passed on Tunstall's and Sampson's opinion of *De unitate*, as well as the substance of a conversation between Starkey and Wriothesley. The latter allegedly said that Sir Geoffrey 'and other of his famylie must nott be made Cok[neyes]', and Starkey added that 'the lord

---

[149] G. R. Elton, *Reform and reformation. England 1509–1558*, 280 takes the conspiracy very seriously, but the standard work remains that by the Dodds sisters, published in 1915. Their book bore the imprint of a heavy bias against the government.

pr[yvey] seal if the king was nott of a good nature for one poles sake wold destroy all poles'.[150] At about the same time, the investigators learned that Starkey had warned Montagu about the plots against his brother the year before.[151] As if all this were not damaging enough, the questioning of Montagu's chaplain, John Collins, revealed that Starkey's servant had brought letters home from the renegade Helyar to Collins. Collins maintained that their content was completely innocuous, but this information emerged immediately after Collins admitted that Geoffrey Pole had burned other missives from Helyar.[152] On the strength of this evidence both Starkey and his unidentified servant were singled out in marginal notes, exactly as were all the conspirators who were latter attainted.[153] This servant was probably Robert Sigbroke. Starkey left sizable bequests to two servants in his will, one of them apparently a relative, but nothing further is known about either this William Starkey or about Robert Sigbroke or Sybroke, except that the latter was also one of Starkey's executors.[154] As the more trusted man of the two, perhaps Sigbroke was more likely to have acted as a courier for Helyar, but why Starkey used him in so dangerous a fashion cannot be certainly established. It may also be that the 'Morgan' whom Philip Hoby recruited as a servant and who had some connection to Starkey was Morgan Wells, one of the principal agents of the 1537 conspiracy. He had sworn to kill anyone who would try to assassinate Pole.[155]

Nevertheless, we may infer that Starkey had more than ideological ties to Helyar, a man over whom the government displayed great concern. He and Starkey may even have met at Oxford, although this is unlikely. Helyar matriculated at Corpus Christi college in 1522, just before Starkey probably left for Italy, and he took his BA the following year. Helyar then became a fellow of his college, perhaps by Wolsey's patronage.[156] This may be what John Bale meant when he noted that Helyar and 'Frogmorton' 'advanced by the cardinal'.[157] If this Frogmorton is Michael Throckmorton, Pole's double agent who successfully hoodwinked Cromwell, then Cromwell would have seen Helyar's pedigree for subversion extending right back to his student

---

150 SP1/138, fols. 215v–216r, Geoffrey Pole's second examination. Lacunae supplied from SP 1/139, fols. 39r–40r (*LP*, XIII:2, 830.i), the fair copy of both second and third examinations.
151 SP 1/138, fol. 174r.
152 SP 1/139, fol. 30v (*LP*, XIII:2, 825.2).
153 SP 1/139, fol. 39r and fol. 45v (*LP*, XIII:2, 830.i and ii). Both notes are probably in the hand of Richard Pollard, one of Cromwell's servants, who may have prosecuted Anne Boleyn and was deeply involved in the aftermath of the Pilgrimage. E. W. Ives, *Anne Boleyn*, 386n.
154 PRO PCC Pynyng, VI, fol. 45r. Starkey's will was also printed in *Somerset medieval wills*, 47–8, where Sigbroke appears as 'Bigbroke'.
155 SP 1/139, fol. 23r (*LP*, XIII:2, 828.2) for Wells's threat and SP 1/103, fol. 162r (*LP*, X, 719), a letter from Hoby to Starkey of 23 April [1536].
156 *DNB*.
157 John Bale, *Index Britanniae scriptorum*, ed. R. L. Poole and Mary Bateson, 216.

days. Helyar studied under Vives, with whom he was still in contact in 1537.[158] Comments on classical authors honed his literary talents and probably helped to fuel fears that he would become another controversialist. Helyar fell foul of Cromwell when he fled from England, first in 1535, and then permanently in 1536. In both cases, Helyar gave religious reasons for his departure.[159] More serious yet, Geoffrey Pole had arranged for Helyar's flight, ordering his servant Hugh Holland to convey Helyar to Paris in 1536 and leave him there. Pole knew this was illegal, because he assured Holland that he had nothing to worry about.[160] Helyar allegedly went to Paris for an education, but soon wound up in Louvain. There he studied the three languages, including Hebrew, under van Kampen's student, Andrew van Gennep.[161] Helyar's mind seems to have been turning to a practical career as a polemicist. He was almost certainly the English student at Louvain who suggested to Pole that fastings and prayers were all very nice, but confutations of English attacks on papal supremacy were also badly needed.[162] More than his education linked Helyar to later seminary priests concerned with the 'reduction' of England. Either in Paris or in Venice he met Ignatius Loyola. The founder of the Jesuits impressed Helyar sufficiently that he copied Loyola's *Spiritual exercises* into his notebook.[163] At Venice Helyar probably met the Spanish consul, Martin de Çornoça, described by Loyola as an *amico antico*, and the man who tried very hard to recruit Pole at about this time.[164] Under Pole's patronage, Helyar later became manager and penitentiary of the English hospice at Rome. He died before December 1541.[165] His servant Henry Pyning later became chamberlain and general receiver to Pole, who left some of his manuscripts in Pyning's charge before he died.[166] Helyar's brother-in-law, John Fowle, shuttled constantly between England and the continent, often carrying messages for Helyar.[167]

As dangerous as Helyar's attainments may have appeared, his real threat arose, like Pole's, from the extent of his support in England.[168] Geoffrey Pole's active encouragement extended right into August 1538.[169] Pole's mother, the

---

[158] De Vocht, *Collegium trilingue*, 423.   [159] *LP*, IX, 128 and XIII:2, 797.

[160] SP 1/138, fol. 191r.   [161] De Vocht, *Collegium trilingue*, 371 and 425.

[162] M. Hallé, *Reginald Pole*, 224.

[163] Marcel Bataillon suggested Paris in an untitled note in *Bulletin hispanique*, 186, while Paul Dudon plumped for Venice in *St Ignatius of Loyola*, 183. For Helyar's copying of the oldest known MS of the *Exercises*, see de Vocht, *Collegium trilingue*, 424.

[164] P. Tacchi Venturi, *Storia della compagnia di Gesù in Italia*, II, 87.

[165] De Vocht, *Collegium trilingue*, 425.

[166] SP 1/138, fol. 191r, and A. C. Southern, *Elizabethan recusant prose 1559–1582*, 479 for the title page of Pole's *Treatie of iustification*, recording its provenance.

[167] *LP*, XIII:2, 797.

[168] For Pole's support, see T. F. Mayer, 'A diet for Henry VIII: the failure of Reginald Pole's 1537 legation', 323–7.

[169] *LP*, XIII:2, 113.

Countess of Salisbury, was patron of Helyar's living in her parish church at Warblington. She had opposed his flight, but left him undisturbed in his benefice.[170] The countess's favour made up only part of Helyar's local support. It ramified more than widely enough to worry Cromwell, who tried to keep tabs on any sort of potentially seditious behaviour in the localities.[171] The circle of Helyar's friends, however, stretched to the centre of English politics. Two landowners in the vicinity of Helyar's second living at East Meon in Hampshire, as well as the patron of the benefice, also protected Helyar. One of those landowners was Sir William Paulet, the leading gentleman of Hampshire and a prominent member of the king's council. According to Holland's testimony, Paulet responded handsomely to Helyar's hopes for assistance. Once, he sent Fowle to Louvain for a certificate to prove that Helyar was studying there in order to have the sequestration of his benefice released.[172] Paulet served on the commission which had tried Anne, and G. R. Elton has recently pointed to his aloof stand during the Pilgrimage as a sign of dissatisfaction with Cromwell.[173] Norfolk had gloatingly executed quite a few of Paulet's tenants in his clearing operation after the Pilgrimage.[174]

The other local grandee was Sir Antony Windsor, who, along with his wife, ran Paulet's parish in his absence. His brother was Sir Andrew, keeper of the Great Wardrobe for forty years and once governor of Princess Mary's household.[175] Windsor's estate lay close by East Meon, as did the principal estate of Arthur, Lord Lisle, for whom Windsor acted as receiver-general. Lisle would be imprisoned in 1540, partly on charges of having secret conference with Pole. Both Windsors held conservative religious opinions. Sir Antony's will committed his soul to God 'and to the blessed Virgin and all the holy company of heaven', and went on to order masses of the five wounds. Whether or not this emblem had a distinctively conservative meaning, it had, after all, appeared on the Pilgrims' badge.[176] Religious conservatism probably accounts for the aid and comfort the Countess of Salisbury, Sir William and Sir Antony offered Helyar. The same factor probably explains why Stephen

---

[170] *Ibid.*, 797 and W. Page, ed., *VCH Hampshire and the Isle of Wight*, III, 135.

[171] Elton, *Policy and police*, chapter 3.

[172] SP 1/138, fols. 191v–2r (*LP*, XIII:2, 797). I have not been able to trace this case. Neither Gardiner's register (Hampshire Record Office MS 21M65/A1/23) nor two volumes of consistory court documents (MS 21M65/Consistory Court Book 6, Depositions 1531–1547, and MS 21M65/Consistory Court Book 7, Act Book 1534–1542) yielded any trace of it.

[173] E. W. Ives, 'Faction at the court of Henry VIII: the fall of Anne Boleyn', 177 and G. R. Elton, 'Politics and the pilgrimage of grace', 213–14.

[174] *LP*, XII:1, 468.

[175] Helyar wrote to Windsor on 10 June (probably 1537), thanking him for handling his parochial affairs. SP 1/121, fol. 91r.

[176] M. St Clair Byrne, ed., *The Lisle letters*, I, 277–9, and J. Youings, *Sixteenth-century England*, 213.

Gardiner, Bishop of Winchester and chief rival to Cromwell, helped Helyar by failing to report his flight until well after the priest was gone.[177]

Hence both Helyar's own talents and the breadth of his domestic support gave Cromwell good cause to cast a jaundiced eye on Helyar himself, as well as anyone who might assist him. When Starkey provided postal service for Helyar, he got himself into very deep trouble. His close ties to the Pole family also implicated Starkey, from the unstable Sir Geoffrey to the disaffected but relatively discrete Lord Montagu. Starkey gave the former only information, but in his will he left the latter both his own bed and a bequest of £4 'to buy him a nagg'.[178] Bosham, the living to which Starkey had retreated in 1536, was only a few miles from the Countess of Salisbury's castle at Warblington and from Sir Geoffrey's more humble house at Lordington. Ties to lesser friends – John Walker and Bernardino Sandro – who had played significant parts in Pole's legation could also have caused difficulties for Starkey, at least once these links came out after the seizure of Starkey's correspondence. In 1538, Walker still held the keys to Pole's house at Sheen, and may have continued to act as the cardinal's English business agent.[179]

The evidence against Starkey was fully as damning as that against most of the rest of the alleged conspirators, and someone directed Richard Pollard to take the last step on the road to formal indictment. Nevertheless, Starkey somehow escaped attainder. The fact that he died before the omnibus bill of attainder passed through parliament in early 1539 probably did not matter much.[180] Perhaps Cromwell spared him out of regard for their former intellectual camaraderie. But it is more likely that some members of the council, who had not been happy about Cromwell's pursuit of Pole in 1536–7 and understandably did not enjoy finding themselves at risk either, managed to limit the full damage of the Exeter business. After all, Paulet and Gardiner were almost as heavily implicated as Starkey. Perhaps in alliance with other conservatives like Sir William Fitzwilliam, Earl of Southampton, or even the council's principal secretary Wriothesley who appears nearly as guilty as Starkey, Paulet and Gardiner managed to curb the scope of Cromwell's vengeance. Then again, if we balance the evidence of the handling of and

---

[177] J. A. Muller, ed., *The letters of Stephen Gardiner*, no. 50. Holland recalled taking Helyar to Paris about 'the beginning of somer was iij or iiij yeres' ago in 1538. SP 1/138, fol. 191r.

[178] Pynyng VI, fol. 45r.

[179] *LP*, XIII:1, 422. It is worth noting that Walker, one of the possible conspirators with Pole in 1537, seems to have escaped even questioning, much less indictment or attainder. Was he, perhaps, really one of those spies some historians have eagerly discovered under each of Pole's beds? If Walker had fled to escape trial and judgment, we might still expect to find him duly attainted. If he were in Cromwell's employ, this casts a different light on his relations with Starkey.

[180] S. E. Lehmberg, *The reformation parliament*, 61 calls this 'the vindictive act of a triumphant faction against a defeated one'.

largely subdued reaction to *De unitate* – which, admittedly, Henry may never have read – including efforts to meet all Pole's demands for a parley in Flanders, combined with Henry's record of forbearance in the face of several earlier monumental provocations by Pole, the most famous of them Pole's rejection of preferment in 1530 and 'escape' to Italy eighteen months later, and the king's large investment in Pole, for whose education he had paid (partly at Pole's request, it must be remembered), and whom he brought along as a diplomat and senior ecclesiastic, only to see both hopes disappointed – all this by Pole's own well-known story of Cromwell's negative reaction to the young pedant and Cromwell's more aggressive actions against Pole in 1537, including even the dispatch of a hand-picked assassin, this suggests that Henry was less than enthusiastic about the attempt to destroy Pole and Poles. The king himself may therefore have applied brakes to Cromwell, either alone or in concert with conservatives on the council, who presented a much more serious threat to Cromwell than to Henry, and for whom Pole served almost as a talisman.[181] Alas, this must all be speculation, but the fact remains that Starkey slipped out from under a crushing burden of proof.

Starkey seems to have realized the tenuousness of his position. In any event, he took himself off to Somerset at the end of his life, where he succumbed on 25 August 1538, probably to a local outbreak of plague.[182] Starkey requested burial in the chancel of St Mary's, North Petherton, and left gifts both to it and the cathedral of Wells.[183] He apparently had no previous ties to this village between Bridgwater and Taunton, but he did to its vicar John Bulcombe. Starkey's activities as patronage secretary to Pole had involved him with Bulcombe in November 1531. Bulcombe had been presented to North Petherton by Sir William Weston, prior of the Order of St John of Jerusalem and a notorious religious conservative, in October of that year.[184] Starkey

---

[181] For the story of Pole's legation, especially Cromwell's own man, Peter Mewtas, who was to shoot Pole, and the mission's role in English faction politics, see my 'A diet for Henry VIII', 319. The plans for a meeting in Flanders, which were canvassed from January through September 1537 and have always been taken as a smoke-screen for other measures, are recorded in *LP*, XII:1, 125 (the council to Pole), 444 (SP 1/116, especially fol. 60v; Pole's reply), XII:2, 619 and 620. Although the king was willing to send (and may actually have sent) Nicholas Wilson, More's fellow resister who had since bowed to the supremacy, the negotiations broke down over Pole's refusal to treat with the English envoys as anything other than a cardinal. For Pole's activities in Paris and the large expectations they both fulfilled and fed, see T. F. Mayer, 'A mission worse than death: Reginald Pole and the Parisian theologians'. And for Pole's embroidery of his response to Henry's offers after his return from Paris, T. F. Mayer, 'Divine intervention in Reginald Pole's confrontation with Henry VIII'.

[182] *Somerset medieval wills*, xx.

[183] The early sixteenth-century brass of a kneeling priest, once indented in the east wall of the sacristy of St Mary's, may well be a memorial to Starkey. Nikolaus Pevsner, *The buildings of England: south and west Somerset*, 261.

[184] *Somerset record society*, LV (1940), no. 412.

may have met Bulcombe in the first place through Oxford ties. Bulcombe had been a fellow of Merton, but long before Starkey arrived.[185] Bulcombe's servants and family nursed Starkey in his final illness, but Starkey carefully avoided naming Bulcombe in his will, despite two references to 'the vicar'. It looks very much as if Starkey had fled to North Petherton to one of the few people he could trust, and wished to keep his old friend out of trouble, if at all possible.

Besides pious and political bequests, Starkey left the bulk of his estate to his father, his best gown to his brother John, and all of his books to his chief executor and old friend Edward Wotton, some for his own children, some for Magdalen, and some for 'suche skollars as maister wotton by his discretion shall see theym apte towardes good lernyng or letters'. Starkey may not have retrieved all his books from Venice, but he must have retained a substantial number even without them.[186] Wotton was by this time a prominent physician, but if Starkey hoped to avoid problems by making him chief executor, he was disappointed. Starkey's will did not go through probate until 1544, an extraordinary delay. Apparently the uncertainty surrounding Starkey's near attainder and the fate of his party deterred Wotton from pressing for probate. Then again, it may only have been the influence he could exert as president of the Royal College of Physicians that saved Starkey's property. Wotton was also the Countess of Salisbury's physician and acted as executor for Lupset's mother in 1543.[187] Starkey was little luckier after death than he had been before, and apparently not much better at understanding faction politics.

[185] H. E. Salter, ed., *Registrum annalium collegii Mertonensis 1483–1521*, 243 and 249.
[186] Pynyng VI, fol. 45r. Harvel twice wrote Starkey in 1536 about his books, which had been threatened by a flood, and which he promised to have shipped to Starkey soon. *LP*, X, 600 and 1142.
[187] *DNB* and J. A. Gee, *Thomas Lupset*, 22. Wotton was president of the Royal College from 1541–3.

CONCLUSION

STARKEY'S LIFE AS A HUMANIST

The nature of English humanism has recently become a topic of debate after decades of general agreement about it. This book in part answers Alistair Fox's call for many case studies to remedy the three major defects he identifies in previous scholarship: reliance on extrinsic rather than intrinsic evidence; excessive generalization; and insufficient clarity about the relations between humanism and religion.[1] The second problem, of course, is easy to avoid in a biography, while the other two ought almost automatically to set the agenda for any successful portrait of an individual. Fox rightly discards most previous definitions of English humanists, offering instead the suggestion that only those who embraced a rather nebulous 'classicism' should qualify. Maria Dowling proposes a very similar standard, but both are vulnerable to George Logan's insistence that humanism must have content as well as formal characteristics, and to the charge of treating England too much in isolation from the continent and continental scholarship.[2] In other words, for all the utility of a restrictive, formal definition instead of the easy acceptance of labels like 'Erasmian' for the whole of English humanism, Fox and Dowling go too far in the direction of ignoring the existential dimension of humanism, what it meant to be a humanist. Starkey's life can help to answer that question, especially if one focuses on his 'civicism' (Margaret King's word), his 'classicism' in both history and rhetoric and the religious tension these helped to induce in him. All three are the warp of Starkey's humanism as they were of those types from which he learned.

Humanism generally was an aristocratic phenomenon, and by birth, education and political and religious affinities, Thomas Starkey was no exception. Born into a family of parish gentry which had once aspired to greater things, Starkey already had large advantages over the majority of Englishmen

---

[1] A. Fox, 'Facts and fallacies: interpreting English humanism', in A. Fox and J. A. Guy, *Reassessing the Henrician age*, 11, 18, 27.

[2] M. Dowling, *Humanism in the age of Henry VIII*, 1 and G. M. Logan, 'Substance and form in renaissance humanism'.

and his Cheshire origins further helped to set him apart. Cheshire was both one of the more politically peculiar areas of England and also had one of the strongest literary traditions outside the South-east. Since the county palatine lacked a resident nobility, its gentry governed in a collective or roughly 'republican' fashion, even if many of them probably still lived in the world of *Sir Gawain and the green knight*. Starkey's native political attitudes thus predisposed him to enjoy his brief experience of republican governance in Oxford, and to absorb Cicero and Aristotle, along with a vocabulary of the commonwealth biased towards republican Rome and classical Greece. Training in disputation further helped to prepare Starkey to write his Dialogue. Robert Whittinton, even if not yet fully a humanist, probably played a key role in all these aspects of Starkey's education. By the end of his career at Magdalen College Starkey had also encountered the permanent humanist dialectic between the *vita contemplativa* and the *vita activa*. While John Colet's thought on the one hand provided Starkey with yet another converging stream of 'civic' language, even if this time it flowed from Augustine, on the other Colet's deep interest in Pauline Christianity together with Whittinton's leanings introduced Starkey to Stoicism. Starkey accepted Colet's criticism of the state of the church and emphasis on its reform from the top down, but it would take a while before he came around to a belief like Colet's Pauline notion of justification.

In the meantime, Starkey followed the example of Colet and other Englishmen in search of the best education and went to Italy. He fitted in quickly and made Paduan and Venetian culture his own. From them he drew not only much of the content and form of his analysis of the English constitution but also the methodological and linguistic tools with which to present it. The intellectual hothouse of Pietro Bembo's circle rooted Starkey's nascent civic humanism, even if many of his teachers and friends may have been *Vernunft-republikaner*. Under pressure of the crises shaking Venice and Florence in the early sixteenth century, the intellectual élite of those two cities produced a hybrid form of constitutional theory in which the concept of the *stato misto* provided the trappings for restored or renewed aristocratic dominance. Despite the high price tag for Italian politics this development bore, it increased the appeal of Italian civic thought to northerners like Starkey who could use its attenuated form to support the nobility's struggle with the king.

From his models, Starkey drew a new conceptual vocabulary as well as the means to present his ideas circumspectly in a literary form beloved of humanists and peculiarly suited to ambiguity, the dialogue. Starkey did not go as far as Sperone Speroni, who thought of his dialogues as jokes, or Marco Mantova Benavides, whose linguistic exuberance regularly overgrew the garden, but aureate diction and dramatic purpose tempted Starkey and help to account for the difficulties of his Dialogue. Further, experiments in the vernacular conducted in Padua no doubt helped to push Starkey toward writing a high-minded political work in English, and thereby launching a new literary tradition. Lastly, Starkey learned a good deal of the resoluto–compositive method of the 'school of Padua', which allowed him to undergird the rhetorical persuasion of his Dialogue with a convincing scientific argument, all presented in the terms of good humanist rhetorical dialectic.

At the turn of the 1530s opportunity offered for Starkey to put his skills to use. Now formally in Pole's service, Starkey watched his patron successfully execute a major diplomatic assignment in Paris, along with their old friend Thomas Lupset and the rising star Edward Foxe. This, together with Starkey's intellectual circumstances in Paris and Avignon, which intensified his earlier leanings toward corporate government, triggered his ambition and led him to devise in his Dialogue a plan for Pole's political advancement which would also offer Starkey an opening to serve the common weal through a *vita activa*. Wolsey's fall ushered in an apparent age of reform as well as a good chance for the religious and political conservatives to whom Starkey probably meant to appeal. They and Starkey hoped Pole would take an active hand, as did Henry VIII. Starkey had no more success with Pole as leader of a revived high nobility than the two wings of the Aragonese party had working together, perhaps because of similar disagreements over the nature of the church. Starkey came much closer to the nobility's anti-clericalism than to Thomas More's (and eventually Pole's) opposition to lay interference in the church. In the moment between 1529 and 1532, Starkey tried to accommodate both political and religious conservatism, partly on the score of the pope's authority, which he would have restricted but not abolished, partly in terms of his view of salvation, which still left plenty of room for human effort and mainly, of course, through his programme to retrain the nobility and make it worthy to head the common weal.

Although the Dialogue failed in its immediate purpose, that did not deter Starkey from continuing to aim at public service, and it may even have led him to approach the king before he once more accompanied his patron to France and Italy in early 1532. Starkey must have known of Pole's refusal to support the divorce project further, and that could only have provided another incentive to leave Pole's service. Unlike Pole, who offered numerous reasons why a divorce would cause trouble for Henry, Starkey distilled his notions about how Henry could free himself from Catherine into an appeal to a general council which would remedy any possible problems. Perhaps Starkey intended to offer the Dialogue to Henry this early, but discovered that he needed other qualifications if he would secure a job, specifically in law and scriptural studies. Starkey pursued these more or less in tandem during his time in Avignon and Padua. Gianfrancesco della Ripa and Jacopo Sadoleto in the former, Mantova and Jan van Kampen in the latter, all helped to redirect

Starkey's energies. Both legists probably appealed to Starkey not only for the technical tools they could give him, but also for their conciliarism and belief in the necessity of church reform, as well as their humanist inclinations. They further put Starkey in touch with the venerable tradition of conciliarism founded by Francesco Zabarella, which was very similar to the Gallican variety Starkey had already learned. Sadoleto inadvertently helped Starkey over the transition from his emphasis on human effort in salvation to a belief much like justification by faith, as well as encouraging his interest in Paul and rather off-beat approach to biblical exegesis, which Kampen, Mantova and almost all of Starkey's acquaintance in Padua helped to make permanent. In the circles around Pole intense religious questing became the rule, even if Pole's friends did not always reach identical ends. A wide range of positions, most loosely clustered under the umbrella of Italian Evangelism, confronted Starkey. Out of the flux surrounding him and his friends in Pole's household, Starkey chose Contarini's activist model over Pole's more self-absorbed version.

As Delio Cantimori argued, there was frequently a close connection between republican politics and unorthodox religion.[3] Given Starkey's earlier heavy reliance on the model of Venice, it was not difficult for him to blaze a path Contarini would follow almost immediately thereafter and turn his primary interest from secular politics to religion. Starkey converted the essence of Evangelism – belief in justification by faith, the necessity of religious reform, and the use of humanist tools to spread these ideals – into a new vocation of precisely the sort expected of a good *spirituale*, that of preacher. Starkey may have chosen to exercise his vocation in England, but in ecumenically Evangelical fashion, he believed he served the same church as Contarini.

So, thought Starkey at first, did Thomas Cromwell. Although they in fact spoke different languages and used them to different ends, for about eighteen months after Starkey approached Cromwell in late 1534, Starkey could satisfy his civic humanist impulses through the service to the commonwealth which Cromwell offered, whether as a key member of Cromwell's intelligence apparatus or as successful controversialist in the *Exhortation*. In both England and Italy Starkey saw great cause for optimism. Religious disagreements had not yet become serious and everyone was convinced that Pole would deliver. Nevertheless, although Pole and Starkey spoke much more nearly the same language than Cromwell and Starkey, he and his former patron put their stress on obedience rather than the active exercise of virtue to quite different ends. While Pole increasingly withdrew, Starkey modified his earlier commonwealth idiom in light of his increasing concern with nonterrestrial felicity. Despite these warning signs or perhaps because of them,

---

[3] D. Cantimori, *Eretici italiani del cinquecento*, 23.

the irenic Starkey spent the time before the Pilgrimage of Grace broke out trying to put together a grand coalition between Cromwell, Henry and Pole for the reform of England. He adjusted his ideas where necessary, whether by moderating his conciliarism, emphasizing the mean and adiaphora, alternately condemning and defending monasticism, or by justifying a large increase in the prince's power. But not even a humanist as adroit as Starkey could hold all these contradictions in tension, especially when political developments left him increasingly isolated.

Although Starkey recovered from disgrace, he was gradually forced into opposition in the last eighteen months of his life. Regarded as of small consequence by Pole and as religiously suspect by Cromwell, both of whom may have manipulated him in their negotiations, Starkey found himself a man in the middle. He tried one or two more times directly with Henry, and seems to have succeeded, but as politics polarized after the upheavals of 1536–7, Starkey forged an ideological, if not actual, political tie with the conservative nobility. His tergiversations about consent are emblematic of his loss of political moorings. Like many conservatives, Starkey accepted the supremacy for political reasons and because of his anti-clericalism, but insisted that it made no difference to doctrine. His anti-clericalism had deep psychological roots and his dissatisfaction with the papacy went back a long way, but his opposition to Anne and support for Mary are harder to explain. Perhaps, as happened to Pole, Starkey's reservations about the executions of 1535 set him on the path to opposition, and led him eventually to embrace the conservatives' attitude to Anne and Mary. Starkey's humanist fondness for complexity cropped up again here in his idiosyncratic religious justification for opposition, compounded of emphasis on human weakness, on faith, on salvation by God's benefit, and providence, which fitted neither the usually semi-Pelagian outlook of king and nobles nor Cromwell's nascent protestantism.

Starkey still tried to attract Cromwell's favour, both by a small fragment of a tract against the Pilgrimage and by undertaking a full-dress attack on Pighe's *Assertio*. He did not succeed. Henry invited his chaplain to preach in early 1538, and Starkey apparently worked closely with Cromwell's secretary Wriothesley, who likely was already less than enthusiastic about his master. But where Starkey had once proposed a thorough reform programme he now found himself unable to find a political platform any stronger than the Pilgrims' appeal to prophecy.[4] The double impact of disillusionment with the nobility (and particularly Pole) and resignation altered most of his positions. Where men had once been to blame for allowing tyrants to rule them, now bad rulers became divine punishments. Ordinary remedies having failed, Starkey put his trust in charismatic solutions, praying for Englishmen to listen to prophets, among them, no doubt, Pole. The only hope lay in penance and

---

[4] J.-P. Moreau, *Rome ou l'Angleterre?*, 229.

newness of life. Starkey's barbed comments on the Old Testament remained private, but he failed to guard his tongue and offered help and counsel to Pole and his family. When Starkey could not secure a broad spectrum of support, he had no choice but to embrace the faction with which he had flirted almost from the beginning. The Exeter conspiracy was the logical culmination of his life. Starkey's flight to Somerset spared him the headsman's axe, but not the knowledge that his career had failed. Like Anne Boleyn, both Starkey's failure and his earlier success were products of cross-cultural incomprehension. Just as Anne's exotic, sophisticated behaviour initially enthralled Henry and his courtiers, only to become an excuse for discarding her later, so Starkey's exotic, sophisticated Italian ideas seemed to offer Cromwell and his allies a powerful new tool of analysis, only to be exposed as radically conservative and, above all, the wrong sort of Evangelical.[5]

Nevertheless, while it lasted, Starkey's subtle combination of a traditional English political agenda with Italian categories of political thought offered an important alternative to the conservative opposition's entrenched alliance with the old church and reliance on prophecy instead of policy. As David Norbrook argues, contact like Starkey's with a different political tradition (or traditions) gave Englishmen a chance to 'experiment with new political values' which need not necessarily make them open radicals, but left their work with radical implications nonetheless.[6] But as John Pocock also notes, a radical in a traditional society could not help but become a reactionary.[7] Such was Starkey. As a result he lived and thought in a web of contradictions and complexities. That he tried to embrace so many apparently incompatible positions might alone almost qualify him as a humanist, but an explanation of how similar tensions arose in other humanists can clarify how Starkey handled them. Pocock offers a comprehensive theory of humanism as an interplay between present and past, a 'conversation' which had 'something ineradicably social and even political about it'.[8] The problem was how to reconcile the particular with the universal. Humanists conceived reality in terms of both, aspiring on the one hand to 'universality in the conduct of particulars', while on the other labouring under the painful awareness that they could never know the universal except intellectually (65). This produced a permanent ambivalence, for which the Aristotelian theory of the *polis* offered a partial curative. The mixed state would render the degeneration of the particular at least much more difficult by fostering the full development of the individual and, therefore, of corporate virtue (66).

[5] Eric Ives, *Anne Boleyn*, 27.
[6] D. Norbrook, *Poetry and politics in the English renaissance*, 12.
[7] J. G. A. Pocock, *Politics, language and time*, 247.
[8] J. G. A. Pocock, *The Machiavellian moment: Florentine political thought and the atlantic republican tradition*, 60 and cf. 64.

Similar motives doubtless lay behind Starkey's plan to reverse the decay of England in exactly this fashion. Pocock's case applies primarily to politics, but George Logan argues that the whole of humanism developed dialectically through 'the emergence and resolution of tensions internal to the tradition'.[9] One of the most important stretched between eloquence and Christian wisdom. It charts exactly Starkey's evolution from an 'Aristotelian, Italianate humanist' (Fox's characterization) into a Pauline, Italianate humanist.[10]

The dynamic between play and seriousness which Richard Lanham posits in humanist rhetoric says even more about Starkey's life and writing. In 'the rhetorical view of life' language is primary, serving a 'fundamentally dramatic' reality, in which any person is 'fundamentally a role player'.[11] As such he must give up a 'central self' together with the comforts of religion, but he gains tolerance and a sense of humour (4–5). As an irreducibly social *persona*, the humanist develops an abiding, self-conscious concern with style, one of the most revolutionary developments in the Renaissance and abundantly evident in Starkey (212). As Lanham argues, style always depends on an audience and its degree of sophistication, and it is therefore incumbent on historians and literary critics to 'imagine the reality for which such a style would be appropriate'. In common with other humanist writing, Starkey's obviously 'academic' or highly ornamented prose 'constantly threatens academic inquiry with comic exposure', exactly as it would have to in order to 'humour' his patron Pole, who was so deeply ambivalent about his role in the commonwealth (26, 28–9). Lanham's theory that rhetorical exuberance may have been a means to 'create' a self also fits Starkey. Not only was he subjected to all the strains associated with proper courtly behaviour but, unlike most of his contemporaries, Starkey immersed himself in Italian culture and became an *inglese italianato* out of his time.[12] Well might he have wondered exactly what his self should be. If Starkey did indeed create a 'dynamic self' through play with language, he could still present 'serious' political proposals for, as a successful courtier knew, there was a time to raise serious issues, to move between 'purpose and game', even if all depended on flattery and hence on the rhetorical self (155). This dichotomy, working at the level of language rather than substance, behaviour rather than psychology,

---

9 G. M. Logan, 'Substance and form in Renaissance humanism', 15 and cf. G. M. Logan, *The meaning of More's 'Utopia'*, 258–9.
10 Logan, 'Substance and form', 29 and Fox, 'Facts and fallacies', 32.
11 R. A. Lanham, *The motives of eloquence: literary rhetoric in the renaissance*, 14.
12 K. R. Bartlett, 'The strangeness of strangers: English impressions of Italy in the sixteenth century', analyses this phenomenon comprehensively and improves on previous accounts by allowing that Pole's circle in Padua anticipated the much more broadly based phenomenon of mid-century. Nevertheless, Bartlett links men like Starkey and Morison, arguing that both went beyond the older view of Italy as just another branch of the *respublica christiana*, but not so far as to regard it as a foreign country, 48–9. Starkey absorbed a good deal more of Italian civilization than Morison, and hence had more trouble readjusting to English circumstances.

further explains how humanists could be simultaneously engaged and detached.

Lanham spells out the implications of his theory for Renaissance political thought and they further help to explain Starkey's love of contradiction. On the one hand, humanist ideals of stasis dominated the Dialogue, but on the other, the language with which Starkey described his immovable commonwealth looked instead 'toward a self-conscious, self-correcting dynamic polis' (213). However self-consciously conservative his programme, it would have required revolutionary action (or at least some – any – human action) to implement it. Starkey's Italian contemporaries were beginning to have a great deal of trouble inhabiting the world of purposive, serious action as a result of the disasters which befell the city states from 1450 on, but he was not quite prepared to abandon the possibility that Englishmen could still change 'reality' and make an impact on their political world. Late in his career, Starkey abandoned the world of both moral action and rhetorical play and withdrew into religion, but for most of his life he held style and substance, play and seriousness in tension.

And yet there is a religious subtext to Starkey's life. With proper regard for its highly schematic and sometimes vague nature, W. J. Bouwsma's dialectic between 'Stoicism and Augustinianism' captures an opposition in Starkey between two philosophical (and, ultimately, psychological) attitudes which helped to produce ambiguity.[13] Starting from a point much like Pocock's and Logan's, Bouwsma develops a dichotomy which includes nearly all the disparate elements in Starkey's intellectual environment and mind.[14] On the Stoic side of the ledger, Starkey argued for a divine spark in man which gave him natural theology and the possibility of rationally comprehending the universe; religious syncretism; the complete dominance of reason and consequently a highly intellectualistic conception of virtue; and a politics which confined government to the hands of those few men capable of contemplating the universal order. Starkey did not adopt Bouwsma's corollary of a world government, but neither did Cicero. Nor did he fully accept history as an irreversible decline from a golden age. As others have noted, Starkey had a much more developed sense of the possibility of change, however much that conflicted with his ideals of permanence.[15]

History was important to Starkey, as it was to all humanists, but he had little more success sticking to one view of it than he did in the case of anything

---

[13] The criticisms are Logan's, 'Substance and form', 30.

[14] W. J. Bouwsma, 'The two faces of humanism. Stoicism and Augustinianism in renaissance thought', *passim*.

[15] A. B. Ferguson, *The articulate citizen and the English renaissance*, 377 and Fox, 'English humanism and the body politic', in Fox and Guy, *Henrician age*, 49–50.

which offered alternatives. In the Dialogue, Starkey wavered between a cyclical and a linear notion, and could not make up his mind whether fortune or divine providence governed history. By 1537 and his notes on the Old Testament, Starkey had adopted an outwardly providentialist conception, but the examples he cited could only have had current relevance if history sometimes moved in cycles. A neat illustration of the humanist difficulty of keeping an eye cocked on past and present at the same time.[16]

The Augustinian end of Bouwsma's spectrum is much less well defined and much harder to isolate in Starkey, especially since many of the traits which Bouwsma identifies as peculiar to Augustinianism also fit Cicero. Nevertheless, the tensions between these two poles roughly map out Starkey's religious evolution. Ultimately, Starkey's attention to the Old Testament at a moment of severe crisis suggests that he had at least begun to change his mind about natural theology, and he definitely emphasized reason much less in his later works than in the Dialogue. While he resisted elevating the will, he gradually turned his religion in a more affective direction. Beyond a shadow of a doubt, he became convinced of human weakness and the necessity of divine aid in the quest for virtue. His attitude to the body was always deeply ambivalent.

Such ambivalence, ambiguity or plain contradiction shaped Starkey's life, as they did other humanists'. Like them, Starkey sought an outlet in literature, especially dialogue, and like them he cast about for classical or historical models to legitimize behaviour which broke with the immediate past. Like many of his fellows, he eventually sought religious solace after one disappointment too many in his secular career. Nevertheless, the most profound dialectic in Starkey's thought lay between conservative ends and radical means, between political ideals and political reality. If he could have, he would have seen the high nobility restored to the dominance it had enjoyed in the early fifteenth century, but through the leadership of a man who owed his education and position to a 'new monarch' who was perhaps not overly enamoured of his nobility. Many would say this programme was a chimera, that Starkey's thought was hopelessly unrealistic. Perhaps it was, but those judgments may benefit too much from hindsight. The humanist Starkey provides another view of an age dominated by the figure of the humanist More, but his is a view not necessarily any more utopian than More's and one which may tell us a good deal more about early sixteenth-century language, perceptions and politics.

[16] K. J. Wilson analyses the humanists' 'binocular vision' in *Incomplete fictions: the formation of English renaissance dialogue*, 93.

BIBLIOGRAPHY

MANUSCRIPT SOURCES

Berkeley, California
  Robbins Law Library, University of California
    Manuscript 63 Lettere di Marco Mantova
Chester
  Cheshire Record Office
    EDA 2/1 Wills and *Inquisitiones post mortem*
Chichester
  West Sussex Record Office
    Ep 1/1/4 Register of Bishop Sherborne, II
London
  British Library
    Additional Manuscripts
    Cotton Manuscripts
    Egerton Manuscripts
    Harleian Manuscripts
    Royal Manuscripts
  Public Record Office
    PCC Pynyng, VI
    SP 1: State Papers, Henry VIII
    SP 6: Theological Tracts
Milan
  Biblioteca Ambrosiana
    MS H 28 inf. 54
Paris
  Archives de l'université de Paris (Sorbonne)
    MS 15 Liber receptoris nationis Angliae, 1493–1530
    MS 91 Conclusiones nationis Angliae
Rome
  Biblioteca apostolica vaticana
    Codex Rossiana 997
    Codices vaticani latini
Venice
  Biblioteca marciana
    Manoscritto italiano X (6606)

Vienna
  Haus-, Hof-, und Staatsarchiv
    Frankreich Varia
Winchester
  Hampshire Record Office
    21M65/A1/23 (Stephen Gardiner's Register)
    21M65/Consistory Court Book 6 (Depositions 1531–47)
    21M65/Consistory Court Book 7 (Act Book 1534–42)

PRINTED WORKS AND TYPESCRIPTS

Aa, A. J. van der and G. D. J. Schotel, eds., *Biographisch wordenboek der Nederlanden*. Haarlem, 1876–88.

Addio, Mario d', *L'idea del contratto sociale dai sofisti alla riforma e il 'De principatu' di Mario Salamonio*. Milan, 1954.

Agricola, Rudolf, *De inventione dialectica,* ed. Alardus Amstreldamus. Frankfurt, 1967; reprint of Cologne, 1523 edition.

Agostini, G. degli, 'Notizie storiche spettanti alla vita e agli scritti di Battista Egnazio Sacerdoto viniziano', in *Raccolta d'opusculi scientifici-filologici,* ed. Angelo Calogerà, ser. 1, XXXIII, 1–199. Venice, 1754.

Albèri, Eugenio, ed., *Relazioni degli ambasciatori veneti al senato,* IV (ser. 1, no. 2). Florence, 1840.

Alberigo, Giuseppe, 'Barbaro, Daniele'. *DBI.*
  'Il movimento conciliare (XIV-XV sec.) nella ricerca storica recente', *Studi medievali,* ser. 3, XIX (1978), 913–50.
  'Vita attiva e vita contemplativa in un'esperienza cristiana del XVI secolo', *Studi veneziani,* XVI (1974), 177–225.

Albertini, Rudolph von, *Das florentinisches Staatsbewusstsein im Übergang von der Republik zum Principat*. Bern, 1955.

Allen, J. W., *A history of political thought in the sixteenth century.* New York, 1960; reprint of 1928 edition.

Allen, P. S., H. M. Allen and H. W. Garrod, eds., *Opus epistolarum Desiderii Erasmi roterodami.* Oxford, 1905–58.

Altman, Joel B., *The Tudor play of mind.* Berkeley, 1978.

Amico, John F., d', *Renaissance humanism in papal Rome: humanists and churchmen on the eve of the reformation.* Baltimore, 1983.

Andrich, Giovanni Alvise, *De natione anglica & scota iuristarum universitatis patavinae ab anno 1222 usque ad annum 1738.* Padua, 1892.

Arber, Edward, ed., *A proper dyaloge betwene a gentillman and a husbandman.* London, 1871.

Archambault, Paul, 'The analogy of the "body" in renaissance political thought', *Bibliothèque d'humanisme et renaissance,* XXIX (1967), 21–52.

Arisi, Francesco, *Cremona literata.* Parma, 1702–41.

Aristotle, *Ethica nicomachea,* trans. W. D. Ross, in Richard McKeon, ed., *Introduction to Aristotle.* New York, 1947.

Armstrong, C. J. R., 'The dialectial road to truth: the dialogue', in Peter Sharratt, ed., *French renaissance studies, 1540–1570: humanism and the encyclopedia.* Edinburgh, 1976, 36–51.

Armytage, G. J. and J. P. Rylands, eds., *The visitation of Cheshire, 1613.* Harleian Society, LIX (1909).

Ascheri, Mario, *Un maestro del 'mos italicus': Gianfrancesco Sannazari della Ripa (1480c.–1535)*. Milan, 1970.

Aston, T. H., 'Oxford's medieval alumni', *Past and present*, LXXIV (1977), 3–40.

Avack, Lorenzo d', 'La teoria della monarchia mista nell'Inghilterra del cinquecento e seicento', *Rivista internazionale di filosofia del diritto*, LII (1975), 574–617.

Avesani, Rino, 'Bonamico, Lazaro'. *DBI*.

Bale, John, *Index Britanniae scriptorum*, ed. R. L. Poole and Mary Bateson. Oxford, 1902.

Barker, Ernest, trans., intro. and notes, *The politics of Aristotle*. Oxford, 1958.

Baron, Hans, *The crisis of the early Italian renaissance: civic humanism and republican liberty in an age of classicism and tyranny*. Princeton, 1966.

'Die politische Entwicklung der italienischen Renaissance', *Historische Zeitschrift*, CLXXIV (1952), 31–56.

Bartlett, Kenneth R., 'The strangeness of strangers: English impressions of Italy in the sixteenth century', *Quaderni d'italianistica*, I (1980), 46–63.

Bataillon, Marcel, 'Untitled note', *Bulletin hispanique*, XXXIX (1928), 184–6.

Baumer, F. L., 'Thomas Starkey and Marsilius of Padua', *Politica*, II (1936), 188–205.

Beccadelli, Ludovico, 'Vita del cardinale Reginaldo Polo', in G. B. Morandi, ed., *Monumenti di varia letteratura*. Bologna, 1797–1804, II, 277–333.

Beck, Joan, *Tudor Cheshire*. Chester, 1969.

Beckmann, K. W., 'Staatstheorie und Kirchenpolitik im Werke des englischen Humanisten Thomas Starkey', unpublished Ph.D. thesis, Universität Hamburg, 1972.

Bellis, Daniella de, 'La vita e l'ambiente di Niccolò Leonico Tomeo', *Quaderni per la storia dell'università di Padova*, XIII (1980), 37–75.

Bembo, Pietro, *Prose e rime*, ed. Carlo Dionisotti. Turin, 1960.

Pietro Bembo's Gli asolani, trans. Rudolf B. Gottfried. Bloomington, 1954.

Béné, Charles, *Érasme et Saint Augustin ou l'influence de Saint Augustin sur l'humanisme d'Érasme*. Geneva, 1969.

Bennett, Michael J., *Community, class and careerism: Cheshire and Lancashire society in the age of Sir Gawain and the green knight*. Cambridge, 1983.

Berkowitz, David S., ed., *Humanist scholarship and public order: two tracts against the pilgrimage of grace by Sir Richard Morison*. Washington, 1984.

Bernard, George W., *The power of the early Tudor nobility: the fourth and fifth earls of Shrewsbury*. Brighton, 1984.

Berti, Enrico, 'Il "regnum" di Marsilio tra la "polis" aristotelica e lo "stato" moderno', *Medioevo*, V (1979), 165–81.

Bevington, David, *Tudor drama and politics: a critical approach to topical meaning*. Cambridge, Mass., 1968.

Bien, Günther, *Grundlegung der politischen Philosophie bei Aristoteles*. Freiburg-Munich, 1973.

Bigane, John E., III, *Faith, Christ or Peter: Matthew 16:18 in sixteenth century Roman catholic exegesis*. Washington, 1981.

Billanovich, Eugenio, 'Intorno a Romolo Amaseo', *Italia medioevale e umanistica*, XXII (1979), 531–3.

Bindoff, S. T., ed., *The house of commons 1509–1558*. London, 1982.

Bisaccia, Giuseppe, *La 'Repubblica fiorentina' di Donato Giannotti*. Florence, 1978.

Blaim, Artur, 'More's *Utopia*: persuasion or polyphony?', *Moreana*, XIX (1982), 5–20.

Block, Joseph, 'Thomas Cromwell's patronage of preaching', *SCJ*, VIII (1977), 37–50.

Boase, C. W., *Register of the university of Oxford*, I, *1449–63 and 1505–71*. Oxford historical society, I (1884).

Bonini, Cissie Rafferty, 'Richard Morison, humanist and reformer under Henry VIII', unpublished Ph.D. thesis, Stanford University, 1974.

Borinski, Ludwig and Claus Uhlig, *Literatur der Renaissance*. Düsseldorf and Bern, 1975.

Bouwsma, W. J., 'The two faces of humanism. Stoicism and augustinianism in renaissance thought', in Heiko A. Oberman and Thomas A. Brady, jun., eds., *Itinerarium italicum: the profile of the Italian renaissance in the mirror of its European transformations*. Leiden, 1975, 3–60.

  Venice and the defense of republican liberty: renaissance values in the age of the counter-reformation. Berkeley, 1968.

Boyle, Marjorie O'Rourke, 'Erasmus and the "modern question": was he semi-Pelagian?', *ARG*, LXXV (1984), 59–77.

Bradshaw, Brendan, 'The Tudor commonwealth: reform and revision', *HJ*, XXII, 455–76.

Brady, Thomas A., jun., *Ruling class, regime and reformation at Strassbourg 1520–1555*. Leiden, 1978.

Braudel, Fernand, *The mediterranean and the mediterranean world in the age of Philip II*, trans. Sian Reynolds. New York, 1972.

Brewer, J. S., *et al.*, eds., *Letters and papers, foreign and domestic of the reign of Henry VIII*. London, 1862–1932.

Briquet, C. M., *Les filigranes. Dictionnaire historique des marques du papier*. Paris, 1907.

Brockliss, L. W. B., 'Patterns of attendance at the university of Paris, 1400–1800', *HJ*, XXI:3 (1978), 503–44.

Brown, Rawdon, ed., *Calendar of state papers and manuscripts, relating to English affairs in the archives and collections of Venice*, IV and V. London, 1871–3.

Brugi, Biagio, 'L'università dei giuristi in Padova nel cinquecento', *Archivio veneto-tridentino* (1922), 1–92.

Burnet, Gilbert, *The history of the reformation of the church of England*, ed. Nicholas Pocock. Oxford, 1865.

Burns, J. H., '*Politia regalis & optima*: the political ideas of John Mair', *History of political thought*, II:1 (1981), 31–62.

Burton, Kathleen M., ed., Thomas Starkey, *A dialogue between Reginald Pole and Thomas Lupset*. London, 1948.

Cairns, Christopher, *Domenico Bollani, bishop of Brescia. Devotion to church and state in the republic of Venice in the sixteenth century*. Nieuwkoop, 1976.

  Pietro Aretino and the republic of Venice: researches on Aretino and his circle in Venice 1527–1556. Florence, 1985.

Calasso, Francesco, 'Bartolo', *DBI*.

Cantimori, Delio, *Eretici italiani del cinquecento. Ricerche storiche*. Florence, 1977; reprint of 1939 edition.

  'Rhetoric and politics in Italian humanism', *Journal of the Warburg and Courtauld Institutes*, I (1937–8), 183–202.

  'Submission and conformity: "nicodemism" and the expectations of a conciliar solution to the religious question', in Eric Cochrane, trans. and ed., *The late Italian renaissance 1525–1630*. London, 1970, 244–65.

Caponetto, Salvatore, ed., *Il 'beneficio di Cristo' con le versione del secolo XVI, documenti e testimonianze*. Florence, 1972.

Carlyle, A. J. and R. W., *A history of medieval political theory in the west*. Edinburgh, 1903–36.

Carroll, Linda L., 'Carnival rites as vehicles of protest in renaissance Venice', *SCJ*, XVI (1985), 487–502.

Caspari, Fritz, *Humanism and the social order in Tudor England*. Chicago, 1954.

Castiglione, Baldesar, *Il libro del cortegiano*, ed. Vittorio Cian. Florence, n.d., but fourth Sansoni edition.

Cervelli, Innocenzo, *Machiavelli e la crisi dello stato veneziano*. Naples, 1974.

Chambers, R. W., *Thomas More*. Ann Arbor, 1958; reprint of 1935 edition.

Chrimes, S. B., *English constitutional ideas in the fifteenth century*. Cambridge, 1936.

Christie, Sharon Kay, 'Richard Morison: an analysis of his life and work', unpublished Ph.D. thesis, West Virginia University, 1978.

Church, F. C., *The Italian reformers, 1534–1564*. New York, 1932.

Cian, Vittorio, *Un decennio della vita di M. Pietro Bembo (1521–1531)*. Turin, 1885.

Cianflone, Gregorio, *Un poeta latino del XVI secolo. Giano Teseo Casopero. I suoi amici – i suoi tempi*. Naples, 1950.

Cicero, Marcus Tullius, *De inventione*, ed. and trans. H. J. Hubbell. Cambridge, Mass., 1968.

De oratore, ed. E. W. Sutton and H. Rackham. Cambridge and London, 1942.

Clarke, H. A., *The history of the ancient parish of Wrenbury (including Combermere Abbey)*. Privately printed, n.d.

Coing, Helmut, ed., *Handbuch der Quellen und Literaturen der neueren europäischen Privatrechtsgeschichte*, II, *Neuere Zeit (1100–1500)*: Teil I, *Wissenschaften*. Munich, 1972.

'Die juristische Fakultät und ihr Lehrprogramm', in H. Coing, ed., *Handbuch der Quellen und Literaturen der neueren europäischen Privatrechtsgeschichte*, II:1, 3–102.

Coleman, Christopher and David Starkey, eds., *Revolution reassessed: revisions in the history of Tudor government and administration*. Oxford, 1986.

Colet, John, *Enarratio in epistolam S. Pauli ad Romanos. Latin text with translation by J. H. Lupton*. Ridgewood, N.J., 1965; reprint of 1873 edition.

Opuscula quaedam theologica. Translated and edited by J. H. Lupton. London, 1876.

Collett, Barry, *Italian Benedictine scholars and the reformation*. Oxford, 1985.

Collingwood, R. G., *The idea of history*. New York, 1956.

Collins, Ardis B., *The secular is sacred: platonism and thomism in Marsilio Ficino's platonic theology*. The Hague, 1974.

Condren, Conal, 'Democracy and the *Defensor pacis*: on the English language tradition of Marsilian interpretation', *Pensiero politico*, XIII:3 (1980), 301–16.

The status and appraisal of classic texts: an essay on political theory, its inheritance, and the history of ideas. Princeton, 1985.

Contarini, Gasparo, *De magistratibus et republica venetorum*, in *Opera*, V, 259–326. Paris: Sebastian Nivel, 1571.

Copleston, F. C., *A history of philosophy: late medieval and renaissance philosophy*, III:1. Garden City, N.J., 1963.

Corrie, G. E., ed., *Sermons and remains of Hugh Latimer*, II. Cambridge, 1845.

Corrigan, Philip and Derek Sayre, *The great arch: English state formation as cultural revolution*. Oxford, 1985.

Cosenza, Mario E., *Biographical and bibliographical dictionary of the Italian humanists*. Boston, 1962.

Coward, Barry, *The Stanleys, lords Stanley and earls of Derby, 1385–1672. The origins, wealth and power of a landowning family*. Manchester, 1983.

Deakins, Roger, 'The Tudor prose dialogue: genre and anti-genre', *Studies in English literature, 1500–1800*, XX (1980), 5–23.

Devereux, E. J., *A checklist of English translations of Erasmus to 1700*. Oxford, 1968.

Dewar, Mary, *Sir Thomas Smith: a Tudor intellectual in office*. London, 1964.

Dickens, A. G. and John M. Tonkin with Kenneth Powell, *The reformation in historical thought*. Cambridge, Mass., 1985.

Dionisotti, Carlo, 'Bembo, Pietro', *DBI*.

Dittrich, Franz, *Gasparo Contarini, 1483–1542. Eine Monographie*. Nieuwkoop, 1972; reprint of 1885 edition.

   Regesten und Briefen des Cardinals Gasparo Contarini (1483–1542). Braunsberg, 1881.

Dolan, John P., *History of the reformation. A conciliatory assessment*. New York, 1965.

Donaldson, Peter S., 'Machiavelli, antichrist, and the reformation: prophetic typology in Reginald Pole's *De unitate* and *Apologia ad Carolum quintum*', in Richard L. DeMolen, ed., *Leaders of the reformation*. Selinsgrove, 1984, 211–46.

Donvito, Luigi, 'La "religione cittadina" e le nuove prospettive sul Cinquecento religioso italiano', *Rivista di storia e letteratura religiosa*, XIX (1983), 431–74.

Douglas, Richard M., *Jacopo Sadoleto (1473–1547), humanist and reformer*. Cambridge, Mass., 1959.

Dowling, Maria, 'Anne Boleyn and reform', *Journal of ecclesiastical history*, XXXV (1984), 30–46.

   'Education of men and women of the early Tudor merchant class: the Withypoll family of London'. Unpublished paper.

   Humanism in the reign of Henry VIII. London, 1986.

   'Humanist support for Katherine of Aragon', *Bulletin of the institute of historical research*, LVII (1984), 46–55.

Driver, J. T., *Cheshire in the later middle ages*. Chester, 1971.

Dudith, Andras, *Vita Reginaldi Poli*, in *ERP*, I, 1–65.

Dudley, Edmund, *The tree of commonwealth*, ed. D. M. Brodie. Cambridge, 1948.

Dudon, Paul, *St Ignatius of Loyola*. Milwaukee, 1949.

Dunn, Thomas F., 'The development of the text of Pole's *De unitate ecclesiae*', *Papers of the bibliographical society of America*, LXX (1976), 455–68.

Dupuigrenet-Desrousilles, François, 'L'università di Padova dal 1405 al concilio di Trento', in Girolamo Arnaldi and M. Pastore Stocchi, eds., *Storia della cultura veneta*, III:2, *Dal primo quattrocento al concilio di Trento*. Vicenza, 1980, 607–47.

Dupuy, R. Ernest and Trevor N. Dupuy, *The encyclopedia of military history from 3500 B.C. to the present*. New York, 1970.

Dyke, Paul van, 'Reginald Pole and Thomas Cromwell: an examination of the *Apologia ad Carolum quintum*', *American historical review*, IX (1904), 696–724.

Egnazio, Giovanni Battista, *De caesaribus libri III a dictatore Caesare ad Constantinum Palaeologum, hinc a Carolo Magno ad Maximilianum caesarem*. Venice: Manutius, 1516.

Ehses, Stephan, ed., *Römische Dokumente zur Geschichte der Ehescheidung Heinrichs VIII von England 1527–1534*. Paderborn, 1893.

Elliott, J. H., 'Revolution and continuity in early modern Europe', *Past and present*, XLII (1969), 35–56.

Elton, G. R., ed., *The new Cambridge modern history*, II, *The reformation*. Cambridge, 1958.

'The body of the whole realm': parliament and representation in medieval and Tudor England. Charlottesville, Virginia, 1969.

England 1200–1640. London, 1969.

'The political creed of Thomas Cromwell', in *Studies in Tudor and Stuart politics and government*, II, *Parliament/political thought*. Cambridge, 1974, 215–35.

Policy and police: the enforcement of the reformation in the age of Thomas Cromwell. Cambridge, 1972.

'Politics and the pilgrimage of grace', in Barbara C. Malament, ed., *After the reformation: essays in honor of J. H. Hexter*. Philadelphia, 1980, 25–56.

Reform and reformation. England 1509–1558. Cambridge, Mass., 1977.

Reform and renewal: Thomas Cromwell and the common weal. Cambridge, 1973.

'Reform by statute: Thomas Starkey's *Dialogue* and Thomas Cromwell's policy', *Proceedings of the British academy*, LIV (1968), 165–88.

The Tudor constitution: documents and commentary. Cambridge, 1960; first edition.

The Tudor revolution in government: administrative changes in the reign of Henry VIII. Cambridge, 1953.

Emden, A. B., *A biographical register of the university of Oxford A.D. 1501 to 1540*. Oxford, 1974.

Farge, James K., *A biographical register of Paris doctors of theology, 1500–1536*. Toronto, 1980.

Fenlon, Dermot, *Heresy and obedience in Tridentine Italy: cardinal Pole and the counter reformation*. Cambridge, 1972.

Ferguson, A. B., *The articulate citizen and the English renaissance*. Durham, NC, 1965.

Clio unbound: perception of the social and cultural past in renaissance England. Durham, NC, 1979.

Ferrai, L. A., 'Pier Paolo Vergerio il giovane a Padova', *Archivio storico per Trieste, l'Istria ed il Trentino*, II (1883), 72–8.

Firpo, Luigi, ed., *Ambasciatori veneti in Inghilterra*. Turin, 1978.

Appunti e testi per la storia dell'antimachiavellismo. Turin, n.d.

Firpo, Massimo, Review of Marcantonio Flaminio, *Lettere*, ed. Alessandro Pastore, *Rivista storica italiana*, XCI (1979), 653–62.

Fish, Stanley Eugene, *John Skelton's·poetry*. New Haven, 1965.

Floriani, Piero, *Bembo e Castiglione: Studi sul classicismo del Cinquecento*. Rome, 1976.

Fortescue, John, *The governance of England*, ed. Charles Plummer. Oxford, 1885.

De laudibus legum Anglie, ed. S. B. Chrimes. Cambridge, 1942.

Foster Watson, J., *Las relaccions de Juan Lluis Vives amb es anglesos i amb l'Angleterra*. Barcelona, 1918.

Fox, Alistair and John Guy, *Reassessing the Henrician age: humanism, politics and reform 1500–1550*. Oxford, 1986.

Fragnito, Gigliola, 'Cultura umanistica e riforma religiosa: Il "De officio viri boni ac probi episcopi"', *Studi veneziani*, XI (1969), 75–189.

Franklin, Julian H., 'Jean Bodin and the end of medieval constitutionalism', in Horst

Denzer, ed., *Jean Bodin: Verhandlungen der internationalen Bodin Tagung in München*. Munich, 1973, 151–66.

Friedensburg, Walter, 'Beiträge zum Briefwechsel der katholischen Gelehrten Deutschlands in der Reformationszeit', *Zeitschrift für Kirchengeschichte*, XXIII (1902), 110–55.

Galen, *Methodus medendi, vel de moribus curandis*, ed. Thomas Linacre. Paris: Didier Maheu, 1519.

Garin, Eugenio, *Storia della filosofia italiana*, II. Turin, 1966.

L'Umanesimo italiano. Filosofia e vita civile nel rinascimento. Bari, 1965.

Gasquet, Adrian, *Cardinal Pole and his early friends*. London, 1927.

de Gazangos, Pascual, *et al.*, eds., *Calendar of letters, despatches and state papers relating to the negotiations between England and Spain*. London, 1862–1954.

Gee, John Archer, *The life and works of Thomas Lupset with a critical text of the original treatises and the letters*. New Haven, 1928.

Geerken, John H., 'Pocock and Machiavelli: structuralist explanation and history', *Journal of the history of philosophy*, XVII (1979), 309–18.

Gerson, Jean, *De potestate ecclesiastica*, in *Oeuvres complètes*, VI, ed. P. Glorieux, *L'oeuvre écclesiologique*. Paris, 1965.

Gewirth, Alan, *Marsilius of Padua and medieval political philosophy*. vol. I of *Marsilius of Padua. The defender of peace*. New York, 1951.

'Republicanism and absolutism in the thought of Marsilius of Padua', *Medioevo*, V (1979), 23–48.

Ghisalberti, A. M., ed., *Dizionario biografico degli italiani*. Rome, 1960–.

Giannotti, Donato, *Lettere a Piero Vettori*, ed. Roberto Ridolfi and Cecil Roth. Florence, 1932.

Della repubblica fiorentina, in Giovanni Rosini, ed., *Opere*, I. Pisa, 1819.

Della repubblica de' Veneziani, in *Opere*, II.

Gibson, Strickland, ed., *Statuta antiqua universitatis oxoniensis*. Oxford, 1931.

Giganti da Fossombrone, Antonio, 'Vita di Monsignor Lodovico Beccadelli', in Morandi, ed., *Monumenta*, I, 1–68.

Gilbert, Felix, 'The date of the composition of Contarini's and Giannotti's books on Venice', *Studies in the renaissance*, XIV (1967), 172–84.

'Religion and politics in the thought of Gasparo Contarini', in T. K. Rabb and J. E. Seigel, eds., *Action and conviction in early modern Europe*. Princeton, 1969, 90–116.

'The Venetian constitution in Florentine political thought', in Nicolai Rubinstein, ed., *Florentine studies*. London, 1968, 463–500.

'Venice in the crisis of the league of Cambrai', in *History: choice and commitment*. Cambridge, Mass., 1977, 247–67.

Gilkey, Dennis M., 'The *Colloquies* of Erasmus and the literature of the renaissance: drama, satire and dialogue', unpublished Ph.D. thesis, University of Colorado, 1983.

Gilmore, Myron, 'Myth and reality in Venetian political theory', in J. R. Hale, ed., *Renaissance Venice*. Totowa, N.J., 1973, 431–43.

Gleason, Elizabeth G., 'Cardinal Gasparo Contarini (1483–1542) and the beginning of catholic reform', unpublished Ph.D. thesis, University of California, Berkeley, 1963.

'On the nature of sixteenth-century Italian evangelism: scholarship, 1953–1978', *SCJ*, IX (1978), 3–25.

ed. and trans., *Reform thought in sixteenth century Italy*. Chico, Calif., 1981.

Grabmann, Martin, 'Die mittelalterliche Kommentare zur Politik des Aristoteles', *Sitzungsberichte der Bayerischen Akademie der Wissenschaften. Philosophische-historische Abteilung*, II, no. 10 (1941), 63ff.

Gray, Hanna H., 'Renaissance humanism: the pursuit of eloquence', originally in *Journal of the history of ideas*, XXIV (1963), reprinted in P. O. Kristeller and P. P. Wiener, eds., *Renaissance essays*, 199–216.

Greenblatt, Stephen, *Renaissance self-fashioning, from More to Shakespeare*. Chicago, 1980.

Gregory, Tullio, ed., *Grande antologia filosofica*, VI, *Il pensiero della rinascenza e della riforma*. Milan, 1964.

Guy, J. A., 'Privy council: revolution or evolution?' in C. Coleman and D. Starkey, eds., *Revolution reassessed*, 59–85.

The public career of Sir Thomas More. New Haven, 1980.

Hallé, Marie (writing as Martin Haile), *Life of Reginald Pole*. London, 1911.

Hanson, Donald W., *From kingdom to commonwealth: the development of civic consciousness in English political thought*. Cambridge, Mass., 1970.

Harcourt, L. W. V., *His grace the steward and the trial of peers*. London, 1907.

Hariman, Robert, 'Composing modernity in *The prince*', *Journal of the history of ideas*, L (1989), forthcoming.

Harris, Barbara J., *Edward Stafford, third duke of Buckingham, 1478–1521*. Stanford, 1986.

Hartmann, Alfred, ed., *Die Amerbach Korrespondenz*, II. Basel, 1943.

Headley, John M., 'Gattinara, Erasmus and the imperial configuration of humanism', *ARG*, LXXI (1980), 64–98.

Heck, Eberhard, *Die Bezeugung von Ciceros Schrift De re publica*. Hildesheim, 1966.

Heiserman, A. R., *Skelton and satire*. Chicago, 1961.

Hennessy, George, ed., *Novum repertorium ecclesiasticum parochiale londinense*. London, 1898.

Herrtage, S. J., *England in the reign of Henry VIII*, I, *Starkey's life and letters*. EETS extra ser., XXXII (1878).

Hexter, J. H., *The vision of politics on the eve of the reformation: More, Machiavelli, and Seyssel*. New York, 1973.

Higham, F. M. G., 'A note on the pre-Tudor secretary', in A. G. Little and F. M. Powicke, eds., *Essays in medieval history presented to T. F. Tout*. Manchester, 1925, 361–7.

Hill, Christopher, *Intellectual origins of the English revolution*. Oxford, 1980; corrected reprint of 1965 edition.

'James Harrington and the people', in *Puritanism and revolution: studies in interpretation of the English revolution of the 17th century*. London, 1962, 299–313.

Hirsch, E. D., *Validity in interpretation*. New Haven, 1967.

Hirsh, Edward L., 'The life and works of George Lily', unpublished Ph.D. thesis, Yale University, 1935.

Hirzel, Rudolf, *Der Dialog. Ein Literarhistorischer Versuch*. Leipzig, 1895.

Hofmann, Hasso. *Repräsentation. Studien zur Begriffsgeschichte von der Antike bis ins 19. Jahrhundert*. Berlin, 1974.

Hook, Walter Farquhar, *Lives of the archbishops of Canterbury*, VIII. London, 1869.

Hoynck van Papendrecht, Cornelius Paulus, *Analecta ad historiam scissi Belgii potissimum attirentia*. The Hague, 1743.

Hudson, Winthrop D., *John Ponet (1516?–1556). Advocate of limited monarchy.* Chicago, 1942.

Hughes, Philip, *The reformation in England,* I, 'The king's proceedings'. London, 1950.

Hunt, Ernest William, *Dean Colet and his theology.* London, 1956.

Huppert, George, 'The idea of civilization in the sixteenth century', in Anthony Molho and J. A. Tedeschi, eds., *Renaissance studies in honor of Hans Baron.* De Kalb, Ill., 1971, 759–69.

Immel, Gerhard, Review of M. Ascheri, *Giovanni Francesco Sannazari della Ripa,* in *Zeitschrift der Savigny-Stiftung für Rechtsgeschichte, Romanische Abteilung,* LXXXIX (1972), 487.

Ives, E. W., *Anne Boleyn.* Oxford, 1986.

'Court and county palatine in the reign of Henry VIII', *Transactions of the historic society of Lancashire and Cheshire,* CXXIII (1972), 1–38.

'Faction at the court of Henry VIII: the fall of Anne Boleyn', *History,* LVII (1972), 169–88.

ed., *Letters and accounts of William Brereton of Malpas. Record society of Lancashire and Cheshire,* CXVI (1976).

Jardine, Lisa, *Bacon: discovery and the art of discourse.* Cambridge, 1974.

'The place of dialectic teaching in sixteenth-century Cambridge', *Studies in the renaissance,* XXI (1974), 31–62.

Jayne, Sears, *John Colet and Marsilio Ficino,* Oxford, 1963.

Library catalogues of the English renaissance. Foxbury Meadow, 1983; reprint of 1956 edition with new notes.

Jedin, Hubert, 'Pflug, Julius', *Lexikon für Theologie und Kirche.* Freiburg, 1957–68.

Studien über die Schriftstellerartigkeit Albert Pigges. Münster, 1931.

Jones, Norman L., *Faith by statute: parliament and the settlement of religion 1559.* London, 1982.

Jones, Richard Foster, *The triumph of the English language: a survey of opinions concerning the vernacular from the introduction of printing to the restoration.* Stanford, 1953.

Jongh, H. de, *L'ancienne faculté de theologie de Louvain au premier siècle de son existence (1432–1540).* Utrecht, 1980; reprint of 1911 edition.

Kampen, Jan, van, *Commentariolus in duas divi Pauli epistolas . . . alteram ad Romanos, alteram ad Galatos.* Cracow: Matthias Scharffenberg, 1534.

Kaufman, Peter Iver, *Augustinian piety and catholic reform: Augustine, Colet and Erasmus.* Macon, Ga., 1982.

'Polydore Vergil and the strange disappearance of Christopher Urswick', *SCJ,* XVII (1986), 69–85.

Kelley, Donald R., 'Civil science in the renaissance: jurisprudence Italian style', *HJ,* XXII (1979), 777–94.

'Horizons of intellectual history: retrospect, circumspect, prospect', *Journal of the history of ideas,* XLVIII (1987), 143–69.

'*Vera philosophia*: the philosophical significance of renaissance jurisprudence', *Journal of the history of philosophy,* XIV (1976), 267–79.

Keohane, Nannerl O., *Philosophy and the state in France: the renaissance to the enlightenment.* Princeton, 1980.

Kessel, Peter J. van, 'The denominational pluriformity of the German nation at Padua and the problem of intolerance in the 16th century', *ARG,* LXXV (1984), 256–76.

Keussen, Hermann, ed., *Der Matrikel der Universität Köln*. Bonn, 1892 and 1919.
Kidd, B. J., ed. *Documents illustrative of the continental reformation*. Oxford, 1911.
King, John N., *English reformation literature: the Tudor origins of the protestant tradition*. Princeton, 1982.
King, Margaret L., *Venetian humanism in an age of patrician dominance*. Princeton, 1986.
Kingdon, Robert M., *The political thought of Peter Martyr Vermigli: selected texts and commentary*. Geneva, 1980.
Knecht, R. J., *Francis I*. Cambridge, 1982.
Kristeller, P. O., and P. P. Wiener, eds., *Renaissance essays from the Journal of the history of ideas*. New York, 1968.
LaCapra, Dominick, 'Rethinking intellectual history and reading texts', in Dominick LaCapra and Steven L. Kaplan, eds., *Modern European intellectual history: reappraisals and new perspectives*. Ithaca, N.Y., 1982, 43–85.
Lanham, Richard A., *The motives of eloquence: literary rhetoric in the renaissance*. New Haven, 1976.
Leader, D. R., 'Professorships and academic reform at Cambridge', *SCJ*, XIV (1983), 215–27.
Lechner, Joan M., *Renaissance concepts of the commonplaces*. New York, 1962.
Lehmberg, S. E., 'English humanists, the reformation and the problem of counsel', *ARG*, LII (1961), 74–90.
    The reformation of cathedrals. Princeton: forthcoming.
    The reformation parliament 1529–1536. Cambridge, 1970.
Le Neve, John, *Fasti ecclesiae anglicanae 1300–1541*, XII, compiled Joyce M. Horn. London, 1967.
Leonico, Niccolò, *Conversio atque explanatio primi libri Aristotelis de partibus animalium*. Basel: Bartholomew Westhemer, 1541.
    Dialogi. Venice: Gregorio de Gregoriis, 1524.
    Dialogi, 2d ed. Louvain: Sebastian Gryphius, 1542.
Lewkenor, Lewes, *The commonwealth and government of Venice*. London: Windet, 1599; STC 5642.
Libby, Lester J., 'Venetian history and political thought after 1509', *Studies in the renaissance*, XX (1973), 7–45.
Lobel, E., 'Cardinal Pole's manuscripts', *Proceedings of the British academy*, 1931, 97–101.
Lockyer, Andrew, 'Traditions as context in the history of political thought', *Political studies*, XXVII (1979), 201–17.
Logan, George M., *The meaning of More's 'Utopia'*. Princeton, 1983.
    'Substance and form in renaissance humanism', *Journal of medieval and renaissance studies*, VII (1977), 1–34.
Lohr, Charles, 'Renaissance Latin Aristotle commentaries', *RQ*, XXX (1977), 681–741.
Lumby, R. J., ed., *Polychronicon Ranulphi Higden monachi cestrensis*. Rolls series, XLI, vol. VIII. London, 1882.
Lupset, Thomas, *An Exhortation to yonge men*. In Gee, *Lupset*, 233–62.
    A treatise of charitie. In Gee, *Lupset*, 205–31.
    A treatise of dieyng wel. In Gee, *Lupset*, 263–90.
Lupton, J. H., *A life of John Colet*. London, 1909.
Macray, W. Dunn, *A register of St Mary Magdalen college, Oxford, from the*

foundation of the college, I, *Fellows to the year 1520*, and II, *Fellows 1522–1575*. London, 1894 and 1897.

McConica, J. K., *English humanists and reformation politics under Henry VIII and Edward VI*. Oxford, 1965.

ed., *The history of the university of Oxford*, III, *The collegiate university*. Oxford, 1986.

'The rise of the undergraduate college', in McConica, *University of Oxford*, 1–68.

McFarlane, K. B., *The nobility of later medieval England*. Oxford, 1973.

McNair, Philip, *Peter Martyr in Italy: an anatomy of apostasy*. Oxford, 1967.

Maddison, Carol, *Marcantonio Flaminio. Poet, humanist, reformer*. London, 1965.

Maitland, Frederick William, *English law and the renaissance*. Cambridge, 1901.

Major, J. Russell, *Representative institutions in renaissance France, 1421–1559*. Madison, 1960.

Mallett, C. E., *A history of the university of Oxford*, I, *The medieval university and the colleges founded in the middle ages*, and II, *The sixteenth and seventeenth centuries*. Oxford, 1924.

Mantova Benavides, Marco, *Observationes legalium libri X*. Louvain: Beringi, 1546.

Marangoni, Giuseppe, 'Lazzaro Bonamico e lo studio padovano nella prima metà del Cinquecento', II, *Nuovo archivio veneto*, n.s. II (no. 42), 301–18; III (no. 43), 131–96 (all 1901).

Maranini, Giuseppe, *La costituzione di Venezia*, II. Florence, 1974; reprint of 1927 edition.

Marius, Richard, *Thomas More. A biography*. New York, 1984.

Marsilio of Padua, *Defensor pacis*, ed. C. W. Previté-Orton, Cambridge, 1928.

Martellozzo Forin, E., ed., *Acta graduum academicorum gymnasii patavini ab anno 1501 ad annum 1525*. Padua, 1969.

Acta graduum academicorum ab anno 1526 ad annum 1537. Padua, 1970.

Mattei, Rodolfo de, 'Il problema della tirannide nel pensiero politico italiano del cinque e del seicento', in *Studi in memoria di Orazio Condorelli*, I, 370–99. Milan,1974.

Mattingly, Garrett, *Renaissance diplomacy*. Baltimore, 1955.

Mayer, T. F., 'A diet for Henry VIII: the failure of Reginald Pole's 1537 legation', *Journal of British studies*, XXVI:3 (1987), 305–31.

'Divine intervention in Reginald Pole's confrontation with Henry VIII', paper presented at the North American Conference on British Studies meeting, Toronto, 1984.

'Faction and ideology: Thomas Starkey's *Dialogue*', *HJ*, XXVIII:1 (1985), 1–25.

'Marco Mantova, a bronze age conciliarist', *Annuarium historiae conciliorum*, XIV (1984), 385–408.

'Marco Mantova and the Paduan religious crisis of the early sixteenth century', *Cristianesimo nella storia*, VII (1986), 41–61.

'A mission worse than death: Reginald Pole and the Parisian theologians', *English historical review*, CIII (October, 1988), 870–91.

'Reginald Pole in Paolo Giovio's *Descriptio*: a strategy for reconversion', *SCJ*, XVI (1985), 431–50.

'The sources of the political ideas of Thomas Starkey', unpublished MA thesis, Michigan State University, 1977.

'Starkey and Melanchthon on adiaphora: a critique of W. Gordon Zeeveld', *SCJ*, XI (1980), 39–49.

'Thomas Starkey's aristocratic reform programme', *History of political thought*, VII:3 (1986), 439–61.

Mazzacurati, Giancarlo, *Conflitti di culture nel cinquecento*. Naples, 1977.

Mehl, James V., 'The first printed editions of the history of church councils', *Annuarium historiae conciliorum*, XVIII (1986), 128–43.

Mendle, Michael, *Dangerous positions: mixed government, the estates of the realm, and the making of the answer to the XIX propositions*. University, Al., 1985.

Merriman, R. B., *Life and letters of Thomas Cromwell*. Oxford, 1902.

Merzbacher, F., 'Die Kirchen- und Staatsgewalt bei J. Almain', in Hans Lentze and Inge Gampl, eds., *Speculum juris et ecclesiarum. Festschrift W. M. Plöchl*. Vienna, 1967, 301–12.

Meschini, Anna, 'Inediti greci di Lazaro Bonamico', *Medioevo e umanesimo*, XXXV (1979), 51–68.

Miller, Helen, *Henry VIII and the English nobility*. Oxford, 1986.

Mingay, G. E., *The gentry: the rise and fall of a ruling class*. London, 1976.

Mitchell, W. T., ed., *Epistolae academicae 1508–1596*. Oxford historical society, n.s., XXVI (1980).

More, Thomas, *Utopia*, ed. J. H. Hexter and Edward Surtz. New Haven, 1964.

Moreau, J.-P., *Rome ou l'Angleterre? Les réactions politiques des catholiques anglais au moment du schisme, 1529–1553*. Paris, 1984.

Moria, Giancarlo, 'Struttura logica e consapevolezza epistemologica in alcuni trattatisti padovani di medicina del sec. XV', in *Scienza e filosofia all'università di Padova nel Quattrocento*, ed. A. Poppi. Triest-Padua, 1983.

Morris, Christopher, *Political thought in England. Tyndale to Hooker*. London, 1953.

Mozley, J. F., *Coverdale and his Bibles*. London, 1953.

Muir, Edward, *Civic ritual in renaissance Venice*. Princeton, 1981.

Muller, J. A., ed., *The letters of Stephen Gardiner*. Cambridge, 1937.

Murphy, Virginia M., 'The debate over Henry VIII's first divorce: an analysis of the contemporary treatises', unpublished Ph.D. thesis, Cambridge University, 1984.

Nardi, Bruno, *Saggi sull'aristotelismo padovano dal secolo XIV al XVI*. Florence, 1958.

Nardi, Paolo, *Mariano Socini, giureconsulto senese del quattrocento*. Milan, 1974.

Nelson, William, ed., *A fifteenth century school book*. Oxford, 1956.

Newcombe, David Gordon, '"Due order & reasonabul mean". Thomas Starkey and the Anglican *via media*', unpublished STM thesis, General Theological Seminary, New York, 1982.

Nicholson, Graham, 'The nature and function of historical argument in the Henrician reformation', unpublished Ph.D. thesis, Cambridge University, 1977.

Nieto, Jose C. *Juan de Valdes and the origins of the Spanish and Italian reformation*. Geneva, 1970.

Noreña, Carlos G., *Juan Luis Vives*. The Hague, 1970.

Norbrook, David, *Poetry and politics in the English renaissance*. London, 1984.

Oakley, Francis, 'Almain and Major: conciliar theory on the eve of the reformation', *American historical review*, LXX (1965), 673–90.

'Conciliarism in the sixteenth century: Jacques Almain again', *ARG*, LXVIII (1977), 111–32.

'Legitimation by consent: the question of the medieval roots', *Viator*, XIV (1983), 303–35.

The political thought of Pierre d'Ailly. The voluntarist tradition. New Haven, 1964.

'On the road from Constance to 1688: the political thought of John Major and George Buchanan', *Journal of British studies*, I:2 (1962), 1–31.

O'Kelly, Bernard and Catherine A. L. Jarrott, eds., *John Colet's commentary on First Corinthians.* Binghamton, NY, 1985.

Ong, Walter J., *Ramus, method and the decay of dialogue: from the art of discourse to the art of reason.* Cambridge, Mass., 1958.

Rhetoric, romance and technology. Ithaca, 1971.

Orme, Nicholas, 'An early Tudor Oxford schoolbook', *RQ*, XXXIV (1982), 11–39.

Education in the west of England 1066–1548. Exeter, 1976.

English schools in the middle ages. London, 1973.

Ormerod, George, *The history of the county palatine and city of Chester (including Leycester's Cheshire antiquities).* London, 1819.

The Oxford English dictionary. Oxford, 1971.

Pagden, Anthony, ed., *The languages of political theory in early-modern Europe.* Cambridge, 1987.

Page, William, ed., *VCH Hampshire and the Isle of Wight*, III. London, 1908.

ed., *VCH Sussex*, II. London, 1907.

Panziroli, Guido, *De claris legum interpretibus*, ed. Ottavio Panziroli. Venice, 1637.

Parekh, Bikhu and R. N. Berki, 'The history of political ideas: a critique of Q. Skinner's methodology', *Journal of the history of ideas*, XXIV (1973), 163–84.

Parks, George B., *The English traveller to Italy*, I, *The middle ages (to 1525).* Rome, 1954.

Paschini, Pio, ed., *Enciclopedia cattolica.* Vatican City, 1948–54, X.

Pascoe, L. B., 'Jean Gerson: mysticism, conciliarism and reform', *Annuarium historiae conciliorum*, VI (1974), 135–53.

Jean Gerson: principles of church reform. Leiden, 1973.

Pastor, Ludwig von, *The history of the popes, from the close of the middle ages*, trans. R. F. Kerr, XI. St Louis, 1950.

Pastore, Alessandro, 'Due biblioteche umanistiche del Cinquecento. (I libri del cardinal Pole e di Marcantonio Flaminio)', *Rinascimento*, ser. 2, XIX (1979), 269–90.

'Un corrispondente sconosciuto di Pietro Pomponazzi: il medico Giacomo Tiburzi da Pergola e le sue lettere', *Quaderni per la storia dell'università di Padova*, XVII (1984), 69–89.

Pastore Stocchi, Manlio, 'Marco Mantova Benavides e i trecentisti maggiori', in I. Favoretto, ed., *Marco Mantova Benavides. Il suo museo e la cultura padovana del Cinquecento.* Padua, 1984, 253–69.

Pecchioli, Renzo, *Dal 'mito' di Venezia all' 'ideologia americana': Itinerari e modelli della storiografia sul repubblicanesimo dell'età moderna.* Venice, 1983.

Perry, A. J., ed., *Dialogus inter militem et clericum, Richard Fitzralph's sermon: 'defensio curatorum' and Methodius: the begynnyng of the world and the end of worlds by John Trevisa.* EETS, o.s., CLXVII (1925).

Pevsner, Nikolaus, *The buildings of England: south and west Somerset.* Harmondsworth, 1958.

and Edward Hubbard, *The buildings of England: Cheshire.* Harmondsworth, 1971.

Piaia, Gregorio, '"Antiqui", "moderni" e "via moderna" in Marsilio da Padova', in A. Zimmermann, ed., *Antiqui und Moderni.* Berlin, 1974, 328–44.

'Democrazia e totalitarismo in Marsilio da Padova', *Medioevo*, II (1976), 363–76.

Marsilio da Padova nella riforma e nella controriforma. Fortuna ed interpretazione. Padua, 1977.

Pighe, Albert, 'Adversus furiosissimum librum Henrici Angliae regis et senatus eius', ed., Vinzenz Schweitzer, in *Concilium tridentinum*, XII. Freiburg, 1930.

Hierarchiae ecclesiasticae assertio. Cologne: Johann Nevizan, 1551.

Pigman, G. W., III 'Versions of imitation in the renaissance', *RQ*, XXXIII:1 (1980), 1–32.

Pineas, Rainer, *Thomas More and Tudor polemics.* Bloomington, 1968.

Pocock, J. G. A., *The ancient constitution and the feudal law: English historical thought in the seventeenth century.* New York, 1967.

'The history of political thought: a methodological enquiry', in P. Laslett and W. G. Runciman, eds., *Philosophy, politics and society*, ser. II. Oxford, 1962, 183–202.

The Machiavellian moment: Florentine political thought and the atlantic republican tradition. Princeton, 1975.

'*The Machiavellian moment* revisited: a study in history and ideology', *Journal of modern history*, LIII (1981), 49–72.

Politics, language and time: essays on political thought and history. New York, 1973.

'Time, institutions and action: an essay on traditions and their understanding', in Preston King and B. C. Parekh, eds., *Politics and experience: essays presented to Professor Michael Oakeshott on the occasion of his retirement.* Cambridge, 1968, 209–37.

Pole, Reginald, 'Apologia ad Carolum quintum caesarem', in *ERP*, I, 66–171.

Défense de l'unité de l'église, ed. Noëlle Marie Égretier. Paris, 1967.

'Epistola ad Eduardum VI Angliae regem', in *ERP*, IV, 306–54.

Pole's defense of the unity of the church, trans. and intro. Joseph G. Dwyer, Westminster, Md., 1965.

Reginaldi Poli ad Henricum octavum Britanniae regem, pro ecclesiasticae unitatis defensione. Rome: Antonio Blado, 1539(?).

A treatie of iustification. Louvain: John Fowler, 1569.

Pollet, J. V., ed., *Julius Pflug Correspondence*, I (*1510–39*). Leiden, 1969.

Post, Gaines, '*Plena potestas* and consent in medieval assemblies', in *Studies in medieval legal thought: public law and the state, 1100–1322.* Princeton, 1964, 91–162.

Postma, Folkert, *Viglius van Aytta als humanist en diplomaat.* Zutphen, 1983.

Pronay, Nicholas and John Taylor, eds., *Parliamentary texts of the later middle ages.* Oxford, 1980.

Prosperi, Adriano, *Tra evangelismo e controriforma: G. M. Giberti (1495–1543).* Rome, 1969.

Quirini, A. M., ed., *Epistolarum Reginaldi Poli.* Brescia, 1744–57.

Randall, John Herman, 'The development of scientific method in the school of Padua', originally in *The school of Padua and the emergence of modern science*. Padua, 1961. Reprinted in P. O. Kristeller and P. P. Wiener, eds., *Renaissance essays*, 215–51.

Rashdall, Hastings, *The universities of Europe in the middle ages*, ed. F. M. Powicke and A. B. Emden, I. Oxford, 1936.

Rawcliffe, Carole, *The Staffords, earls of Stafford and dukes of Buckingham.* Cambridge, 1978.

Richmond, Colin, 'After McFarlane', *History*, LXVIII (1983), 46–60.

Ripa, Giovanni Francesco Sannazzari della, *In primum decretalium librum commentarium*, in *Opera omnia*, V. Venice: Giunta, 1569.
Responsa in quinque libros decretalium. Venice: Giunta, 1569.
Roberti, Melchiorre, 'Il collegio padovano dei dottori giuridici nel secolo XVI', *Rivista italiana per le scienze giuridice*, XXXV (1903), 171–249.
Ronconi, Giorgio, 'Il giurista Lauro Palazzolo, la sua famiglia e l'attività oratoria, accademica e pubblica', *Quaderni per la storia dell'università di Padova*, XVII (1984), 3–65.
Ross, James Bruce, 'Gasparo Contarini and his friends', *Studies in the renaissance*, XVII (1970), 192–232.
'Venetian schools and teachers fourteenth to early sixteenth century: a survey and a study of Giovanni Battista Egnazio', *RQ*, XXIX (1976), 521–66.
Rossetti, Lucia, *L'università di Padova: Profilo storico*. Milan, 1972.
Rubinstein, Nicolai, 'The history of the word *politicus* in early modern Europe', in A. Pagden, ed., *The languages of political theory in early-modern Europe*, 41–56.
'Marsilio da Padova e il pensiero politico italiano del Trecento', *Medioevo*, V (1979), 143–62.
'Marsilius of Padua and Italian political thought of his time', in J. R. Hale, J. R. C. Highfield and B. Smalley, eds., *Europe in the late middle ages*. London, 1965, 44–75.
Rylands, J. P., ed., *The visitation of Cheshire, 1580*. Harleian Society, XVIII (1882).
Sadoleto, Jacopo, *Epistolae quotquot extant proprio nomine scriptae*, ed. V. A. Costanzi. Rome, 1760–4.
In epistolam ad Romanos commentariorum [libri], in *Opera*, IV.
Opera quae exstant omnia. Englewood, N.J., 1964; reprint of Verona, 1738 edition.
St Clair Byrne, Muriel, ed., *The Lisle letters*. Chicago, 1981.
Saitta, Giuseppe, *Il pensiero italiano nell'Umanesimo e nel rinascimento*, I. Florence, 1961.
Salter, H. E., ed., *Registrum annalium collegii Mertonensis 1483–1521*. Oxford historical society, LXXVI (1923).
Santangelo, Giorgio, *Il Bembo critico e il principio d'imitazione*. Florence, 1950.
ed., *Le epistole 'de imitatione' di Giovanfrancesco Pico della Mirandola e di Pietro Bembo*. Florence, 1954.
Santosuosso, Antonio, 'Pier Vettori e Benedetto Lampridio', *La bibliofilia*, LXXX (1978), 155–69.
Sarri, Francesco, 'Giovanni Fabrini da Figlione (1516–1580?)', *La rinascita*, II (1939), 617–40.
von Savigny, Friedrich Carl, *Geschichte des römischen Rechts im Mittelalter*, 2nd edn, III. Heidelberg, 1834.
Sawada, P. A., 'Two anonymous Tudor treatises on the general council', *Journal of ecclesiastical history*, XII (1961), 197–214.
Scarisbrick, J. J., *Henry VIII*. Berkeley, 1968.
The reformation and the English people. Oxford, 1984.
Scattergood, John, *John Skelton: the complete English poems*. New Haven, 1983.
Schenk, Wilhelm, *Reginald Pole, cardinal of England*. London, 1950.
Schillings, A., ed., *Matricule de l'université de Louvain*. Louvain, 1952–1967, III–IV.
Schmitt, Charles B., *Aristotle and the renaissance*. Cambridge, Mass., 1983.
Schottenloher, Karl, *Jakob Ziegler aus Landau an der Isar. Ein Gelehrtenleben aus der Zeit des Humanismus und der Reformation*. Münster, 1901.

Schutte, Anne Jacobsen, *Pier Paolo Vergerio: the making of an Italian reformer.* Geneva, 1977.
de Seyssel, Claude, *The monarchy of France*, trans. J. H. Hexter, ed. and intro. D. R. Kelley. New Haven, 1981.
Shapiro, Barbara, Review of Lauro Martines, *Society and history in English renaissance verse, American historical review*, XCI (1986), 1191.
Shennan, J. H., *The parlement of Paris.* Ithaca, 1968.
Simoncelli, Paolo, *Il caso Reginald Pole: eresia e santità nelle polemiche religiose del cinquecento.* Rome, 1977.
  Evangelismo italiano del cinquecento. Questione religiosa e nicodemismo politico. Rome, 1979.
  'Pietro Bembo e l'evangelismo italiano', *Critica storica*, XV (1978), 1–63.
Skeel, C. A. J., 'The influence of the writings of Sir John Fortescue', *Transactions of the royal historical society*, 3rd ser., X (1916), 77–114.
Skinner, Quentin, *Foundations of modern political thought*, I, *The renaissance*, and II, *The reformation.* Cambridge, 1978.
  'History and ideology in the English revolution', *HJ*, VIII (1965), 151–78.
  'The ideological context of Hobbes's political thought', *HJ*, IX (1966), 286–317.
  'The limits of historical explanation', *Philosophy,* XLI (1966), 199–215.
  Machiavelli. New York, 1981.
  'Meaning and understanding in the history of ideas', *History and theory*, VIII (1969), 3–53.
  'On performing and explaining linguistic actions', *Philosophical quarterly*, XXI (1971), 1–21.
  'Sir Thomas More's *Utopia* and the language of renaissance humanism', in A. Pagden, ed., *The languages of political theory in early–modern Europe*, 123–57.
  '"Social meaning" and the explanation of social action', in P. Laslett, W. G. Runciman and Q. Skinner, eds., *Philosophy, politics and society*, ser. IV. Oxford, 1972, 136–57.
  'Some problems in the analysis of political thought and action', *Political theory*, II (1974), 277–303.
Slavin, A. J., 'Profitable studies: humanists and government in early Tudor England', *Viator*, I (1970), 307–25.
Smith, Lacey Baldwin, *Treason in Tudor England: politics and paranoia.* Princeton, 1985.
  Tudor prelates and politics, 1536–1558. Princeton, 1953.
Somerset medieval wills. Somerset record society, XXI (1905).
Somerset record society, LV (1940).
Southern, A. C., *Elizabethan recusant prose 1559–1582.* London, 1950(?).
Speroni, Sperone, *Dialogo delle lingue*, ed. and trans. Helene Harth. Munich, 1975.
  Opera di M. Sperone Speroni degli Alvarotti, ed. Marco Forcellini and Natal dalle Laste. Venice, 1740.
Spini, Giorgio, 'Bibliografia delle opere di Antonio Brucioli', *La bibliofilia*, LII (1940), 129ff.
  Tra rinascimento e riforma: Antonio Brucioli. Florence, 1940.
Stanier, R. G., *Magdalen school. A history of Magdalen college school, Oxford.* Oxford historical society, n.s., III, 1940.
Starkey, David, 'The lords of the council: aristocracy, ideology and the formation of the Tudor privy council', paper delivered at the American Historical Association meeting in Chicago, December 1986.

'Public debate and public policy: the course of reform, 1440–1540'. Unpublished paper.

The reign of Henry VIII: personalities and politics. New York, 1985.

'Stewart serendipity: a missing text of the *Modus tenendi parliamentum*', *Fenway court 1986*, 39–51.

Starkey, Thomas, *An Exhortation to the people instructynge theym to Unitie and Obedience.* London: Thomas Berthelet, 1536; STC 23236.

Starn, Randolph, *Donato Giannotti and his epistolae.* Geneva, 1968.

Stella, Aldo, 'Tradizione razionalistica patavina e radicalismo spiritualistico nel XVI secolo', *Annali della scuola normale superiore di Pisa. Lettere, storia e filosofia*, ser. 2. XXXVII (1968), 275–302.

Stephen, Leslie and Sidney Lee, eds., *Dictionary of national biography.* Oxford, 1917.

Stintzing, Roderich, *Geschichte der deutschen Rechtswissenschaft.* Munich, 1880.

Stone, Lawrence and Jeanne C. Fawtier Stone, *An open elite? England 1540–1880.* Oxford, 1984.

Stout, Harry S., 'Marsilius of Padua and the Henrician reformation', *Church history*, XLIII (1973), 308–18.

Stow, John, *Survey of London and Westminster*, expanded by John Strype. London, 1720.

Strype, John, *Memorials of the most reverend father in God Thomas Cranmer*, II. Oxford, 1812.

Surtz, Edward, *Henry VIII's great matter in Italy: an introduction to representative Italians in the King's divorce, mainly 1527–1535.* Ann Arbor, 1978.

Tacchi Venturi, Pietro, *Storia della compagnia di Gesù in Italia*, II, *Dalla nascita del fondatore alla solenne approvazione dell'ordine (1491–1540).* Rome, 1922.

Tarlton, Charles D., 'History, meaning and revisionism in the study of political thought', *History and theory*, XII (1973), 307–28.

Tateo, Francesco, *Tradizione e realtà nell'Umanesimo italiano.* Bari, 1967.

Taylor, John, *The universal chronicle of Ranulf Higden.* Oxford, 1966.

Tedeschi, John A., 'Notes toward a genealogy of the Sozzini family', in *Italian reformation studies in honor of Laelius Socinus.* Florence, 1965, 275–318.

Terpening, Ronnie H., 'Pietro Bembo and the cardinalate: unpublished letters to Marco Mantova', *Lettere italiane*, XXXII (1980), 75–86.

Teule, Alexandre-Edilbert de, *Chronologie des docteurs en droit civil de l'université d'Avignon.* Paris, 1887.

Tierney, Brian, '"Divided sovereignty" at Constance: a problem of medieval and early modern political theory', *Annuarium historiae conciliorum*, VII (1975), 238–56.

Tolomeo da Lucca, *De regimine principum*, in Thomas Aquinas, *De regimine principum ad regem Cypri et de regimine judaeorum*, ed. Joseph Mathis. Turin, 1948.

Tracy, James D., 'Humanism and the reformation', in S. E. Ozment, ed., *Reformation Europe: a guide to research.* St Louis, 1982, 33–57.

Tuck, Richard, *Natural rights theories: their origin and development.* Cambridge, 1979.

Twyne, John, *De rebus Albionicis, Britannicis atque Anglicis, commentariorum libri duo*, ed. Thomas Twyne. London: Edmund Bollisant, 1590; STC 24407.

Ullmann, Walter, '*De Bartoli sententia: concilium repraesentat mentem populi*', in *Bartolo da Sassoferrato: studi e documenti per il VI centenario.* Milan, 1962, II, 705–34.

Valor ecclesiasticus tempore Henrici VIII auctoritate regia institutus. London?, 1810.

Vasoli, Cesare, *La dialettica e la retorica dell'Umanesimo: 'invenzione' e 'metodo' nella cultura del XV e XVI secolo*. Milan, 1968.

'The Machiavellian moment: a grand ideological synthesis', *Journal of modern history*, XLIX (1977), 661–70.

Verkamp, Bernard J., *The indifferent mean: adiaphorism in the English reformation*. Athens, Ohio, 1977.

Verrua, Pietro, *Umanisti ed altri 'studiosi viri' italiani e stranieri di qua e di là dalle Alpi e dal mare*. Geneva, 1924.

Villoslada, Ricardo Garcia, *La universidad de Paris durante los estudios de Francesco de Vitoria O. P. (1507–1522)*. Rome, 1938.

Vives, Juan Luis, *Opera omnia*, ed. Gregorius Majansius. Valencia, 1782–90.

de Vocht, Henry, 'Excerpts from the register of Louvain university from 1405 to 1527', *English historical review*, XXXVII (1922), 89–105.

History of the foundation and rise of the collegium trilingue lovaniense. Louvain, 1951–55.

John Dantiscus and his Netherlandish friends as revealed by their correspondence 1522–1546. Louvain, 1961.

Monumenta humanistica lovaniensa: texts and studies about Louvain humanists in the first half of the sixteenth century. Louvain, 1934.

Vona, Piero di, *I principi del defensor pacis*. Naples, 1974.

Walbank, F. W., *Polybius*. Berkeley, 1972.

Warner, G. F. and J. P. Gilson, *British museum: catalogue of western manuscripts in the old royal and king's collections*. London, 1921.

Warnicke, Retha M., 'The fall of Anne Boleyn: a reassessment', *History,* LXX (1985), 1–15.

'Sexual heresy at the court of Henry VIII', *HJ*, XXX:2 (1987), 247–68.

Weiss, James Michael, *'Ecclesiastes* and Erasmus: the mirror and the image', *ARG*, LXV, 83–108.

White, Beatrice, ed., *The vulgaria of John Stanbridge and the vulgaria of Robert Whittinton*, EETS, orig. ser., CXXXLVII, 1932.

Whittinton, Robert, *Opusculum Roberti Whittintoni*. London: de Worde, 1519; STC 25540.5.

trans., *A Frutefull worke of Lucius Anneus Senecae. Called the myrrour or Glasse of maners and wysedome*. London: William Myddleton, 1547; STC 17502.

trans. *The thre bookes of Tullius offyce*. London: de Worde, 1534; STC 5278.

Wilkins, David, ed., *Concilia magnae Britanniae et Hiberniae ab anno 1356 ad annum 1545*, III. London, 1745.

Wilkinson, Bertie, *Constitutional history of England in the fifteenth century 1399–1485*. London, 1964.

Constitutional history of medieval England, 1216–1399, III. London, 1958.

Wilks, Michael, *The problem of sovereignty in the later middle ages*. Cambridge, 1963.

Willen, Diane, *John Russell, first earl of Bedford: one of the king's men*. London, 1981.

Wilson, K. J., *Incomplete fictions: the formation of English renaissance dialogue*. Washington, 1985.

Winckelmann, Otto, 'Die Armenordnung von Nürnberg (1522), Kitzingen (1523), Regensburg (1523) und Ypern (1525)', *ARG*, X (1912/1913), 242–80.

Youings, Joyce, *Sixteenth-century England*. Harmondsworth, 1984.

Zeeveld, W. G., *Foundations of Tudor policy*. Cambridge, Mass., 1948.

Zimmermann, Athanasius, *Kardinal Pole, sein Leben und seine Schriften. Ein Beitrag zur Kirchengeschichte des 16. Jahrhunderts*. Regensburg, 1893.

INDEX